THE
BIAS-FREE
WORD FINDER

THE
BIAS-FREE
WORD FINDER

a dictionary of nondiscriminatory language

ROSALIE MAGGIO

BEACON PRESS
Boston

TO DAVID
Liz, Katie, Matt

Beacon Press
25 Beacon Street
Boston, Massachusetts 02108-2892

Beacon Press Books
are published under the auspices of
the Unitarian Universalist Association of Congregations.

Printed in the United States of America

99 98 97 96 95   8 7 6 5 4 3

Library of Congress Cataloging-in-Publication Data

Maggio, Rosalie.
   The bias-free word finder: a dictionary of nondiscriminatory
language / Rosalie Maggio.
        p. cm.
   Originally published as: The dictionary of bias-free usage /
Rosalie Maggio. 1991.
   ISBN 0-8070-6003-8
   1. English language–Usage–Dictionaries. 2. Pluralism (Social
sciences)–Dictionaries. 3. Nonsexist language–Dictionaries.
4. Discrimination. 5. Prejudices. I. Maggio, Rosalie. Dictionary
of bias–free usage. II. Title.
PE1460.M26 1992
428'.003–dc20
                                             92-4694
                                               CIP

Contents

User's Guide vii

Acknowledgments x

WRITING GUIDELINES 1

    Introduction 3

    Definition of Terms 6

    Sex and Gender 9

    Naming 10

    General Rules 13

    Pseudogeneric "He" 16

    Pseudogeneric "Man/Men/Mankind" 19

    Special Problems 21

    Further Reading 25

    Your Help Wanted 26

THE BIAS-FREE WORD FINDER. 27

User's Guide

George Orwell recommended the "scrapping of every word or idiom that has outgrown its usefulness." This dictionary is designed to help you scrap outdated, stereotypical, and damaging language. Those of you who have used the first edition will notice that in addition to terms that are prejudicial to women this edition also includes terms that are prejudicial to men as well as words and phrases that are biased against people because of their race, age, sexual orientation, disability, ethnic origin, or belief system.

To best use the book, first familiarize yourself with the Writing Guidelines section, which provides you with many specific kinds of help: a rationale for unbiased language; logical ways of ensuring your material is inclusive; suggestions for replacing masculine pronouns; paragraphs on such things as sex-linked metaphors and our language on prostitution; help with special situations (letter salutations, for example); and practical, easy-to-use guidelines.

The book contains 5,000 entries with 15,000 alternatives. The great majority of these entry words and phrases are biased in some way. When an entry term requires a substitute, it is immediately followed by one or more alternatives. These alternatives (in italics) are listed in order of usefulness and are separated by semicolons when they are for different meanings of the entry. Sometimes notes or comments follow the synonyms. If the entry term is not biased or if alternatives are optional, you may have to read further for synonyms (if any). Cited works are given simply by author and title—enough information to allow readers to locate the works, but not enough to overwhelm the entries, many of which are very brief.

And, as humorist Dave Barry would say, we didn't make any of this up. All entry terms and alternatives have been gathered from reference works, from daily newspapers and weekly magazines, and from standard, everyday speech and writing. This is nothing more than a collection of the ways people have found to deal with the bias in our language. Unbiased language is not being legislated somehow "from above." Ordinary people have chosen to replace linguistic pejoration and disrespect with words that grant full humanity and equality to all of us.

You will not agree with everything in this book. There is imperfect consensus today on which words are biased and on what constitutes an adequate substitute for those that are. For example, some people find the words *master*, *fellow*, and their compounds and derivatives sexist; others do not. Still others accept *fellow*, but not *master*. Some readers will see the inclusion of terms like *bull market*, *jackpot*, *charley horse*, *kaiser roll*, *lazy Susan*, and *cock of the roost* as nitpicking. Others will appreciate the cumulative and largely covert effect of the many male-based expressions in the language, and will be glad to have alternatives. Some readers will choose never to use a sexist or ageist term, for example, no matter how limited its substitutes or how difficult it is to get around it; others will believe that the use of a mildly biased word now and then is defensible.

In addition to entries that consist of biased words and phrases, several other types of entries are included to help you avoid bias in more subtle ways.

1. **Definition entries**. The following entries provide you with brief definitions: adultism, ageism, classism, discrimination, ethnocentrism, exclusive language, handicappism, heterosexism, homophobia, inclusive language, looksism, racism, sexism.

2. **Occupation entries**. Occupations that have in the past been limited to one sex are included. Statistics are often given so that in discussing these occupations you will have some idea of what is reality today. For example, although most people know that both men and women may be either dentists or dental hygienists, it may be instructive to see that approximately 91% of dentists are male and more than 98% of dental hygienists are female. In the same way, most people know that CEO (chief executive officer) positions are held by women, but it may be critical to our understandings of social process to see that, as of this writing, only a dozen of the 6,400 top-ranking CEOs are women.

3. **Key concept entries**. Several dozen entries consist of words or phrases that are not biased themselves but that are difficult to discuss realistically and fairly without understanding the biases that underlie them. Examples of this type of entry include: advertising, body image, comparable worth, divorce, education, family, gender roles, mental health, poverty, rape, sex differences, and violence. These entries will sometimes provide specific usage suggestions, but more often will simply alert you to the kinds of bias that should be taken into account when you write or speak about these issues.

The aim of this book is not to tell anyone how they must speak or write. Both editions have been a response to my own need for such a work. I recognize biased words when I see them, but I don't always know what to do with them—without spending a lot of time looking for alternatives. I wanted all the biased terms in the language in one place for handy reference.

At least once you will find an entry that causes you to smite your forehead and say, "How petty can you get!" Marie Shear talks about the tyranny of sexist trifles: "Individually, too trivial to protest; collectively, potent enough to humiliate, enrage, and incapacitate." She reminds us that although the Lilliputians were less than six inches tall, they managed to capture the full-sized Gulliver because there were so many of them. So, too, a word here and a word there look fairly harmless—and would probably be harmless if there weren't so many others like them. The dictionary attempts to give you, the reader, the broadest possible range of choices. If you come here looking for substitutes for the handful of common offenders (*handicap, mankind, busboy*), you will be as well served as the person determined to use no bias, no matter how trivial. The dictionary is thus self-adjusting; readers may choose words at their own levels of understanding and commitment.

Replacing biased words and phrases with terms that treat all people respectfully can be satisfying and rewarding. It can also be difficult and frustrating, and it is good to admit that.

It is also necessary to acknowledge that there can be no solution to the problem of bias in society on the level of language alone. Replacing *handicap* with *disability* does not mean a person with disabilities will find a job more easily. Using *secretary* inclusively does not change the fact that only 1% of U.S. secretaries are men. Deleting *black* and *white* from our vocabularies will not do away with racism in society. The language we use is symptomatic of our attitudes and beliefs. Changing the language does not automatically affect the way we think. However, research indicates that language powerfully influences attitudes, behavior, and perceptions. To ignore this factor in social change would be cultural suicide.

One writer says inclusive language is an illusion, that it changes nothing. However, if one accepted no other rationale for unbiased language, there is one that has high meaning: alleviating people's pain. "It hurts me when you describe me that way." "I feel left out when they never include my race, my sex, my group." "I feel bad when I hear that word." We may not always understand why a certain word hurts. We don't have to. It is enough that someone says, "That language doesn't respect me."

It is impossible to think that we would *not* change language that "has outgrown its usefulness," language that hurts people. Moving toward bias-free language is a small, but absolutely necessary step in encouraging our collective full human development. And the payoffs are enormous: we assure justice and equal treatment to all in a country that at least nominally prizes equality; we clarify fuzzy, illogical, and unrealistic thinking; and our writing becomes more sharply expressive and dynamic. And yes, George, useful.

Acknowledgments

The following wordsmiths were helpful and generous with their suggestions, criticisms, and support: Sanford Berman, Mary Kaye Medinger, John Wall, Judith Stoughton, Lucy Knoll, Mary Maggio, Bonnie Goldsmith, Joanna Cortright, Sarah Cardin, Maureen Williams, Ralph Slovenko, and Judy Johnston. Laura Gintz Jasper shared with me her excellent thesis, "Nonsexist Alternatives to Sexist Words: A Thesaurus." She and I wrote the same "book" at the same time, neither of us knowing of the other or her work.

I owe a great deal to all the thoughtful people who wrote or helped with comments and information, especially Rabbi Cheryl Rosenstein, Michael Nicholson-Beer, E. Mendelsohn, Ann Daly Goodwin, Joe Claus, the Reverend Sandy Stephens, Kevin M. Mitchell, Dr. Ian Hancock, Albert Weissman, Dr. Janet Spector, Bill Dudley, Betty-Ann Buss, Nancy Greiner, Bob Epstein, Linda Atkinson, Eleanor Graham, Cammie Callan Farrell, Margaret Houston, Sandra Hack, Randy Kloko, Jean Remke, Judy Ryan Haaversen, and Marc S. Mentzer.

I am particularly grateful to Irene and Paul Maggio, who knew how to raise their eight children in a bias-free manner even before any books were written on the subject. I am also much indebted to such pathfinding women and men as Casey Miller and Kate Swift, Cheris Kramarae, Paula Treichler, Mary Daly, Simone de Beauvoir, Dale Spender, Mary Ritchie Key, Ann Oakley, Bobbye D. Sorrels, Dennis Baron, Alleen Pace Nilsen, Nancy Henley, Robin Lakoff, Marlis Hellinger, Julia Penelope, Barrie Thorne, and Varda One (among others) who have worked in powerful, insightful, and inspiring ways to tell us how our biased language came to be, how it hurts all of us, and what we can do about it.

WRITING GUIDELINES

Writing Guidelines

INTRODUCTION

Language both reflects and shapes society. The textbook on American government that consistently uses male pronouns for the president, even when not referring to a specific individual (e.g., "a president may cast his veto"), reflects the fact that all our presidents have so far been men. But it also shapes a society in which the idea of a female president somehow "doesn't sound right."

Culture shapes language and then language shapes culture. "Contrary to the assumption that language merely reflects social patterns such as sex-role stereotypes, research in linguistics and social psychology has shown that these are in fact facilitated and reinforced by language" (Marlis Hellinger, in *Language and Power*, ed., Cheris Kramarae et al.).

Biased language can also, says Sanford Berman, "powerfully harm people, as amply demonstrated by bigots' and tyrants' deliberate attempts to linguistically dehumanize and demean groups they intend to exploit, oppress, or exterminate. Calling Asians 'gooks' made it easier to kill them. Calling blacks 'niggers' made it simpler to enslave and brutalize them. Calling Native Americans 'primitives' and 'savages' made it okay to conquer and despoil them. And to talk of 'fishermen,' 'councilmen,' and 'longshoremen' is to clearly exclude and discourage women from those pursuits, to diminish and degrade them."

The question is asked: Isn't it silly to get upset about language when there are so many more important issues that need our attention?

First, it's to be hoped that there are enough of us working on issues large and small that the work will all get done—someday. Second, the interconnections between the way we think, speak, and act are beyond dispute. Language goes hand-in-hand with social change—both shaping it and reflecting it. Sexual harassment was not a term anyone used twenty years ago; today we have laws against it. How could we have the law without the language; how could we have the language without the law? In fact, the judicial system is a good argument for the importance of "mere words"; the legal profession devotes great energy to the precise interpretation of words—often with far-reaching and significant consequences.

On August 21, 1990, in the midst of the Iraqi offensive, front-page headlines told the big story: President Bush had used the word *hostages* for the first time. Up to that time, *detainee* had been used. The difference between two very similar words was of possible life-and-death proportions. In another situation—also said to be life-and-death by some people—the difference between *fetal tissue* and *unborn baby* (in referring to the very same thing) is arguably the most debated issue in the country. So, yes, words have power and deserve our attention.

Some people are like George Crabbe's friend: "Habit with him was all the test of truth, / it must be right: I've done it from my youth." They have come of age using *handicapped, black-and-white, leper, mankind*, and pseudogeneric *he*; these terms must therefore be correct. And yet if there's one thing consistent about language it is that language is constantly changing; when the *Random House Dictionary of the English Language: 2nd Edition* was published in 1988, it contained 50,000 new entries, most of them words that had come into use since 1966. There were also 75,000 new definitions. (Incidentally, *RHD-II* asks its readers to "use gender-neutral terms wherever possible" and it never uses *mankind* in definitions where *people* is meant, nor does it ever refer to anyone of unknown gender as *he*.) However, few supporters of bias-free language are asking for changes; it is rather a matter of choice—which of the many acceptable words available to us will we use?

A high school student who felt that nonsexist language did demand some changes said, "But you don't understand! You're trying to change the English language, which has been around a lot longer than women have!"

One reviewer of the first edition commented, "There's no fun in limiting how you say a thing." Perhaps not. Yet few people complain about looking up a point of grammar or usage or checking the dictionary for a correct spelling. Most writers are very fussy about finding the precise best word, the exact rhythmic vehicle for their ideas. Whether or not these limits "spoil their fun" is an individual judgment. However, most of us accept that saying or writing the first thing that comes to mind is not often the way we want to be remembered. So if we have to think a little, if we have to search for the unbiased word, the inclusive phrase, it is not any more effort than we expend on proper grammar, spelling, and style.

Other people fear "losing" words, as though there weren't more where those came from. We are limited only by our imaginations; vague, inaccurate, and disrespectful words can be thrown overboard with no loss to society and no impoverishment of the language.

Others are tired of having to "watch what they say." But what they perhaps mean is that they're tired of being sensitive to others' requests. From childhood onward, we all learn to "watch what we say": we don't swear around our parents; we don't bring up certain topics around certain people; we speak differently to friend, boss, cleric, English teacher, lover, radio interviewer, child. Most of us are actually quite skilled at picking and choosing appropriate words; it seems odd that we are too "tired" to call people what they want to be called.

The greatest objection to bias-free language is that it will lead us to absurdities. Critics have posited something utterly ridiculous, cleverly demonstrated how silly it is, and then accounted themselves victorious in the battle against linguistic massacre. For example: "So I suppose now we're going to say: He/she ain't heavy, Father/Sister; he/she's my brother/sister." "I suppose next it will be 'ottoperson'." Cases have been built up against the mythic "woperson," "personipulate," and "personhole cover" (none of which has ever been advocated by any reputable sociolinguist). No grist appears too ridiculous for these mills. And, yes, they grind exceedingly small. Using a particular to condemn a universal is a fault in logic. But then ridicule, it is said, is the first and last argument of fools.

One of the most rewarding—and, for many people, the most unexpected—side effects of breaking away from traditional, biased language is a dramatic improvement in writing style. By replacing fuzzy, overgeneralized, cliché-ridden words with explicit, active words and by giving concrete examples and anecdotes instead of one-word-fits-all descriptions you can express yourself more dynamically, convincingly, and memorably.

"If those who have studied the art of writing are in accord on any one point, it is on this: the surest way to arouse and hold the attention of the reader is by being specific, definite, and concrete" (Strunk and White, *The Elements of Style*). Writers who talk about *brotherhood* or *spinsters* or *right-hand men* miss a chance to spark their writing with fresh descriptions; they leave their readers as uninspired as they are. Unthinking writing is also less informative. Why use the unrevealing *adman* when we could choose instead a precise, descriptive, inclusive word like *advertising executive, copywriter, account executive, ad writer*, or *media buyer*?

The word *manmade*, which seems so indispensable to us, doesn't actually say very much. Does it mean artificial? handmade? synthetic? fabricated? machine-made? custom-made? simulated? plastic? imitation? contrived?

Communication is—or ought to be—a two-way street. A speaker who uses *man* to mean *human being* while the audience hears it as *adult male* is an example of communication gone awry.

Bias-free language is logical, accurate, and realistic. Biased language is not. How logical is it to speak of the "discovery" of America, a land already inhabited by millions of people? Where is the accuracy in writing "Dear Sir" to a woman? Where is the realism in the full-page automobile advertisement that says in bold letters, "A good driver is a product of his environment," when more women than men influence car-buying decisions? Or how successful is the ad for a dot-matrix printer that says, "In 3,000 years, man's need to present his ideas hasn't changed. But his tools have," when many of these printers are bought and used by women, who also have ideas they need to present? And when we use stereotypes to talk about people ("isn't that just like a welfare mother/Indian/girl/old man"), our speech and writing will be inaccurate and unrealistic most of the time.

DEFINITION OF TERMS

Bias/Bias-Free

Biased language communicates inaccurately about what it means to be male or female; black or white; young or old; straight, gay, or bi; rich or poor; from one ethnic group or another; disabled or temporarily able-bodied; or to hold a particular belief system. It reflects the same bias found in racism, sexism, ageism, handicappism, classism, ethnocentrism, anti-Semitism, homophobia, and other forms of discrimination.

Bias occurs in the language in several ways.

1. Leaving out individuals or groups. "Employees are welcome to bring their wives and children" leaves out those employees who might want to bring husbands, friends, or same-sex partners. "We are all immigrants in this country" leaves out Native Americans, who were here well before the first immigrants.
2. Making unwarranted assumptions. To address a sales letter about a new diaper to the mother assumes that the father won't be diapering the baby. To write "Anyone can use this fire safety ladder" assumes that all members of the household are able-bodied.
3. Calling individuals and groups by names or labels that they do not choose for themselves (e.g., *Gypsy, office girl, Eskimo, pygmy, Bushman, the elderly, colored man*) or terms that are derogatory (*fairy, libber, savage, bum, old goat*).
4. Stereotypical treatment that implies that all lesbians/Chinese/women/people with disabilities/teenagers are alike.
5. Unequal treatment of various groups in the same material.
6. Unnecessary mention of membership in a particular group. In a land of supposedly equal opportunity, of what importance is a person's race, sex, age, sexual orientation, disability, or creed? As soon as we mention one of these characteristics—without a good reason for doing so—we enter an area mined by potential linguistic disasters. Although there may be instances in which a person's sex, for example, is germane ("A recent study showed that female patients do not object to being cared for by male nurses"), most of the time it is not. Nor is mentioning a person's race, sexual orientation, disability, age, or belief system usually germane.

Bias can be overt or subtle. Jean Gaddy Wilson (in Brooks and Pinson, *Working with Words*) says, "Following one simple rule of writing or speaking will eliminate most biases. Ask yourself: Would you say the same thing about an affluent, white man?"

Inclusive/Exclusive

Inclusive language includes everyone; exclusive language excludes some people. The following quotation is inclusive: "The greatest revolution of our generation is the discovery that human beings, by changing the inner attitudes of their minds, can change the outer aspects of their lives" (William James). It is clear that James is speaking of all of us.

Examples of sex-exclusive writing fill most quotation books: "Man is the measure of all things" (Protagoras). "The People, though we think of a great entity when we use the word, means nothing more than so many millions of individual men" (James Bryce). "Man is nature's sole mistake" (W.S. Gilbert).

Sexist/Nonsexist

Sexist language promotes and maintains attitudes that stereotype people according to gender while assuming that the male is the norm—the significant gender. Nonsexist language treats all people equally and either does not refer to a person's sex at all when it is irrelevant or refers to men and women in symmetrical ways.

"A society in which women are taught anything but the management of a family, the care of men, and the creation of the future generation is a society which is on the way out" (L. Ron Hubbard). "Behind every successful man is a woman—with nothing to wear" (L. Grant Glickman). "Nothing makes a man and wife feel closer, these days, than a joint tax return" (Gil Stern). These quotations display various characteristics of sexist writing: (1) stereotyping an entire sex by what might be appropriate for some of it; (2) assuming male superiority; (3) using unparallel terms (*man and wife* should be either *wife and husband/husband and wife* or *woman and man/man and woman*).

The following quotations clearly refer to all people: "It's really hard to be roommates with people if your suitcases are much better than theirs" (J.D. Salinger). "If people don't want to come out to the ball park, nobody's going to stop them" (Yogi Berra). "If men and women of capacity refuse to take part in politics and government, they condemn themselves, as well as the people, to the punishment of living under bad government" (Senator Sam J. Ervin). "I studied the lives of great men and famous women, and I found that the men and women who got to the top were those who did the jobs they had in hand, with everything they had of energy and enthusiasm and hard work" (Harry S. Truman).

Gender-Free/Gender-Fair/Gender-Specific

Gender-free terms do not indicate sex and can be used for either women/girls or men/boys (e.g., *teacher, bureaucrat, employee, hiker, operations manager, child, clerk, sales rep, hospital patient, student, grandparent, chief executive officer*).

Writing or speech that is gender-fair involves the symmetrical use of gender-specific words (e.g., *Ms. Leinwohl/Mr. Kelly, councilwoman/councilman, young man/young woman*) and promotes fairness to both sexes in the larger context. To ensure gender-fairness, ask yourself often: Would I write the same thing in the same way about a person of the opposite sex? Would I mind if this were said of me?

If you are describing the behavior of children on the playground, to be gender-fair you will refer to girls and boys an approximately equal number of times, and you will carefully observe what the children do, and not just assume that only the boys will climb to the top of the jungle gym and that only the girls will play quiet games.

Researchers studying the same baby described its cries as "anger" when they were told it was a boy and as "fear" when they were told it was a girl (cited in Cheris Kramarae, *The Voices and Words of Women and Men*). We are all victims of our unconscious and most deeply held biases.

Gender-specific words (for example, *alderwoman, businessman, altar girl*) are neither good nor bad in themselves. However, they need to be used gender-fairly; terms for women and terms for men should be used an approximately equal number of times in contexts that do not discriminate against either of them. One problem with gender-specific words is that they identify and even emphasize a person's sex when it is not necessary (and is sometimes even objectionable) to do so. Another problem is that they are so seldom used gender-fairly.

Although gender-free terms are generally preferable, sometimes gender-neutral language obscures the reality of women's or men's oppression. *Battered spouse* implies that men and women are equally battered; this is far from true. *Parent* is too often taken to mean *mother* and obscures the fact that more and more fathers are very much involved in parenting; it is better here to use the gender-specific *fathers and mothers* or *mothers and fathers* than the gender-neutral *parents*.

Generic/Pseudogeneric

A generic is an all-purpose word that includes everybody (e.g., *workers, people, voters, civilians, elementary school students*). Generic pronouns include: *we, you, they*.

A pseudogeneric is a word that is used as though it included all people, but that in reality does not. *Mankind, forefathers, brotherhood*, and *alumni* are not generic because they leave out women. When used about

Americans, *immigrants* leaves out all those who were here long before the first immigrants. "What a christian thing to do!" uses *christian* as a pseudogeneric for *kind* or *good-hearted* and leaves out all kind, good-hearted people who are not Christians.

Although some speakers and writers say that when they use *man* or *mankind* they mean everybody, their listeners and readers do not perceive the word that way and these terms are thus pseudogenerics. The pronoun *he* when used to mean *he and she* is another pseudogeneric.

Certain generic nouns are often assumed to refer only to men, for example, *politicians, physicians, lawyers, voters, legislators, clergy, farmers, colonists, immigrants, slaves, pioneers, settlers, members of the armed forces, judges, taxpayers*. References to "settlers, their wives, and children," or "those clergy permitted to have wives" are pseudogeneric.

In historical contexts it is particularly damaging for young people to read about settlers and explorers and pioneers as though they were all white men. Our language should describe the accomplishments of the human race in terms of all those who contributed to them.

SEX AND GENDER

An understanding of the difference between sex and gender is critical to the use of bias-free language.

Sex is biological: people with male genitals are male, and people with female genitals are female.

Gender is cultural: our notions of "masculine" tell us how we expect men to behave and our notions of "feminine" tell us how we expect women to behave. Words like *womanly/manly, tomboy/sissy, unfeminine/unmasculine* have nothing to do with the person's sex; they are culturally acquired, subjective concepts about character traits and expected behaviors that vary from one place to another, from one individual to another.

It is biologically impossible for a woman to be a sperm donor. It may be culturally unusual for a man to be a secretary, but it is not biologically impossible. To say "the secretary. . .she" assumes all secretaries are women and is sexist because the issue is gender, not sex. Gender describes an individual's personal, legal, and social status without reference to genetic sex; gender is a subjective cultural attitude. Sex is an objective biological fact. Gender varies according to the culture. Sex is a constant.

The difference between sex and gender is important because much sexist language arises from cultural determinations of what a woman or man "ought" to be. Once a society decides, for example, that to be a man means to hide one's emotions, bring home a paycheck, and be able to discuss football standings while to be a woman means to be soft-spoken, love shopping, babies, and recipes, and "never have anything to wear," much of the population becomes a contradiction in terms—unmanly men and unwomanly women. Crying, nagging, gossiping, and shrieking are assumed to be women's lot; rough-housing, drinking beer, telling dirty jokes, and being unable to find one's socks and keys are laid at men's collective door. Lists of stereotypes appear silly because very few people fit them. The best way to ensure unbiased writing and speaking is to describe people as individuals, not as members of a set.

Gender Role Words

Certain sex-linked words depend for their meanings on cultural stereotypes: *feminine/masculine, manly/womanly, boyish/girlish, husbandly/ wifely, fatherly/motherly, unfeminine/unmasculine, unmanly/unwomanly*, etc. What a person understands by these words will vary from culture to culture and even within a culture. Because the words depend for their meanings on interpretations of stereotypical behavior or characteristics, they may be grossly inaccurate when applied to individuals. Somewhere, sometime, men and women have said, thought, or done everything the other sex has said, thought, or done except for a very few sex-linked biological activities (e.g., only women can give birth or nurse a baby, only a man can donate sperm or impregnate a woman). To describe a woman as unwomanly is a contradiction in terms; if a woman is doing it, saying it, wearing it, thinking it, it must be—by definition—womanly.

F. Scott Fitzgerald did not use "feminine" to describe the unforgettable Daisy in *The Great Gatsby*. He wrote instead, "She laughed again, as if she said something very witty, and held my hand for a moment, looking up into my face, promising that there was no one in the world she so much wanted to see. That was a way she had." Daisy's charm did not belong to Woman; it was uniquely hers. Replacing vague sex-linked descriptors with thoughtful words that describe an individual instead of a member of a set can lead to language that touches people's minds and hearts.

NAMING

Naming is power, which is why the issue of naming is one of the most important in bias-free language.

Self-Definition

People decide what they want to be called. The correct names for individuals and groups are always those by which they refer to them-selves. This "tradition" is not always unchallenged. Haig Bosmajian (*The Language of Oppression*) says, "It isn't strange that those persons who insist on defining themselves, who insist on this elemental privilege of self-naming, self-definition, and self-identity encounter vigorous resistance. Predictably, the resistance usually comes from the oppressor or would-be oppressor and is a result of the fact that he or she does not want to relinquish the power which comes from the ability to define others."

Dr. Ian Hancock uses the term *exonym* for a name applied to a group by outsiders. For example, Romani peoples object to being called by the exonym *Gypsies*. They do not call themselves Gypsies. Among the many other exonyms are: the elderly, colored people, homosexuals, pagans, adolescents, Eskimos, pygmies, savages. The test for an exonym is whether people describe themselves as "redmen," "illegal aliens," "holy rollers," etc., or whether only outsiders describe them that way.

There is a very small but visible element today demanding that gay men "give back" the word *gay*—a good example of denying people the right to name themselves. A late-night radio caller said several times that gay men had "stolen" this word from "our" language. It was not clear what language gay men spoke.

A woman nicknamed "Betty" early in life had always preferred her full name, "Elizabeth." On her fortieth birthday, she reverted to Elizabeth. An acquaintance who heard about the change said sharply, "I'll call her Betty if I like!"

We can call them Betty if we like, but it's arrogant, insensitive, and uninformed: the only rule we have in this area says we call people what they want to be called.

"Insider/Outsider" Rule

A related rule says that insiders may describe themselves in ways that outsiders may not. "Crip" appears in *The Disability Rag*; this does not mean that the word is available to anyone who wants to use it. "Big Fag" is printed on a gay man's T-shirt. He may use that expression; a non-gay may not so label him. One junior-high student yells to another, "Hey, nigger!" This would be highly offensive and inflammatory if the speaker were not African American. A group of women talk about "going out with the girls," but a co-worker should not refer to them as "girls." When questioned about just such a situation, Miss Manners replied that "people are allowed more leeway in what they call themselves than in what they call others."

"People First" Rule

Haim Ginott taught us that labels are disabling; intuitively most of us recognize this and resist being labeled. The disability movement originated the "people first" rule, which says we don't call someone a "diabetic" but rather "a person with diabetes." Saying someone is "an AIDS victim" reduces the person to a disease, a label, a statistic; use instead "a person with/who has/living with AIDS." The 1990 Americans with Disabilities Act is a good example of correct wording. Name the person as a person first, and let qualifiers (age, sex, disability, race) follow, but (and this is crucial) only if they are relevant. Readers of a magazine aimed at an older audience were asked what they wanted to be called (elderly? senior citizens? seniors? golden agers?). They rejected all the terms; one said, "How about 'people'?" When high school students rejected labels like kids, teens, teenagers, youth, adolescents, and juveniles, and were asked in exasperation just what they would like to be called, they said, "Could we just be people?"

Women as Separate People

One of the most sexist maneuvers in the language has been the identification of women by their connections to husband, son, or father—often even after he is dead. Women are commonly identified as someone's widow while men are never referred to as anyone's widower. Marie Marvingt, a Frenchwoman who lived around the turn of the century, was an inventor, adventurer, stunt woman, superathlete, aviator, and all-around scholar. She chose to be affianced to neither man (as a wife) nor God (as a religious), but it was not long before an uneasy male press found her a fit partner. She is still known today by the revealing label "the Fiancée of Danger." If a connection is relevant, make it mutual. Instead of "Frieda, his wife of seventeen years," write "Frieda and Eric, married for seventeen years."

It is difficult for some people to watch women doing unconventional things with their names. For years the etiquette books were able to tell us precisely how to address a single woman, a married woman, a divorced woman, or a widowed woman (there was no similar etiquette on men because they have always been just men and we have never had a code to signal their marital status). But now some women are Ms. and some are Mrs., some are married but keeping their birth names, others are hyphenating their last name with their husband's, and still others have constructed new names for themselves. Some women—including African American women who were denied this right earlier in our history—take great pride in using their husband's name. All these forms are correct. The same rule of self-definition applies here: call the woman what she wants to be called.

Name-Calling

Some printable epithets are also biased and are included in the dictionary (see, for example, **bastard; bitch; ethnic and racial slurs; fag/faggot; son of a bitch**). Animal and food names are also used to label people; see **animal names for people; food names for people**.

GENERAL RULES

Parallel Treatment

Parallel treatment is essential when discussing different groups (e.g., persons with and without disabilities, Christians and Jews, or heterosexual, bisexual, and homosexual groups). Beware false parallels: "white" and "nonwhite" are not parallel. "White" is specific while "nonwhite" simply lumps together everyone else. The problems with nonparallel treatment are most easily seen in gender asymmetries.

If you refer to a woman as Margaret Schlegel, refer to a man in the same material as Gavan Huntley. If he is Huntley, she will be Schlegel, or if she is Margaret, he will be Gavan, and if she is Ms. Schlegel, he is Mr. Huntley.

Half the time use "girls and boys," half the time "boys and girls." Because of a grammatical "convention" based on the belief that the masculine was the more worthy gender, the male word has always had the right to be placed first. Thus we have Mr. and Mrs., husband and wife, male and female, etc. Vary this half the time (although be prepared for odd looks if you try Mrs. and Mr.).

Do not make of one sex a parenthetical expression: "hats off to the postal employees who manned (and womanned) the Olympic stamp cancellation booths"; "male (and female) students"; "his (or her)".

When sex-specific words are used, maintain sexual symmetry. Male-female word pairs are troublesome in three ways. (1) Certain words are used as parallel pairs, but are in fact asymmetrical, for example, camera-girl/cameraman, man Friday/girl Friday, mermaid/merman, makeup girl/makeup man. The worst offender in this category is man/wife; the correct pairs are man/woman and wife/husband. (2) Other words are so unequivalent that few people confuse them as pairs, but it is revealing to study them, knowing that they were once equals: governor/governess, patron/matron, courtier/courtesan, master/mistress, buddy/sissy, hubby/hussy, dog/bitch, patrimony/matrimony, call boy/call girl, showman/showgirl, Romeo/Juliet. We all know what a Romeo is, but if we didn't we could look it up in the dictionary; this is not true of a Juliet. A call boy is a page; a call girl is a prostitute. Buddy is affectionate; sissy is derogatory. A study of word pairs shows that words associated primarily with women ultimately become discounted and devalued. Muriel Schulz (*Language and Power*) calls it "semantic derogation." (3) Acceptable words and constructions become unacceptable sometimes because of the nonparallel way they are used. For example, *a male and three women, aldermen and women*, and *two girls and a man* should read: *a man and three women, aldermen and alderwomen*, and *two women and a man* (or *two girls and a boy*).

"Feminine" Endings

Suffixes like *-ess, -ette,* and *-trix* do three things. (1) They perpetuate the notion that the male is the norm and the female is a subset, a deviation, a secondary classification. A poet is defined as "one who writes poetry" while a poetess is defined as "a female poet"; men are thus "the real thing" and women are sort of like them. (2) These endings specify a person's sex when gender is irrelevant. (3) They carry the sense of littleness or cuteness (consider how even nonhuman *-ette* words don't carry much weight: dinette, featurette, luncheonette, sermonette).

The purpose of a suffix is to qualify the root word. Why qualify a standard word describing a standard human activity? A poet should be a poet—without qualification. Which would you rather be, a governor or a governess? An adventurer or an adventuress? A master or a mistress? The discounting and devaluation of the female member of a word pair is the biggest argument against "feminine" endings. Invariably the parallelism, if it ever existed, breaks down, and the female word ends up with little of the prestige and acceptability of the male word.

If the individual's sex is critical to your material, use adjectives ("At a time when male actors played female roles . . .") or pronouns ("The poet interrupted her reading . . .").

The following words with "feminine" endings should generally be replaced as shown (but see the dictionary entries for additional information).

actress/actor
adulteress/adulterer
adventuress/adventurer
ambassadress/ambassador
ancestress/ancestor
anchoress/anchorite
authoress/author
aviatrix, aviatress/aviator
benefactress/benefactor
canoness/canon
coadjutress/coadjutor
co-heiress/co-heir
comedienne/comedian
deaconess/deacon
directress/director
doctoress/doctor
enchantress/enchanter
equestrienne/equestrian
executrix/executor
farmerette/farmer

giantess/giant
goddess/god
governess/governor
heiress/heir
heroine/hero
hostess/host
huntress/hunter
inheritress/inheritor
inspectress/inspector
instructress/instructor
Jewess/Jew
laundress/launderer
majorette/major
manageress/manager
mayoress/mayor
mediatress, mediatrix/mediator
murderess/murderer
Negress/African American,
  black
ogress/ogre

patroness/patron
peeress/peer
poetess/poet
portress/porter
priestess/priest
procuress/procurer
prolocutrix/prolocutor
prophetess/prophet
proprietress/proprietor
protectress/protector
Quakeress/Quaker
sculptress/sculptor
seamstress/sewer
seductress/seducer
seeress/seer
shepherdess/shepherd

songstress/singer
sorceress/sorcerer
starlet/star
stewardess/steward
suffragette/suffragist
temptress/tempter
testatrix/testator
tragedienne/tragedian
traitress/traitor
tutoress/tutor
usherette/usher
victress/victor
villainess/villain
votaress/votary
waitress/waiter
wardress/warder

-Woman, -Man, -Person

Words that end in *-woman* and *-man* are generally listed in this dictionary as a last resort for three reasons: (1) in most cases it is unnecessary to
specify sex; (2) male-female word pairs rarely get equal treatment and thus
are better avoided; (3) the other alternatives are almost always a better
linguistic choice. *Mailcarrier* and *mail handler*, for example, are more
descriptive than *mailman/mailwoman*.

Sometimes the *-man* and *-woman* words are preferable in order to
emphasize the presence or participation of both sexes in some activity or
position: "Local businesswomen and businessmen donated their weekends
to do plumbing, electrical, and carpentry work in the new downtown
shelter for the homeless."

When using these suffixes, however, be sensitive to sex symmetry.
Salesmen and women should be *salesmen and saleswomen; spokesman and
spokesperson* should be *spokesman and spokeswoman*.

The weak, awkward, and annoying suffix *-person* is not generally
recommended. It was useful in making the transition to inclusive language because it was so easy to tack *-person* onto words, but it not only
looks contrived, it is contrived. Because the *-person* suffix comes so readily
to mind, we don't look any further and thus miss out on other more
dynamic and descriptive words.

Sexist Quotations

Sometimes you need to use a quotation, but it is sexist: "The best use
of laws is to teach men to trample bad laws under their feet" (Wendell
Phillips). There are several ways of handling this.

Omit the quotation marks and paraphrase the remark (still attributing it to the author): Wendell Phillips suggested that the best use of laws is to teach people to trample bad ones underfoot.

Replace the sexist words or phrases with ellipsis dots and/or bracketed substitutes: "The best use for laws is to teach [people] to trample bad laws under their feet" (Wendell Phillips).

Use "[sic]" to show that the sexist words come from the original quotation and to call attention to the fact that they are incorrect: "The best use of laws is to teach men [sic] to trample bad ones under their feet" (Wendell Phillips).

Quote only part of it: Wendell Phillips said the best use for laws was to teach people "to trample bad laws under their feet."

And of course you always have the choice of replacing the quotation with one that doesn't exclude anyone.

Hidden Bias/Context

Writing may be completely free of biased terms yet still carry a biased message. According to a radio news item, "More women than ever before are living with men without being married to them. And more unmarried women than ever before are having babies." An accurate, unbiased report would have said: "More men and women than ever before are living together without being married. And more unmarried couples than ever before are having babies."

Too often language makes assumptions about people—that everyone is male, heterosexual, able-bodied, white, married, between the ages of twenty-six and fifty-four, of European extraction, etc. Until it becomes second nature to write without bias, re-read your material as though you were: a gay man, someone who uses a wheelchair, a Japanese American woman, an eighty-year-old man, or other "individuals" of your own creation. If you do not feel left out, discounted, and ignored but instead can read without being stopped by some incongruence, you have probably avoided hidden bias. It is also wonderfully helpful to ask people from a group with which you aren't familiar to read your work; they can quickly spot any insensitivity.

PSEUDOGENERIC "HE"

The use of *he* to mean *he and she* is to be strictly avoided. It is ambiguous, the grammatical justification for its use is problematic, and it is not perceived as including both women and men. Donald G. McKay (in *The Voices and Words of Women and Men*, ed., Cheris Kramarae) points out that each of us hears the pseudogeneric *he* over a million times in our lifetime and that the consequences of this kind of repetition are "beyond the ken of present-day psychology." He says pseudogeneric *he* has all the characteristics of a highly effective propaganda technique: repetition, covertness/ indirectness, early age of acquisition, and association with high-prestige sources. "Although the full impact of the prescriptive *he* remains to be explored, effects on attitudes related to achievement, motivation, persever- ance, and level of aspiration seem likely."

Young children, who are unfamiliar with the grammatical rule that says *he* really means *he and she* and who are also fairly literal-minded, hear *he* thousands of times and understand it to refer to males only. They come to think of maleness as the general state of being and femaleness as some- thing peripheral. In a study by Steven Gelb of Toronto's York University, young children were asked to describe pictures of gender-indeterminate bunnies, dinosaurs, and babies; 97% of the time boys labeled them male, and 81% of the time the girls also labeled them male. By the use of pseudogeneric *he*, parents and teachers unconsciously teach youngsters that maleness and humanness are equivalent.

The ubiquity of *he* is not to be underestimated. When the Minnesota legislature ordered the removal of gender-specific language from state statutes, the Office of the Revisor of Statutes deleted or replaced some 20,000 sex-specific pronouns; only 301 of them were feminine.

Defenders of the convention most often claim that it is a point of grammar and certainly not intended to offend anyone. That it does in reality offend large numbers of people does not appear to sway some grammarians, nor does the fact that their recourse to the laws of language is on shaky ground. *He* was declared generic and legally inclusive of *she* by an Act of the English Parliament, which was following a rule invented in 1746 by John Kirby, who decreed that the male gender is "more compre- hensive" than the female. Grammarians articulated the policy that be- tween an error of number ("to each their own") and an error of gender ("to each his own") it was preferable to make an error of gender. Thus this "convention" of grammar is based on the indefensible and illogical prem- ise that the male gender is more comprehensive. In fact, a case can be made that the female gender is more comprehensive than the male both linguistically (*she* contains *he*) and genetically (see dictionary entry **Eve**).

A little-mentioned by-product of the use of pseudogenerics is that some valuable words have been lost to men. One man said he was always jealous that women had their own word, *she*, whereas men had to share their word, *he*, with women. Today when men are reclaiming male solidarity, they find that the word *brotherhood* has grown misshapen from so much loose application; it lacks the punch and immediacy of *sisterhood*. When we say *womankind*, it conveys something precise; *mankind* no longer does. By avoiding pseudogeneric usage, we may be able to reclaim the narrow and graphic meanings of some of these words.

The pronoun *he* (when used in any way except to refer to a specific male person) can be avoided in several ways.

- Rewrite your sentence in the plural: "Everyone is a genius at least once a year; a real genius has his original ideas closer together" (G. C. Lichtenberg). Everyone is a genius at least once a year; real geniuses have their original ideas closer together.

- Substitute *we/us/our*: "From each according to his abilities, to each according to his needs" (Karl Marx). From each of us according to our abilities, to each of us according to our needs.

- Use the second person: "No man knows his true character until he has run out of gas, purchased something on the installment plan and raised an adolescent" (Marcelene Cox). You don't know what your true character is until you have run out of gas, purchased something on the installment plan and raised an adolescent.

- Recast in the passive voice: "Pessimist: One who, when he has the choice of two evils, chooses both" (Oscar Wilde). Pessimist: One who, when given the choice of two evils, chooses both.

- Omit the pronoun entirely: "Repartee: What a person thinks of after he becomes a departee" (Dan Bennett). Repartee: What a person thinks of after becoming a departee. "The American arrives in Paris with a few French phrases he has culled from a conversational guide or picked up from a friend who owns a beret" (Fred Allen). The American arrives in Paris with a few French phrases culled from a conversational guide or picked up from a friend who owns a beret.

- Replace the masculine pronoun with an article: "Can't a critic give his opinion of an omelette without being asked to lay an egg?" (Clayton Rawson). Can't a critic give an opinion of an omelette without being asked to lay an egg?

- Replace the pronoun with words like *someone, anyone, one, the one, no one*: "He who can take advice is sometimes superior to him who can give it" (Karl von Knebel). Someone who can take advice is sometimes superior to one who can give it. "Everyone can master a grief but he that has it" (Shakespeare). Everyone can master a grief but the one that has it. Or, as La Rochefoucauld put it: "We all have the strength to endure the misfortunes of others."

- Use *he and she* or *her and his*, but only if there are not a great many of them. *S/he* is not recommended for anything but brief memos or notes. There are times when it is better to use *he or she* as, for example, when you want to raise consciousness about both sexes being involved in a certain activity: the new parent . . . he or she; the plumber . . . she or he. "Education is helping the child realize his potentialities" (Erich Fromm). Education is helping the child realize his or her potentialities.

- Replace the pronoun with a noun (or a synonym for a noun used earlier): "He is forced to be literate about the illiterate, witty about the witless and coherent about the incoherent" (John Crosby). The critic is forced to be literate about the illiterate, witty about the witless and coherent about the incoherent. "To find a friend one must close one eye—to keep him, two" (Norman Douglas). To find a friend one must close one eye—to keep a friend, two.

- When *he* refers to an animal whose sex is unknown or irrelevant, replace with *it*: "When you see a snake, never mind where he came from" (W.G. Benham). When you see a snake, never mind where it came from. "When you have got an elephant by the hind legs and he is trying to run away, it is best to let him run" (Abraham Lincoln). When you have got an elephant by the hind legs and it is trying to run away, it is best to let it run.

- Singular *they* ("to each their own") has strong supporters (see dictionary entry **singular "they"**). "Only a mediocre person is always at his best" (Somerset Maugham). Only a mediocre person is always at their best.

- Use genderless nouns (*the average person, workers*, etc.) or substitute job titles or other descriptions for the pronoun.

- Use masculine and feminine pronouns in alternating sentences, paragraphs, examples, or chapters, although this technique should be used sparingly as it can be annoying to read.

PSEUDOGENERIC "MAN/MEN/MANKIND"

Much of the debate on inclusive language centers on the use of *man*. Some say *man* is defined not only as "an adult male human being" but also as "a human being," "a person," "an individual," or "the whole human race." They claim that the use of *man* does not exclude women but is nothing more than a grammatical convention: man embraces woman.

Not everybody, however, reads dictionaries or, having read them, uses words the way they are defined there. Researchers who studied the hypothesis that *man* is generally understood to include women found "rather convincing evidence that when you use *man* generically, people do tend to think male, and tend not to think female" (letter from Joseph Schneider and Sally Hacker, quoted in Casey Miller and Kate Swift, *Words and Women*). According to Miller and Swift, that study and others "clearly indicate that *man* in the sense of *male* so overshadows *man* in the sense of *human being* as to make the latter use inaccurate and misleading for purposes both of conceptualizing and communicating."

Citing dictionary definitions as proof of a word's meaning is an iffy business at best. One definition of *virago* is: "a woman of great stature, strength, and courage" (*Webster's Ninth New Collegiate Dictionary*). But the average person is almost certainly more likely to think of a virago in terms of the word's other definition, "a loud, overbearing woman: termagant."

If you use *virago* in its positive sense and your audience "mis-hears" you, it's unproductive to insist that you really meant the other definition.

Few wordsmiths will tolerate an ambiguous word, especially if there is an unambiguous one available. Imagine discussing giraffes and zebras, where sometimes *zebras* is used to include both giraffes and zebras but sometimes it means simply zebras. The audience would never know when it heard *zebras* whether it meant only zebras or whether it meant zebras and giraffes.

A high school senior explained that the reason his Western civilization textbook used only the words *man* and *mankind* was because "women were dogs. You might as well say men and their dogs plowed the fields. Or men and their dogs tanned hides. The reason women aren't mentioned in our book is that women did nothing, were nothing." His startling conclusion shows practically and graphically what happens when a word means one thing (*women and men*) but is heard as another (*men*).

How people hear a word is far more important than its etymology or dictionary definition. Jeanette Silveira (in *The Voices and Words of Women and Men*, ed., Cheris Kramarae) says "there is ample research evidence that the masculine 'generic' does not really function as a generic. In various studies words like he and man in generic contexts were presented to people who were asked to indicate their understanding by drawing, bringing in, or pointing out a picture, by describing or writing a story about the person(s) referred to, or by answering yes or no when asked whether a sex-specific word or picture applied to the meaning." In all these studies (fourteen of them are summarized in *Women's Studies International Quarterly*, vol. 3, no. 2, 1980), women/girls were perceived as being included significantly less often than men/boys. Both women and men reported that they usually pictured men when they read or heard the masculine pseudogeneric.

Saying that man embraces woman is illogical on two counts. (1) In terms of language alone, it would seem more sensible to have *woman* embrace *man* and *she* embrace *he* since *man* is found in *woman* and *he* is found in *she*—but not vice versa. (2) The justification for man becoming the set and woman the subset is linguistically, sociologically, philosophically, and psychologically indefensible. (Early grammarians didn't know that genetically man comes from woman. Would it have made a difference?) The term *human being* clearly includes both man and woman. With such a simple, commonsensical alternative available, it seems unnecessary to defend a convention that is almost surely on its last manly legs.

Finally, Dennis Baron says (*Grammar and Gender*) that attempts today to justify the use of the masculine generic "are but thin masks for the underlying assumption of male superiority in life as well as language; despite the attempts of the wary language commentators to include women under masculine terms, the effect is to render women both invisible and silent."

Not all words containing *man, men*, or *boy* are sexist. When in doubt, see individual entries (e.g., **boycott; highboy; dragoman; menopause**) or the entries **man-/-man; -men**.

We are so accustomed to *-man* compounds that we feel helpless without them and their replacements somehow don't "sound right" to us. However, *-man* nouns are outnumbered by the common and useful *-er* and *-or* words. *Fisher* seems alien to people, yet has a far stronger precedent in the language than *fisherman*. The same is true of *waiter* for *waitress, flagger* for *flagman, deliverer* for *deliveryman*, and *repairer* for *repairman*. If we had grown up hearing *shoeman*, would we balk at *shoemaker*? What about *roofman* for *roofer, gardenman* for *gardener*, and *teachman* for *teacher*? The following sample list may help those alternatives for *-man* words sound a little more "right" to us:

angler, barber, batter, bottler, brother, builder, butcher, buyer, canoer, caregiver, caretaker, carpenter, catcher, commissioner, consumer, customer, dealer, doer, dressmaker, driver, employer, executioner, farmer, father, fitter, gambler, gamester, gardener, golfer, hairdresser, handler, healer, hunter, insurer, jogger, jokester, laborer, landscaper, leader, lexicographer, lithographer, lover, maker, manager, manufacturer, member, messenger, mother, nurturer, officer, outfielder, owner, painter, performer, pitcher, planner, player, plumber, practitioner, producer, promoter, provider, race-walker, reporter, retailer, retainer, rider, robber, roofer, runner, shoemaker, sister, speaker, speechmaker, storekeeper, striker, subscriber, teacher, trader, treasurer, trucker, waiter, whaler, woodworker, worker, writer; actor, administrator, ambassador, ancestor, arbitrator, auditor, author, benefactor, coadjutor, conqueror, contractor, counselor, director, doctor, editor, executor, facilitator, governor, inspector, instructor, janitor, legislator, liquidator, major, mayor, mediator, navigator, negotiator, operator, professor, proprietor, protector, purveyor, sculptor, surveyor, testator, traitor, vendor, victor.

SPECIAL PROBLEMS

Fellow, King, Lord, Master

Fellow, king, lord, and *master* have three things in common. (1) Either from definition, derivation, or people's perceptions of them, they are very male-oriented words. *King, lord*, and *master* are also hierarchical, dominator society terms. (2) They are root words: many other words, phrases, and expressions are formed from them, thus extending their reach. (3) Not everyone agrees whether all forms of them are biased. Someone who might admit that a fellow sitting next to them at lunch can only be a man might see nothing unacceptable in the expression *fellow student*. Those who agree that the master of a certain house is a man might believe that mastering a skill is fair language.

The recommendation in this dictionary is that these four words be used only in their narrowest, male-defined terms; all other uses are provided with alternatives. Consider, for example, the cumulative effect on the language when such a masculine and slavery-related word as *master* is encountered in so many everyday ways: *master bedroom, master builder, master class, masterful, master hand, master key, master list, mastermind, masterpiece, master plan, master stroke, master switch, master tape, master teacher, masterwork, mastery, overmaster, past master, postmaster, poundmaster, prizemaster, self-mastery, trickmaster, truckmaster, weighmaster, wharfmaster, yardmaster.*

For specific information on *fellow, king, lord, master,* see the dictionary entries.

Prostitute/Prostitution

The words that we use to describe people involved in prostitution are some of the most interesting and revealing in the language. Prostitution involving adults is a takes-two-to-tango operation and could not survive without the active and continued participation of both parties. Yet our language does not reflect this reality; in no way does it treat prostitute and prostitute's customer equally. If there is an imbalance, if anyone is a victim, it is the prostitute; prostitutes are often disadvantaged, compelled by poverty, homelessness, a pimp, or drugs to maintain the system. The prostitute's "customer" does not suffer from similar life-and-death compulsions. Yet by naming prostitutes pejoratively, society apportions to them all the blame, all the "badness." There are several hundred synonyms for *prostitute* (see the entry **prostitute/prostitution** for a few of them), but when it comes to the men who do with prostitutes that which supposedly makes the prostitutes bad women, we presently have only four generally used words for them: *john, trick, score, date. John* is a nice word; many people name their sons John. *Trick* and *score* are not too shabby either; they are both used (although not in that sense) in polite society. And *date* is even more innocuous. Virtually none of the prostitute words have this double life; they live only on the streets.

Until we find and use words for prostitute and prostitute's customer that are inclusive or symmetrical, we perpetuate a coverup for half the people involved in prostitution. A good start is to avoid all terms for prostitutes except *prostitute*. This matter-of-fact word is as informative and descriptive as it needs to be. It can also be used inclusively for male and female prostitutes. Tarting up the business with expressions like *lady of pleasure* and *pavement princess* is the worst kind of doublespeak.

For want of a better term, the prostitute's partner might be called *prostitute's customer*. What is essential is to associate the user directly with the prostitute.

Eliminate also coverups like *outcall service, escort service, red light district, call girl service, brothel, bordello, call house*; they are *houses of prostitution* or *prostitution services*. Only by using neutral, symmetrical, direct terms can we remove the wholly inappropriate sexist bias on prostitution from our language and begin to face what prostitution is and what it does to people.

Sex-Linked Expressions

Our rich and colorful language contains thousands of striking, evocative, and useful metaphors, expressions, and figures. Many identify a real or fictional person by a feminine or masculine name.

As is true of the rest of the language, these phrases are dominated by male images. There is nothing wrong with any of them per se, although their cumulative effect tends to be overpowering. It is the story of Lilliput again: one Lilliputian is harmless enough, but an army of them can overtake a Gulliver. An individual male-based expression is acceptable; to use only male metaphors is not. This dictionary lists alternatives for several dozen expressions, *not so that they can be removed from the language*, but so that you will have alternatives available if you want to balance your writing and speaking or if you need one (e.g., when you prefer not to use a male metaphor for a woman).

The long-term solution to the overabundance of male-based images is not to avoid the powerful ones we have but to look for or create new ones that are female-based or inclusive. Are we less inventive, less poetic, less expressive than our predecessors?

Letter Salutations

A state commission on the economic status of women reports receiving a surprising number of letters addressed "Dear Sir" or "Gentlemen." "Pueblo to People," a nonprofit organization of craft and agricultural cooperatives run by very low-income people in Central America and the Philippines, notes in their catalog under "When Writing to Us": "Please remember we are a cooperative of women and men. We prefer to be addressed in terms that include all of us, such as 'Friends,' 'Folk,' or 'People,' rather than exclusive terms such as 'Gentlemen' and 'Sir.' May we also note that over half of our products are made by women: weavers, basketmakers, carpenters, seamstresses, and cashew processors." Below are some other suggestions for inclusive letter openings. The standard "Dear . . . " salutation in business letters seems to be giving way in many cases to the memo format, a subject line instead of a salutation, or beginning the letter directly after the name and address (no salutation).

Dear Agent
    Board Member
    Citizen
    Committee Member
    Councilor
    Credit Manager
    Customer
    Director
    Editor
    Employee
    Executive
    Friend
    Homeowner

Dear Manager
    Mr./Ms.
    Neighbor
    Owner
    Parent/Guardian
    Personnel Officer
    Publisher
    Reader
    Resident
    Subscriber
    Taxpayer
    Teacher
    Voter

Dear Friends of the Library
    Members of the . . .
    Parishioners
    Supporters
    Volunteers

Dear Ellen Howard-Jeffers
    Acme Drycleaning
    K. Koskenmaki
    Tiny Tots Toys
    Office of the Bursar

Dear Superintendent Bennett
    Vice-President Morris
    Senior Research Specialist Jordan
    Administrative Assistant Maki

Greetings!
Hello!

To the Chief Sales Agent
To the Consumer Relations Department
To the Freestyle Credit Department
TO: The Commission on Language Abuse
TO: Parents/guardians of Central High School students
TO: J. G. Frimsted

  Or omit the salutation entirely and begin with:
    Re: Account # 4865-1809-3333-0101
    Subject: Reprints of your article on hearing loss
    Please send me a copy of the most recent committee report.
    I am ordering six copies of your publication.
    Enclosed please find complete payment for . . .

Miscellaneous

Avoid ascribing one sex or the other to animals and nonhuman things. If the sex of an animal is known (and is important to your material), specify it. When the sex is unknown or unimportant, use *it*. Also use *it* instead of *she* to refer to nature, nations, churches, ships, boats, cars, engines, gas tanks, etc., and *it* instead of *he* to refer to the enemy, the devil, death, time, etc. (These items are included in the dictionary.)

Generally retain "sexist" names for nonhuman items, for example, timothy grass, daddy longlegs, alewife, sweet william, myrtle. (These and similar items are included in the dictionary.)

Avoid changing official titles that contain biased language, although you may add "[sic]" to indicate that it is the official title and to underline its bias.

Be sensitive about rewriting history. *Fathers of the Church* is a historically correct term. But we commonly refer now to the Founding Fathers as the Founders. Many biased words are used as they are in historical contexts because they reflect that time and culture. Rewriting literature is not done either, although a classroom discussion of bias in great literature is always highly recommended.

The following words can be used in conjunction with more specific words to arrive at nonsexist phrases: agent, anyone, artisan, artist, assistant, associate, attendant, builder, chief executive, citizen, civilian, clerk, clinician, coach, colleague, commissioner, companion, consumer, contractor, correspondent, counselor, crew, customer, dealer, deputy, employee, engineer, everybody, everyone, executive, expert, fabricant, facilitator, folks, guide, hand, handler, individual, inhabitant, inspector, intermediary, laborer, loader, machinist, maker, manufacturer, mechanic, member, messenger, motorist, nobody, nominal head, no one, notable, officer, one, operator, owner, patriot, performer, person, planner, politician, practitioner, producer, professional, program director, promoter, proprietor, purveyor, repairer, reporter, representative, retailer, scientist, servant, someone, specialist, student, steward, subscriber, technician, tender, tutor, vendor, worker, writer.

FURTHER READING

A good many excellent works deal with sexist language; you can find them under such library catalog classifications as Language and Languages—Sex Differences; Nonsexist Language; Sexism in Language; Sex and Language; Sexism in Communication. There is very little material on biased language in general, and you may have to look under narrow topics (Racism in Language, Homophobia) or under very broad topics (Journalism; Sociolinguistics). The classic and pathbreaking *The Language of*

Oppression by Haig A. Bosmajian (University Press of America, 1983) is cataloged solely under Freedom of Speech and under Civil Rights, although the subject of the book is biased language.

The single most helpful work on sexist language is *The Handbook of Nonsexist Writing: For Writers, Editors and Speakers*, second edition, by Casey Miller and Kate Swift (New York: Harper & Row, 1988). Another excellent work is *Language, Gender, and Professional Writing* by Francine Wattman Frank and Paula A. Treichler (New York: Modern Language Association, 1989). *The Nonsexist Communicator: Solving the Problems of Gender and Awkwardness in Modern English* by the late Bobbye D. Sorrels (Englewood Cliffs, NJ: Prentice-Hall, 1983) is a standard. In addition to those authors, look for works by Cheris Kramarae, Barrie Thorne, Nancy Henley, Alleen Pace Nilsen, Dale Spender, and Ann Oakley.

YOUR HELP WANTED

Our language is constantly changing, especially perhaps now as it begins to reflect the fullness and richness of our human diversity and oneness. This edition was greatly enhanced by those who responded to the "Your Help Wanted" request in the first edition. If you disagree with something here, if you find biased terms not listed, or if you know of additional alternatives for biased terms, please send your comments to: Rosalie Maggio, Beacon Press, 25 Beacon Street, Boston, MA 02108-2892. Thank you!

THE BIAS-FREE WORD FINDER

a

Since the concepts people live by are derived only from perceptions and from language and since the perceptions are received
and interpreted only in light of earlier concepts, [we come]
pretty close to living in a house that language built.

Russell R.W. Smith

abbess/abbot retain these terms; "abbess" is one of the few exceptions to
the rule on avoiding feminine endings; abbesses were generally equal
to abbots in power, influence, and respect. In the generic sense of
"abbess" or "abbot," use *religious, ascetic, superior, administrator,
director.*

abigail *See* lady's maid; maid.

abominable snowman *yeti, the yeti.* "Yeti" is in any case the preferred
term.

Abraham, Isaac, and Jacob these traditional ancestors of Jews and Christians should be joined by their partners, also authentic and important
ancestors: Sarah, Rebecca, Leah, and Rachel. "The God of Abraham"
would read "the God of Abraham and Sarah."

according to Hoyle when using expressions like this, be aware of how
many are male-based. Some of the time use female-based expressions, creative expressions of your own, or alternatives: *according to/
by the book, according to/playing by the rules, absolutely correct, cricket, in
point of honor, on the square, proper/correct way to do things.* *See* Writing
Guidelines for a discussion of sex-linked expressions.

accountant approximately half the nation's accounting majors and half the
new recruits at the Big Eight accounting firms are women; however,
only 10% of new partners in accounting firms are women, and
percentages are even lower in the Big Eight (e.g., 2.1% at Price
Waterhouse, 3.1% at Arthur Andersen).

Achilles' heel when using expressions like this, be aware of how many
are male-based. Some of the time use female-based expressions,
creative expressions of your own, or alternatives: *vulnerable point/spot,
vulnerability, only weakness, chink in one's armor, where the shoe pinches.*
See Writing Guidelines for a discussion of sex-linked expressions.

acid-conditioning man *acid-conditioner.*

acid-correction man *acid-correction hand, acid-corrector.*

acid man (explosives) *nitrating-acid mixer.*

acolyte usage varies; in the Roman Catholic Church, women can function as acolytes (one of the minor orders of the diaconate) but may not be officially installed as acolytes. When it means "attendant," an acolyte can be either sex. *See also* altar boy.

acquaintance rape *See* date rape.

act like a man/be a man/take it like a man *be brave/bold, put on a bold face, defy, meet danger/trouble head on, bear up, meet/confront with courage/ bravery/valor/boldness, hold up one's head, screw one's courage to the sticking point, look in the face, nerve oneself, hold out against, take heart, have plenty of backbone, come up to scratch, face the music, act coura- geously/bravely/wisely/straightforwardly/honorably, show fortitude/ patience/determination/strength/vigor, stand up for oneself, be independent/ resolute/unflinching/earnest, sit tall in the saddle, stand tall, keep one's chin up.* Expressions like these limit, bewilder, and oppress men while also implying that women are not bold, courageous, straightforward, hardy, etc. (Alternatives are for both sexes.) Paul Theroux says that "be a man" really means "Be stupid, be unfeeling, obedient and soldierly, and stop thinking." Writing in *About Men: Reflections on the Male Experience*, Russell Baker says, "Before you were old enough to think for yourself, they were preparing you for a lifetime of feeling like a disgrace to your sex. What was this 'man' you were supposed to take it like, to act like, to be?" He decided that these "men" were blessed with utter fearlessness, a zest for combat, and indifference to pain. "Men would rather have their eyes blackened and teeth loosened than let the whole world see that they hate being severely beaten." *See also* coward/cowardly/cowardice; manful/manfully; manlike/manly.

actress *actor.* Many women call themselves actors, pointing out that they are members of the Actors' Guild. "Actor" was used for both sexes for about seventy-five years before the appearance of "actress"—"a woman who is an actor." The specification of gender supports the male-as-norm system ("actor" being the standard and "actress" being the deviation). However, of all the words ending in "-ess" or "-ette," this is one of the least biased; it should be used for women who so label themselves.

Adam's apple there is no good substitute for this term other than a lengthy description ("the projection in the front of the neck formed by the largest cartilage of the larynx"). The expression comes from a combination of the mythical belief that Adam's ruinous apple got stuck halfway down (since Eve hadn't eaten any, women generally do not have an Adam's apple) and a translation error. In a post-biblical form of Hebrew "tappuah ha adham" means "bodily projection on a person." However "tappuah" also means "apple," and "adham" also means "Adam." The word "apple" is not mentioned in Genesis; the fruit was more likely an apricot.

Adam's rib there are two biblical creation stories (one in Genesis 1, one in Genesis 2). In the second, much-older story, God works very hard to find a "suitable partner" for Adam. The words "bone of my bones and flesh of my flesh" emphasize that both are of the very same substance; the "Adam's rib" metaphor need not be taken negatively. In the first story Eve and Adam are created simultaneously, which also emphasizes male-female equality. Dennis Baron (*Grammar and Gender*) says that the phrase "Adam's rib" (as womankind's point of origin) should be put in quotes to show its dubiousness and reserved for discussions of the term itself. Science's contribution to the who-came-first exchange is that the original human chromosome was carried by the female; in the genetic sense, men spring from women. "A man is really a female with testosterone" (Dr. Claude Migeon, chief, pediatric endocrinology clinic, Johns Hopkins Hospital). *See also* Eve.

adman *advertising executive, creative/art director, copywriter, ad agent/writer/ creator, account executive/manager/supervisor, media buyer, ad rep, advertising representative.* Generic plurals: *advertising executives, ad agency staff, advertising people.* When possible use specific job titles.

adulteress *adulterer.* In 1990 a Wisconsin woman was prosecuted for adultery although neither her husband—who admitted to an affair of his own—nor her partner was so charged. This imbalance is also seen in "cuckold," where the man whose wife has been unfaithful has a special label showing the high harm done him; there is no label for a woman whose husband has been unfaithful. *See also* cuckold.

adultism a lack of respect for those who are too young, adultism discounts children and teenagers as too immature to know what's good for them and too inexperienced to do anything valuable. Some believe that adultism lays the foundation for accepting racism, sexism, and other oppressive relationships. The United States considers itself child-centered, but statistics say otherwise: millions of children live in poverty, are physically and sexually abused, and are involved in largely unrestricted kiddie sex and child pornography operations.

advance man *advance agent, booker, agent, promoter, publicity/press agent, publicist, rep, representative, go-between, negotiator, talent coordinator, producer.*

adventuress *adventurer.* Also: *sensation-seeker, explorer, pacesetter, globetrotter, bird of passage, gadabout, vagabond, gambler*—all equally applicable to women or men. "Adventurer" and "adventuress" have different cultural overtones and definitions; the latter seeks to support herself by "questionable means" where the former courts danger and risk.

advertising   advertising creates and maintains numerous sexist stereotypes: women are sex objects and men are success objects; women live to please men and men live to take care of women; men are hopeless at the simplest household tasks while women are fulfilled doing the simplest household tasks; all women really want is male sexual attention and all men really want is a fast car and a good beer. Women are shown primarily as housewife or sex partner, appear in fewer ads than men, tend to promote beauty, home, food, and clothing products, and are shown primarily at home rather than at work. The most harmful role is that of the pouting, inviting woman who signals very clearly her sexual availability. When real-world women fail to live up to the image, resentment and even rage follow. Rapists believe women are teases who try to control them; advertising reinforces the notion. Sex sells, but women pay. Advertising doesn't do much better by men, especially in recent years. Dr. Joyce Brothers says that now men "are the ones who come off looking like jerks." Partly because of the growing strength of the women's movement and partly because women are major consumers, poking outright fun at women has become financially risky as well as politically incorrect. In a year-long study of over 1,000 print and television ads, Men's Rights Inc. concluded that men are portrayed as ignorant, incompetent, and at the mercy of women. Men's roles as parents and caregivers are largely ignored. In any ad in which a man and a woman appear, and one of them is a jerk, the man gets the job. Studies show that male-bashing ads are remembered far better than others. In a survey of 18,000 commercials and 70,000 print ads in its New York creative library, ad agency J. Walter Thompson found that stereotypes used for men in 1960 are still being used today, for example, the Lone Wolf (the Marlboro man), Mr. Success (the Rolex guy), the Expert, the Lover, the Stud, and the Husband. Where are catchy, memorable ads that don't demean or stereotype either sex?

advertising layout man   *advertising layout planner.*

adzman   *adzer.*

afflicted with   when speaking of people with disabilities, avoid this phrase. Substitute "affected by" or rephrase it to read "a person who has/a person with" a certain condition (not an "affliction").

aficionada/aficionado   *fan, enthusiast, devotee, nut, hound, buff.*

African American/Afro-American   currently favored terms, although "black" is also still used; African American is seen more often than Afro-American. The trend is away from hyphenation (African American, Asian American, Italian American). *See also* black-and-white (adj.); black/Black (noun); black/black-; Negress/Negro.

ageism although age discrimination is prohibited in the workplace, our cultural preoccupation with youth results in attitudes, behaviors, and policies that keep older people invisible and undervalued.

agent provocateur the masculine-gender French is used in both French and English for women and men. If you prefer something that sounds more inclusive, use *infiltrating agent*.

aggressive numerous pan-cultural studies indicate that in general men are more aggressive than women. Testosterone levels appear related to aggression as well as to general behavior changes where aggression is a by-product. It also appears that genetic predisposition to aggression can be somewhat altered by the social environment. Factors that increase aggression in men include cultural values that say men are aggressive and women are not; male models of aggression in the culture; exposure to television violence; and uncaring, rejecting, or punishing parents. Some women have more aggression than the culture thinks is "womanly" and some men have less aggression than the culture thinks is "manly." Avoid using "assertive" for women and "aggressive" for men. Ann Hopkins, one of eighty-eight candidates (and the only woman) for a partnership at Big Eight accounting firm Price Waterhouse, had the best record for generating new business and securing multimillion-dollar contracts. She lost her bid for the partnership, however, because she was considered too aggressive. In the lead opinion in the court case that followed, William Brennan wrote, "An employer who objects to aggressiveness in women but whose positions require this trait places women in an intolerable and impermissible Catch-22: out of a job if they behave aggressively and out of a job if they don't." Pollster Celinda Lake asked observers to rate women and men reading the same text at identical decibel levels. Invariably the women were described as louder, more aggressive, and shrill. *See also* coward/cowardly/cowardice; glass ceiling; testosterone; violence.

agribusinessman *farmer, agriculturist; agribusinesswoman and agribusinessman* (both terms have appeared in print). *See also* farmer; farm wife/farmer's wife.

aide (medical) *nursing assistant, nurse assistant, N.A.* Traditionally, aides and orderlies did the same work, but all aides were women and all orderlies were men. Most hospitals and nursing homes now use the inclusive terms.

aide de camp today both military and civilian aides can be women or men; historically an aide de camp was a man.

aidman *medical aide.*

AIDS "an equal opportunity pathogen," the AIDS virus crosses all cultural, economic, racial, sex, sex-preference, and social lines. It is not ever "a gay disease"; it is "a sexually transmitted disease." (In

some parts of the world it is predominantly a heterosexual issue.)
The World Health Organization (WHO) says six to eight million
people worldwide have contracted the virus; one million Americans
are believed to be infected. In some areas of Africa as much as one-
third of the population—men, women, children—test positive for
HIV. In major cities of the Americas, Western Europe, and sub-
Saharan Africa, AIDS is now the leading cause of death for women
between the ages of twenty and forty. When disseminating information about AIDS, don't use the vague shortcut terms "intimate sexual
contact" and "bodily fluids"—tell exactly what kinds of sexual
contact and exactly what kinds of bodily fluids can transmit AIDS. A
person with AIDS is not "an AIDS victim" or "someone afflicted
with/suffering from AIDS." Use instead *person living with AIDS,
someone with AIDS, person who has AIDS.* Note that the correct term is
often "HIV" (human immunodeficiency virus), not "AIDS." *See also*
afflicted with; handicappism; handicapped; high-risk group; homophobia; innocent victim; "people first" rule; victim.

airdox man *airdox fitter.*

airhead *out to lunch, space ranger, flake, out of it, on another planet, with one's
head in the clouds, not all there, missing some marbles, with a mind like a
sieve, impractical, irresponsible, slaphappy, woolgathering, dreamy, mindless, brainless wonder, dense, muddleheaded, shallow, inane, foolish.* Along
with birdbrained, emptyheaded, featherbrained, harebrained, and
scatterbrained, this word is used almost exclusively for girls/women.

airman *aviator, pilot, flier, airline/test pilot, co-pilot, navigator, flight/aeronauti-
cal engineer, aerial navigator, flying officer, bombardier, air marshal,
aeronaut, balloonist, aviation/aircraft worker, glider, skydiver, paratrooper,
parachutist, airborne trooper, member of the U.S. Air Force.* The official
U.S. Air Force publication is *The Airman* and the Air Force calls its
members airmen, although all ranks are open to both sexes (12.5% are
women). Until the Air Force itself changes this term, it will continue
to be used, although it can be circumvented with "member of the U.S.
Air Force." Outside the Air Force, some 3% of all airplane pilots and
navigators are women.

airman basic/airman first class man or woman. *See also* airman.

airmanship *aerial navigation/flying/piloting skills, flying ability, aeronautical/
flying/piloting expertise.*

airplane steward/airplane stewardess *See* steward/stewardess.

airport serviceman *airport attendant/servicer.*

alcoholic more than one-third of all alcoholics in the U.S. are women.
Texts have customarily referred to the alcoholic as "he" and to the co-
dependent as "she." Because of the public perception that women
aren't or can't be alcoholic many women delay naming and treating
their problem. This also unfairly stereotypes men as alcoholics.

alderman *council/city council member, city/municipal councilor, chancellor, city representative, commissioner, councilor, member of the council, municipal officer, ward manager; alderman and alderwoman.*

alewife (fish) OK as is.

alewife (woman) *barkeep, barkeeper, bartender.*

alien *undocumented immigrant/resident.* An "alien" is strange, threatening, and very much "other" to us; avoid this usage.

alimony other terms are sometimes more appropriate: *back salary, reparations, permanent maintenance, permanent spousal maintenance, rehabilitative/temporary alimony/maintenance.* The newer terms avoid the implication that one spouse is receiving unearned financial support from the other. Either sex may receive alimony or maintenance.

all boy/all girl/all man/all woman replace these vague, stereotypical expressions with specific descriptions. No two people will agree, for example, on what "He's all man!" means: he plays baseball and spits? What is fairly typical is that "all boy/all man" refers to action while "all girl/all woman" refers to physical appearance.

alleyman *alley cleaner, bowling alley cleaner.*

all men are created equal *all men and women/women and men are created equal, all people/we are all/all of us are created equal.* At the first American Woman's Rights Convention (1848), the proposed "Declaration of Sentiments" began: "We hold these truths to be self-evident: that all men and women are created equal; that they are endowed by their Creator with certain inalienable rights" (Susan B. Anthony, *History of Woman Suffrage*, 1889). One hundred years earlier, Frenchwomen realized that the liberty, equality, and fraternity won for Frenchmen in the 1789 French Revolution were truly that: for Frenchmen. In 1790 playwright and revolutionary Olympe de Gouges published "The Declaration of the Rights of Women" modeled on the "Declaration of the Rights of Man and the Citizen." (Three years later, after opposing Robespierre and the Jacobins, she went to the guillotine.)

all the king's men *everybody, one and all, every last one, the whole world, everybody under the sun, all the monarch's soldiers.* **See also** all the world and his wife; everybody and his grandmother/brother; every Tom, Dick, and Harry.

all the world and his wife *all the world and little Billing, everyone, everybody, the whole world, every last one of them, all the world and their offspring.* **See also** all the king's men; everybody and his grandmother/brother; every Tom, Dick, and Harry.

all work and no play makes Jack a dull boy *you know what they say about all work and no play; you know what they say, "all work and no play . . ."; all work and no play makes us pretty dull sorts; all work and no play makes Jill a dull girl/Jack a dull boy.*

alma mater this gender-specific term (from the Latin for "fostering/ bounteous mother") is not perceived as particularly biased. However, for truly inclusive forms use *the university I (he/she/we/they/you) attended, school attended, my (your/his/her/our/their) graduating institution, my (her/his/their/our/your) college or university.* For the school song, use *my school song/anthem, the school song, the University of Iowa school song.*

almsman *pauper, suppliant, mendicant, beggar, beneficiary, pensioner, recipient, welfare recipient.*

altar boy *server, acolyte, attendant, helper; altar girl and altar boy.*

alterations woman *alterer, tailor. See also* dressmaker; seamstress; sewing woman.

alto an alto is always a woman, although you will find both men and women singing in the alto range; the countertenor is the highest male voice and the contralto ("alto" is a contraction of contralto) is the lowest female voice.

alumna/alumnae/alumnus/alumni when used correctly to describe respectively a woman/women/a man/men, these Latin terms are gender-fair. The most common errors are the use of "alumnus" to refer to a woman and the use of "alumni" to describe both women and men. However, the trend is away from the more pedantic sex-linked Latin and toward pithier inclusive terms: *graduate(s), alum(s), member(s) of the class of 1996, postgraduate(s), former student(s), ex-student(s).* If you must for some reason use the Latin, write *alumna/us* or *alumnus/a* and *alumni/ae* or *alumnae/i.*

amaurotic family idiocy *Tay-Sachs' Disease.*

Amazon/amazon in Greek mythology Amazons were fabulous female warriors. The 1970 edition of the *Encyclopaedia Britannica* explains (although a later edition deletes it): "The only plausible explanation of the story of the Amazons is that it is a variety of the familiar tale of a distant land where everything is done the wrong way about; thus the women fight, which is man's business." The word "amazon" is loaded with cultural and historical meanings; it has been used as a pejorative to describe certain women and certain kinds of women, but in other contexts it is a term of respect that women appropriate for themselves. (For example, The Amazon Bookstore, founded in 1970, is the oldest and one of the largest feminist bookstores in the country.) Use the term only if you understand its history and multiple connotations. For the casual use of "amazon" meaning a tall, strong, or belligerent woman, substitute those or other descriptive adjectives. *See also* combat; warrior.

ambassadress *ambassador.*

amiga/amigo *friend.* Or, use the terms gender-fairly ("amiga," feminine, and "amigo," masculine).

amputee do not refer to a person by a surgical procedure or missing body part. Question the need to refer to a disability at all. When it is highly relevant to your material, the information can be neutrally conveyed without labeling the entire person by something that is only one part of their life. *See also* handicapped.

analysis girl *silver solution mixer.*

ancestress *ancestor. See also* fathers (pseudogeneric); forefather.

anchoress *anchorite.* Although the base term is preferred, "anchoress" has remained a strong and positive term not discounted over time, perhaps because of its association with such women as anchorite Julian of Norwich, the first English woman of letters and the first theologian of either sex to write originally in English.

anchorman (black jack) *third base.*

anchorman (newscasting) *anchor, news anchor, newscaster, broadcaster, telecaster, sportscaster, announcer, reporter, TV reporter, commentator, communications artist, news analyst, narrator.*

ancient man *ancient people/peoples, ancient civilization, ancient humanity.*

androgynous/androgyny the ultimate in inclusive, these words contain the roots for both man ("aner") and woman ("gyne"). "Androgyny suggests a spirit of reconciliation between the sexes; it suggests, further, a full range of experience open to individuals who may, as women, be aggressive, as men, tender; it suggests a spectrum upon which human beings choose their places without regard to propriety or custom" (Carolyn G. Heilbrun, *Toward a Recognition of Androgyny*). According to *The Opposite Sex* (Dr. Anne Campbell, ed.), it is the androgynous person who shows the most satisfactory psychological and social adjustment. Gloria Steinem (*Outrageous Acts and Everyday Rebellions*) says the concept of androgyny "raised the hope that the female and male cultures could be perfectly blended in the ideal person; yet because the female side of the equation has yet to be affirmed, androgyny usually tilted toward the male. As a concept, it also raised anxiety levels by conjuring up a conformist, unisex vision, the very opposite of the individuality and uniqueness that feminism actually has in mind." John A. Sanford (*The Invisible Partners*) says, "Men are used to thinking of themselves only as men, and women think of themselves as women, but the psychological facts indicate that every human being is androgynous." And Samuel Taylor Coleridge said, "The truth is, a great mind must be androgynous." On the other hand, radical feminist Mary Daly (*Gyn/Ecology*) refers to the word androgyny as a "semantic abomination": "The word is misbegotten—conveying something like 'John Travolta and Farrah Fawcett-Majors scotch-taped together'."

angel (woman) use with great caution. In many cultures and for many men, women are either angels (perfect and innocent) or they are evil

tempters. Our ideas of both angels themselves and women-as-angels
are highly mythic and in some cases insulting to real angels and real
women. The association of women with angels is a little puzzling. In
the Jewish and Christian scriptures, there were no female angels; they
were generally represented as men, although in one case they appear
to be neuter. They also must be fearsome; their first words are
always "Do not be afraid."

angel of the Lord *angel of God, angel. See also* Lord.

Anglo this ersatz synonym for "white" is inaccurate (not all whites have
an Anglo-Saxon heritage) and offensive (those who have suffered
from Anglo-Saxon oppression—the Irish, for example—do not
appreciate being called Anglos).

anima/animus in Jungian psychology, "anima" (the feminine form of the
Latin for "soul") refers to the female component in a man's personality, while "animus" (the masculine form) refers to the masculine
component in a woman's personality. Use as they are.

animal (man) calling men "animals" carries with it a what-can-you-expect
attitude and builds tolerance for behavior that is not particularly
normative for men. Often referring to sexual overaggressiveness, the
label is mistaken by some men for a compliment—much like the
"no!" that is clear and unambiguous to women but heard as "sounds
fine to me" by some men. *See also* animal names for people.

animal/he if you know the animal's gender and it is important for your
audience to also know it, use it; otherwise refer to all animals of
unknown or irrelevant gender as "it."

animal husbandman *animal scientist.*

animal names for people using animal names to refer to people is insensitive and socially unattractive. In addition, most pejorative animal
names are also sexist. "Men's extensive labeling of women as parts
of body, fruit, or animals and as mindless, or like children—labels
with no real parallel for men—reflects men's derision of women and
helps maintain gender hierarchy and control" (Thorne, Kramarae,
and Henley, *Language, Gender and Society*). Avoid: ape, baboon, bat,
beast, bird, brood mare, buck, bull, bunny, cat, cow, dog, dumb ox,
filly, fox, gay dog, goose, gorilla, heifer, hellcat, kitten, lapdog, mare,
old bat, old goat, ox, pig, pussy, pussycat, sex kitten, she-cat, sow,
stag, stud, swine, tigress, tomcat, top dog, turkey, vixen. A few
terms seem descriptive without being derogatory; lamb is used
affectionately of both sexes. Metaphors that compare people to
animals in some particular are seldom sexist and thus are acceptable,
for example, merry as a cricket, wise as an owl, happy as a lark,
feeling one's oats. To distinguish between pejorative descriptions
and acceptable descriptions, ask first whether the expression is
limited to one sex, and then determine whether a person is being

labeled an animal or whether the person is being likened to some animal characteristic. Calling someone an eager beaver implies not so much that the person is a beaver but that the person is eager as a beaver is eager. Strong writing depends on metaphors—even metaphors based on animals—but there is a difference between labeling people and creating vivid word associations. *See also* animal (man); bitch (noun); chick/chicken/chickie-baby (girl/woman); food names for people; fox/fox trap/foxy/foxy lady; hen party; lone wolf; stag line; stag movie; stag party; wolf (man).

anthropology the Greek word "anthropos" ordinarily means "human being" although in some contexts it can be translated "man." In practice, "anthropos" words like anthropology, anthropocentric, anthropoid, anthropomorphism, philanthropic, philanthropist, philanthropy, and others are defined, used, and perceived as inclusive.

antifeminist nonsexist; not all antifeminists are men.

any man's death diminishes me unless you are quoting Donne, use *anyone's death diminishes me.*

"ape-man" *early human, anthropoid ape.*

Apostolic Fathers leave as is; historically correct.

apron strings, tied to *dependent/overly dependent on, clinging, immature, timid, childish, youthful, pampered, protected, hang on the sleeve of, dance attendance on, can't make a move without, no mind of one's own.*

architect 15% of U.S. architects are women.

armed forces women make up 11% of the two-million-member armed forces, but fewer than 2% of the top officers are women as are less than 1% in the ranks of brigadier general and above. Sexual harassment of women remains "a significant problem" in spite of clear policy guidelines, and facilities in some locations are not equal for women and men. *See also* combat; males-only draft; serviceman (armed forces).

armful (referring to a woman) avoid this belittling and objectifying term.

artilleryman *artillery personnel, gunner.* "Artilleryman" is used in the army but can refer to either sex.

artist although 60% of U.S. artists are women, only 2% to 5% of the works in U.S. art museums are by women. In one of the most widely used texts, *History of Art* by H. W. Janson, a woman artist was not mentioned until the book's sixteenth edition (1985).

artiste used for either sex.

Asian American Shirley Geok-Lin Lim notes that this homogenizing label includes "hundreds of tribes, language groups, a variety of immigration histories (from first-generation Chinese Americans, arriving from Taiwan or Hong Kong or the mainland, who have different stories to tell, to the Sansei, third-generation Japanese Americans

whose American roots go back to the early nineteenth century)."
There are times when "Asian American" may be appropriate, but
generally try to replace it with a specific designation.

as one man *unanimously, simultaneously, as one person/body, without exception, of the same mind, of one accord, at one with each other, willing, agreed
on all hands, in every mouth, in concert, carried unanimously/by acclama-
tion, everyone, all.*

asphalt-heater man *asphalt-heater tender.*

assemblyman (manufacturing) *assembler.*

assemblyman (politics) *assembly member, state assembly member, member of
the assembly, legislator, representative.*

assembly-room foreman *assembly-room supervisor.*

assistant cameraman *dolly pusher.*

attaboy!/attagirl! these terms seem to be used equally often and to be
equally harmless.

augerman *rotary auger operator.*

au pair girl *au pair, live-in sitter/child-minder/family helper, family helper.*
There do not appear to be any male au pairs.

authoress *author.*

auto mechanic fewer than 1% of U.S. auto mechanics are women.

automobile/she *automobile/it.*

automotive parts man *automotive stock clerk.*

average man *average person/citizen/human being/voter, common person/citizen/
human being/voter, ordinary person/citizen/human being/voter, citizen,
voter, layperson, taxpayer, resident, homeowner, landowner, passerby,
nonspecialist, commoner, one of the people/masses, rank and file.*

aviation survivalman this Coast Guard title can refer to either sex. For
non-official alternatives, try *aviation survivalist/rescuer, aviation rescue
equipment supervisor/manager/steward/chief/officer/clerk.*

aviatress/aviatrix *aviator. See also* airman.

avuncular there is no equally tidy equivalent for a woman, but you might
be able to use "auntly" or "auntlike." ("Amitate" is a narrow term
referring to a relationship in some cultures between a niece and her
paternal aunt.) Otherwise try adjectives with related meanings for
both sexes: *indulgent, kindly, genial, expansive, conspiratorial, friendly,*
etc.

axman *axer.*

b

The most violent element in society is ignorance.

Emma Goldman

babble *ramble, mutter, mumble, stutter, stammer, sputter, blather, splutter, gibber, blurt out, let slip, reveal foolishly, divulge secrets, spout/talk nonsense, talk through one's hat, run off at the mouth, talk idly, shoot the breeze, make chin music, rattle away, bend someone's ear.* Not sexist per se, "babble" is reserved for babies and women (originally it belonged only to babies). *See also* bull session; chatter; chatterbox; gabby; gossip; gossipy; yenta.

babe/baby/baby doll (woman) avoid. Picturing women as children and playthings has been highly damaging. For the use of "big baby" referring to men, *see* coward/cowardly/cowardice.

babysitter this inclusive word is used in one highly sexist manner. Todd Melby, Minneapolis, says when he's out with his child, he's been "complimented" by people for babysitting. Melby says he is parenting, "not just giving Mom a few minutes away from the kids." Where mothers are never considered to be babysitting their children, fathers often are.

bachelor *man.* Something that is only one part of a person's life (being single) becomes the whole of the person when "bachelor" is used. If a reference to marital status is necessary (it rarely is), use an adjective instead of a noun: *single, unmarried, unwed, celibate.* However, "unmarried" and "unwed" perpetuate a marriage-as-norm attitude. We write and speak as though marriage and parenthood somehow grant validity to a person when in fact married and unmarried often have more in common than not. Note the nonparallel connotations of the supposedly parallel "bachelor" and "spinster." Women go from bachelor girl to spinster to old maid but men are bachelors forever.

bachelor girl/bachelorette *woman. See also* bachelor; spinster.

bachelor pad *apartment, home.* The term has been give a new and invidious sexist twist in the "bachelor pads" available today: bikini-clad women decorate computer mouse pads from Computer Giftware. They were a "response to consumer requests."

bachelor's degree *B.A., B.S., undergraduate degree, college degree, four-year degree, baccalaureate.* "Baccalaureate" means a college or university undergraduate degree and is therefore an exact synonym for "bachelor's degree" without gender-specific overtones (although its Latin roots are masculine).

backcourt man *backcourt player.*

backdoor man *illicit lover.*

backroom boys *power brokers, wheeler-dealers, politicos, strategists, movers and shakers.*

back-shoe girl *back-shoe worker.*

back-up man *back-up, back-up worker, backer-up.*

backwoodsman *settler, wilderness settler, backsettler, pioneer, woodlander, woodcutter; hermit, recluse; backwoodsman and backwoodswoman.*

bad guy *bad actor/news, villain.* There are few good alternatives because virtually all the "bad guy" words in our language are perceived as referring to men, even those that are not sexist per se. In theory the following words could be used of a woman; in practice they very rarely are: bounder, brigand, bully, cad, cheat, crook, deviate, double-crosser, evildoer, four-flusher, gangster, geek, goon, heel, hoodlum, hooligan, louse, mobster, mountebank, mugger, outcast, outlaw, punk, rascal, rat, renegade, reprobate, rogue, rotter, ruffian, scalawag, scoundrel, scum/scumbag/scuzzbag, sleaze/sleazebag/ sleazeball, slimebag/slimeball/slime bucket, suspect, thug, two-timer. Negative words for women focus on sexual promiscuity (there are ten times as many words for sexually promiscuous women in our language as there are for men); negative words for men focus on moral vileness (almost all terms for moral vileness are for men). *See also* animal (man); provider; success object (man); ugly customer.

badman *thief, robber, outlaw, gangster, desperado, bank robber, cattle/horse thief, rustler, villain. See also* gunman.

bad workman quarrels with his tools, a *a bad worker quarrels with the tools, bad workers quarrel with their tools.*

bag/old bag (woman) avoid. There is no parallel for a man.

baggageman *baggage checker/handler/agent.*

bag lady/bag man (homeless) *bag woman/bag man, street person.* The gender-fair use of "bag woman" and "bag man" (avoid the nonparallel "lady/man") is sometimes appropriate although we tend to hear a great deal more about the bag woman than we do about the bag man even though more men than women end up trying to survive on the streets. In the plural, use *the homeless, street people.*

bagman (British) *traveling sales agent/representative.*

bagman (collector/distributor of illicit funds) *bagger, go-between, shark, racketeer, peculator, receiver.*

bailsman *bail agent, bond agent, bail bond agent/poster; provider, guarantor, bonding institution, underwriter.*

balcony man *platform worker.*

ball/bang these slang terms for sex convey a number of twisted and sexist attitudes: they are violent; they are nonreciprocal; they make objects of the partner; they belong to the unfortunate it-itches-so-I-scratch school of sex. Avoiding these words won't change attitudes, but an awareness of language brings with it an awareness of underlying values.

ball and chain (woman) avoid. Although women being held back/ enchained/weighed down by men has been a predominant feature of society for centuries, no term like "ball and chain" for men ever got into the (male-dominated) language.

ball boy *tennis court attendant, ball/court attendant, ball tender/fetcher.*

ballerina a ballerina is a principal (but not the principal) female dancer in a company, a soloist. Although the term is commonly used to refer to any female ballet dancer, this is not, strictly speaking, correct. The French word for a female solo dancer is "danseuse"; "ballerina" is the Italian equivalent, the term most commonly used in the United States. Retain "ballerina" for its narrow meaning within ballet companies, but for anyone who dances ballet nonprofessionally use *ballet dancer. See also* danseur/danseuse; premier danseur; prima ballerina.

ballet master/ballet mistress these titles are fairly standard within professional ballet companies, but for all others, use *ballet instructor/teacher.*

balls acceptable sex-specific word when it means testicles. For the inclusive metaphorical use substitute *guts, moxie, courage, nerve, bravery, self-assurance, confidence, determination, spunk.* For "ballbreaker/ballbuster" meaning a difficult or complicated task or situation, use *gutbuster, bunbuster, tough row to hoe, killer, bad news, hell on wheels, no picnic, hell of a note, tall/large order, tough grind/one, tough sledding, uphill job.* For "ballbreaker" meaning a woman, *see* castrate/ castrating; shrew.

ball the jack *speed, go all out/full speed/full speed ahead, stake everything on one throw/attempt, no holds barred, all or nothing effort, anything goes.*

bandsman *member of the band, band player/member/musician, player in the band.* Or, be specific: *trumpeteer, drummer, saxophone player, pianist.*

banshee retain; this female spirit has no male counterpart, but she plays an important part in Gaelic folklore.

barber almost half of all barbers are women, and the woman cutting your hair is not a "lady barber," "barberette," or "barberess." She is a barber.

bar boy *bartender/bar helper, bar assistant/server, waiter.*

bard not itself sex-based, "bard" has acquired masculine overtones, probably from its close association with "the" bard, Shakespeare, and you may sometimes want more inclusive-sounding alternatives: *poet, poet-singer, epic/heroic poet, heroic versifier, minstrel, balladsinger.*

bargeman *barge hand, deckhand.*

bargemaster *barge captain.*

bar girl avoid; with drinking age limits, the "girl" is obviously inappropriate, and the term has come to usually mean a prostitute who works out of bars. (Note the different path "bar boy" has taken.)

barmaid *bartender/bar helper, bar assistant/server, waiter, cocktail server.*

barman *bartender, bar attendant, barkeeper, barkeep.* Half of U.S. bartenders are women.

barracuda (woman) avoid; too often directed at a forceful woman, this term penalizes one sex when it is as aggressive as the other. *See also* aggressive.

barren *sterile, infertile.* The alternatives are used for both sexes. "Barren," which is used only for women, carries an unwarranted stigma and many negative associations (synonyms include words like impoverished, desolate, arid, fruitless, unproductive, meager, ineffective, incompetent, useless, worthless, valueless, devoid, deficient). Saying that someone is "childless" or "has no children" is not recommended; these phrases support a children-as-norm stereotype. *See also* infertile; sterile.

barrow boy *costermonger, street vendor.*

baseman (baseball) *base player, baser; first/second/third baser; first-base/second-base/third-base player; first, second, third; first-base/second-base/third-base position; 1B, 2B, 3B (baseball notation); first/second/third sacker.* There is good traditional support for the alternatives. According to Stuart Berg Flexner (*Listening to America*), "first base, second base, and third base" have referred to both the positions and the players since the 1840s, while "first," "second," "third," and "base player" were already being used in the 1860s. Note that other baseball terms use the common -er ending: outfielder, infielder, pitcher, catcher, batter. Base players may be girls/women or boys/men; in 1989 the first girl competed in a Little League World Series.

bassman (music) *bassist.*

bastard avoid. When you mean someone whose parents were not married at the time of their birth, use *offspring/child/son/daughter of unmarried parents/of single parent/of unknown father.* Most often the status of a person's birth is gratuitous information; refer to it only when it is relevant and then relay it in a neutral way, e.g., "She never knew who her father was." Or, "His birth certificate was blank after 'father's name.'" When you mean "bastard" in the sense of "a wretched and repellent male" (Richard A. Spears, *NTC's Dictionary of American Slang and Colloquial Expressions*) you'll have to be creative—most alternatives are unacceptable on grounds of sexism, handicappism, ageism, or unprintable language. Try *ignoramus, saphead, stinker, ratfink, snake in the grass, creep, heel, jerk, bum, lowlife.* "Bastard" is sexist because it is used only for men and because the insult also slyly impugns the man's mother. *See also* bad guy; illegitimate/illegitimate child.

batboy *batkeeper, bat attendant/tender/fetcher.*

bathing beauty *sunbather.* *See also* beauty queen.

batman *aide.*

batsman (cricket) *batter.*

battered wife/woman retain sex-specific terms: *battered wife or battered husband, battered man or battered woman.* When inclusive terms are needed use *battered spouse/partner, spouse/domestic abuse, domestic/marital/family violence.* Gender-neutral terms obscure the pattern of explicit violence perpetrated on overwhelming numbers of women compared to men. Some men's organizations claim more men than women are victims of domestic abuse. However, of cases taken through the courts, 95% result in conviction of men, 5% of women— most of whom are retaliating against abuse. The 95%/5% breakdown also appears in most studies of the issue. The federal Centers for Disease Control reported in August 1990 that assaults involving people who are related, sharing a household, or otherwise intimate are a major public health problem in which victims are predominantly female and perpetrators are predominantly male. (Battering is not, however, solely a male-female problem; partner-battering is also a problem for lesbians and gay men.) Nearly six million U.S. women are abused by partners every year; a woman is beaten every fifteen seconds. The FBI estimates that one of every two women will be physically abused at some point in her life and says that 34% of all female homicide victims older than fifteen are killed by their husbands or intimate partners. National studies have found battering to be the greatest single cause of injury to women, exceeding rapes, muggings, even car accidents. Businesses lose $3 to $5 billion per year as a result of absenteeism due to spouse abuse and medical costs reach $10 million per year (22% to 35% of women who visit emergency departments have abuse-related symptoms).

battle-ax (woman) *tyrant, grouch, bully, petty despot, ornery/quarrelsome/domineering/strong-willed/high-handed/combative/hostile/battlesome/hot-tempered person.*

"battle of the sexes" don't perpetuate the adversarial approach to female-male relations. This term legitimizes a certain hopelessness about women and men being able to coexist peaceably. Riane Eisler (*The Chalice and the Blade*) describes early partnership societies in which the sexes cooperated with each other on every social level. She says that as long as there are imbalances of power between individual men and women, there will be imbalances of power in the larger society, leading to a dominator, warlike model of society. We still have the choice to be a partnership society or a dominator society; "battle of the sexes" gives us to think there is no choice. *See also* opposite sex.

bawd/bawdy house *prostitute/house of prostitution.*

bawdy despite the connection with "bawd," this adjective can be used of both sexes.

beach bum/beach bunny although "bum" and "bunny" carry some cultural pejoratives for their respective sexes, these terms are at least moderately parallel and will probably continue to be used.

beadsman/beadswoman (or bedesman/bedeswoman) *suppliant, licensed beggar, almhouse inmate, professional penitent.* "Beadswoman" or "beadsman" may sometimes be the correct choice, especially in certain historical contexts, but avoid using "beadsmen" as a pseudo-generic.

be a man *See* act like a man/be a man/take it like a man.

beau "beau" and "belle" are the masculine and feminine forms of the same French word, but the English meanings for the two words are nonparallel. For a sex-nonspecific word use *friend, lover, sweetheart. See also* belle/belle of the ball, boyfriend.

beau idéal although inclusive, this term looks sexist because of the masculine "beau" (the French noun "idéal" is grammatically masculine in gender and thus takes a masculine adjective). If you prefer, use *perfect model/type/example, standard model/type/example, paradigm.*

beautician *cosmetologist, hairdresser, hairstylist, hair designer, haircutter.* Some people in the field still prefer "beautician," although that refers to someone who does only women's hair. *See also* barber.

beauty queen *beauty contest/beauty pageant winner; beautiful/attractive woman.*

bedfellow *bedmate, ally, partner, associate, cohort, companion, mate, pair, colleague, sidekick, chum, buddy.*

Beefeater has always been a man.

bee in one's bonnet *one-track mind, fixation, obsession, fixed idea/idée fixe, ruling passsion.* This is a fairly harmless phrase (except for the bee, of course), but alternatives are offered for the times it might sound silly to say "he's got a bee in his bonnet."

before you can say Jack Robinson when using expressions like this, be aware of how many are male-based. Balance them with female-based expressions, creative expressions of your own, or alternatives: *in two shakes of a lamb's tail, on the double, in a jiffy, immediately if not sooner, before you can say "knife," right off the bat, in one fell swoop, in a pig's whisker, pronto, straightaway, lickety-split, in the same breath, in the wink/ twinkling of an eye, at the drop of a hat, in double-quick time, on the spot, at once, immediately. See* Writing Guidelines for a discussion of sex-linked expressions.

beget in the general sense of creating something, half the time use *give birth to*. *See also* father (pseudogeneric verb).

beggarman/beggarwoman *beggar.*

bellboy *bellhop, attendant, hotel/passenger attendant.*

belle/belle of the ball *charming/popular/attractive person, flirt, center of attention, success, stunner, head-turner.* The language never had a "beau of the ball," nor are many men described in "belle"-type terms—probably because women's successes have always been closely identified with the way they look and how they "behave" while men's successes correlate with what they have done and how they "perform."

bellman *bellringer, crier, herald, trumpeteer.*

belly dancer in the Middle East, belly dancing is a traditional women's folk dance and there are no public performances by male dancers. In the United States, however, there are professional male belly dancers who perform publicly.

bench jockey/bench warmer can refer to boy/man or girl/woman.

benchman *bench technician, bencher; sugar tester; bench baker.*

benefactress *benefactor.*

benjamin when using expressions like this, be aware of how many are male-based. Balance them with female-based expressions, creative expressions of your own, or alternatives: *youngest/favorite child. See* Writing Guidelines for a discussion of sex-linked expressions.

be one's own man/be your own man *stand on one's own two feet, be one's own person, be a do-it-yourselfer, be independent/inner-directed/self-ruling/ self-reliant, self-regulated/individualistic/outspoken/self-confident, be a free-thinker/free spirit, be at one's own disposal, be nobody's lackey.*

best boy *gaffer assistant, assistant to chief electrician, chief electrician's assistant, assistant, gofer.* These positions are held by both sexes.

best-laid schemes of mice and men, the unless quoting Burns use simply *the best-laid schemes.*

best man "best man" is acceptable only if his partner is "best woman." Otherwise use *attendant, attendant of honor, honor/wedding/groom's attendant.* Use a parallel term for the female attendant. Male and female wedding attendants did not originally have the same duties, which is perhaps why nonparallel terms developed. Centuries ago, men enlisted the help of their friends to kidnap a future wife or to prevent her from being kidnapped by someone else.

best man for the job *best choice/candidate/applicant/person/ worker for the job.*

better half *spouse, partner, wife/husband, mate, best friend.* The perfect marriage has erroneously and destructively been touted as two half-people who are now a whole. If you must think in halves, at least use "other half" instead of "better half."

Bible although there is often disagreement about inclusive-language translations of the Bible going too far or, conversely, not going far enough, most individuals and churches can find something today to help meet their needs. The degree of inclusiveness varies. For example, the 1990 *New Revised Standard Version* has no "man" or "men" when the reference is to all people, but it retains male references to God. *An Inclusive Language Lectionary* avoids all gender-specific words, including pronouns for God (or it refers to God as male and female). Among other publications are *The New Jerusalem* and *Psalms Anew: In Inclusive Language*. Although many people worry that "changing the language" means being unfaithful to the scriptures, there is much theological and linguistic support for the changes; in the introduction to the *Lectionary for the Christian People*, the editors say, "It is astounding how often masculine designations have entered the text in English translations and have no basis in the original language." Just as "thee"s and "thou"s are considered archaic and irrelevant and the products of translation, so are male-centered terms. Father Joseph Arackal says that going back to the original language of the scriptures does away with almost 90% of the exclusive words in our English translations. The "newest" translations often turn out to be the "oldest" with their reliance on ancient Greek and Hebrew texts rather than on intermediate translations. *See also* hymn.

Bible thumper *fundamentalist.*

bicker *wrangle, argue, quarrel, have words, squabble, cross swords, disagree.* Alternatives are given because "bicker" is reserved for women.

big boss/cheese/enchilada/fish/gun/noise/shot/wheel/wig these can refer to either sex. Avoid the violent "big gun" and "big shot."

Big Brother unless referring specifically to the Stalin-like figure unceasingly watching everyone via television ("Big Brother is watching you") in George Orwell's 1949 novel *1984*, you may use inclusive alternatives: *mind police, dictator, omnipresent totalitarian authority, government spy, infiltrator, stakeout, monitor, watchdog, mole, surveillant, guard, someone who keeps tab on/a sharp eye upon/a watchful eye upon.*

bigot woman or man.

billionaire man or woman.

bimbette this word, apparently meaning "a young bimbo," actually enjoyed a Warholian fifteen minutes of fame (in a well-publicized British libel suit). Some newspapers even described one of the participants as "an aging bimbette."

bimbo from the Italian for "little boy" or "little kid," this word now has a range of meanings: sexually loose woman, giddy woman, clown-like or klutzy person of either sex. It's been used in recent years chiefly to describe women involved with men involved with trouble (for example, Donna Rice, Fawn Hall, and Jessica Hahn with, respectively, Gary Hart, Oliver North, and Jim Bakker). Why the women get the label while the men who do the running around, arms dealing, and bilking still remain just guys is a peculiarity of our value system. Avoid "bimbo" or use it equally for both sexes.

bindle man *bindle stiff, hobo, wanderer, itinerant, migrant, harvest worker, lumberjack.*

bird/bird-dog/bird-watcher these terms, which refer respectively to a woman/girl, someone who "takes" another man's woman, and someone who watches women or girls, are all demeaning; avoid them. *See also* animal names for people; owner.

birdbrained *See* scatterbrained.

birdman *aviator.* If you need to use "birdman," use the equivalent "ladybird," which, even though it suffers from nonparallelism ("man/lady") and includes "lady," has a history and associations that make it fairly innocuous. *See also* airman.

birth control this issue belongs to both men and women; avoid associating it solely with women. Other acceptable terms include *contraception, family planning, fertility control, reproductive freedom. See also* population control.

bisexual woman or man. The increasingly visible bisexual community reports frequent antagonism from both the heterosexual and homosexual worlds; watch for speaking or writing that implies people are either gay or straight.

bishop depending on the religious denomination, a bishop could be a man or a woman.

bitch (noun) when used of a woman, this is one of the most loaded of the sexist words. Vague and stereotypical, it says more about the name-caller than about the name-callee; it is usually the knee-jerk response of a defensive person with a small vocabulary. Richard A. Spears (*NTC's Dictionary of American Slang and Colloquial Expressions*) calls this term a verbal weapon. Sometimes the correct alternative to "bitch" is simply *woman, person, individual.* Sometimes use an inclusive noun: *grumbler, grouch, griper, malcontent, sourpuss, sorehead, bellyacher, crab, crank, kvetcher.* Other times you may want an adjective: *hell on wheels, ruthless, aggressive, domineering, controlling, powerful, tyrannical, overwhelming, overpowering, spiteful, malicious, cruel, wicked, vicious, cold-hearted, hard-hearted, merciless.* In the sense of a complaint, use instead *gripe, complaint, problem, bone to pick, objection.* In the sense of something that is difficult, unpleasant, or problematic ("a bitch" or "a real bitch"), use *tough row to hoe, tough nut to crack, heavy sledding, hornet's nest, between a rock and a hard place, bad news/one, killer, tough grind/one, large order, predicament, no picnic, thorny/knotty problem, uphill job, gutbuster, bunbuster, backbreaker, dilemma, bind, tangle, mess, fine pickle, hell of a note.*

bitch (verb) *complain, gripe, kvetch, grouse, grumble, badmouth, harp on, sound off, beef, bellyache, carp, crab, criticize, denounce, disapprove, dissent,* *object, protest, reproach, backbite, bawl out, call/dress down, call on the carpet/mat, call names, cuss, make cutting remarks/dirty digs/cracks, give someone hell/the devil/a going-over, lambaste, give someone lip, make it hot for, pick on, pitch into, put down, put someone in their place, tell someone where to get off.* When you mean "to spoil or bungle" ("bitch something up") use *botch*.

bitch goddess Success unless quoting William James, avoid this term. Consider the psychology involved in attributing one's successes and failures to a powerful, capricious, female Other. *See also* Dame Fortune.

bitch session *gripe session.*

bitchy *grouchy, cranky, crabby, spiteful, moody, rude, ill-tempered, bad-tempered, irritable, surly, complaining, cantankerous, peevish, out of sorts.*

black/Black (noun) current style generally lowercases "black," but some people prefer it capitalized. Because of the current debate about "black" versus "African American," know your audience and their preferences. For some people "black," "black power," and "black is beautiful" still convey racial pride. Others want to move beyond color-coding to "African American," a term like those chosen by other Americans (e.g., Italian Americans, Chinese Americans). They say color cannot classify human distinctions as suitably as an ethnic/national taxonomy and that the use of "black" and "white" over-dramatizes whatever real differences exist. Terms like Afro-American and Euro-American, which are less evaluative, less contrasted, and more descriptive, have been gaining acceptance in recent years, although not everyone agrees. Some blacks say they have never seen Africa, their parents and grandparents have never seen Africa—why would they want to be called African Americans? They say blacks are as American as any other ethnic group and shouldn't dilute their nationality by naming themselves after the continent of their ancestors. A problem also arises with respect to West Indies blacks, Indic peoples, and Australoid peoples; an across-the-board usage of African American necessarily misidentifies large segments of society. The term "people of color" is another possibility for some. The importance of the debate is that people are naming themselves instead of being named by others—as they were in the cases of "Negro" and "colored." Once racial equality is achieved, the question of identity and naming may not be so critical. In the meantime, call people what they want to be called—and accept that this may vary from group to group. Do not identify people as "black" or "African American" when this information is irrelevant to your material, as it most often is; would "white" be equally appropriate in a similar instance? *See also* African American/Afro-American; black-and-white (adj.); black/black-; Negress/Negro; niggardly; nonwhite; white man's burden.

black/black- Martin Luther King, Jr. pointed out that there are some 120 synonyms for "blackness" of which at least half are offensive. Almost all the 134 synonyms for "whiteness" are favorable. "The symbolism of white as positive and black as negative is pervasive in our culture" (Robert B. Moore, in *Racism and Sexism* by Paula S. Rothenberg). The good guys wear white hats and ride white horses, and everybody knows what the bad guys wear and ride. Dictionary definitions of black refer in part to evil, the devil, disaster, condemnation, dirt, sullenness, and darkness while definitions of white refer to innocence, purity, harmlessness, good fortune, and lightness. Avoiding words that reinforce the negative connotations of black will not do away with racism, but it can lessen the everyday pain these expressions cause readers. The following terms can be replaced by those in parentheses: blackball (ostracize); "black day in our nation's history" ("bleak" or "sad"); black deed (evil deed); blacken (slander, defile, defame; smirch, soil, tarnish); black eye (mouse, shiner; bad name); blackguard (scoundrel, villain, ne'er-do-well); blackhearted (wicked); black humor (satire, sinister humor); blackletter day (evil/tragic day); blacklist (denounce, condemn, proscribe, ostracize); blackly (darkly, gloomily, hopelessly); blackmail (hush money, payola, extortion, shake-down; extort, bleed, put the arm on, shake down); black mark (mark against one, blot on one's copybook); black market (illegal market/trade/trafficking); black moment (dark moment); black outlook (bleak outlook); black sheep (outcast, pariah, reprobate, renegade, idler, prodigal, born/family loser, ne'er-do-well, bad apple in the barrel, family rebel). *See also* black-and-white (adj.); white.

black-and-white (adj.) *either-or, simple, all good or all bad, one extreme or the other, either here or there, binary, dogmatic, definite, unequivocal, absolute, positive, categorical, polar opposites, diametric opposites, day and night, chalk and cheese.* This highly racist expression (it refers to things being sharply divided into good and evil groups, sides, or ideas) perpetuates the positive evaluation of white and the negative evaluation of black. *See also* black/black-; white.

blackjack although based on a man's name, this term has specific associations and no substitutes. It is also rarely perceived as sexist or racist; leave as is.

black Maria *patrol/paddy wagon, police van.*

blacksmith *farrier.* The preferred "farrier" is perceived as more inclusive.

blind *visually impaired, partially sighted, sight/vision disability; naive, unaware, ignorant, obtuse, dense, unreasoning, senseless, thoughtless, uncritical, undiscerning, insensitive, unfeeling, indifferent.* Avoid once-I-was-blind-but-now-I-see metaphors, which associate physical vision loss with negative personal characteristics. Refer to "blind persons/

individuals" rather than to "the blind" (thus defining entire individuals by something that is only one aspect of their life). *See also* handicappism; handicapped; "people first" rule.

blindman's bluff/blindman's buff this game has been played for many centuries under a number of different names, some of them neither sexist nor handicappist: *blufty, hoodwink play, the brazen fly* (Iona and Peter Opie, *Children's Games in Street and Playground*).

blonde *blond*. Use the shorter base word as noun or adjective for both sexes. *See also* divorce/divorcee.

blood brother the term blood sister is also used; in the plural use *blood brothers and blood sisters/blood sisters and blood brothers*.

blue long associated with boys, especially babies, this color was once thought to ward off the evil spirits that inhabited nurseries, perhaps because of its association with the sky (and thus with well-disposed heavenly spirits). According to David Feldman (*Imponderables: The Solution to the Mysteries of Everyday Life*), boys were held to be very valuable by parents, so blue clothing was used as a cheap form of insurance. No such insurance was desired or apparently needed for girl babies. *See also* pink.

Bluebeard the original Bluebeard, Gilles de Rais, abducted, raped, and murdered between forty and one hundred peasant boys: "The most amazing part of the Gilles de Rais story is that the legend of Bluebeard's Castle that we know today has metamorphosed from a terrifying account of a sex-murderer of small boys to a glorified fantasy of a devilish rake who killed seven wives for their 'curiosity'" (Susan Brownmiller, *Against Our Will*). According to Brownmiller, it is more palatable to the sex in power to accept women in the role of victim than themselves. Do not perpetuate the recast Bluebeard story.

blue boys (police) *blue coats, blues*.

bluesman *blues musician/player/singer*.

bluestocking *intellectual, member of the literati, wit, artistic/learned person, egghead, dilettante, dabbler, amateur, culture vulture*. This derisory term for educated or literary women was originally used for both sexes, although no parallel term developed for men when this one became limited to women—even though the blue stockings worn at the small literary assemblies hosted by Elizabeth Montague, Portman Square, London, belonged to a certain Mr. Stillingfleet.

board boy/board girl *board maker*.

board man *board member*.

boat/she *boat/it*. *See also* ship/she.

boatman *boater, boat worker/dealer/operator*. *See also* seaman.

boatswain "swain" refers to a servant or a boy, and boatswains have traditionally been men. However, "boatswain" could be used for a woman as its sex link is related more to the lack of female boatwains than to its etymology. More neutral-appearing alternatives might include *bosun, bosun's mate, ship's bosun, ship warrant officer/petty officer, deck crew/topside supervisor, hydraulic mate, rigging boss.*

bobby in Great Britain both women and men police officers are called bobbies. Sir Robert ("Bobby") Peel organized the London police force in the early 1800s and is responsible for the other popular police nickname: "peeler." *See also* policeman.

bobsled nonsexist; this term is not based on a man's name, although its etymology is uncertain (perhaps from the Middle English "bobbe" meaning "bunch" or "cluster" and referring to the coupling of sleds or the paired runners).

Bob's your uncle when using expressions like this, be aware of how many are male-based. Some of the time use female-based expressions, creative expressions of your own, or alternatives: *there you are! there you have it! that's it! voilà! everything's great!* For a discussion of sex-linked expressions, *see* Writing Guidelines.

bodyguard because bodyguards were only men for so long, you may want to use a term that sounds more inclusive: *personal protection agent/operative, personal security agent/operative/consultant.*

body image we speak and write about men's bodies and women's bodies in very different ways. Minneapolis writer Mary Morse Marti sees a direct association between a study showing that adolescent girls are almost twice as likely as boys to be depressed—primarily because of their poor body image—and, for example, media emphasis on women's bathing suit fashions that extols such virtues as "constructed bust lines" to "enhance smaller chests," "bottoms to flatter round stomachs and hips," and even suits with "built-in shape" for women and girls unfortunate enough to have none. Morse Marti wonders if she can expect to see similar articles on men's swimwear that feature "size-enhancing groin pads, rear-end boning (for that all-important pert look), and retro 'Dad' full-cut boxer trunks (for men and boys with something to hide)." There are virtually no general-interest books telling teenage boys how to dress, how to control weight, how to feel more comfortable about their bodies; countless fiction and nonfiction books address these issues for teenage girls. Twice as many women ages 30–64 as men in the same age group think they are overweight; 58% of seventeen-year-old girls said they were overweight when actually only 17% were; some 90% to 95% of those with eating disorders are female. *See also* lookism.

bogeyman *bogey/bogy, bogeymonster, goblin, hobgoblin, bugaboo, gremlin, phantom, spook, specter, ghost.*

boilerman *boiler tender operator.*

bomb disposal man *bomb disposal specialist, explosives expert/specialist.*

bombshell/blonde bombshell (woman) avoid; militaristic, violent, and sexist. There is no parallel for a man and the term paints women as destructive to men, even though on the surface it appears complimentary.

BOMFOG coined around 1960 by New York reporter Joe Shannon, BOMFOG came from a phrase repeatedly used by the late Nelson Rockefeller: "The brotherhood of man under the fatherhood of God." The acronym is used to indicate vague political rhetoric, but women have also used it to describe the overwhelmingly male system under which they live.

bondman/bondwoman *bondslave, bond servant, slave, serf.*

bondsman (law) *bonding/bond/bail/bail bond agent, surety provider, guarantor, bonding institution, lender.*

bondsman/bondswoman (slave) *See* bondman/bondwoman.

bonhomie *good-naturedness, geniality, cheerfulness, light-heartedness, optimism, happiness, joy, liveliness, friendliness, affability.* From the French for "good man," this is most often applied to men and groups of men, which is why alternatives are suggested. However, there is nothing against using it to refer to women and to groups of women and men.

bon vivant the French is grammatically masculine and this term has become associated primarily with men over the years, but women are using it too: Catherine Deneuve—female and French—says, "I'm a bon vivant, a reveler." For times when you need something more neutral-looking try *connoisseur, hedonist, epicure, aesthete, sensualist, high-liver, sophisticate, enthusiast, someone with joie de vivre.*

bookman *bookseller, publisher's representative, book dealer/collector/salesclerk, bookstore clerk/owner, bibliophile, bookworm, librarian.*

boom man *log sorter.*

bordello *house of prostitution.*

border patrolman *border guard/patrol, member of the border patrol.*

born out of wedlock avoid this dated and judgmental expression. *See also* bastard; illegitimate/illegitimate child; wedlock.

borrow from Peter to pay Paul when using expressions like this, be aware of how many are male-based. Some of the time use female-based expressions, creative expressions of your own, or alternatives: *borrow from the left hand to pay the right, juggle the bills, keep one step ahead of the bailiff, indulge in creative accounting, six of one and half a dozen of the other.*

bosom buddy nonsexist. The noun "bosom" is defined as the human chest; the adjective is defined as "close" or "intimate."

boss lady/boss man *boss, straw/job boss.* Note the nonparallel "lady/man." *See also* forelady/foreman/forewoman; lady (noun).

boulevardier *See* man about town.

bouncer there may be isolated exceptions, but for all practical purposes bouncers are men. Bouncing is associated primarily with bars, but similar work is done in nonbar environments by women, who are then called *security officers/guards/consultants, crowd controllers, patrols, bodyguards.*

bowman (boats) *bow paddler, rower, boater.*

bowman (weapons) *archer.*

box boy *carryout clerk, bagger.*

box man (gambling) *box boss/supervisor/collector.*

boy (referring to a man) *man, young man.* "Boy" usually refers to someone no more than sixteen and sometimes no more than twelve or thirteen, depending on the context and on the boy/young man himself. It is absolutely unacceptable when used of African American men.

boycott nonsexist; named after English land agent Captain Charles Cunningham Boycott (1832–1897), who was so harsh on the Irish tenants of his employer, Lord Erne, during a period of crop failures and famines that his neighbors shunned him and the tenant farmers refused to pay rent, stopped harvesting, and formed the Irish Land League. They drove off his servants, intercepted his mail, and tried to cut off his food supplies.

boyfriend *friend, man friend* (if "woman friend" is also used), *male friend* (if "female friend" is also used), *best friend, escort, date, companion, constant/longtime/loving/live-in/intimate/domestic companion, romantic interest, heartthrob, significant other, mate, housemate, partner, domestic/ life partner, partner of long standing, steady, paramour, lover, longtime love, live-in, live-in lover, fiancé, betrothed, sweetheart, main/major squeeze* (and, for stars, *offscreen squeeze*), *my reason for living, the love/light of my life, the man in my life.* **See also** fiancé/fiancée.

boyish replace this vague word with specific inclusive adjectives: *ingenuous, naive, childlike, innocent, open, friendly, eager, youthful, immature, self-conscious, inept, bright-eyed, optimistic, cheerful, adolescent, childish, sophmoric, juvenile, kiddish, infantile, callow, unsophisticated.*

boys and girls half the time use *girls and boys.* Sometimes use *children, students, young people.* In 1990 the 1.5-million member Boys Clubs of America, which had been quietly accepting girls as members since the late 1880s, changed its name to Boys and Girls Clubs of America. Although individual clubs are not required to accept girls, 91% of them do. Also in 1990 the 250,000-member Girls Clubs of America, Inc. changed its name to Girls Inc. to "better reflect the seriousness of its mission and its leadership as an advocate for girls."

boy scout there is nothing particularly sexist about the terms "boy scout" and "girl scout" (although the goals, activities, and attitudes of the two groups have often been based on sexist concepts). Inclusive terms are being seen more often: *youth scout, scouter.*

boys in blue (armed forces) the armed forces now consists of both girls and boys, so use instead *soldiers, members of the armed forces, armed forces personnel.*

boys in blue (Civil War) *Union soldiers, bluecoats, the Blue, Army blue.*

boys in gray (Civil War) *Confederate soldiers, graycoats, graybacks, the Gray.*

boys in the backroom See backroom boys.

boys will be boys *children will be children, kids will be kids.* Sometimes used archly of men when they indulge in games, adult "toys," or practical jokes, the expression has also served to excuse the inexcusable. When a young woman at the U.S. Naval Academy was dragged from her dormitory room and handcuffed to a urinal by male classmates while others taunted her and took pictures, the administration determined that the incident was "a good-natured exchange that got out of hand." Translation: boys will be boys.

bozo *clown, jerk, fool.* Alternatives are given since "bozo" is most often reserved for men.

bra burner this term is inaccurate. Women protesting at the 1968 Miss America Pageant in Atlantic City threw brassieres into a trash can, thereby shedding what they considered a symbol of female oppression. Although burning was in fact outlawed by a municipal fire ordinance and never did occur, newspapers mistakenly reported "bra burning." In many cases, the use of this incorrect term betrays a hostile, anti-woman attitude.

braggart technically inclusive, this word is more often associated with men. Alternatives are only slightly more inclusive-appearing: *bragger, boaster, show-off, loudmouth, windbag, blowhard.*

brakeman *braker, brake tender/holder/coupler/controller/ operator, yard coupler; conductor's assistant.*

brass (high-ranking officers) includes both sexes.

brazen *fearless, dauntless, bold, daring, brash, defiant, audacious, plainspoken, outspoken, candid, frank.* "Brazen" is usually ascribed to women (e.g., "brazen hussy").

breadwinner 28% of all households are headed by a woman. *See also* bring home the bacon; provider.

brethren/brothers (pseudogeneric) *brothers and sisters/sisters and brothers, people, congregation, assembly, colleagues, friends, associates, peers, community, companions, family, kin, believers, the faithful, children of God, neighbors.* In direct address, use *my dear people, sisters and brothers/ brothers and sisters, friends, dear friends.*

brewmaster *brewing director, head brewer.*

bridal *wedding, nuptial, marital, connubial.* Use terms that include both parties. A bridal consultant, for example, is a wedding consultant, and bridal showers are more often becoming wedding showers for the couple, thus de-emphasizing kitchen and houseware gifts for the woman under the assumption that domestic matters are her affair.

bride and groom OK. Or, *wedding couple*. *See also* bridegroom; give
away the bride.

bride burning also called dowry death, bride burning is the murder
(often disguised as a domestic accident) of a Hindu newlywed
because she does not bring enough money to the marriage; the man is
then free to remarry and claim another dowry. There is nothing
remotely parallel for men. In 1989 there were 110 dowry deaths in
Delhi; fewer than 5% of such incidents result in conviction. Human
rights groups suggest sanctions against countries that practice gender
apartheid and tolerate violence against women. *See also* widow
burning.

bridegroom *groom.*

bride of Christ although this is one of the important titles of the Roman
Catholic Church, it may be a metaphor that needs to be soft-pedaled
when possible because of the rampant sexism it enshrines. While
there is nothing unacceptable or inconsistent about picturing the
church as subordinate to Christ, the bride image says by implication
that brides are also subordinate to their god-like husbands. *See also*
church/she; God.

bridesmaid *attendant*. *See also* best man; maid/matron of honor.

bring home the bacon both women and men bring home the bacon today
(28% of U.S. households are headed by women) and one of the
derivations of the phrase is also egalitarian: according to ancient
custom in Dunmow, England, a flitch of bacon is awarded "to any
married couple who can take an oath that they have never once
during the year wished themselves unmarried" (Charles Earle Funk,
A Hog on Ice: And Other Curious Expressions). *See also* provider.

brinkmanship/brinksmanship *gamesplaying, gameplaying, courting catas-
trophe, risk-taking bluff, bluffing, savvy, gambling, playing chicken.*

bro although there is no parallel slang term for women, the popular and
affectionate "bro" isn't negatively sex-linked.

broad (woman) no.

broken home *single-parent home/family.*

brothel *house of prostitution.*

brother (religion) retain because of narrow meaning and because all
orders with brothers consist of men; there are orders with sisters, but
"brother" and "sister" do not signify entirely parallel roles.

brotherhood (pseudogeneric) *unity, unity among humans, humanity,
compassion, peace, companionship, goodwill, amity, friendship, comradeship, camaraderie, conviviality; family, the human family, kinship, shared/
human kinship; community, society, association, organization, social
organization, common-interest group, club, corporation, federation, union,
group, partnership, society; brotherhood and sisterhood.* It may be particularly important to protect "brotherhood" from pseudogeneric use; the
word has been gaining new, legitimate, and exciting use as men find

that other men can sometimes best understand, discuss, and reflect common joys and problems ("brotherhood" thus developing along the same lines that "sisterhood" developed as a description of a meaningful sex-specific bond). "Brotherhood" has been used since 1340 as a synonym for "guild"; we still see today, for example, the International Brotherhood of Electrical Workers. But another group calls itself the United Electrical Workers and "solidarity" is also useful in this context (for example, the Newspaper Union Solidarity Committee).

brotherhood of man *human family/community/bond/solidarity, bond of humanity, humanity, humankind.* **See also** BOMFOG.

brotherliness (pseudogeneric) *neighborliness, affection, concern, warmth.* **See also** brotherly love (pseudogeneric).

brotherly this is a useful and accurate sex-specific word in most cases. Sometimes, however, it is used stereotypically when other words would be more descriptive: *affectionate, loving, caring, kindly, supportive, sympathetic, protective, indulgent, friendly, humane,* etc.

brotherly love (pseudogeneric) *kindheartedness, goodwill, philanthropy, charity, goodnaturedness, generosity, benevolence, loving kindness, geniality, human feeling, benignity, beneficence, humanity, compassion, unselfishness, friendship, amiability, tolerance, consideration, affectionate/human love, love of others/of neighbor, other love, love of people, agape.* **See also** City of Brotherly Love.

brothers (pseudogeneric) *See* brethen/brothers (pseudogeneric).

brother's keeper *See* I am not my brother's keeper.

bruiser as this is by definition a big, rough, husky man, there are no inclusive alternatives or parallel terms for a woman.

brunette *brunet.* The preferred dictionary usage is "brunet," although we tend to see "brunette" more often. However, using "brunette" reinforces the male-as-norm pattern; that is, like "blond/blonde," "brunet" is the standard and "brunette" is the deviation. *See also* divorcé/divorcée.

brushman *brusher; brush seller.*

brute/brute force use sparingly. These terms are strongly associated with men and there are no parallels for women. Although sometimes some men may be correctly described this way, the words will lose their truth if carelessly used.

buccaneer *See* pirate.

buckaroo *See* cowboy.

buck naked *stark naked, naked, starkers, naked as a jaybird, without a stitch on, in the altogether/raw/buff, in one's birthday suit, au naturel, unclad.* "Buck naked" refers either to the male animal or to the color of buckskin (which isn't everybody's shade); on either count the term is better replaced.

buddy woman/girl or man/boy. This word comes from the word "brother" and is a positive term denoting closeness and friendship, whereas its counterpart, "sissy" (from "sister"), is never used positively. In spite of its masculine associations, "buddy" can be used of either sex.

bull *lies, exaggeration, tall tale/story, snow/snowjob, hot air, bunk, nonsense; police officer, private detective, guard; speculator.*

bull dyke (woman) this term is disliked by some lesbians, but it is used by others. It follows the "insider/outsider" rule, which means its use is unacceptable for those outside the lesbian community. *See also* butch (woman); dyke (woman); femme/fem; homophobia; homosexual.

bullfighter almost, but not quite all bullfighters are men. Raquel Martinez, possibly the world's only professional woman matador (she earned the "alternativa" certificate), is still discriminated against after ten years of bullfighting. Very few other matadors will share a booking with her, and she's been booed and had beer bottles thrown at her. A sports news director says, "the time, in Mexico, for women matadors has not come."

bullish/bullish on America *escalating, rising, inflationary; optimistic about the U.S. economy.* Stock market terms using "bull" are some of the least overtly offensive sexist terms we have, and some readers will view their inclusion here as nitpicking. Others, appreciating the cumulative and largely covert effect of the many such expressions in the language, may want to replace them with sex-neutral expressions when not quoting. In addition, the use of "America" is ethnocentric when the reference is to the United States. *See also* bull market.

bull market *rising/improving/escalating/buy/favorable market.* *See also* bullish/bullish on America.

bull session "bull" does not refer to the animal but to fraud or deceit, from the word "boule." However, for a more neutral-appearing term (especially since men tend to have "bull sessions" while women have "gabfests"), use *buzz/rap/brainstorming session, parley, talk, chat, free-for-all/informal discussion.*

bully boy/man or girl/woman. "Bully" is mostly defined in terms of men and it has a masculine feel to it, but it is currently used for both sexes. For a more inclusive-sounding noun, use *meanie, tormentor, browbeater, aggressor, terrorist, dictator, menace.* For the verb use *browbeat, mistreat, tyrannize, terrorize, threaten, domineer, bulldoze, intimidate, oppress, menace.*

bum although this theoretically inclusive term can refer to either sex, it tends to be reserved for men. You may want to use instead *street person, homeless person.* "Bum" and its traditional synonyms (beggar, hobo, vagabond, sponger, scrounger, vagrant, parasite) are pejorative and insensitive; many of the homeless today are victims of a combination of societal values, political decisions, the economy, ill health, and bad luck. *See also* bad guy.

bumpkin *See* hayseed.

burgomaster *mayor*. Or, leave as is for European towns that use it.

busboy *busser, busperson, dining room attendant, kitchen helper, dish carrier, waiter's helper/assistant, serving/server's assistant, room service assistant/ attendant, porter, runner.*

Bushman/Bushmen *San.* These people refer to themselves as San, categorically rejecting "Bushman/Bushmen." Library cataloger Sanford Berman notes that Africanists, anthropologists, and other educated people avoid the racist, sexist, Eurocentric, and inauthentic "Bushman/Bushmen." He warns against replacing these terms with the also ethnocentric and racist "native/natives" or "tribe/tribes."

businessman *executive, business executive/associate/professional, member of the business community, business leader/manager/owner, professional, merchant, shopkeeper, entrepreneur, industrialist, financier, manager, investor, speculator, buyer, trader, capitalist, retailer, wholesaler, mogul, magnate, tycoon.* Richard A. Spears (*NTC's Dictionary of American Slang and Colloquial Expressions*) offers two colloquial alternatives for either sex: *pinstriper, vest.* If used gender-fairly, *businessman and businesswoman* are additional possibilities although not high on the list, and *businessperson* comes in a poor last choice. Or, be specific: *stockbroker, advertising executive, chief executive officer, public relations officer, banker,* etc. Plural: *people in business, businesspeople.* Women now own 30% of all U.S. businesses. *See also* career girl/career woman; entrepreneur.

businessman's lunch *working lunch, business lunch.*

busman's holiday *bus driver's holiday, working vacation.* Some 49% of U.S. bus drivers are women.

busy as a hen with one chick *never idle, going full tilt, have many irons in the fire, have one's hands full, not a moment to call one's own, in the thick of things, doesn't let the grass grow under one's feet, on the go/move/fly, tireless, up to one's eyebrows/ears in, not have a moment to spare, in full swing, not a minute to waste.* This is a harmless enough expression, but alternatives are offered because of the hen; most of our images of parenting emphasize mothers.

butch (woman) usage of "butch" follows the "insider/outsider" rule, that is, it is acceptable for lesbians who want to use the term; it is generally unacceptable for non-lesbians to use it. Describing a lesbian relationship with the outdated and stereotyped "butch" and "femme" roles is a misleading oversimplification: avoid it.

butcher 7% of butchers are women.

butler invariably a man.

butter-and-egg man *butter-and-egger, nouveau riche.*

button man *button, button player/soldier, soldier, gangster, mobster.*

buxom avoid. *See also* sweater girl.

C

Why shouldn't we quarrel about a word? What is the good of words if they aren't important enough to quarrel over? Why do we choose one word more than another if there isn't any difference between them?

G. K. Chesterton

cabana/cabin boy *cabana/cabin attendant.*
cabbages and kings unless quoting Lewis Carroll use *this and that, odds and ends, threads and thrums.*
cabinet member woman or man. However, before 1933, when Frances Perkins was appointed, all U.S cabinet members were men.
cabman *cabdriver.* Some 12.5% of cab drivers and chauffeurs are women.
caddymaster *caddyboss, caddy supervisor/leader/director/captain.*
cadet in the service academies, 10% of the cadets are women. "Cadet" can also refer specifically to a younger brother or son. For the slang, use instead *pimp.*
cadette *cadet*
Caesar's wife for a gender-free substitute use *someone whose conduct is impeccable, someone about whom there hovers the odor of sanctity, someone who is beyond reproach/above suspicion/irreproachable/unimpeachable/ innocent/blameless/sinless/clean-handed.*
calendar girl *calendar model.*
call a spade a spade *get to the point, speak plainly/straight from the shoulder/ straight out, be up front/frank/on the up and up/aboveboard.* The expression is associated with a racial slur and should be avoided.
call boy *page, caller.*
call girl/call girl service/call house *prostitute/prostitution service/house of prostitution.* Note the nonparallel "call girl" and "call boy."
camaraderie an inclusive term, although it has often been thought the province of men to share this feeling of unity and goodwill. *See also* brotherhood (pseudogeneric); fellowship (social bond).
cameragirl/cameraman *photographer, camera operator/technician, cinematographer, camera crew.*

camp follower if you mean prostitute, use *prostitute*. If you mean a politician who switches parties for reasons of personal gain, the term can be used for either sex.

can-can dancer this has always been a woman; there is no equivalent for a man.

candy-striper *volunteer, junior/teen/hospital volunteer*. These volunteers are both girls/young women and boys/young men.

canoness *canon*. Depending on the denomination, a canon might be a woman or a man.

car/she *car/it*. Referring to cars as "she" is part of the association of the feminine with men's possessions. Everything that dominator societies have traditionally run or overpowered has been imaged as female: church, nations, nature, ships, cars, etc. *See also* fill 'er up (gas tank).

carboy nonsexist; from the Persian "qaraba" for "large bottle."

card boy *card doffer*.

career girl/career woman *professional, business executive, executive trainee, longtime/full-time employee, careerist*. Or, be specific: *sales rep, paralegal, career scientist, industry representative, P.R. agent, social worker, professor, engineer, administrative assistant*. When tempted to use "career woman," consider how "career man" would sound and then handle the situation the way you would have for a man. A 1990 Parker Brothers Inc. game, "Careers for Girls," has six career choices: supermom, schoolteacher, rock star, fashion designer, college graduate, animal doctor. Susan Engeleiter, administrator of the U.S. Small Business Administration said the game shows an "insensitivity to modern realities in a society where women are making breakthroughs in almost every profession." *See also* businessman.

caretaker if you mean someone who looks after the daily needs of another, use *caregiver*.

carpenter 1.5% of carpenters are women.

cart boy *cart attendant*.

Casanova if you need an inclusive alternative use *heartthrob, heartbreaker, lover, great romantic, dashing lover, flirt, make-out artist, smooth operator, God's gift to women/men*.

cash boy *cash messenger*.

Caspar Milquetoast *See* milquetoast/milksop (man).

castrate/castrating if you must use these terms metaphorically, be sure you are on sound psychological ground. They blame women for something that takes two to accomplish. It is not possible to "castrate" a secure, independent person; the man is not an anesthetized patient in this type of surgery. For "castrate" use *disarm, disable, incapacitate, undermine, unhinge, unnerve, deprive of power/strength/ courage/vigor, devitalize, attenuate, shatter, exhaust, weaken, disqualify,* invalidate, paralyze, muzzle, enervate, tie the hands of, draw the teeth of, clip the wings of, spike the guns of, take the wind out of one's sails, put a spoke in one's wheels. For "castrating": ruthless, aggressive, domineering, controlling, powerful, tyrannical, overwhelming, overpowering.

cathouse *house of prostitution.*

cat may look at a king, a *a person can dream, can't they? (see* singular "they"), *someone who lives in a fool's paradise/has airy hopes/hopes against hope/catches at a straw/makes sheep's eyes at/eyes wistfully/longingly.*

cattleman *cattle owner/raiser/buyer/grower/producer, rancher, farmer.*

catty *malicious, spiteful, snide, sly, underhanded, disingenuous, envious.* "Catty" is used exclusively of women; the alternatives can refer to either sex.

cavalryman *cavalry soldier/officer, horse soldier.*

caveman (man who behaves primitively toward women) *clod, slob, fumbler, boor, insensitive/ill-mannered person, masher.* It is difficult to render this concept inclusively since it refers by definition to a man, but the alternatives are less sexist-appearing than "caveman," which is also an ethnocentric and inaccurate metaphor.

caveman/cavewoman *cave dweller.* Plural: *cave people.* The use of "cavemen" as a pseudogeneric and the cartoon image of a cavewoman being dragged away by her hair have obscured women's role in history. Researchers now say that, contrary to common assumptions, it was women who were probably responsible for making tools and pottery and for such major technological innovations as horticulture, agriculture, basketmaking, weaving, and textiles. In any case, anthropologists do not use "cave" terms to refer to any past peoples; it is more a media and lay press term.

cellarman *cellar clerk/laborer, winery worker.*

centerfold girl *centerfold model.*

CEO (chief executive officer) approximately a dozen of the 6,400 top-ranking CEOs are women.

cerebral palsied *someone with/who has cerebral palsy/C.P.* Cerebral palsy is a condition, not a disease. C.P. can be used to name the condition, but not the person. Do not use palsied, spastic, or spaz. *See also* handicapped.

chainman *surveyor's assistant, chain surveyor helper; chain offbearer; pattern assembler.*

chairman (noun) *chair, moderator, committee/department head, presiding officer, presider, president, chairer, convener, coordinator, group coordinator, leader, discussion/group/committee leader, head, speaker, organizer, facilitator, officiator, director, supervisor, manager, overseer, administrator, monitor, clerk, chairperson.* Some people accept "chairwoman" and "chairman" when they are used equally and fairly in a passage, but it is generally better to keep this term gender-free because "chair-

woman" is perceived as a less weighty word. "Chairperson" is
awkward, and seems to be used mostly for women. There is much
linguistic support for "chair"; it was, in fact, the original term (1647),
with "chairman" coming into the language only later (1654). The
verb "chair" is highly preferred to the rarely seen "chairman." ("He
chairmaned the committee"?) Using "chair" as both noun and verb
nicely parallels the use of "head" for both noun and verb. (People
who are upset about being called "a piece of furniture" apparently
have no problem with the gruesome picture of a "head" directing a
department, division, or group.) Note too the longstanding noun use
of "chair" in music ("first chair"). *See also* CEO (chief executive
officer).

chairmanship *chair, leadership, presidency.*

chamberlain historically a man. Sometimes you can use for both sexes
   treasurer, chief officer.

chambermaid *room attendant, servant, cleaner, housekeeper.*

chancellor man or woman.

"change, the" avoid this term, which often predisposes women to expect
   more change than many of them actually experience. *See also*
   menopause/menopausal.

change booth man *cashier.*

chanteuse *singer, vocalist, balladeer.*

chaperone *chaperon. See also* divorcé/divorcée.

chaplain woman or man.

chapman *peddler.*

chargé d'affaires man or woman.

charley horse retain; this popular and instantly grasped term is harmless
   as sex-linked terms go. The problem is not with the term per se, but
   with the fact that it is one of hundreds of male-oriented terms that
   give the language an overwhelming male "voice." There is nothing
   wrong with using male expressions, as long as they are balanced with
   female expressions. If you want an alternative try *strain, bruise,
   contusion, stiffness, muscular stiffness, cramp.*

charwoman *char, charworker, cleaner, janitor, maintenance worker, custodian.*

chaste/chastity in the past these terms have been used almost entirely for
   women; except for priests and monks, men were not held to any
   sexual standards. With the advent of AIDS, it was speculated that
   chastity might make a modest comeback as the only truly effective
   preventive. Use the terms for both sexes or not at all.

chatelaine retain in historical contexts.

chatter avoid this sexist term, which tends to be reserved for women,
   children, birds, and squirrels, and which implies a certain value
   judgment—that the conversation is trivial and irrelevant. Use
   instead for the verb *shoot the breeze, talk idly, make small talk, bandy*

words, pass the time of day, make chin music, beat one's gums, jaw, talk one's arm/head off, be talkative/loquacious/garrulous, ramble, run off at the mouth, rattle/ramble on, pour forth, talk oneself hoarse, talk at random, talk a donkey's hind leg off. For the noun use *small/idle/empty talk, blather, palaver. See also* babble; bull session; chatterbox; gabby; gossip; gossipy; yenta.

chatterbox *windbag, blatherskite, excessive talker, jabberer, blabbermouth, hot-air artist, magpie, palaverer. See also* chatter.

chauffeuse *chauffeur.*

cheap-jack *huckster.*

checkout girl/checkout man *checker, checkout/desk clerk, cashier.* Note the nonparallel "girl/man."

checkroom girl/checkroom woman *checkroom attendant.*

cheerleader man/boy or woman/girl.

cheesecake *See* food names for people.

chef until recently, men have always been chefs and women have always been cooks; even fifteen years ago the idea of a woman chef was considered absurd. Today, however, women in the United States, France, and England are gaining for themselves the full title of chef. At the Culinary Institute of America, 25% of the 1,850 students are women, and the American Culinary Federation has more than tripled its female membership since 1986.

cherchez la femme! a mystery story favorite implying that wherever there is dirty work afoot, there must be a woman involved. On one level it is fairly harmless, but it should be used cautiously because of its covert message.

chessman *chess/game piece.*

Chicana/Chicano use these gender-specific terms ("Chicana," female, "Chicano" male) for people who so label themselves. Some people of Mexican descent in the United States might prefer other terms (Mexican, Mexican American, Latina/Latino); know your context and ask your audience how it wants to be addressed. *See also* Hispanic; Latina/Latino.

chick/chicken/chickie-baby (girl/woman) avoid. These terms imply women are cute little fluffy helpless things. For the use of "chicken" for men, *see* coward/cowardly/cowardice. *See also* animal names for people; sex object.

chief/chief justice/chief master sergeant/chief master sergeant of the Air Force/chief petty officer/chief warrant officer/chief of staff/chief of state man or woman.

child/he (pseudogeneric) avoid. There are several solutions when you need to use a pronoun with "child." Switch to the plural: "Children are remarkable for their intelligence and ardor . . ." (Aldous Huxley). Avoid the pronoun altogether: "One of the most obvious facts about grownups to a child, is that they have forgotten what it is like to be a child" (Randall Jarrell). Use "it": "Who will show a child, as it really is? Who will place it in its constellation and put the measure of distance in its hand?" (Rilke). "People murder a child when they tell it to keep out of the dirt. In dirt is life" (George Washington Carver). "The finest inheritance you can give to a child is to allow it to make its own way, completely on its own feet" (Isadora Duncan).

childcare avoid treating childcare as a women's issue; it is a family, social, political, business issue (companies that have innovative policies on childcare and family-friendly benefits say they are not motivated by benevolence—their programs make good business sense). Although 64% of large companies offer some kind of childcare assistance to employees, only 9% of those companies provide what many working parents think is the most essential service: employee-sponsored childcare centers.

childcare worker 97% of childcare workers are women. The average median earnings of a full-time caregiver were less than $10,000/year in 1989, usually unaccompanied by any benefits. Turnover is 41% annually.

child custody damaging gender-based stereotypes about both sexes play a role in child custody. While joint custody seems consistent with equal rights and equal responsibilities, it is often not in the child's best interest; when shared responsibility, equal rights, and coopera-tion do not exist pre-divorce, it is almost impossible to legislate them during a custody suit and ensure compliance later. In some courts, women are almost automatically given custody simply because they are women, yet men might have been the more suitable custodial parent in some of the cases. According to the Coalition of Free Men, only 10% of men succeed in child custody suits. With the growth of the fathers' rights movement, however, men are more often being given custody—but sometimes for the wrong reasons. Reviewing *Child Custody and the Politics of Gender* (ed. Carol Smart and Selma Sevenhuijzen), Nancy D. Polikoff concludes that the book "presents devastating evidence that mothers are losing custody of their chil-dren because of economic disadvantage, because they are judged by a 'good mother' standard vastly different from the 'good father' standard, because women's nurturing of children (as opposed to men's) is profoundly undervalued, and because, more than anything, the rhetoric of equality has outdistanced the realities of parenting." For example, when fathers act as individuals, their acts are not construed as conflicting with their children's interests, but mothers' interests as individuals rather than as mothers appear to courts as antagonistic to those of their children. Child custody issues are highly complex and have profound, long-lasting, and sometimes devastating effects on all concerned. There are no simple, fair rules, but eliminating decisions based solely on gender might ensure that the child has the most suitable custodial parent. *See also* alimony; courts (judicial); displaced homemaker; divorce; divorced father/ divorced mother; noncustodial parent.

child is father of the man, the unless quoting Wordsworth, use *the child is parent to the adult, the child begets/gives birth to the adult, the oak tree sprouts from the acorn, the seeds of the future lie in the past/present.*

chimney sweep girls and women have not historically been chimney sweeps; today in the United States both men and women own, operate, and work for chimney cleaning companies, although neither actually climb inside chimneys anymore.

Chinaman *Chinese.* The offensive "Chinaman" is racist as well as sexist; use "Chinese" for both sexes.

Chinaman's chance *not a prayer, not an earthly chance, no chance, no chance at all, not a hope in hell, fat/slim chance, a snowball's chance in hell, as much chance as a snowflake in hell, doomed, unlucky, ill-omened, ill-fated, unblessed.* "Chinaman's chance" is racist as well as sexist.

chip off the old block the child and parent here could be either sex, but as this phrase is so often used to indicate fathers and sons, you may want to use instead *the spit and image, the spitting image, following in the footsteps of, the very image/picture of, cast in the same mold, for all the world like, a carbon copy of, as alike as two peas in a pod.*

chit (girl/young woman) avoid; there is no parallel for a boy/young man.

chivalrous *courteous, considerate, protective, courtly, brave, civil, generous, honorable, kindly, heroic, mannerly, gracious, well-bred, upstanding.* See *also* chivalry.

chivalry except when speaking or writing about medieval history, use alternatives: *courtesy, honor, high-mindedness, consideration, bravery, courage, civility, valor, fidelity, manneriness.* Sexist attitudes underlie the concept and historical sense of chivalry. The belief that women need protection ("for their own good"), special courtesies, and kid-glove treatment results in superficial pleasantness but deep-seated discrimination, paternalism, and oppression. What chivalry says is that women can't take care of themselves, are not the equals of men in most respects, and certainly cannot do certain heavy, dirty, dangerous (and high-paying) work. In addition, "chivalry" and "chivalrous" are words reserved for men. *See also* lady (noun).

choirboy *choir member/singer, member of the choir, singer, vocalist.*

choirmaster *choir/music/song director/leader/conductor, director of the choir.*

chorine *cabaret/nightclub dancer, chorus member, member of the chorus.*

chorus boy/chorus girl *chorus member/dancer/performer/singer, member of the chorus, singer, vocalist, dancer, musical cast member.*

Christ *See* Jesus Christ.

christen *name, baptize, dedicate, identify, label, denote, designate, entitle.*
"Christen" comes from and refers to Christian denominations'
baptismal rituals.

christian in recent years "christian" and "judeo-christian" have come to
be casually used as inappropriate synonyms for morality. Use
instead *ethical, moral, decent, upstanding, righteous, upright, high-minded,
honorable, principled, conscientious, moralistic, right, good.* During the
Middle East war of 1948 the U.S. Ambassador to the United Nations
urged the Arabs and Jews to resolve their disagreements "like good
Christians."

christian name *baptismal/first/given name, forename.*

Christmas with the widespread commercialization and increasingly
extended celebration of this religious (for some) holiday, those who
are not Christian are barraged with the word "Christmas." The
assumption that everyone celebrates Christmas ignores that Hannu-
kah, for example, another major—but uncommercialized—religious
holiday, falls in the same season. Use instead *holiday greetings/season/
gifts/cards/ decorations/music, season's greetings, year-end sales, New
Year's greetings/sales.*

church/she *church/it.* Everything that dominator societies have traditionally run or overpowered has been imaged as female: church, nations,
nature, ships, cars, etc. This is particularly inimical in religious
matters because the image has the weight of moral "rightness"
behind it. The longtime God-is-male, church-is-female thinking has
inspired and maintained the logical but ultimately untenable conclusion that male must be better than female. *See also* bride of Christ;
God.

church father if you are referring to one of the Fathers of the Church,
leave as is for historical accuracy. When referring to someone who
was not acknowledged as one of the apostolic or patristic Fathers, use
instead, for example, *fourth-century religious writer, bishop, great
Christian teacher, early Christian philosopher, post-Nicene writer,* etc.

churchman *church member/worker, churchgoer, believer, member of a church;
churchwoman and churchman if they are used gender-fairly.* Also:
*religious, clergy, ecclesiastic, priest, presbyter, pastor, imam, minister,
confessor, elder,* etc. *See also* clergyman.

cigarette girl *cigarette vendor.*

circumcision specify female circumcision or male circumcision. For
many male Jews, circumcision is an important religious rite. Medi-
cally there is no clearcut and universal position on the advantages
and disadvantages of circumcision, but many men feel it is invasive
and more properly thought of as sexual mutilation. Female circumcision (a rite undergone by more than eighty million African women)
differs radically from male circumcision in that it is always sexual

mutilation, it is performed without anesthesia by nonprofessionals and most often with unsterilized razors, and it often leads to infection, painful intercourse, infertility, difficult childbirth, and death. There are many organizations campaigning against female circumcision and laws have been passed in some affected countries; the choice here would be for concerned outsiders to take a supportive but nondominating back seat to leaders in those countries who are working on the issue.

city councilman *city councilor, city council member; councilwoman and councilman.*

city fathers *city leaders/founders/councilors/elders/officials/legislators/administrators/bureaucrats, the powers that be.*

city hostess *goodwill ambassador.*

City of Brotherly Love William Penn named Philadelphia after a city in Asia Minor that was the seat of one of the seven early Christian churches and known for its goodwill and generosity; "Philadelphia" comes from the Greek "phil-" ("love") and "adelphos" ("brother"). "The City of Human Love" is seen occasionally but it seems unlikely to replace the centuries-old "City of Brotherly Love."

claim(s) man *claim(s) agent.*

clairvoyante *clairvoyant. See also* divorcé/divorcée.

clansman *clan member, member of a clan.*

classism the United States believes itself a fundamentally classless society, yet the income gap between rich and poor (measured by the percentage of total income held by the wealthiest 20% of the population versus the poorest 20%) is approximately 11 to 1, one of the highest ratios in the industrialized world—Japan's is 4 to 1 (Paula S. Rothenberg, *Racism and Sexism*). Half the population holds less than 3.5% of U.S. wealth. Class differences affect educational opportunity and achievement, material well-being, lifestyles, health, and death rates. According to Benjamin DeMott (*The Imperial Middle*), the myth that upward mobility is available to everyone shapes our response to poverty; social programs pretend most needs are temporary (the stopgag welfare system) or narrow (nutritional supplements for pregnant women). Classist writing is subtle ("welfare mother," for example) and difficult to weed out.

cleaning girl/cleaning lady/cleaning woman *cleaner, domestic/office cleaner, household/domestic/maintenance worker, housecleaner, houseworker, housekeeper, janitor, custodian, charworker.*

clergyman *clergy, cleric, member of the clergy, spiritual leader.* Or, be specific: *pastor, rabbi, minister, priest, deacon, presbyter, elder, ecclesiastic, confessor, bishop, prelate, rector, parson, dean, imam, vicar, chaplain, preacher, missionary,* etc. Along with the Conservative, Reform, and Reconstructionist branches of Judaism, some eighty-four Christian denominations have women clergy; at least eighty-two still do not. Approximately 9% of clergy are women. *See also* bishop; imam; minister; priest; rabbi.

cleric/clerical may refer to either sex.

clod/clodhopper *See* hayseed.

close shave this can be used of either sex as it does not refer to shaving whiskers but to removing a thin layer of anything and proceeding with difficulty, as in "scraping by" or "close scrape."

clotheshorse *fashion plate, fancy/fashionable/sharp/conspicuous dresser, tailor's/ sartorial dream, a person it pays to dress, one who keeps the tailor in business, clothes-conscious person.* "Clotheshorse" usually refers to a woman, although there is another kind of clothes sexism: women today are free to borrow from what have traditionally been men's wardrobes (pants, suits, ties, hats), but men are still culturally restrained from borrowing from women's wardrobes or accessories.

clothes make/don't make the man *clothes make/don't make the person/ individual, clothes can break/make a person, clothes aren't everything, dress for success, the right clothes make a difference, don't judge a book by its cover, appearances are deceptive, all that glitters is not gold, you can't make a silk purse out of a sow's ear, a monkey dressed in silk is still a monkey.*

clubman/clubwoman *club member, member of the club, enrollee, cardholder; clubber, joiner, belonger, social person.*

coachman *coach driver, driver, chauffeur.* Retain "coachman" in some historical contexts.

coadjutress *coadjutor.*

coastguardsman *coastguard, coastguarder, member of the Coast Guard.* About 15% of Coast Guard members are women.

coatcheck girl *coatchecker, coatroom attendant/clerk, coat attendant/checker, checkroom attendant.*

co-chairman *co-chair.* *See also* chairman (noun).

cock-a-hoop *feeling one's oats, flushed with victory, happy as a lark, merry as a cricket, lighthearted, jubilant, exultant, triumphant, jaunty; awry, out of shape, askew.*

cock-and-bull story the male imagery here doesn't make this expression particularly prejudicial to either sex. (The original long, boring seventeenth-century tale featured a cock and a bull.) If you want a neutral-sounding alternative use *snow job, nonsense, a lot of nonsense, stuff and nonsense, tall tale, yarn, preposterous/improbable story, canard, moonshine, bunkum, poppycock, hot air, hogwash, banana oil, balderdash, not true, applesauce.*

cock of the roost *arrogant, conceited, careless, overbearing, in high feather, on a high horse, sitting pretty, riding tall in the saddle.*

cock of the walk *crème de la crème, flower of the flock; tyrant, dictator, leader, ruler.* ("The walk" was the chicken yard.) *See also* high man on the totem pole.

cocksure/cocky this is used of both sexes although it comes from the male fowl. If you want a strictly sex-neutral term use *self-confident, overconfident, arrogant, self-important, in love with oneself, pushy, overbearing, swaggering, aggressive, conceited, haughty, supercilious, jaunty, brash, cheeky, flippant, saucy, nervy, impertinent, insolent, careless.*

coed (noun) *student.* In theory a coed is a student at a coeducational school; in practice it is always a young woman. Several generations ago, Joe College and Betty Coed were the neat generic couple on campus, but Joe got to be the whole college while Betty was the coed, the exception to the old rule that higher education was reserved for men. From the *Wall Street Journal*: "In a plane-crash story we called one female victim a coed, bringing this well-taken protest: 'Coed carries with it the connotation of perky little female students in tight sweaters, or of women who have only recently been allowed to study with their more deserving male counterparts. Only men are students; women are just co-educated.'" Commented the paper: "'Tis truly sad to let go of such a headline-short word in newspapers, but let us put it on our list of sexist words to be avoided." *See also* perky.

coffee girl/coffee man *coffee maker/server.* Note the nonparallel "girl/man."

co-heiress *co-heir.*

coiffeur/coiffeuse *hairdresser. See also* barber; beautician.

college girl *college/university student.* The masculine equivalent is "college man," not "college boy." If necessary to specify sex, use "college man" and "college woman."

colonist colonists have been both sexes and several races. Avoid using the word pseudogenerically (for example, "colonists, their wives, and families") or of implying that they were only white.

coloratura retain as is for the soprano who specializes in ornately figured vocal music.

colored as a description of African Americans, "colored" is unacceptable except in established titles (e.g., National Association for the Advancement of Colored People). One possible reason for the persistence of this term: "colored people" are perceived to "know their place" better than uppity, threatening blacks or African Americans. "People of color" is used for those who so name themselves.

colporteur although this French word is grammatically masculine, it is used in French and English to refer to both sexes. To avoid the masculine flavor, use *religious book peddler.*

combat women are not permitted to serve in combat positions—by law in the Navy, Air Force, and Marines, and by policy in the Army. However, women fill jobs where the line between combat and combat-related is increasingly blurred: they train men for missions they can't carry out themselves; they command units in which they can't serve;

Air Force women ferry troops and supplies over hostile areas and refuel jet fighters, but they can't fly the fighters; in the Navy, they are barred from permanent assignment on combat ships such as carriers, destroyers, and submarines, but they can serve on repair and supply ships in the same waters. Although few of the 192,000 enlisted women in the armed forces are actually pining for combat duty, the situation is different for the 33,000 female officers, who know that their exclusion from combat commands creates a glass ceiling; advancement to top ranks often depends on leading combat units. Women who qualify for combat should be allowed to fight, they say, as they already do in some other Western countries (in 1989 Canada abolished laws barring women from combat, and opened all military jobs, except on submarines, to women). Not all women qualify, but neither do all men; in the Army, for example, 72% of male recruits qualify for combat while 8% of female recruits qualify. It's being asked if it is fair to ask men to risk their lives while giving women special treatment—treatment that at least some of them do not want. Barring an ideal world in which neither men nor women need to go to war, it seems reasonable to allow those women who want combat positions and who qualify for them to have them. The increasing number of women in the armed forces (11% of the total) means that fewer men who don't want to be in the armed forces will end up there; it is largely women, by making up for the shortfall in male volunteers, who allow the suspension of the compulsory draft to continue. It may be, too, that only when women are full participants in war will we rethink the way we have used men as pawns, cannon fodder, and "death objects." Ellen Goodman writes: "Are Americans ready to see women come home in body bags? I hope not. But new risks and roles may force us to ask a deeper question: Why are we ready to see men come home in body bags? . . . In the end, this must be said: Any war that isn't worth a woman's life isn't worth a man's life." *See also* armed forces; males-only draft; serviceman (armed forces).

combination girl/combination man *short-order cook.* Note the nonparallel "girl/man."

comedienne *comedian, comic, comic actor, entertainer.*

come-hither look this look often exists more in the eye of the beholder than in the person supposedly giving it. Because advertisements constantly use the look, it is perhaps not surprising that some men see it when it isn't there. Rapists have claimed they were given the come-on although their victims denied it. In a survey on how men know when women don't want their advances, one man said the only way he would know if a woman didn't want to have sex with him was if she fought and screamed the whole time. *See also* provoke; "she asked for it."

come on like gangbusters from a 1936 radio show with startlingly loud opening music, this expression can be used today of either sex even though the original gangbusters were male.

come to man's estate *come of age, attain majority, settle down, become adult, mature, come into one's own.*

commander-in-chief in the United States, this is the president, and thus gender depends on the person in office.

committeeman/committeewoman *member of the committee, committee member; ward leader, precinct leader.* "Committeewoman" and "committeeman" are not as equal as they seem; "committeewoman" is a much less weighty term.

common-law husband/common-law wife *common-law spouse*, except when sex-specific terms are necessary. Beware the prevailing sexist tendency to discount the woman in this household and not the man. In a few states, common-law spouses are regarded as legally married; disapproval based on lack of marriage lines is misplaced.

common man *common citizen/person/human/human being/voter, average citizen/person/human/human being/voter, ordinary person/citizen/human/human being/voter, everyday person, layperson, taxpayer, voter, resident, householder, homeowner, landowner, passerby, one of the people, citizen, the nonspecialist, commoner, rank and file.* "The common man" translates well to "ordinary people."

company man originally someone who led a company union and represented management's hope of keeping away outside unions, a company man today is someone who always sides with the boss or the company. It's a difficult term to replace as it says so much to us in two words. Today, however, there are company women, too, but "company woman" may not be understood in the same way. For both sexes use instead *loyal employee/worker, staunch supporter.* Or, use adjectives: *loyal, faithful, devoted, trustworthy, true-blue.* **See also** organization man.

comparable worth this term refers to pay schedules that offer equal pay for jobs similar in education requirements, skill levels, work conditions, and other factors. "Comparable worth" differs from "equal pay"; the latter means people doing the same job receive equal pay—for example, female and male nurses of equal seniority working on the same hospital floor receive the same pay. Comparable worth means that a female clerk-typist might earn the same as a male warehouse employee. Despite the 1963 law mandating equal pay for women and men doing equal work, women still earn only about 70% of what men earn; it is hoped that comparable worth can redress this inequity. However, even the most careful comparable worth plans have serious difficulties weighting job dimensions. Dr. Marc S. Mentzer gives the following example: women historically have been concentrated in jobs requiring communication skills (secretaries, telephone operators, teachers) while men have historically been concentrated in jobs requiring physical skills (manual laborers, construction workers). In a job evaluation plan in which two of several dimensions might be communications skills and physical skills, how should these two be weighted? Are communication skills equal to, double, or half the weight of physical skills? In so subjective a judgment, a biased employer could tinker with the weights to produce a number of favorable (to the company) results. Job evaluation is not an objective, scientific process. And the business community will always oppose comparable worth since it conflicts with business's unfounded faith that market forces are fair. Another factor is a set of underlying attitudes so deeply entrenched that it will take more than legislation to arrive at comparable worth: Marilyn French (*Beyond Power: On Women, Men and Morals*) writes, "In just about every [society], whatever men do or produce is valued more highly than what women do or produce, even though what a man does in one society is done by women in another society. In most societies, it is not the thing done, nor the objects produced, but the sex of the doer that confers distinctions upon acts or products." *See also* equal pay/equal pay for equal work; executive; glass ceiling; wage earner.

compatriot although "compatriot" has masculine roots (from the Latin for "land of my father"), the word seems to be used in an inclusive manner today.

complain don't use this of women unless they are truly complaining (griping); it discounts what they are saying. "Complain" is often seen in examples like this: "Women are more likely to complain of discrimination." Depending on the meaning of the article, it should have read "to report discrimination" or "to experience discrimination." This usage may have sprung from legal terminology in which a complainant "complains," but using that sense in everyday language results in ambiguity.

computer programmer 32% are women. In related positions, 29% of computer systems analysts are women as are 88% of data entry keyers and 9% of data processing equipment repairers.

conceive when you want the broader meaning of this term as opposed to its narrow biological meaning, use alternatives that are not sex-linked: *imagine, dream up, think, invent, fashion, create, formulate, design, devise, contrive, concoct, hatch, form, originate, initiate, bring about. See also* beget; seminal.

concertmaster *concert leader/director, assistant conductor, first violinist.* Some concert directors, both women and men, prefer to retain "concertmaster."

concierge woman or man.

concubine this word, meaning "to lie with," refers to a woman who lives with a man outside marriage. The person she is presumably lying with has no label; he is simply a man. Our sexist values assert themselves countless times in the pejorative labeling of women alone for something men and women do together. *See also* kept woman; loose woman; mistress; pickup (woman).

conductress *conductor*.

confessor the role of confessor originated with the development of the Keltic "anamchara" or "soul friend" (fifth to tenth centuries) who could be female or male, single, married, or celibate. It was not until 1215 that the Fourth Lateran Council defined "confessor" in terms of a priest. Today we return to inclusive usage: *spiritual director, confidant, adviser, counselor, mentor, preceptor, therapist, mother confessor/father confessor*.

confidante *confidant. See also* divorcé/divorcée.

confraternity *society, union, association, organization, group, club, religious society*. "Confraternity" is based on the Latin for "brother."

confrere *colleague, associate, co-worker, teammate, collaborator, partner, companion, comrade, confederate, counterpart, accomplice*. "Confrere" comes from the French (and before that the Latin) for "brother."

congressman *member of Congress, representative, congressional representative, legislator, member of the United States House of Representatives, delegate, assembly member; congressman and congresswoman* if they are used fairly—and if "congressman" is not used as a false generic. "Congressperson" is not recommended, although it is seen in print from time to time. There are presently thirty women in the House, two in the Senate; twenty-six blacks in the House (no seated senators, although both "shadow senators" from Washington, D.C are African American); twelve Hispanics in the House (no senators); five Asian Americans in the House and two in the Senate.

con man/confidence man *con artist, swindler, hustler, confidence operator, operator, chiseler, flimflammer, flimflam artist, fraud, cheat, faker, charlatan, mountebank, trickster, quack, shark, crook, dodger, defrauder, deceiver, sharpie, scoundrel, hoodwinker, phony, imposter, shortchange/bunko artist, scammer, snollygoster*. Although all these terms are inclusive, many of them tend to be thought of first as male. *See also* bad guy.

constable depending on locale, a constable might be either a woman or a man.

construction worker 2% of construction workers are women; they earn 25% less than male hardhats. *See also* tradesman.

consumer women have traditionally been given the consumer label for purchasing household and similar products, but recent market research shows that women also account for 40% of the buying base for business products and office equipment. They also buy nearly half of all cars sold in the United States, influence 80% of all new-car sales, buy 20% of all light trucks and 5% of all full-size pickups, and purchase 22% of compact vans. However, a recent study shows that racism and sexism are alive and well in the car showroom; for the same model car with exactly the same options, a white woman pays about $150 more than a white man, a black man pays about $400 more, and a black woman may pay $900 more.

contact man *advance agent, song plugger.*

control man *control panel operator, control operator, controller.*

conveyor belt man *conveyor belt repairer/tender/worker.*

copy boy/copy girl *copy messenger/carrier/clerk/distributer, runner.*

copy man *copywriter.*

coquette *flirt.* There is only one alternative given because all other co-quette-type words are specific for women (tease, vamp, belle, hussy) or for men (playboy, masher, wolf, sheik).

Cornishman use also *Cornishwoman.* Plural: *inhabitants of Cornwall, Cornishfolk, Cornishwomen and Cornishmen* (but not "Cornishmen and women").

corpsman *medical aide; corps member.* "Corpsman" is still used by the Marine Corps but it may refer to either sex.

costerman *costermonger, street vendor.*

councilman *councilor, council member, member of the council/city council, city representative, municipal officer, ward manager, commissioner; councilwoman and councilman.* Beware of "councilman" as a false generic. "Councilperson" is not recommended, although it is seen and heard from time to time.

countergirl/counterman *counter attendant/server, waiter.* Note the nonparallel "girl/man."

country/she *country/it.* See also ship/she.

country bumpkin this term tends to be used more of a man than of a woman, although it is not in itself gender-specific. However, it supports a pejorative, anti-farmer stereotype and should be avoided on that ground.

countryman *compatriot, citizen, inhabitant, native, resident, indigene; counterpart; country dweller, ruralist, farmer; countrywoman and countryman.* Or, be specific: *African, Japanese, Norwegian,* etc. See also compatriot.

couple in the sense of two people with emotional, domestic, or sexual ties to each other, a couple is not always a woman and a man; it might equally well be two men or two women. Instead of "married couple" try the inclusive "domestic partners." See also boyfriend; family; girlfriend; husband and wife.

courtesan *high-class prostitute.* A courtesan used to be the female equivalent of a courtier; "courtier" retains most of its former meaning, but "courtesan" has been completely devalued and there is no remaining parallel.

courtesy boy (grocery store) *courtesy help, carry-out.*

courtesy titles *See* social titles.

courtier *attendant; flatterer. See also* courtesan.

courts (judicial) gender bias in the judicial system has been the subject of a number of court-sponsored studies in Colorado, Minnesota, New Jersey, New York, and Rhode Island; about twenty more states are working on the issue. The conclusion in New York was that unfairness and gender bias against women as litigants, attorneys, and court employees was a pervasive problem. In Minnesota discrimination against women was found in areas such as divorce, domestic abuse, sexual assault, employment discrimination, and access to courts. The group also found examples of judges and lawyers addressing female litigants and witnesses by first names or by such terms as "dear" or "honey" while they did not do this to men. In child custody cases, there was judicial bias against men and also against working women and poor women. One study found that other factors being equal, plaintiffs tend to receive higher awards for disfigurement if they are women and for loss of future earning capacity if they are men. The bias begins in law school. Carl Tobias (in the *Golden Gate University Law Review*) analyzed the most widely used torts casebook in American law schools and reported it to be overwelming male: "All of the illustrations of people, including the legal heroes, torts scholars and judges, are males." The casebook relies almost exclusively on masculine pronouns (even when the litigants are women), it omits historical information useful in evaluating women's concerns before the law, and depicts "numerous female parties pursuing what appear to be frivolous, vindictive, or unsubstantiated litigation or otherwise seem to be crazy, inconsiderate or weak people." *See also* child custody; dear/dearie; divorce; honey/hon; lawyer.

couturière *high fashion designer, proprietor of a haute couture establishment.*

cover girl *cover model.*

cover that man (sports) *cover that receiver/player, cover them.*

coward/cowardly/cowardice avoid; nonsexist per se, these terms are almost entirely reserved for men/boys. From the Latin "cauda" for "tail," "coward" refers to a dog with its tail between its legs. According to Stuart Berg Flexner (*Listening to America*), "It doesn't seem to be until the 1850s that boys began to taunt each other with being timid, cowardly, or unmanly, perhaps because earlier frontier days had produced fewer such boys, or because now new diversity meant tough frontier and rural youths were meeting some milder boys." In one of the great social double standards, we hold boys/men to impossibly high and arbitrary standards of courage that we never hold women to because of a cultural discounting that associates women with weakness and says women cannot and should not

accept challenges that call for courage or risk-taking. In an ideal
world there would be no external evaluation of a person's moral or
physical courage and no gender lines along a continuum for bravery;
we could each determine our own standards. In the real world,
however, boys/men are acculturated never to show fear, inadequacy,
uncertainty, or weakness and to be deeply stung by taunts of "coward." Variants on "coward" that are technically inclusive but that are
generally applied to men include: big baby, chicken, chicken-hearted,
chicken-livered, creampuff, featherweight, fraidy cat, gutless wonder,
jellyfish, lily-livered, Miss Nancy, nebbish, pantywaist, pussyfooter,
quitter, rabbit, shirker, sissy pants, softie, spineless, traitor, twerp,
weakling, weenie, wimp, worm, wuss/wussy. Especially for men:
are you a man or a mouse? *See also* act like a man/be a man/take it
like a man; crybaby; milquetoast/milksop; namby-pamby; sissy;
weak sister; yellow/yellow-bellied/yellow-bellied coward/yellow
belly/yellow streak down one's back.

cowboy *cowhand, cowpuncher, ranch hand, hand, rancher, herder, cowpoke,
wrangler, range rider, drover, buckaroo, rodeo rider/roper, cowgirl and
cowboy* (in some contexts). Although some of the terms in the list
have a masculine flavor, there is nothing to contravene their being
used for girls/women.

cowboy hat *stetson, ten-gallon/western-style/rodeo hat.*

cowboy shirt *western-style/buckskin/fringed/rodeo shirt.*

cowgirl *roper, rider, rodeo entrant; cowgirl and cowboy* when referring to
teenage rodeo participants. *See also* cowboy.

cowman *rancher, cattle owner/buyer/grower/producer, farmer, cowherd.*

coxswain "swain" refers to a servant or a boy, and most coxswains are
and have been men. However, "coxswain" could be used for a
woman as its sex link is related more to the lack of female coxswains
than to its etymology. Or, use the more neutral-sounding *bosun*,
derived from boatswain. (A "cock" was a small boat, so coxswain
and boatswain are related.) Today most coxswains are found in the
Navy, on small craft, and in racing shells.

crackerjack (adj.) the "jack" here is rarely thought of as sex-linking this
term. If for some reason you need something strictly neutral use *first-
rate, exceptionally fine, smashing, fantastic, marvelous, tiptop, remarkable,
wonderful, super.*

cracksman *safecracker, burglar, housebreaker.*

craftsman *artisan, crafts worker, craftworker, skilled worker, skilled craft
worker, handworker, handiworker, handicrafts worker, handicrafter, trade
worker, artificer, technician, craftsman and craftswoman; craftsperson* (use
only as a last resort). Plural: *craft workers, artisans, skilled workers,
handworkers, handicrafts workers, handicrafters, trade workers, handiwork-
ers, artificers, craftspeople, craftsmen and craftswomen.* Or, be specific:
potters, weavers, woodworkers, etc.

craftsmanship *artisanry, artisanship, craft, handiwork, skilled-craft work, expertise, handicraft, skill, artistry, quality, crafts skills, expertness, expertise.* Or, mention the characteristics that contribute to the piece's beauty or the specific skills that went into its making.

cragsman *climber, rock/cliff climber.*

craneman *crane operator.*

Creatrix *Creator, Maker. **See also** God.*

crewman *crew member, member of the crew, hand, employee, personnel, staff member, worker; crew/deck hand, sailor, mariner.*

criminal *See* bad guy; juvenile delinquent; murderess; prisoner.

crip/cripple *person/individual with a disability/orthopedic disability/physical disability/functional limitation, someone who is mobility impaired, someone with paraplegia/arthritis.* Omit any reference to a disability if it is not strictly necessary to your material. "Crip" and "cripple" follow the "insider/outsider" rule, that is, they are derogatory and unacceptable when used by those outside the group, but acceptable when used by people with disabilities among themselves. Avoid all forms of this word; do not, for example, refer to a disease or a condition as a "crippler." *See also* handicapped; wheelchair-bound.

Cro-Magnon man *Cro-Magnon(s).*

crone avoid the pejorative use. In other times, the Crone was a wise, balanced, powerful elder honored by her society. Although this role is generally unacknowledged today, some women are reclaiming it, asking why we do not have some of our many wise older women alongside our wise older men at public events, in newspaper columns, on speaker podiums, at society's head tables.

crooner "crooner" tends to be associated with male singers, so either use it also for women or try a more inclusive alternative: *pop singer, popular singer, vocalist, balladeer, blues singer.*

crossbowman *crossbow archer, archer.*

crown prince/crown princess OK. Or, *heir apparent, heir to the throne.*

crybaby used as a taunt for children of either sex or as a criticism of a whiny adult, also of either sex, this disparagement carries a special sting for boys/men, who are perhaps allowed to cry, but only for extremely important things. *See also* coward/cowardly/cowardice.

cubmaster *cub scout/pack leader.*

cuckold avoid this term; there is no equivalent for a woman. Speak instead of one partner being unfaithful or of the other partner being betrayed.

cureman *curer.*

curmudgeon *grouch, grumbler, bad-tempered/peevish/cranky/petulant person, crosspatch, faultfinder, fire-eater, complainer, pain in the neck, nitpicker, troublemaker.* Alternatives are given because "curmudgeon" is usually defined and used in reference to men.

"curse"   avoid this slang term for menstruation. It perpetuates the myth that women do not operate on all cylinders throughout the month and it fosters incorrect and harmful attitudes in preadolescent and adolescent girls and boys.

cut the Gordian knot   when using expressions like this, be aware of how many are male-based. Some of the time use female-based expressions, creative expressions of your own, or alternatives: *solve the riddle, solve an intricate/unsolvable problem, find the key, crack a hard nut, figure it out, find a way out, unravel something.* *See* Writing Guidelines for a discussion of sex-linked expressions.

d

One must be chary of words because they turn into cages.

Viola Spolin

daddy long legs leave as is.

dairy husbandman *dairy scientist.*

dairymaid/dairyman *dairy worker/employee/milker/hand; dairy scientist.* The nonparallel "maid/man" goes more than skin deep; while dairy-maids were appearing in entry-level jobs in fairy tales, dairymen were becoming scientists.

dalesman *dale inhabitant/dweller.*

damage controlman *damage controller, handler.*

dame/damsel *woman, person, adult; young woman, teenager, adolescent, child, youngster.* "Dame" and "damsel" are outdated and inappropriate, and "dame" is belittling when used as slang.

Dame Fortune *fortune/Fortune, luck, chance, happy chance, wheels of fortune/chance, roll/throw of the dice, turn of the cards, luck of the draw, lucky stroke, the way things fall, how the cookie crumbles, the breaks, how the ball bounces, serendipity, happenstance, destiny, kismet, fate, fickle finger of fate, fortuity, whirligig of chance.*

dancing girl *dancer.*

dandy *fashion plate, fancy/sharp/conspicuous/fashionable dresser, tailor's/sartorial dream, a person it pays to dress, one who keeps the tailor in business, clothes-conscious person.*

danseur/danseuse a danseur is a principal (but not the principal) male dancer in a company, a soloist, and a danseuse is a principal (but not the principal) female soloist. Retain "danseur" and "danseuse" for their narrow meaning within ballet companies, but to describe a woman or a man who dances ballet nonprofessionally use *ballet dancer.* *See also* ballerina; premier danseur; prima ballerina.

darkest Africa never use this phrase; it is Eurocentric, ethnocentric, and inaccurate (only 20% of the African continent is wooded savanna).

date inclusive term for someone of the same or opposite sex one goes out with. For the person who has to pay for sex, use *prostitute's customer.* For a discussion of our language on prostitution, *see* Writing Guidelines.

date rape date rape may account for as much as 80% of all sexual assaults. According to figures presented to the Senate Judiciary Committee in 1990, one in seven college women will be raped by the time she graduates, most often by someone she knows. One of the special problems associated with date rape is that prosecutors and police investigators tend to give less credit to a charge of rape from someone who knew or who may even have had previous consensual sex with the rapist. A helpful analogy: the benefactor who often gives to a certain charity is justified in laying a charge of theft if that charity breaks into the benefactor's house one night to obtain additional funds. Beware the heterosexist assumption that date rape involves a woman and a man. *See also* provoke; rape; rape victim; sexual harassment; "she asked for it"; victim; violence.

daughterboard *board*. *See also* motherboard.

daughter cell leave as is; this is a biology term with specific meanings.

daughter track this media catch phrase describes women whose careers may be threatened because of time spent caring for elderly relatives; 11% of working caregivers (almost all of whom are women) quit or are fired. U.S. women spend an average of eighteen years helping their parents.

David and Goliath when using expressions like this, be aware of how many are male-based. Some of the time use female-based expressions, creative expressions of your own, or alternatives: *unequal contest, unequal contestants, unexpected defeat*. This evocative phrase is particularly difficult to replace as its meaning is so specific. There is nothing wrong with it per se, so if you are not using male metaphors and expressions to the exclusion of female images, use this one with good cheer. *See* Writing Guidelines for a discussion of sex-linked expressions.

Davy Jones's locker when using expressions like this, be aware of how many are male-based. Some of the time use female-based expressions, creative expressions of your own, or alternatives: *ocean/sea bottom, the briny deep*. *See* Writing Guidelines for a discussion of sex-linked expressions.

deaconess *deacon*, except when specific denominations designate "deaconess" as the office for women; in some churches "deaconess" is the functional equal of "deacon." Although most translations of the Bible use "deaconess," the original Greek used the same word—"diakonos"—for both sexes. In the early church both men and women functioned as deacons. Whenever possible use the more authentic "deacon."

dead man (empty liquor/beer bottle) *dead one*. "Dead soldier" and "dead marine" are sometimes seen as alternatives, but they are too ugly and violent to be recommended.

dead men tell no tales *the dead tell no tales.*

deaf/deaf and dumb use "deaf" only for someone with a total hearing loss and then only as an adjective ("deaf persons," not "the deaf"). For less than a total hearing loss use *hearing impaired, someone with a partial hearing loss/with a hearing disability.* Avoid "deaf and dumb" or "deaf mute"; most deaf people can speak or communicate with sign. If someone truly cannot speak use *nonverbal person, someone without speech. See also* handicapped.

dear/dearie these words are patronizing and inappropriate when used by a man or a woman to someone (most often a woman) who has not given permission to be so addressed. These terms especially do not belong in the workplace or in social interactions with strangers where the lower-power person gets stuck with unwanted and insincere intimacy. *See also* courts (judicial); honey/hon.

dear John letter, send a *give someone the air, give the gate to someone, whistle someone down the wind, send someone packing.* Or, *send a dear Jane letter.*

dear sir *See* salutations.

death the word is inclusive, but death itself is both sexist and racist today: men of all ages die at greater rates than women, and black men die at even greater rates than white men. Depending on age, black men's rates of death are two and a half to nearly six times that of white women. Of all those who die prematurely—that is, of illnesses that could be cured or treated by routine medical care—80% are African Americans (who make up 13% of the population). In general, men die an average of eight years earlier than women.

deathsman *executioner.*

debonair *jaunty, lighthearted, vivacious, breezy, nonchalant, free and easy, merry, cheery, sunny, sporty; well-mannered, well-bred, polite, refined, civil, charming, suave, courteous, urbane, gracious, graceful, obliging, affable.* These alternatives are suggested because "debonair" is used to describe only men, although it need not be (in *L'Allegro* Milton used it to describe a goddess).

debutante *debutant,* except where the "feminine" spelling is still used for a young woman making her formal debut into society. *See also* divorcé/divorcée.

deckman *log roller, deck worker.*

defenseman *defensive/defense player.* Or, use specific term: *goalie, goalkeeper, goaltender, guard, linebacker,* etc. *See also* line man (sports).

delivery boy/delivery man *delivery driver/clerk/person, merchandise deliverer, deliverer, porter, messenger, carrier, courier, runner.*

demijohn leave as is because of its specific meaning and lack of alternatives. The word is actually a mistranslation of the French "damejeanne" meaning Lady Jane.

demimondaine if you mean prostitute, use *prostitute*. If you mean someone on the fringes of society, use *lowlife, riffraff, outcast, down-and-
outer*.

den mother *den/group leader*.

dental assistant/hygienist over 98% are women.

dentist approximately 9% of dentists are women. They are not particularly new to the profession; the School of Dentistry of Paris, founded
in 1884, acccepted students of both sexes from the beginning.

depot master *depot supervisor/chief*.

deserter always a man so far. *See also* draft dodger; males-only draft.

deskman *desk clerk/jockey*.

detail man *detailer, pharmaceutical sales agent, pharmaceutical company
representative, representative, sales rep*.

deus ex machina this Latin phrase, "god from a machine" (because
sometimes in Greek and Roman plays a god arrived onstage by
means of a crane to produce a "providential" ending), is appropriate
for either a woman or a man. However, since "deus" is in the
masculine gender and since it is used most often in masculine contexts, you may want alternatives: *last-minute rescuer, eleventh-hour
deliverer; contrived solution*.

devil/he *devil/it*.

devotee woman or man. Unlike similar words borrowed from French—
divorcé/divorcée, fiancé/fiancée, habitué, protegé/protegée—this
one is used in the feminine form and without its accent for both
sexes. Some have suggested using "-ee" for all such words as is done
in "employee."

diamond in the rough this has always been used for men, although there
is no reason it couldn't also refer to women. If you want something
less male-associated, use *rough/gauche/crude/ unpolished/untutored
person, raw material, someone with rough edges/a little rough around the
edges, someone with hidden talents/potential*.

diamonds are a girl's best friend avoid this inane sexist phrase, which
originated in the 1930s with a DeBeers ad campaign.

dick this slang term has three main meanings: (1) For "dick" meaning
"detective" use *gumshoe, private eye, tail, shadow, flatfoot*. (2) For
"dick" meaning "penis" leave as is. (3) For "dick" meaning a stupid
person, use the more inclusive *dork*.

die man *die designer*.

dingbat *kook, nitwit*. Thanks to Archie Bunker, this technically inclusive
word seems reserved for women.

directress *director*. There remain serious race and sex inequalities on
boards of directors: a 1990 congressional study says directors of the
Federal Reserve are overwhelmingly white men, most of whom have
close ties to the banking industry. Despite a 1977 law requiring

diversity of membership and public participation on the Federal Reserve boards, of the seventy-two regional directors, only three are women and all but two are white. According to *Fortune* magazine, of the 4,012 highest paid officers and directors of the nation's largest industrial and service corporations, only nineteen are women—less than .5%. Women hold fewer than 5% of the directorships available at the top 1,000 companies and they are even more under-represented as inside directors of their own companies. *See also* glass ceiling.

dirty old man ageist as well as sexist, this stereotype conveys very little real information. Describe instead what the person is doing, thinking, or saying. *See also* lech/lecher; pederast; pedophile; satyr; womanize/womanizer.

"discovery" of America only by a strange twist of white ethnocentrism can one be considered to "discover" a continent inhabited by millions of people. The forty-year period following Columbus's arrival in the western hemisphere produced one of the greatest losses of human life in history. Columbus and his men had no interest in or respect for nature and human beings, but a high interest in and respect for gold and wealth—attitudes still seen today in the lack of respect society has for "nonproductive" individuals. Do not teach or perpetuate the idea of Columbus's "discovery"; give a complete picture of its ramifications and effects. *See also* savage.

discrimination discrimination exists when people's choices of and access to employment, education, housing, resources, and other public goods are limited by their race, sex, age, religion, disability, or national origin.

diseur/diseuse *professional reciter*. Or, use the base term, "diseur," for both sexes.

displaced homemaker generally defined as a woman whose principal job has been homemaking and who has lost her main source of income because of divorce, separation, widowhood, spousal disability, or loss of eligibility for public assistance; "displaced homemaker" has been a sex-specific term. However, federal legislation and funding dictate that financial assistance for people in this situation be available to men as well as to women. An estimated 40% of homemakers fall into poverty following displacement; 58% are over sixty-five; one in four is a minority woman. The first year after divorce, the standard of living for women and their children declines 73% while the standard of living for men rises 42% (*Congressional Caucus for Women's Issues*). According to Emily Card, California attorney and author of *The Ms. Money Book*, a judge will not award a woman with children more than 40% of her ex-husband's net income, which means that while the ex-husband gets 60%, the woman and her children have to live on less than half the prior family income. Approximately 60% of displaced homemakers are classified poor or near-poor; 45% do not have a high-school diploma. *See also* alimony; child custody; divorce; wage earner; working mother; working wife.

display man *displayer, merchandise displayer, sign painter.*

district lineman *district line maintainer.*

ditz/ditzy *out to lunch, space ranger, flake, out of it, on another planet, with one's head in the clouds, not all there, missing some marbles, with a mind like a sieve, mindless, brainless wonder, dense, muddleheaded, not bright, half-witted, dull-witted, dim-witted, thick-headed, thick-witted, inane.* These relatively new terms are associated with girls/women, which is why inclusive alternatives are provided.

divorce avoid phrases like "he divorced her" or "she divorced him" unless you know this was the case. Use instead *they were divorced, they filed for divorce, they divorced.* Divorce in the United States is often sexist and racist. When it first appeared over twenty years ago, the no-fault divorce was hailed as a quick and equitable solution to an unsalvageable marriage. However, according to Fred Moody (in the *Seattle Weekly*), "Instead of reducing inequality between the sexes, no-fault divorce has widened the gap in status between men and women, and is the leading cause of the well-documented feminization of poverty in America." Lenore Weitzman (*The Divorce Revolution*) agrees: "No fault was taken to mean no responsibility," resulting in "a systematic impoverishment of women and children." (Over half the eighteen million poor children in this country are living in single-parent homes caused by divorce.) Five years after a divorce, a woman's income is 30% of what it was during the marriage; a man's is 14% more. The lack of alimony and lax child-support enforcement in no-fault contribute to the problem, with black women hurt the most; they are half again as likely as white women to be awarded alimony, and much less likely than white women to get property settlements. Weitzman suggests that husband and wife "both share the burdens of divorce in America." *See also* child custody; courts (judicial); displaced homemaker.

divorcé/divorcée *divorced person, divorcé.* Or, *unmarried/unwed/formerly married person.* It is always better to omit a person's marital status; it is so seldom relevant. For many years, it has been the woman who is called a divorcée (often with pejorative overtones), while a man is referred to as unmarried, a bachelor, or as someone who is divorced. If you need to mention marital status, use parallel terms for both sexes. Casey Miller and Kate Swift (*The Handbook of Nonsexist Writing*) persuasively recommend the standard form of French words, that is, "divorcé" for both sexes. This guideline can also be applied to such words as blond, brunet, chaperon, confidant, clairvoyant, debutant, fiancé, habitué, protegé.

divorced father/divorced mother *single parent.*

dizzy avoid as an adjective for a woman (or a blond). For inclusive alternatives *see* scatterbrained. *See also* ditz/ditzy.

dockman *dockhand, dockworker, docker, stevedore, shoreworker, shorehand, longshore worker, longshorehand, wharfworker, wharfhand.*

dockmaster *dock supervisor/boss.*

doctoress *doctor.* One-fifth of U.S. physicians are women. Do not use "woman doctor" where sex is irrelevant or where you would not use "man doctor."

doll/dollie-bird/dolly-bird/China doll/Kewpie doll/dolled up/all dolled up these terms are patronizing, belittling, inaccurate, and objectifying. The terms "dolled up/all dolled up" are generally reserved for women, but can be, and have been, used of men. As long as we have Ken, men can be dolls too, although it is not perceived as quite so patronizing to call them "dolls." *See also* living doll.

domestic not sexist per se, "domestic" is sometimes used to further a sexist context—for example, the assumption that all domestic matters belong a priori to the nearest woman. When you see the word "domestic," check the environs carefully.

dominatrix *dominator.*

dominie always a man. *See also* clergyman; schoolmarm/schoolmaster/schoolmistress.

don to mean a Spanish gentleman, grandee, or Mafia leader, "don" is correct and always refers to a man. To mean a university professor however, use *professor, college/university professor, teacher, tutor, head, lecturer.*

Don Juan this sex-specific term has no parallel for a woman and is virtually irreplaceable for a man. If you need a sex-neutral term try *lover, dashing lover, great romantic, paramour, heartthrob, flirt, sexually aggressive/sexually active person, seducer, bedhopper, swinger.*

don't know from Adam the commonly used partner to this sex-specific expression is *don't know from Adam's aunt.*

doorman *doorkeeper, door attendant, security guard, caretaker, doorkeep, attendant, porter, concierge, sentry, gatekeeper, commissionaire, guard, warder, beadle.*

doubting Thomas when using expressions like this, be aware of how many are male-based. Some of the time use female-based expressions, creative expressions of your own, or alternatives: *skeptic, doubter, unbeliever, disbeliever, nonbeliever, cynic, questioner, pessimist, defeatist, someone from Missouri.* The tongue-in-cheek "doubting Thomasina" is sometimes seen. *See* Writing Guidelines for a discussion of sex-linked expressions.

doughboy use as is in historical context. Also: *World War I soldier.*

dowager avoid; there is no parallel for a man. One definition of "dowager" reflects on a woman's marital status (widowed) while the other reflects mainly on her age. Decide if this information is relevant and then use descriptive terms that apply to both men and women. It should not be difficult to get along without the word; we have talked about men for centuries without using a similar term.

doyen/doyenne *dean*.

draft dodger this currently can be only a young man/man because of the males-only draft. It is a values-laden, judgmental, sexist, and even classist term that is best avoided. During certain periods of our history, it was a common and perfectly legal practice to hire a substitute to fight in one's place. Grover Cleveland hired a substitute rather than fight in the Civil War. This was not a problem for him in the presidential campaign of 1884, however, because his Republican opponent, James Blaine, had also hired a soldier substitute. One did, of course, need to be able to afford such a tactic; poor men did not have the option. This legacy continues today. The lawmakers who make the wars do not become footsoldiers in these wars; neither, generally, do their sons or the sons of other rich, powerful individuals. *See also* coward/cowardly/cowardice; males-only draft.

draftsman *drafter, artist, copyist, landscape artist, limner, drawer, sketcher, delineator, designer, architect, designer, engineer*. Women make up 16% of drafting technicians.

draftsmanship *drafting, drafting expertise/skill*.

drag/drag queen these terms usually refer to gay men, especially transvestites, cross-dressers, or female impersonators. The "insider/outsider" rule applies: the terms are derogatory when used by those outside the gay community, usually acceptable when used within.

dragoman nonsexist; the "man" is from the Italian for "hand." If the word's sexist appearance is a problem, use *interpreter, travel agent, guide*.

drayman *dray driver*.

dredgemaster *dredge operator*.

dressmaker *tailor, custom tailor, clothier, garment designer/worker, mender, alterer, alterations expert, stitcher*.

drillmaster *drill sergeant/instructor*.

droit de seigneur a highly sexist concept that is no longer part of our vocabulary in the same way it was. However, the term may be useful (in quotation marks) to describe what happens in certain cases of sexual harassment of women where there is unequal power: professors and students, bosses and staff, political candidates and campaign workers, etc. There is no parallel term for the absolute power of a woman over a subordinate man (probably because these cases have been so rare), but the "droit de seigneur" metaphor could still be used effectively and understood in context.

drudge *menial, common laborer, toiler, plodder, hard worker, industrious/hard-working person*. Alternatives seem indicated since "drudge" is used for women only, although the word itself is not sex-specific.

drug czar/drug lord/drug king *drug dealer/chief/boss/tycoon/ bigwig/distributor*.

drugs one way in which the flourishing drug culture attracts young people is by establishing an "insider" vocabulary of colorful terms that make drugs and drug dealers seem harmless and fun. All drug-related street slang, including the following short list of sex-linked terms, ought to be replaced with words that reflect reality (in parentheses): Aunt Hazel (heroin); auntie (opium); Aunt Mary (marijuana); baglady/bagman (drug dealers); Barbies/Barbie doll (barbiturates); big Harry (heroin); blue johnnies (delirium tremens); boy (heroin); brother (heroin); businessman's lunch (amphetamines); candy man (drug pusher/dealer); Christinas (amphetamines); chick (cocaine); dollies (methadone); George smack (heroin); golden girl (cocaine); good-time man (drug dealer); Harry/Hazel/Henry (heroin); jane (marijuana); jug man/jug broad (drug user, but note grossly nonparallel "man/broad"); junker man or J-man (marijuana smoker); ken doll (barbiturates); kick man (drug dealer); Lady/Lady Snow/Lady White (cocaine); Lady H (heroin); Mary (morphine); Mary Jane/ maryjane/Mary J. (marijuana); Mary Warner/Mary Werner/Mary Worner (marijuana); Miss Emma (morphine); pink ladies (barbiturates); schoolboy (codeine); simple simon (psilocybin); sister (morphine); swingman (drug connection/seller); tambourine man (drug dealer); white girl/white lady (cocaine); white goddess (morphine).

drugstore cowboy there doesn't seem to be an equally pithy and colorful inclusive substitute for this phrase, especially as it's generally defined as a man who hangs around drugstores or other public places trying to impress women. If you need to describe a woman who hangs around drugstores, etc., "drugstore cowgirl" would probably be understood.

drum majorette *drum major, baton twirler*.

drunk as a lord *drunk, intoxicated, tight, loaded, well-oiled, stewed to the gills, plastered, smashed, three/four sheets to the wind, half seas over, under the table, lit to the gills, pickled, high as a kite, out of it*. You might want to consider the wisdom of dressing up something that really isn't very attractive; the plain word "drunk" may be the best choice here.

dude to mean vacationers at a dude ranch both women and men can be dudes. The slang term, either as a form of address or to mean a male friend, a boy/man, or a swinging, attractive man, has no parallel for women but doesn't demean either sex and seems unlikely to be abandoned in casual conversation and writing in the near future. For alternatives to "a fancy dresser," *see* dandy.

duenna *chaperon*.

dukedom *duchy*.

dumb blond avoid this overworked, meaningless, and inaccurate cliché. *See also* blonde.

dumpman *dumper*.

dustman *cleaner, sweeper, sweep; garbage collector/hauler, trash/refuse collector, sanitation worker*.

Dutch courage *sham courage, courage from a bottle*. The term is ethnocentric.

Dutchman *Hollander, Dutch citizen, Dutchwoman and Dutchman*. Plural: *Hollanders, Dutch people, Dutchfolk, Dutchwomen and Dutchmen* (but not "Dutchmen and women").

dutch treat this term has probably not caused many people to think less of the Dutch or to consider them cheapskates. However, it is mildly pejorative, and if you want to get around it use *separate checks, I insist on paying for myself*.

Dutch uncle, talk to like a *See* talk to like a Dutch uncle.

dweeb girl/woman or boy/man.

dyke (woman) this term is unacceptable to some lesbians, but it is used and enjoyed by others. It follows the "insider/outsider" rule, which means its use is generally unacceptable for those outside the lesbian community. Writer Denise Ohio says that dyke is "a word being reclaimed by the people it's normally used to denigrate. It was a total insult before; now it's showing power, solidarity." *See also* bull dyke; butch; femme/fem; Gay Rights Movement; heterosexism; homophobia; homosexual.

dyslexia both boys/men and girls/women can have dyslexia; it affects 10% to 15% of the population. For the past century, it has been widely believed that dyslexia strikes mostly boys, and entire research programs have been set up to find the biological basis for the presumed gender difference. However, three recent studies say girls are just as likely to be reading impaired, but that teachers are far more likely to diagnose the condition in boys, to the point that too many boys are in special-education classes (they also typically account for 80% of those treated at dyslexia clinics) and too many girls with reading problems are struggling in silence. The frequent diagnosis of dyslexia in boys and failure to diagnose it in girls is caused partly by teachers' and parents' expectations that boys, not girls, will have problems.

e

The investigation of the meaning of words is the beginning of education.

Antisthenes

each man for himself *See* every man for himself.

Eagle Scout boys/young men only.

early to bed, early to rise, makes a man healthy, wealthy, and wise *early to bed, early to rise, will make us all healthy, wealthy, and wise.*

earth mother there is no parallel term for a man and no inclusive term conveys quite the same idea. Despite the generally negative association of women with nature, this term seems positive and descriptive enough to retain. *See also* Father Sky; Mother Earth; Mother Nature; nature/she.

ecofeminism coined by French writer Françoise d'Eaubonne in 1974, the term describes the synthesis of feminist and ecological concerns. According to Lindsy Van Gelder ("It's Not Nice to Mess with Mother Nature," *Ms.*, Jan./Feb. 1989), "Ecofeminists believe that the domination of women and of nature comes from the same impulse . . . . In an ecofeminist society, no one would have power over anyone else, because there would be an understanding that we're all part of the interconnected web of life." Ecofeminists say environmental problems grow out of a logic of domination that oppresses and exploits women and nature, and that the best hope of saving the world lies in traditionally female (cooperation/partnership) values. *See also* male-dominated society; Mother Earth; Mother Nature; nature/she.

economist about 35% of economists are women.

education education has not been, and is often still not, an equal opportunity or parallel experience for boys/young men and girls/young women or for minority groups. Multiple studies have found that teachers tend to pay more attention to boys than to girls; call on boys more often; maintain stronger eye contact with them; remember their names more often; expect more of them (especially in math and science); take their ideas and contributions more seriously; and allow them to dominate discussions (in undergraduate classrooms they talk up to twelve times longer than female students, according to data gathered from videotaped classes). When girls have trouble with math, they are advised to drop the class; when boys have trouble, tutors are suggested. Boys taking a keyboarding class were oriented toward computer programming; called typing, the very same class oriented girls toward clerical careers. On the other hand, boys are disciplined more often than girls, have more behavioral problems, and are more likely to repeat grades. Much is being done to provide education that is fair and effective; much remains to be done.

effeminate although this word could be used in a positive sense (and, in fact, a men's movement called Revolutionary Effeminism has consciously struggled against masculinism), in its most commonly understood sense, it is pejorative and sexist, loaded with cultural stereotypes about what it means to be a man or a woman today. Choose instead one of the following inclusive words, which are not synonyms but seem, rather, to be what most people are trying to convey with "effeminate": *passive, gentle, timid, weak, agreeable, docile, fussy, particular.*

elder statesman *senior/longtime/career diplomat, skilled/career/experienced politician, foreign relations expert, power behind the throne.*

Electra complex acceptable sex-specific term; the parallel is "Oedipus complex."

Elks (lodge members) males only.

emasculate this may very occasionally be the appropriate word to use, but too often it is used carelessly; it indicts something or someone (often a woman) for a process that depends just as importantly on a man's willingness to be emasculated, and unflatteringly implies that he is a passive victim. There are no parallel terms relating to women for "emasculate," "unman," and "castrate." For "emasculate" substitute *disarm, disable, weaken, incapacitate, undermine, deprive of courage/ strength/vigor/power, unhinge, unnerve, devitalize, attenuate, shatter, exhaust, disqualify, invalidate, paralyze, undo, muzzle, enervate, tie the hands of, draw the teeth of, clip the wings of, spike the guns of, take the wind out of one's sails, put a spoke in one's wheels, render hors de combat. See also* castrate/castrating.

embezzler 36% of embezzlers are women.

émigré woman or man.

éminence grise the nickname of Père Joseph, French monk, diplomat, and confidant of Cardinal Richelieu, is used today to describe a confidential agent of either sex or, in popular usage, a renowned expert. "Grise" ("gray") was not the color of his hair, but of his habit.

emotional in our culture being "emotional" is not an admired trait; the word is most often used as an antonym for "rational" or "intelligent." Although women have been allowed to be emotional, the tradeoff was that this cultural permission carried a patronizing, they-can't-help-it attitude—and was liable to turn to disapproval at whim. The usually sneering "touchy-feely" shows how we react to explorations of our emotional side. Largely because of changing social attitudes toward women, "emotional" is not used as often as it once was to rebut a woman's arguments or generally discount her as a thinking human being. The problem today, says M. Adam (in *Men Freeing Men,* ed. Francis Baumli), is that "women can now wax logical while men look silly waxing emotional." Until men are free to wax emotional and "emotional" is a positive word for both men and women, use it cautiously. *See also* irrational.

empress acceptable sex-specific official title. An empress may be the wife or widow of an emperor or an imperial titleholder in her own right.

emptyheaded *out to lunch, space ranger, flake, out of it, on another planet, with one's head in the clouds, not all there, missing some marbles, with a mind like a sieve, impractical, irresponsible, slaphappy, woolgathering, dreamy, mindless, brainless wonder, dense, muddleheaded, shallow, inane, foolish.* Along with airhead, birdbrained, featherbrained, harebrained, and scatterbrained, this word is reserved for women.

enchantress *enchanter.*

endman this term has such a specific meaning that it is not easily rendered gender-free, the more so since historically minstrels were men; for a woman use *endwoman, end comic.*

enemy/he *enemy/it, enemy/they.*

enfant terrible although this French expression is grammatically masculine, "enfant" refers to both sexes and the term is used inclusively in English-speaking countries as well.

engineer 7.5% of engineers are women.

engineman *engine operator.*

Englishman *Britisher, Briton, Brit* (slang), *English/British citizen/subject, Englander; Englishwoman and Englishman.* Plurals: *the English, English people/citizens, the British, Britons, Englishwomen and Englishmen* (but not "Englishmen and women"). The terms "English" and "British" are not synonymous. Great Britain consists of England, Scotland, Wales, and Ulster, so the Scottish, the Welsh, and the Ulsters, all Keltic peoples, are British, but they are not English, and would not care to be so named. Only those born of Anglo-Saxon parentage, wherever they live in Great Britain, are happy to be named English. To refer to the English when actually meaning the British is to exclude the Scottish, the Welsh, and the Ulsters.

enlisted man *enlistee, service member, recruit, enlisted member/person/personnel/soldier/sailor, soldier, sailor; enlisted man and enlisted woman.*

entrepreneur in French the word is grammatically masculine, but it is functionally inclusive in both English and French. Almost 30% of sole proprietorships are owned by women.

entryman *entry miner.*

equal pay/equal pay for equal work the Equal Pay Act of 1963 requires that women and men receive equal pay for equal work. *See also* comparable worth.

Equal Rights Amendment (ERA) this proposed amendment, which failed to obtain ratification of two-thirds of the states, consists of three brief sections. The first says, "Equality of rights under the law shall not be denied or abridged by the United States or by any state on account of sex." The second states that Congress shall have the power to enforce the article, and the third says the amendment will take effect two years after ratification. This extremely simple amendment (different by only one word from the amendment ensuring racial equality) has been bitterly resisted for several reasons: many people have never actually read the simple, sensible words of the amendment; equal rights for women have been confused with androgyny, sameness of function, and even a supposed loss of rights for women; and perhaps, as someone once pointed out, the equality of women means the eradication of a servant class—and this may be what fuels some fear. In 1915 former President Theodore Roosevelt described a new world—one that has yet to arrive: "No one who is not blind can fail to see that we have entered a new day in the great epic march of the ages. For good or for evil the old days have passed; and it rests with us, the men and women now alive, to decide whether in the new days the world is to be a better or a worse place to live in, for our descendants. In this new world women are to stand on an equal footing with men, in ways and to an extent never hitherto dreamed of."

equerry has always been a man.

equestrienne *equestrian.*

errand boy/errand girl *errand runner, runner, messenger, courier, page, gofer, clerk, office helper.*

escape man *escape artist.*

escort service *prostitution service.* If there are legitimate escort services, they should probably consider using another term as this phrase has been preempted by prostitution services.

Eskimo *Inuit.* "Eskimo," meaning "Eaters of Raw Meat," is the name given to the Inuits by the Algonquin Indians; it is not their own name for themselves. Use "Eskimo" only for those few Inuit groups that call themselves Eskimo.

Esq./Esquire it is correct to address a letter to a U.S. attorney of either sex using this courtesy title, for example, Marian Chernov, Esq. (In Great Britain "Esq." signifies rank and is used only for men.)

ethnic and racial slurs epithets and slurs label people as less-than-human objects, which then makes them easier to discount, degrade, and destroy. In *Contreras* v. *Crown Zellerbach, Inc.* (1977) the Washington Supreme Court held that "racial epithets which were once part of common usage may not now be looked upon as 'mere insulting language.'" They constitute instead a tort of outrage, or "intentional infliction of emotional distress." Richard Delgado (*Harvard Civil Rights-Civil Liberties Law Review*, vol. 17, 1982) says, "The racial insult remains one of the most pervasive channels through which discriminatory attitudes are imparted." Terms like the following range from moderately to deeply offensive and, depending on the context, may even be actionable: brave, chink, coon, dago, frog, gook, goy, gringo, honkie/honky, jap, kike, kraut, limey, mick, nigger, oreo, pickaninny, pollack, spic/spick, squaw, wetback, whitey, wop.

ethnocentrism the belief that one's own group is superior to other groups is ethnocentrism.

eunuch use this word only in the literal sense of a castrated man, in which case it is a legitimate sex-specific word. For its metaphorical use substitute *weakling, coward, wimp, pushover, doormat, lightweight, loser, craven. See also* castrate/castrating; emasculate; namby-pamby (noun/adj.); sissy; unman.

Eve Eve has traditionally symbolized the tempter, the one by whom evil came into the world. Do not perpetuate this stereotype, which incidentally leaves Adam looking suggestible, inept, and "belly-oriented," as one writer puts it. Be extremely cautious in referring to the biblical Eve; this story has profoundly contributed to negative attitudes toward women throughout history, largely because of misogynistic and patriarchal interpretations that labeled her evil, inferior, and seductive. Interpreters who argue Eve's inferiority and subordination to Adam because he was created first fail to apply the argument logically: in the story, God created light, water, land, plants, stars, animals, and finally man. According to this later-is-better hierarchy of creation, woman would be God's final, most glorious effort. As "first woman," Eve may be in for some rehabilitation; scientists tell us that the original human chromosome was carried by the female. This mitochondrial mother, our common ancestor, is popularly called Eve. *See also* Adam's rib.

even-steven *equally divided, share and share alike, fifty-fifty, even, balanced, go halves, six of one and half a dozen of another.*

everybody and his grandmother/brother *everybody and their grandmother, all the world and their offspring, all the world and their dog, everybody and their second cousin, one and all, the whole world, everybody under the sun, every citizen of heaven and earth, everybody, everyone, crowd. See also* singular "they."

every dog has his day, and every man his hour *every dog has its day.* Also: *talent will out, cream will rise, to everything there is a season.* In Mexico it's "Every little chapel has its little fiesta" (Suzanne Brock, *Idiom's Delight: Fascinating Phrases and Linguistic Eccentricities*).

every inch a king   leave as is when referring to a king and for a queen use *every inch a queen*; otherwise use *a noble person, a regal bearing, an air of command*.

everyman/Everyman   *the typical/ordinary person, the archetypical human being, Everyman and Everywoman* (always use together). *See also* average man; common man; man in the street.

every man a king   *share the wealth*. From Huey Pierce Long's political campaign, this term referred to his share-the-wealth program.

every man for himself   *everyone for themselves* (*see* singular "they"), *you're on your own, the devil take the hindmost, look out for number one, no time to be lost*. Or, if you like foreign expressions, there is the nonsexist French equivalent: *sauve qui peut!* ("Save yourself if you can!")

every man has his price   *everyone has a price*.

every man is a king in his own castle   *everyone wears a crown in their own castle* (*see* singular "they"); *we are all kings and queens in our own castles; in our own castle, each of us wears a crown; aboard our own ship each of us is captain; we are all rulers in our own castles; I am monarch of all I survey; home is where the heart is*.

every man jack   *everyone, every single person, every last one of them. See also* everybody and his grandmother/brother.

every man's death diminishes me   *See* any man's death diminishes me.

every mother's child/son   *every last one of them. See also* all the world and his wife; everybody and his grandmother/brother; every Tom, Dick, and Harry.

every Tom, Dick, and Harry   *every stranger off the street, every so-and-so, any old body, anyone, doesn't matter who it is. See also* all the world and his wife; everybody and his grandmother/brother.

evil men do, the   *the evil we/people do. See also* man's inhumanity to man.

exciseman   *excise agent/officer/collector, tax/duty collector*.

exclusive language   speech and writing that excludes, intentionally or unintentionally, certain groups of people and their experiences, and makes them invisible to others and less valuable in their own and others' eyes. They become symbolically annihilated. For years most of the advertising, writing, teaching, and speaking in our culture has been directed toward white, middle-class, christian, heterosexual, able-bodied men. There is nothing wrong with this category of people; they have in fact contributed enormously to society. The problem is that there are many other members of society who do not belong to this category and whose existence has been ignored by exclusive language.

executive   a 1990 survey of 698 top executives at the 1,000 biggest companies found that fewer than 5% of the managers were women or minorities. "Top jobs in corporate American are still overwhelmingly the province of white males," says Lester Korn, head of Korn/Ferry International, which did the survey with UCLA'S Anderson Graduate School of Management. Figures have changed only slightly since Korn/Ferry's first study in 1979—1% of top executives were women and .4% were black, Asian, or Hispanic; today women represent 3% and minorities slightly more than 1%. Partly because women have not been in management as long as men and partly because of institutionalized sexism, there are still serious inequities between men and women executives: a 1989 *Savvy* magazine survey found that the highest-paid woman executive in corporate America made $1.3 million that year while her male counterpart earned $14.6 million; at the vice presidential level or higher women are paid 42% less than men with comparable titles; according to *Fortune* magazine, in 799 of the nation's largest industrial and service corporations, only 19 of the 4,012 highest-paid officers and directors were women—less than 0.5%; *Fortune* also found that just 465 of the nearly 9,300 people listed as officers in the annual reports of 255 major companies were women—about 5%; according to a study of fired executives, female executives earn an average of $63,339 after relocation while male executives earn an average of $86,134. Getting to the top involves personal inequities too: only about 40% of top female executives have children, compared to 95% of their male peers. In one way, female and male executives are similar: women chief executives work 56.2 hours a week; male chief executives work 54.9 hours. *See also* glass ceiling; mommy track; wage earner.

executrix *executor*. In some certain narrow legal senses "executrix" is still used.

expatriate/ex-pat although based on the Latin for "country," "patria" (and thus on "pater," "father"), these words are functionally inclusive and their roots not as obtrusive as some "pater"-based words ("paternal," for example). If you prefer, use *American abroad, exile, displaced person, émigré*.

expert a 1989 study of ten major U.S. newspapers found that only 11% of those quoted on the front pages were women. (And that was an average; the *New York Times* quoted women as sources in only 6% of one month's front-page stories.) A 1990 survey of the three major newsmagazines showed that women were referred to for any reason only 12% of the time. When journalists and writers want a quick opinion, quote, or information from an expert, the tendency is to seek out a white, middle-aged man, even when equally expert women, minorities, older people, gay individuals, and people with disabilities are available. Watch the word "expert" to see how often it falls into a rather narrow range of available humans. There was good reason in the past for most experts from the same set; these were (and still are, in many cases) the people who are running things. However, if you regularly check with experts in a certain field, you should be able to compile a list of non-white, non-male, non-straight, non-ablebodied people of all ages who can answer your questions equally competently.

ex-serviceman *ex-service member, ex-soldier, ex-member of the armed forces.*

f

Language makes culture, and we make a rotten culture when we abuse words.

Cynthia Ozick

factory boy/girl/man/woman *factory worker.*

faculty wives *faculty spouses.* Casey Miller and Kate Swift (*The Handbook of Nonsexist Writing*) say that tacking on identifiers like "faculty/Senate/service/corporate wives" makes women appendages of both a man and an institution while detracting from their own lives and roles. The terminology also assumes that all members of the institution are men. Where are the "corporate husbands," "Senate husbands," and "faculty husbands"?

fag/faggot (man) these terms follow the "insider/outsider" rule: they are extremely derogatory when used by non-gays, but usually acceptable when used positively among gay men. By reclaiming the words for themselves, gay men defuse the hostility of these words and the power such words had over them.

fair-haired boy/fair-haired girl *the favorite, the apple of someone's eye, privileged person, someone with pull, front runner, person after one's own heart, in one's good graces, persona grata, teacher's pet.* "Fair-haired" is problematic because (1) making fair-haired the preferred coloring is racist and ethnocentric; (2) the phrases are used of adults, which makes the boy/girl designation inappropriate; (3) "fair-haired boy" is common, while "fair-haired girl" is not.

fair sex, the this phrase has lost whatever meaning it ever had.

fairy (legend) fairies are both male and female, although they most often materialize in our culture as female (e.g., fairy godmother, Tinkerbell, Walt Disney's fairies, the tooth fairy).

fairy (man) this essentially derogatory term follows the "insider/outsider" rule: gay men might use it in a friendly and positive way among themselves, but others should avoid it.

fairy godmother retain in traditional fairy tales and add fairy godfathers to modern tales. Also: *good fairy/genie/genius, guardian angel, benefactor, savior, hero.*

faith of our fathers *faith of our ancestors/mothers and fathers.*

fakir *wonder-worker, ascetic, mendicant; dervish; impostor, swindler.* "Fakir" comes from the Arabic for "poor man"; fakirs are generally men and the word is perceived as male.

Falashas *Beta Israel.* Ethiopian Jews reject the term "Falashas," which signifies "landless aliens," and prefer the self-selected "Beta Israel."

fallen woman if you mean prostitute, use *prostitute.* Otherwise use for either sex *someone who is unfortunate/unlucky/sexually active/promiscuous, someone who has fallen on hard/evil times/from grace.*

fall guy/fall man *scapegoat, dupe, goat, sucker, victim, fool, laughingstock, loser, greenhorn, sitting duck, soft mark, mark, target, pushover, sap, nebbish. See also* whipping boy.

fall of Man *fall of the human race, the Fall.*

family use "family" in ways that reflect contemporary realities; the "family of nostalgia" ("Father Knows Best," "Leave It to Beaver," "Ozzie and Harriet") that is still pictured as the "real" family was actually only an aberration that predominated for several decades after World War II. The legalistic definition of family is a group of people related by blood, marriage, or adoption, but the real-world definition is much broader; in a 1989 Massachusetts Mutual Life Insurance Company study almost three-quarters of the respondents chose the description, "A group of people who love and care for each other." In 1988 fewer than 27% of the nation's ninety-one million households fit the traditional model of a family; the Census Bureau counted 1.6 million same-sex couples living together and 2.6 million unmarried opposite-sex couples sharing a household. Domestic partners ordinances that have been passed or are being passed in some U.S. cities officially recognize as families "committed adult partners" (unmarried heterosexuals and gay and lesbian couples who have registered their relationship with the city clerk). These partners, who must live together, be unmarried to anyone else, and be jointly responsible for living expenses, then have the same rights as married couples to bereavement and sick leave, health insurance, and fringe benefits. So far these ordinances benefit only municipal employees, but activists are urging the adoption of similar policies by unions and public employers. The short civil ceremony, in which couples pay a fee, exchange vows, and obtain a certificate of domestic partnership, is being referred to as "partnering."

family man *homebody, stay-at-home, family head, home-lover, family-oriented/family-centered/home-centered person, someone devoted to the family.*

family planning this sex-neutral term ought not to be presented as the exclusive province/responsibility of women. *See also* birth control.

family of man *the human family, humanity, humankind, the human family tree.*

fancy girl/fancy lady/fancy man/fancy woman *prostitute/prostitute's pimp/ prostitute.*

farm boy (employee) *farm hand/worker.*

farmer approximately two-thirds of all farmers in the world are women. "And yet," writes Lee Egerstrom (*St. Paul Pioneer Press*), "of all the job descriptions in the English language, few jobs have a more masculine connotation than the title 'farmer.' . . . In most cultures, agriculture becomes 'men's work' when it progresses to the point of being a successful commercial industry. When that happens, women are shoved back to perform related commercial activities, while also tending children." Casey Miller and Kate Swift (*The Handbook of Nonsexist Writing*) note that "most farmers in the developing world are women. According to United Nations estimates, women produce 60% to 80% of the food supply in Africa and Asia." Sign of progress: newspapers referred to the Iowa woman who found the missing parts of the United Airlines DC-10 that crashed in Sioux City in 1989 as a "farmer."

farmerette *farmer.*

farm wife/farmer's wife most often, this woman is a farmer in all but name; give her the name. In one survey of farm women, nearly 95% were heavily involved in farm management, including basic farm labor and decision-making; 86% did the farm recordkeeping; 75% cared for the animals; 72% harvested crops. Sometimes farm wives have not only not been called farmers, they have not even been called persons. In 1988 a federal judge had to rule against the U.S. Department of Agriculture, which claimed that a farm couple was only one person. Although a father and his son or a brother and a sister farming in partnership were regarded as two people, a husband and wife were counted as only one person for USDA purposes. U.S. District Court Judge Joyce Hens Green officially rejected "the archaic notion that husbands and wives are one 'person.'"

father (clergy) leave as is in direct address ("Father Frank Friar") but when referring to someone use the inclusive *priest, minister, pastor. See also* clergyman; priest.

Father (God) When Jesus Christ speaks to or refers to God as his Father, the word "Father" should be retained, according to those who believe that the name "Father" that Jesus gives to God indicates a very specific relationship and may not be changed. Others, however, look back to the Gnostic and Semitic traditions from which the words "Father" and "Son" emerged, and say that these words have nothing to do with roles like father and son, or indeed with any familial roles, but that they were rather the closest worshipers could come to expressing in personal terms the concepts of Uncreated Source (God) and Reflected Image (Jesus). For these people, using metaphors for

God (God as nurturing mother or loving father) is acceptable, but the idea of God having a gender is not. There is nothing wrong with thinking of God as Father—indeed, it is a strong, beautiful metaphor. The problem is that we have overused that one metaphor until it has taken on a spurious life of its own. God is only *like* a father; the metaphor does not mean God is a father or that God is male. We need to create new metaphors for God and build on the others that we have. God is also light, rock, potter, mother, bread, wind, water, sun, fire, wisdom, judge, homemaker, physician, warrior, midwife, lion, leopard, she-bear, mother eagle, and shepherd, for example. The question of God's gender or lack of it poses a dilemma for people who are equally sensitive to the Word of God, theological truth, sexist language, and the person in the pew. The latter often sees inclusive language (particularly the elimination of God as Father) as unconscionable tampering, and finds the challenge to faith over-whelming. In the Old Testament, where the issue is not so much the "fatherness" of God as the "Godness" of God, the word "Father" can be replaced by one of the following: *Advocate, Almighty/the Almighty, Author, Being, Blessed One, Creator, Creator God, Creator of all things, Defender, the Deity, Divine Light/One, Elohim, the Eternal, Eternal One, Ever-present God, Exalted One, First Cause, First and Last, Friend, Glory, God, Godhead, God in Heaven, God my Rock, God my Rock and my Redeemer, God of Abraham and Sarah (or God of Abraham and Sara, of Isaac and Rebecca, of Jacob, Leah and Rachel), God of Grace/Heaven/Hosts/ Israel, God of our ancestors/forebears, God of the Nations, Good Parent, Ground of Being, Guide, Healer, Heavenly Creator/One/Parent, Helper, Holy One/the Holy One, Holy One of Blessing/Israel, the Infinite, Just One, Liberator, Living God, Maker, Majesty of the Universe, Merciful God, Mighty One, Most High/the Most High, Most Loving God, Nurturer, O God my God, O Gracious God, Omnipotent One, our Refuge and our Strength, Powerful One, Preserver, Protector of Sarah and Shield of Abraham, Providence, Redeemer, Rock, Rock of Refuge, Ruler, Savior, Shepherd, Shepherd of Israel, Source/the Source, Source of Life, Sovereign, Spirit, Supreme Being, Sustainer, the Truth, Wisdom.* When using the Father metaphor, avoid as much as possible masculine pronouns in order to mitigate the strongly male orientation. *See also* Father, Son, and Holy Spirit/Ghost; God; God/he; God/his; Holy Spirit (Ghost)/ he; Lord; Son of Man (Christ).

father (parent) when writing about men as fathers, avoid stereotypes— that they are absent, inept, distant, or cold. Some may well be, but perpetuating these vague and oftentimes unfounded notions does a disservice to men who are committed, loving, and effective fathers. It also breeds social tolerance for second-rate fathering. When writing or speaking about fathers, give them a full range of behaviors, attitudes, and emotions. Although there are many nurturing, involved "new fathers," there are significant numbers of absent fathers; one of every four U.S. children is growing up without a father in the home, more than twice as many as in 1960. *See also* advertising; parent.

father (pseudogeneric noun) *parent, progenitor, procreator, mother and father; source, ancestor, forebear; originator, founder, inventor, promoter.* *See also* forefather; mother and father.

father (pseudogeneric verb) *parent, nurture, support, protect, take care of, care for, look after, be responsible for, rear/raise children, caregive, supervise; procreate, create, co-create, reproduce, breed, propagate, give life to, bring to life, bring into being, bring about, call into existence, cause to exist; produce, make, found, author, originate, generate, engender, establish, invent, introduce.* Alternate gender-specific words such as *father/mother, beget/ give birth to, conceive/beget.*

father absence this is acceptable when paired with "mother absence." It has all too frequently been paired with the much more emotional and judgmental "mother deprivation." If you use "mother deprivation," use also "father deprivation."

father and mother *See* mother and father.

Father Christmas *See* Santa Claus.

father figure *role model, father figure and mother figure.* "Father figure" has a specific meaning and should be retained even though the potentially parallel term "mother figure" is not used very often (we have mother figures, but we are not so apt to label them). There does not seem to be any galloping sexism behind the fact that we use "father figure" but don't use "mother figure."

fatherland *homeland, native land/country/soil, home, home/birth country, land of one's ancestors, natal place, the old country, country.*

fatherless (pseudogeneric) *orphaned, parentless.*

fatherly replace this vague adjective with precise ones: *warm, nurturing, loving, kind, kindly, protective, supportive, caring, solicitous, considerate, interested, benevolent, good-natured, fond, affectionate, devoted, tender, gentle, demonstrative, sympathetic, understanding, indulgent, obliging, forbearing, tolerant, well-meaning, sheltering, generous.* These adjectives also apply to women; they are not synonyms for "fatherly" but rather what the culture understands by the word.

fathers (pseudogeneric) *ancestors, forebears, progenitors, precursors, predecessors, forerunners, leaders, pioneers, founders, trailblazers, innovators, fathers and mothers.*

Father's Day first celebrated in Spokane, Washington, in 1910, Father's Day was suggested by Mrs. John Bruce Dodd whose father, William Smart, had raised his children after his wife died. Prompted by Mrs. Dodd and by the new popularity of Mother's Day (1908), Spokane ministers, newspapers, and stores promoted acceptance of the idea.

Father Sky the use of "Father Sky" is not recommended as it reinforces the sexist stereotype of the distant, uncaring father. In addition, the use of its traditional but better-known partner, Mother Earth or Mother Nature, is not recommended either because of negative sexist associations. *See also* Mother Nature.

Fathers of the Church leave as is; historically accurate. *See also* church father.

Father, Son, and Holy Spirit/Ghost *God, Jesus, and Holy Spirit; Creator, Christ/Word, and Holy Spirit; Source of all Being, Eternal Word, and Holy Spirit; Maker, Jesus, and Holy Spirit; Creator, Savior, and Healer; Source, Servant, and Guide; Creator, Liberator, and Advocate; the grace of the Lord Jesus Christ and the love of God and the communion of the Holy Spirit; Creator, Redeemer, and Comforter/Sustainer/Sanctifier/Sanctifier God; Source of All Being, Eternal Word, Holy Spirit; the Holy Trinity; Three in One; One in Three; the Triune God.* When choosing alternatives note that some describe who God is ("God, Jesus, and Holy Spirit") while others describe what God does ("Creator, Savior, and Healer"). Some people object to the overuse of God-as-function terms.

Father Time *time/Time, progress, ravages/march of time.*

father upon *saddle with, lay at the door of, ascribe to, bring home to, charge with.*

favorite son candidate *state favorite, favorite candidate/citizen, favorite citizen candidate.*

featherbrained *See* scatterbrained.

fellow (noun/adj.) this is one of the most problematic words in language gender issues. "Fellow" is often judged inclusive; women receiving academic fellowships are called fellows, for example, and among its dictionary definitions are many wonderfully inclusive concepts. However, because one definition is "a familiar synonym for man, male person" (*Oxford English Dictionary*) it is often difficult to determine whether a writer or speaker is using "fellow" in the inclusive or exclusive sense. A convincing argument for its being exclusive is the common perception of the word. If someone says, for example, "Today I saw a fellow downtown throwing away hundred-dollar bills," there is no doubt in anyone's mind that the distributor of largesse was a man. The folksy "fella/feller" are also incontestably masculine. Substitutes for the noun include *person, partner, colleague, co-worker, companion, counterpart, associate, ally, comrade, friend, acquaintance, peer, affiliate, equal, mate, pair, double, twin, match.* For the adjective use *similar, alike, analogous, comparable, parallel, matching, corresponding, coinciding, like, something like, other, related, akin, equal, equivalent, associate(d), united, connected.* For the academic "fellow" you can sometimes use *scholar, recipient, postgraduate student.*

OCKHOLDERS

ORPORATION
DIRECTORS

CHAIRMAIN OF THE
EXECUTIVE COMMITTEE
TED MEREDITH

SIDENT/
UTIVE OFFICER
KERR

REAL ESTATE GROUP
PRESIDENT
ALLEN SABBAG

Finance
Legal
Public Relations
Human Resources
Information Systems

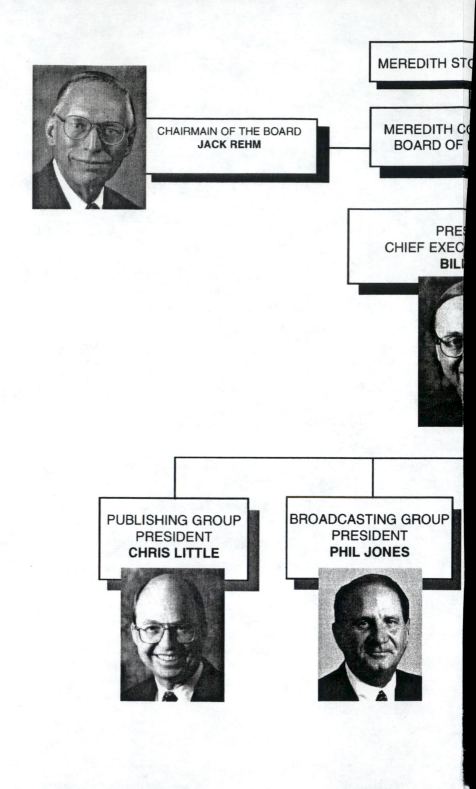

CHAIRMAIN OF THE BOARD
JACK REHM

MEREDITH ST

MEREDITH C
BOARD OF

PRES
CHIEF EXEC
BIL

PUBLISHING GROUP
PRESIDENT
CHRIS LITTLE

BROADCASTING GROUP
PRESIDENT
PHIL JONES

fellow countrymen *friends and neighbors, all of us, compatriots.* Rework the sentence to avoid this term if the alternatives don't suit. *See also* compatriot; fellow man/men.

fellow feeling *sympathy, understanding, compassion, commiseration, empathy, rapport, link, bond, union, tie, closeness, affinity, friendship, agape, pity, walking in someone else's shoes, putting oneself in someone else's place.*

fellow man/men in most cases "fellow" is superfluous. We are so used to hearing this catch-all term in certain contexts that we don't stop to ask if it is necessary. Be specific: *other people, you, citizens, workers, another human being, all of us here, the average person,* etc.

fellowship (scholarship) *scholarship, assistantship, stipend, subsidy, honorarium.* In its narrow meaning retain "fellowship."

fellowship (social bond) *friendship, companionship, solidarity, communion, union, unity, unity of mind and spirit, association, camaraderie, comradeship, partnership, togetherness, collaboration, esprit de corps, neighborliness, sharing, amity, good will, bonding, friendliness, conviviality, sodality, human community/kinship, kinship, humanity, family, the human family; society, assembly, community, organization, club, group, federation, corporation.* The substitute most often used for "fellowship" in religious materials is "communion." *See also* brotherhood (pseudogeneric); fellowship (scholarship).

fellow traveler *traveling companion, other traveler.*

fellow worker *co-worker, colleague, associate, teammate, partner.*

female (adj.) although it is generally preferable to use "woman" or "women" as adjectives, there will be times when "female" seems more appropriate. Use it, however, only when you would use "male" in a similar situation or when it is necessary for clarification; sex-specific adjectives are often gratuitous and belittling (for example, one sees "the female lawyer" but not "the male doctor"). Watch especially for nonparallel usage ("two technicians and a female mechanic"). *See also* female (noun).

female (noun) avoid the use of "female" as a noun except in technical writing, for example, in medicine, statistics, police reports, sociology. It is most often reserved for biological or nonhuman references. When using "female," use the parallel "male," not "man." It is sometimes thought that "female" is sexist because it has "male" in it. Dennis Baron (*Grammar and Gender*) says, "Actually *female* derives from the Latin *femella*, a diminutive of *femina*, 'woman.' It is completely unrelated to *male*, which comes to us via Old French from Latin *masculus*, a diminutive of *ma*, 'male, masculine.'" *See also* female (adj.).

feminine avoid this vague stereotype that conveys different meanings to different people according to their perceptions of what a woman ought or ought not do, say, think, wear, feel, look like. These subjective, cultural judgments have nothing to do with sex and everything to do with gender. Use instead specific descriptive adjectives: *gracious, warm, gentle, thoughtful, sensitive, loyal, receptive, supportive, compassionate, expressive, affectionate, tender, charming, nurturing, well-mannered, cooperative, neat, soft-spoken, considerate, kind*, etc. All these adjectives may be used equally appropriately of a man; they are not synonyms for "feminine" but rather what most people mean when they use the word.

feminine intuition *intuition.*

feminine mystique from Betty Friedan's landmark 1963 book of the same title in which she exposed "the problem that has no name" (women's unhappiness with their role and status in society), this term refers to the then-narrow definition of women primarily as housewives.

feminine wiles *wiles.*

femininity notions of femininity are based on culturally defined gender roles and how closely a woman fulfills these arbitrary expectations. Because the concept is so subjective, "femininity" may mean different things in Louisiana, Maine, Kansas, and California. Choose specific words for the qualities you want to describe: *warmth, graciousness, compassion, expressiveness, softness, self-confidence, strength, assurance, poise, charm, kindliness*, etc. These words can also be applied to men; they are not synonyms for "femininity" but rather what the culture often takes it to be.

feminism feminism has no strictly organized agenda but advocates equal rights and opportunities for both sexes, the ERA, comparable worth, and, in general, abortion rights (although many pro-life women call themselves Christian feminists). Most people now accept feminism as a historical, enduring movement that has promoted changes beneficial to society as a whole, although other, more conservative, elements of the population see it as a destructive and inimical force. Contrary to myth, feminism is not a white, middle-class, U.S.-dominated movement: while 56% of U.S. white women say they are feminists, 65% of U.S. black women say they are; 60% percent of the participants at the 1985 world conference on women were from nonaligned countries. An international bill of rights for women ("Convention on the Elimination of All Forms of Discrimination Against Women") spells out the equivalent of the U.S. Equal Rights Amendment in sixteen articles. This document is now an international treaty ratified by ninety-seven nations (the United States is not among them).

feminist a feminist is a person who believes in "the full humanity of women" (Gloria Steinem). It is primarily women who identify themselves as feminists, but some men do too. The Reverend Jerry Falwell is not one of them: "I listen to the feminists and all those radical gals—most of them are failures. They've blown it. . . . These women just need a man in the house. That's all they need. Most of these feminists need a man to tell them what time of day it is and to lead them home. And they blew it and they're mad at all men. Feminists hate men. They're sexist. They hate men—that's their problem" (quoted in *Ms.*, December 1985, p. 81). Rebecca West's 1913 remark is still true in many places today: "People call me a feminist whenever I express sentiments that differentiate me from a doormat or a prostitute."

fem lib *feminism, women's liberation movement, women's liberation, women's movement, female liberation movement.* The use of the shortened form is insulting.

femme/fem these terms, which are not heard so much anymore, follow the "insider/outsider" rule: they may be used among lesbians, but should be avoided by non-lesbians. Describing a lesbian relationship with the outdated and stereotyped "butch" and "femme" roles is a misleading oversimplification; avoid it.

femme fatale avoid; there is no parallel for a man, and this term perpetuates the myth of woman as Eve/tempter/siren. One of the most valuable rules in good writing or speaking is "show, don't tell." Instead of telling that someone is a "femme fatale," show how that person affects others.

ferryman *ferry operator/pilot/captain/driver/boat operator.*

fiancé/fiancée these sex-specific terms are acceptable to most people and are still widely used. However, the trend is toward using only the base word (fiancé). *See also* divorcé/divorcée.

fickle *unpredictable, changeable, unaccountable, unreliable, impulsive, impetuous, indecisive, uncertain, unsteady, irresolute, vacillating, unfaithful, disloyal, inconstant, treacherous, tricky.* Except for that notorious finger of fate, only women wear the "fickle" label.

fieldman *fielder, field player; canvasser, commercial traveler, field worker/representative/technician/contractor/buyer.*

fighting man *fighter, soldier, pugilist, belligerent, belligerent/aggressive individual/person.*

filial/filiation although these words come from the Latin for "son," they are defined and used inclusively in terms of children and offspring of both sexes.

fill 'er up (gas tank) *fill it up. See also* car/she.

filterman *filter press tender, filter operator/tender, ripening room attendant.*

finishing school *private school.* There are no finishing schools for boys; the cultural parallel has been the military school.

fireman *firefighter.* Slightly over 2% of firefighters are women.

fireman (locomotive/ship) *fire/furnace tender, firer, stoker, oil feeder.*

fire patrolman *fire patroller/ranger/guard.*

first baseman *See* baseman (baseball).

First Lady the wife of a U.S. president has been given this honorary term, but it is not an official title. Thus, the "problem" of what to do with a female president's spouse is moot. He will be known simply as "Mr. Last-Name." The usefulness of the term "First Lady" is questionable; it is seen less and less often in print. Recent presidential spouses have preferred to be known by a name, rather than by a role.

fisherman *fisher, angler, fish catcher, fishing licensee* (for some legal purposes); *fisherman and fisherwoman* if used gender-fairly. Do not be afraid of "fisher." In the following series of -er words, "fisherman" would be the odd man out: camper, hunter, canoer, fisher, hiker, mountain climber, birdwatcher, biker, nature lover. "Fisher" is appearing more often in print; newspapers like its length for headlines. Author, library cataloger, and wordsmith Sanford Berman says the Random House II dictionary gives "a fisherman" as the primary definition of "fisher"; the Library of Congress has replaced the sexist catalog heading "fishermen" with "fishers"; and the Hennepin County Library (Minneapolis) has been using "fishers" since 1974. He adds that a venerable example of such usage appears in Matthew 4:19 and Mark 1:17: "I will make you fishers of men" (King James Version). Incidentally, the "men" in that phrase were actually "human beings" in the original Greek. The phrase can be translated "fishers of souls."

fisherman's bend (knot) leave as is.

fishman *fishmonger, fish porter.*

fishwife *fishmonger, fish porter.* Avoid the word to mean an abusive, scolding woman; there is no parallel for a man and we tend to attribute those qualities to women. *See also* shrew.

fit for a king *fit for royalty/for the best, magnificent, noble, magnificent, splendid, luxurious, sumptuous, one in ten thousand/in a million, of the best quality.*

fix-it man *fixer-upper, fix-it expert, fixer, repairer. See also* handyman.

flag girl *flag bearer.*

flagman *signaller, flagger, traffic controller, signal giver; flag waver/carrier.*

flagman ahead *construction/signal/signaller ahead, watch for signal.*

flapjack *pancake.* Or leave as is.

flapper use in historical context. Note, however, that before World War I a flapper was considered a sprightly, knowing female teenager, while afterwards the term developed some negative connotations, and flappers were thought to be rather "fast."

flasher *exhibitionist.* Use "flasher" to describe a woman if you want, but without any identifying pronouns, the word will commonly be assumed to be male.

flimflam man *flimflam artist. See also* con man/confidence man.

floor boy/floor girl *floor worker.*

floorlady/floorman *operator, supervisor, floor supervisor/worker.* Replace the stock market term "floor man" with *floor broker.*

flower girl (vendor) *flower seller/vendor, florist.*

flower girl (wedding) *flower carrier.*

flyboy *pilot, aviator, flier, high-flier, glamorous pilot, member of the Air Force.* *See also* airman.

Flying Dutchman leave as is.

flyman *flyhand, stagehand, flyworker*

foeman *foe, enemy, opponent, rival, competitor.*

foilsman *fencer.*

food names for people while many food names for people purport to be positive, ultimately they are belittling, trivializing, and objectifying. They are also often sexist. Reflecting on all the connotations of people as food may help you avoid such terms as: babycakes, beefcake, cheesecake, cookie, creampuff, cupcake, cutie pie, dish, fruit, fruitcake, fruit salad, honey, honeycakes, lambchop, marshmallow, peach, pudding, pumpkin, sugar, sugar and spice, sweetie pie, sweet potato pie, tart, tomato, top banana. The difference between positive and negative uses of food terms depends on whether the term is limited to one sex (a man would never be referred to as a cookie, nor would the word beefcake be used of a woman) and whether the food word is a direct label ("she's a dish") or whether it is simply comparing the person in some metaphorical way to a food. For example, "apple of my eye" can be said of either sex and it doesn't mean the person is an apple in the same way a woman is called a tomato—but rather that he or she is like the best apple from the tree. Strong writing depends on metaphors—even metaphors based on food—but there is a difference between labeling people and creating vivid word associations. *See also* animal names for people.

fool and his money are soon parted, a *fools and their money are soon parted.*

footboy *page, attendant.*

footman leave as is in historical contexts; a footman was always a man. Or, *servant.*

forefather *forebear, forerunner, ancestor, predecessor, precursor, pioneer; forefather and foremother.* Also, in some senses, *colonist, patriot, founder.* An interesting sidelight on "forefather" is that because genes sort randomly, "It is possible for a female to end up with all her genes from male ancestors, and for a male to end up with all his genes from female ancestors" (Sally Slocum, "Woman the Gatherer: Male Bias in Anthropology," *Toward an Anthropology of Women*).

foreign service one-third of those who enter the Foreign Service today are women; about 6% of senior officers are women. Long a bastion of male diplomats, the Foreign Service is becoming an equal opportunity department, largely due to lawsuits brought against it. Women have traditionally been pigeonholed in administrative and consular positions rather than in the fast-track economic and political posts. Suits have also contended, and the State Department has acknowledged, that for a number of years it discriminated against its female foreign service officers in hiring, assignments, and honors.

forelady/foreman/forewoman *supervisor, lead/floor supervisor, line manager/ supervisor, section head, manager, boss, job/straw boss, chief, task sergeant, monitor, overseer, overlooker, superintendent, super, inspector, director, head, leader, floor leader.* The British use *chargehand.*

foreman (jury) *head juror, jury supervisor/chair/chief/representative/leader, forewoman and foreman, foreperson.* When it recently mandated juror guidelines revised to avoid sexist language, the Florida Supreme Court ensured that all future foremen in Florida would be forepersons.

foremanship *supervisory duties/skills, supervision.*

foremother *forebear, forerunner, ancestor, predecessor, precursor, pioneer; forefather and foremother.* While "forefather" is often used as a false generic, the use of "foremother" may be valid to emphasize that there were indeed women before us even though they so seldom appeared in the history books, classrooms, or public halls. *See also* forefather; foresister.

foresister when a sex-specific term is useful, some people prefer this term to "foremother."

foretopman *foretopper, sailor, foretop sailor.*

forewoman *See* forelady/foreman/forewoman; foreman (jury).

for Pete's sake!/for the love of Mike! *good grief! for pity's/heaven's sake! for crying out loud!*

fossil man *fossil human/remains, fossil, early human.*

Founding Fathers *the Founders, writers of the Constitution, Founding Mothers and Founding Fathers; founders, pioneers, colonists, forebears, patriots.* Beware of assuming that these groups were all men, for example, by saying "pioneers and their wives and children."

fountain girl/fountain man *fountain/counter server, fountain attendant/ tender/waiter, lunchcounter waiter.* Note the nonparallel "girl/man."

fox/fox trap/foxy/foxy lady it is generally acceptable to use the adjective "foxy" but less acceptable to use the noun "fox" (the distinction lies in saying someone is like an animal or saying someone is an animal). "Foxy lady" is not acceptable because of "lady," and "fox trap" (a customized car designed to attract women) perpetuates the man-the-hunter, woman-the-prey attitude. *See also* animal names for people; lady (noun); score; sex object.

frameman *framer, frame wirer.*

fraternal unless speaking of a brother, choose sex-neutral words: *warm, loving, friendly, kindly, teasing, protective, sympathetic, intimate,* etc. Use also *sibling*. Because the feminine parallel for "fraternal" ("sororal") has never gained a foothold in the language—an example of the severe discounting of female words—even women's groups have used "fraternal." The Degree of Honor Protection Association, founded over a hundred years ago, describes itself as "a fraternal insurance organization of women" and engages in "fraternal activities." "Fraternal" is used here as a synonym for "benevolent." *See also* sororal.

fraternal order of *order of, benevolent order of. See also* fraternal.

fraternal organization *organization, society, association, common-interest group.*

fraternal twins *distinguishable/dizygotic/nonidentical twins.*

fraternity *organization, society, association, union, secret society, club, federation, fraternity and sorority, common-interest group; comradeship, unity, community, companionship, friendship, family, kinship. See also* brotherhood (pseudogeneric); fellowship (social bond); fraternity/frat (Greek).

fraternity/frat (Greek) these terms no longer refer strictly to male bastions: there are some coed fraternities and some sororities are officially called fraternities. For sex-neutral alternatives use *Greek society/ system, Greek-letter organization, Greek-letter society/group.* Although most fraternities have social service goals and almost all have nondiscriminatory membership codes, in practice they are often exclusionary. Robin Warshaw (in *The Nation*) says, "Universities across the country are proclaiming diversity—social, sexual, ethnic, racial, economic, and cultural—as the guiding spirit behind their pursuit of academic growth and excellence. At the same time, fraternities— whose members usually select one another on the basis of conformity to homogeneous group standards—are experiencing their highest membership levels ever. As a result, colleges find themselves trying to impart the bias-free goals of the 1990s to students who are clustering, in ever greater numbers, in the exclusionary communities of the 1950s. . . .it's not the blood drives, charity fund-raiser, or improved résumé potential that brings in new members; it's an attraction to a culture that often seems to say, 'Become one of us and you'll get loaded, you'll get laid, you'll become a man.'" Referring to the "inherently destructive influence of fraternities," Warshaw says, "most fraternity cultures are still centered on proving manhood in acccordance with three basic beliefs: that women are sex objects to be manipulated at will; that drinking and drug-taking are endurance sports; and that all non-members, be they other male students, professors, or college administrators, are deficient weenies. Because fraternities are essentially closed shops, both morally and intellectually, members are unlikely to have those beliefs disputed in any way they will find convincing."

fraternization/fraternize *association, socialization, mingling, banding to-gether, keeping company, hobnobbing, mixing, consorting, clubbing to-gether, rubbing shoulders with; associate, socialize, mingle, band together, befriend, keep company, hobnob, mix, consort, club together, rub shoulders with.* There is no parallel based on the Latin for "sister," "soror."

frau *woman.* There is nothing wrong with this word in German; the problem arises when it is used in English to convey a certain disdain for a narrowly defined role for women. There is no parallel term for men. *See also* hausfrau.

freedman *freed/former slave, ex-slave, free-issue black; freedman and freed-woman.*

Freedmen's Bureau, the/Freedmen's schools retain for historical accuracy.

freeman *citizen, citizen of a free country; freeman and freewoman.* "Free-woman" has had other connotations in the feminist movement; *The Freewoman,* one of the earliest feminist newspapers, was published in Great Britain as a "weekly feminist review" in 1911-1912.

Freemason "Freemason" (member of the Free and Accepted Masons or Ancient Free and Accepted Masons) always refers to a man; women cannot be Freemasons. The Order of the Eastern Star is an affiliate, however, to which both women and men belong.

Frenchman *French native/citizen, French-born, Franco-, French person; French-man and Frenchwoman.* Too often "Frenchman/Frenchmen" are used as false generics. Plurals: *the French, French citizens/people/persons, Frenchwomen and Frenchmen.*

freshman *first-year/first-semester/second-semester student, freshperson, frosh, fresher, class of 1995, beginning/entering student; beginner, novice, new-comer, greenhorn, tenderfoot.* Plurals: *freshpeople, freshers, frosh, freshfolk.* People currently on college campuses will recognize the alternatives. Those who are not may be appalled and suspicious. However, all the listed alternatives can be found on campuses throughout the country, especially in student-run publications. The old "freshman/fresh-men" lives on primarily in outsider and administration-headed publications.

freshman congressman *first-year member of Congress.*

frigid *unaroused, unresponsive, uninterested, anorgasmic, nonorgasmic.* "Frigid" is unscientific and sexist. Beware orgasm-as-norm thinking (contrary to cultural myth, it is possible to live a full life without being frequently orgasmic or, indeed, orgasmic at all). Men who cultivate reputations as high performers in the bedroom will be particularly careful not to label partners "frigid" as the word is out now: "frigidity" is most often traceable to an insensitive lover.

frivolous *lighthearted, easygoing, trivial, insignificant, superficial, inane, vacuous, shallow, flimsy, idle, immature.* "Frivolous" is used almost exclusively of women and their interests and activities.

frogman *military/deep-sea/scuba diver, skin-diver, underwater swimmer/ explorer, diver, frog; frogman and frogwoman.*

front-end man *front-end mechanic.*

frontiersman *frontier settler, pioneer, backsettler; frontierswoman and frontiersman.*

front man *front, figurehead.*

front man (industry) *stevedore, dockhand.* **See also** longshoreman; wharfman.

front man (music) *lead singer, vocalist, star, leader, front musician/player.*

frump/frumpy *slob, sloven, unkempt person, stick-in-the-mud; dowdy, slovenly, unkempt, tacky, drab, old-fashioned, unfashionable, out-of-date, staid.* Alternatives are given because one of the two definitions of "frump" is an unattractive girl/woman and because in everyday use the terms are reserved for women.

fugleman *file leader, lead soldier, leader.*

Fuller Brush man *Fuller Brush agent/rep.* About 80% of "Fuller Brush men" are women today.

funnyman *comedian, comic, humorist, wit, clown, jokesmith, jokester, jester, mime; joker, practical joker, prankster, wisecracker, punster, satirist, comedist.*

furnaceman *furnace installer/tender/stoker/repairer/cleaner.*

g

The language is perpetually in flux: it is a living stream, shifting, changing, receiving new strength from a thousand tributaries, losing old forms in the backwaters of time.

E.B. White

gabby *talkative, loquacious, garrulous, voluble, fluent, glib, effusive, exuberant, talky, wordy, verbose, long-winded, windy, big-mouthed, talking a blue streak.* Nonsexist per se, "gabby" is functionally sexist and ageist because it is used exclusively for women and older men. *See also* babble; bull session; chatter; chatterbox; gossip; gossipy; yenta.

gaffer woman or man.

gag man *gag writer, comedian.*

gal *woman.* Like many word pairs, "gal" and "guy" have gone separate ways. "Gal" has few acceptable uses while "guy" is very common and in the plural can refer to both sexes.

gal-boy this prison slang may have a certain limited legitimacy, although there is no parallel for women and no inclusive alternative.

gal Friday *See* girl Friday.

galley queen are there no lazy male flight attendants who hide out in the galley? Use instead *galley mouse.*

gamesman *gamesplayer, gamester, gambler, someone who sails suspiciously close to the wind/skates on thin ice/cuts corners/squeaks home, risk-taker, high-flyer.*

gamesmanship *gamestership, sailing close to the wind, sharp playing, expertise, skill; suspiciously shrewd playing, slight of hand, trickery.*

garageman *garage worker/attendant, gas station attendant/worker.* Over 6% are women.

garbageman *garbage collector/hauler, trash/refuse collector, sanitation worker.*

gasman *gas fitter, gas pipe repairer/installer, gas appliance repairer/installer.*

gateman *gatekeeper, gate tender/attendant.*

gathered to one's fathers *gathered to one's ancestors/forebears/mothers and fathers.*

gaucho always a man; there is no parallel for a woman and no inclusive term. *See also* cowboy.

gay (adj.) can modify issues, events, and places of relevance to gay men and lesbians. For example, gay rights activists work for rights for both lesbians and gay men. However, the preference is for binary adjectives: "gay and lesbian activism" or "lesbian and gay readership." Do not use the adjectives "gay" and "lesbian" gratuitously; a person's sexual orientation is irrelevant to most discussions. *See also* gay man; heterosexism; homophobia; homosexual; lesbian (noun/adj.).

gay blade/gay dog *high-flyer, fun-lover, high-spirited person; hedonist, sensualist, flirt, bedhopper, free spirit, swinger.* The word "gay" could be ambiguous in this context, and the terms are sexist insofar as they are used only of men. *See also* ladies' man; man about town; womanize/womanizer.

gay man this is the preferred term for a man with a same-sex emotional and sexual orientation. *See also* gay (adj.); Gay Rights Movement; heterosexism; homophobia; homosexual.

Gay Rights Movement the beginnings of the movement, originally called the Gay Liberation Movement, can be traced to New York City's 1969 Stonewall Rebellion (also Stonewall Uprising or Stonewall riots) when gay men and women fought back against a police raid on a gay bar. Goals of the movement now include equal rights for lesbians and gay men, educating about AIDS and homosexuality, and working to eradicate hate crimes. Queer Nation/queer nation, which emerged in 1990 in New York as a response to the significant increase in gay-bashing incidents, has spread quickly throughout the country; this may come to be the umbrella term for the gay rights movement.

geisha always a woman; there is no parallel for a man and no inclusive term. Use only in its narrowest definition, that is, a Japanese woman with special training in the art of providing lighthearted entertainment, especially for men.

gendarme bien sûr, when in France, use "gendarme" even though it is a masculine word (it means "men of arms"). There are, however, both female and male gendarmes with identical job descriptions. At one time the French experimented with the term "gendarmette" for its new female members, but the term was deemed profoundly sexist, was caricatured in a movie, and has since been given a decent burial.

gender understanding the difference between sex and gender is crucial to the correct use of language. Sex is biological: people with male genitals are male, and people with female genitals are female. Gender is cultural: our notions of "masculine" tell us how we expect men to behave and our notions of "feminine" tell us how we expect women to behave—but these may have nothing to do with biology. When deciding whether a word is restricted to one sex or the other, the only acceptable limitation is genetic sex. A woman cannot be a sperm donor because it's biologically impossible. It may be culturally unusual for a man to be a secretary, but it is not biologically impossible. To assume all secretaries are women is sexist because the issue is gender, not sex. Gender signifies an individual's personal, legal, and social status without reference to genetic sex; gender is a subjective cultural attitude while sex is an objective biological fact.

gender-fair language words that treat both sexes equally constitute gender-fair language. The words may or may not reveal the person's sex. For example, "girls and boys" specifies sex but because both are included, the phrase is gender-fair. Terms like "mail carrier," "firefighter," and "lawyer" are also gender-fair because they could be either sex.

gender-free language words that do not specify gender constitute gender-free language. "Students," "police officers," and "laypeople" are gender-free terms; "businessman" and "businesswoman" are not.

gender gap used in politics, economics, sociology, education, and other fields, this term gained prominence in 1982 when, for the first time in opinion-polling history, a significant sex difference in the job-approval rating surfaced during Ronald Reagan's first term; 61% of men thought he was doing a good job, but only 42% of women did. "Gender gap" has also been commonly used with respect to standardized test scores, where girls/young women used to score higher on verbal tests and boys/young men scored higher on math tests. In a discussion of these differences, a male director of math studies at Johns Hopkins said, "I wish the feminists would get busy and do careful longitudinal research on kids from kindergarten through high school." It was not clear why research in this area was the responsibility of "the feminists." Researchers of both sexes have since discovered that the gender gap has all but disappeared in verbal scores and has greatly narrowed in math scores.

gender roles gender roles (sometimes called sex roles) involve attitudes and behaviors that society expects *because* someone is a woman or *because* someone is a man. Roles traditionally assigned to men are "provider" and "protector." Women have been assigned "caregiver" and "sex object" roles. Biologically, both women and men can provide, protect, nurture, or be a sex object, but most often "cultural influences have been misrepresented as biological imperatives" (Deborah Rhode, *Theoretical Perspectives on Sexual Differences*). Lucile Duberman (*Gender and Sex in Society*) says "the truth is our gender roles are not innate and God-given, nor are they necessarily irrevocable. Society creates gender roles, and society can alter them." Biologist Robert Trivers and others suggest that there was a fairly reasonable perpetuation-of-the-species basis for these roles: to ensure that one of his many small and fragile gametes reproduced his kind, the man needed to fertilize as many women as possible—and they needed to be attractive to him and young enough to bear children, thus his emphasis on seeing women as "sex object"; a woman, on the other hand, with many fewer fertilization opportunities for her larger, less numerous gametes, needed quality rather than quantity—a partner with enough resources (a "provider") to maintain her and her child through the nine-month gestation and the growing-up period. This at least partly explains the stereotypical assumptions that men want women's bodies, and women want men's money.

gentleman except for the still-acceptable generic public address of "ladies and gentleman" and for an occasional, "He is a real gentleman," this word ought to be retired. Its true mate, "gentlewoman," is long gone, and its other partner, "lady," has been shelved in spite of herself. The word has lost its original meaning; Marjorie Luft, St. Paul, Minnesota, collects published reports of such "gentle" men as the "gentleman" who beat his dog to death, the arsonists whose work resulted in the death of two women (Crime Stoppers asked the public to help bring "these gentlemen to justice"), or serial killer Ted Bundy—also referred to in news articles as a gentleman. *See also* gentlewoman; lady (noun).

gentleman farmer *hobby/Sunday/weekend/amateur farmer, farmer.*

gentleman friend *See* boyfriend.

gentlemanlike/gentlemanly this vague stereotype conveys different meanings to different people according to their perceptions of what a man ought or ought not to do, say, think, wear, feel, look like. These words have nothing to do with sex and everything to do with gender. Use instead *courteous, civil, refined, polite, well-mannered, polished, mannerly, brave, thoughtful, considerate, agreeable, accommodating, decent, discreet, dependable, punctilious, civilized, cultivated, dignified,* etc. These adjectives can be used equally well of women. They are not synonyms for "gentlemanlike/gentlemanly" but rather what society hears by those terms.

gentleman's agreement *unwritten/informal/oral/honorable/verbal agreement, verbal/oral promise/contract, handshake, your word, mutual understanding.*

gentlemen of the press *representatives of the press. See also* newsman/newspaperman.

gentle sex, the avoid; in its quiet way it does violence to both women and men.

gentlewoman this would be appropriate when used with "gentleman" (although it never is), but it should especially not be used alone as it has developed along very different lines from "gentleman." We might say, "He's a real gentleman" or "That gentleman over there is waiting to speak to you," but we would never say, "She's a real gentlewoman" or "That gentlewoman over there is waiting to speak to you." *See also* gentleman.

giantess *giant.*

gigolo *lover, prostitute.* "Gigolo" might be roughly comparable to "gold digger" or "kept woman"; in an ideal world "gold digger" would refer to both sexes and there would be "kept men" as well as "kept women." French slang uses "gigolette," meaning a woman of "easy morals." *See also* gold digger; kept woman; toyboy.

GI Joe *GI.* This nickname for U.S. armed forces personnel comes from "government issue" and thus is not gender-specific.

gingerbread man *gingerbread cookie/figure, gingerbread man and gingerbread woman.*

gird (up) one's loins perceived as sexist because it is assumed to refer to men, this term comes from Proverbs 31:17 where the loins in question actually belong to a woman. If you want an alternative use *prepare, prepare for battle, buckle on one's armor, get the steam up, get in gear, batten down the hatches, grit one's teeth.*

girl (referring to a woman) *woman, young woman.* "Girl" is reserved for pre-teens or at least for those fifteen or under; it is objectionable and demeaning when used for young women or women. Some women may refer to themselves and their women friends as "girls" either out of long habit, local custom, or because they still think of themselves that way. However, for an outsider to refer to them this way is unacceptable. *See also* girl Friday; "insider/outsider" rule; office boy/office girl.

girl Friday *assistant, office assistant/specialist, administrative/executive/ program assistant, clerk, right hand, secretary, aide, office helper, gofer; man Friday and woman Friday* if used gender-fairly, although it is generally only "woman Friday" that is used, and even then there is reluctance to use "woman" instead of "girl." *See also* girl (referring to a woman); office boy/office girl.

girlfriend *friend, woman friend* (if "man friend" is also used), *female friend* (if "male friend" is also used), *best friend, escort, date, companion, constant/longtime/loving/live-in/intimate/domestic companion, romantic interest, heartthrob, significant other, mate, housemate, partner, domestic/ life partner, partner of long standing, steady paramour, lover, longtime love, live-in, live-in lover, fiancé, betrothed, sweetheart, main/major squeeze* (and for stars, *offscreen squeeze*), *my reason for living, the love/light of my life, the woman in my life. See also* fiancé/fiancée.

girlie there are no circumstances in which this word is acceptable.

girlie magazine/movie *pornographic magazine/movie.*

girlie show *X-rated "entertainment."*

girlish *ingenuous, naive, childlike, innocent, open, friendly, eager, youthful, immature, self-conscious, inept, bright-eyed, optimistic, cheerful, adolescent, childish, sophomoric, juvenile, kiddish, infantile, callow, unsophisticated.* "Girlish" is vague and almost always pejorative.

girls and boys *See* boys and girls.

girl scout there is nothing particularly sexist about the terms "girl scout" and "boy scout" (although the goals, activities, and attitudes of the two groups have often been based on sexist concepts). Inclusive terms are being seen more often: *youth scout, scouter.*

give away the bride *escort the bride to the altar, accompany the bride down the aisle.* Women are not "given" by their fathers to their husbands.

give her/'er the gun (motor/engine) *give it the gun, rev it up.*

give someone Harry when using expressions like this, be aware of how many are male-based. Balance them with female-based expressions, creative expressions of your own, or alternatives: *dress down, chew out, scold, reprimand, castigate, call someone on the carpet, read someone the riot act, tell someone where to get off.* *See* Writing Guidelines for a discussion of sex-linked expressions.

glamour girl/glamour puss *glamorous woman.* But use sparingly.

glass ceiling the glass ceiling is a symbol of all the barriers, overt and covert, that corporate, industry, military, and professional women keep banging their heads against. According to corporate research firm Catalyst, 80% of CEOs admit that male managers stereotype and discriminate against women employees: women are excluded from the men's communication network where men who are still more comfortable with other men can maintain the status quo; women find it difficult to find mentors and role models; they are often harassed and must deal with stereotypical language and sexist behavior on the part of superiors and peers; in a Catch-22, women with family responsibilities are seen as lacking commitment to the organization, while women who are fully committed to the organization are often seen as "abrasive and unfeminine." Mary Dingee Fillmore (*Women MBSs: A Foot in the Door*) asked one woman what she would need to win a top slot in her corporation. The answer: "A sex-change operation." *See also* directress; executive; manageress; mommy track; wage earner.

glassman *glassmaker, glass dealer/retailer/repairer.*

gloomy Gus *spoilsport, killjoy, crapehanger, party-pooper, prophet of doom and gloom, gloom and doomer, grinch, wet blanket.*

G-man *government/federal/FBI/plainclothes/secret/undercover agent, government investigative agent, intelligence officer, member of the FBI, spy.* About 8% of FBI agents are women.

God although we would never consider assigning God a race, an ethnic origin, or an age, we have apparently thought nothing of assigning a gender. Contrary to what most people understand, however, theology has never ruled that God is male. In the fourth century, St. Gregory of Nazianzus summed up traditional thought when he wrote that "Father" and "Son" as applied to the persons of the Trinity did not name their natures or their essences but rather were metaphors for their relationship to each other. John 4:24 says that God is pure Spirit (and thus is genderless) and the words for God in both Greek and Hebrew are sex-neutral. Sandra M. Schneiders (*Women and the Word*) lists some of the many metaphors we have for God and then says, "While we are immediately aware that the personal God is not really a rock or a mother eagle, it is easy enough to imagine that God is really a king or a father . . . . We create the metaphor to say something about God; but then God seems to be saying something about the vehicle of the metaphor. Thus, if God is a king, there is a tendency to see kings as divine. If God is male, then males are divine and masculinity becomes normative of humanity . . . ." Theologian Mary Daly says simply, "If God is male, then male is God." God's presumed masculinity has provided a religious legitimization of the social structures and attitudes that treat women as second-class, non-normative, derivative human beings. The key to inclusive God-language is to be conscious that we are using metaphors ("God is like a . . . " but not "God is a . . .") to make a pure Spirit more accessible to us. Therefore, use a variety of metaphors to enlarge our images of God, balance male and female metaphors, and use masculine or feminine pronouns only for specific, limited metaphorical uses (otherwise avoid sex-specific pronouns). When writing to Orthodox Jews, use "G-d" instead of "God"; in their tradition, anything with "God" written on it must be respectfully buried. *See also* Father (God); Father, Son, and Holy Spirit/Ghost; God/he; God/himself; God/his; God of our Fathers; Holy Spirit; Lord; Son of Man; Yahweh.

God/he avoid gender-specific pronouns by: (1) replacing "he" or "him" with "God" or another name for God; (2) recasting the sentence; (3) replacing the pronouns with "you/yours" or "who/whom/that." *See also* God; God/himself; God/his.

God/himself some people are using "Godself." "God himself" can sometimes be "that very God." Since the word "God" is sex-neutral, the correct pronoun should also be sex-neutral. You can often circumlocute to avoid the reflexive pronoun (sometimes this is best done by changing the verb that takes the pronoun). *See also* God; God/he; God/his.

God/his replace phrases like "his goodness," "his love," or "by his mercy" with sex-neutral expressions ("divine goodness," "eternal love," or "out of mercy") or with the second person: "Your Goodness," "Your Mercy." The proper possessive pronoun for God is "God's," for example, "God's goodness," "God's mercy." *See also* God; God/he; God/himself.

goddess *god; god and goddess*. Retain "goddess" in references to feminist spirituality that uses the term and to the goddess religions, which point to a historical truth about the importance of women in certain societies and eras (evidence indicates that the first human religions were female-centered.) When "goddess" indicates a lesser god, replace it with "god."

godfather/godmother OK. Or, *godparent, sponsor, guardian.* Popularized by Mario Puzo's 1969 book *The Godfather*, the term "godfather" has no comparable "godmother" partner and alternatives are mostly male-oriented: *boss of bosses, head don, capo di tutti capi, don, capo.*

God of our Fathers *God of our ancestors/of all generations/of our forebears/of our mothers and fathers.*

go-go boy *go-go manager, go-go broker.* Fast-moving speculative funds called go-go funds were usually handled by an up-and-coming young man. Note the nonparallel "go-go boy" and "go-go girl."

go-go girl *go-go dancer.*

gold digger parallel male terms in some cases might be "gigolo" or "toyboy," but try instead to describe the trait you have in mind with inclusive terms: *greedy, grasping, avaricious, self-seeking, rapacious, out for all one can get.*

gondolier there are only about 320 gondolas left in Venice, and all of them are plied by men.

Good Humor man *Good Humor/ice cream vendor.*

good Joe *good sort, agreeable/good-natured/good-humored person.*

goodman/goodwife these are both obsolete. But note the nonparallel "man/wife."

good old boy/good ole boy *loyal Southerner, Southern supporter, supporter, sidekick, crony, pal, goombah.* These terms were particularly popular in the mid-1960s when they referred to the Texas cronies of President Lyndon B. Johnson. Women don't often choose to play a "good ole boy" role. Sometimes this might be the appropriate term for a particular man. *See also* old-boys' network; old-girls' network.

goody two shoes the original Little Goody Two Shoes from the nursery rhyme by Oliver Goldsmith was a girl who earned an undeserved reputation as a self-righteous, affected little do-gooder, but the phrase is scarcely perceived as sex-linked today. If you need strictly inclusive alternatives use *goody-goody, do-gooder.*

gossip not sexist per se (it originally meant "godparent"), "gossip" is functionally sexist because the term is reserved for women. For the verb use *talk, talk idly, talk over, talk up a storm, converse, discuss, shoot the breeze, pass the time of day, make small talk, jaw, make chin music, wag tongues, rattle away, run off at the mouth, beat one's gums, bend someone's ear, talk someone's arm/head off, talk the hind legs off a donkey; repeat everything one hears, tell secrets, spread rumors/stories, mudsling, dish the dirt.* For the noun use *rumormonger, whisperer, talebearer, blabbermouth, big mouth, mudslinger, motormouth, jawsmith, loose tongue, chin wag,* *newsmonger, windbag, idle talker; palaver, idle/small/empty talk, scuttle-butt, hearsay, chin music, talkfest, an earful.* **See also** babble; bull session; chatter; chatterbox; gabby; gossipy; yenta.

gossipy *long-winded, big-mouthed, talkative, curious, loquacious, garrulous, gregarious, windy; rumormongering.* **See also** gossip.

governess to refer to a female governor, use *governor.* For someone who teaches young children, use *tutor, private teacher, teacher, child mentor, instructor.* Note what happened to the formerly parallel word pair "governor/governess" over the years. Three of the fifty U.S. governors are women. One governor (a man) is African American.

gownsman *academic, academician, scholar, professional, licentiate.*

grandaddy/daddy of them all this type of sex-linked expression is fairly benign (and if so much of our language weren't male-based, it wouldn't even have to be mentioned), but if you need a sex-neutral substitute use *biggest/oldest/grandest of them all.*

grand duchess retain for official title, which can refer either to the wife of a duke or to the ruler of a duchy.

grande dame this may be appropriate in certain circumstances, but there is no precise equivalent for a man. You might use the inclusive "éminence grise."

grandfather aid this legislative term must probably be left as is; those who have experimented with calling it "grandparent aid" find that others don't recognize it.

grandfather clause leave as is in legal uses. Otherwise use *escape clause, exemption, retroactive exemption, grandparenting.* Some women who have been covered by the clause speak of being *grandmothered.*

grandfather clock/grandmother clock retain; these terms indicate to the initiated the size of the clock. The fact that all grandmothers are not shorter than all grandfathers is evidently irrelevant here. For an inclusive term use *floor clock.*

grand master *excellent chess player, expert player.*

granny/grannie OK; "gramp/gramps" is for a man.

granny dress/gown *old-fashioned/Victorian/high-necked dress/gown.*

granny knot this sexist term (it describes an insecure knot made inadvertently when one is trying to tie a square knot) has no "gramps" parallel and no good synonym.

grantsman *grantwriter.*

grantsmanship *the fine art of obtaining grants, grant-getting, the knack of attracting grants, grant-getting/grant-writing skills.* There is no one-word substitute for this handy, but sexist, term.

grass widow/grass widower both terms refer to someone who is divorced, separated, or whose spouse is temporarily away, but "grass widow" has additional dictionary definitions (albeit rarely used ones) referring to a discarded mistress or an unmarried mother. "Grass widow" is also used more often than is "grass widower." Use the terms equally of both sexes, or not at all. *See also* widow/widower.

greater love than this has no man *greater love than this has no one.*

Green Mountain Boys leave as is (historical term).

greensman *greens planter/worker, landscape artist.*

grisette if you mean prostitute, use *prostitute.* Otherwise use *member of the working class, working class person.* There is no male parallel.

groceryman *grocer, grocery store owner/worker.*

groomsman *best man, attendant.* Avoid "groomsman"; its opposite number ("bridesmaid") is nonparallel ("maid/man"). "Best man" is used with "best woman," and "attendant" is used when the bride's witness is also called an attendant.

groundsman *groundskeeper, grounds/yard worker, caretaker, landscaper, gardener.*

groupie *admirer, fan, follower, worshiper at the throne.* "Groupie" has come to be associated with young women, and there is no parallel for young men.

guardsman *guard, soldier, guardian, member of the guards, guard member/officer, National Guard member.*

Guerilla Girls correct term for the mysterious group of art-world women who have been papering sections of New York City with smartly designed black-and-white posters since 1985. Using sarcasm, statistics, and bold graphics, the posters charge galleries, museums, collectors, critics, and white male artists with sexism and racism. This term reflects the principle that people can call themselves what they want; it is their choice to call themselves "girls" and to give the term a new twist by associating it with the aggressive "guerilla." *See also* artist; "insider/outsider" rule.

gumshoe this term, from the shoes with gum-rubber soles they wore, no longer belongs exclusively to male detectives like Dashiell Hamett's Sam Spade, Raymond Chandler's Phillip Marlowe, and Ross MacDonald's Lou Archer; we now have among others Marcia Muller's Sharon McCone, Sara Paretsky's V.I. Warshawski, Linda Barnes's Carlotta Carlyle, and Sue Grafton's Kinsey Millhone.

gunman *killer, armed/professional killer, assassin, robber, intruder, slayer, gun, trigger, hired gun/assassin, gunfighter, gunner, shooter, thug, gunslinger, gun-wielder, gun-toter, gunsel, sharpshooter, sniper, attacker, outlaw, bandit, terrorist, gangster, racketeer, mobster, hoodlum, liquidator, executioner, enforcer, croaker.*

gun moll *accomplice, gun-toting accomplice, sidekick, confederate in crime, gangster's companion.* *See also* girlfriend; gunman.

guru *oracle, sage, spiritual guide/teacher/leader, leader, counselor, advisor.* Although you could refer to a woman as a guru, the term is usually perceived as masculine.

guy "guy" seems here to stay even though its companion term "gal" would rarely be appropriate in similar situations. When used colloquially, the plural "guys" has become acceptable for both sexes.

guys and gals *folks, people.*

gyp *cheat, defraud, rip off, soak, fleece, hoodwink, swindle, deceive, victimize, pull the wool over someone's eyes, take in, buffalo, con, sting, put across, put one over on, rig, fix, rook, gull, exploit, take advantage of, diddle.* Avoid the ethnocentric and pejorative "gyp."

Gypsy/Gypsies *Rom, Romani* (singular), *Roma, Roms, Romanies* (plural), *Romani* (adj.), as in the International Romani Union. If these terms are unfamiliar to your audience, and you need to relate them to "Gypsy," capitalize the word. Whenever possible refer to specific Romani groups (Romanichal, Kalderash, Bashaldo). For centuries the Roma have been been severely oppressed and regarded as second-class citizens (and in some countries as no citizens at all). There is virtually no mention of the Roma in references to the Holocaust; although there is some debate about the actual figures, it is possible that up to 80% of the Romani population perished. Ten to twelve million Roma live in Europe today, where they are currently facing a surge of anti-Rom slogans and activities by neo-fascist groups in Eastern Europe.

h

Every language reflects the prejudices of the society in which it evolved.

Casey Miller and Kate Swift

habitué grammatically masculine in French (the feminine would be habituée) "habitué" is used for both sexes in English—a convention that has been suggested for similar terms. *See also* divorcé/divorcée.

hackman *cabdriver.*

hag although there are attempts to reclaim this word's older meaning—a mature wise-woman—it is better avoided in its more widespread pejorative meaning.

hail-fellow-well-met *backslapping, hearty, jovial, breezy, extroverted, heartily informal, convivial, comradely, jocular, playful, full of life, in high spirits, glad hand.*

hair-do *hair style.* "Hair-do" is used almost exclusively for women.

handicappism the attitudes, practices, and physical obstacles that lead to unequal and unfair treatment of people with disabilities constitute handicappism. A handicappist society has a high tolerance for bias and discrimination against those with disabilities, sometimes seeming unaware of their presence in society and oftentimes seeming to value the nondisabled more than the disabled. *See also* handicapped.

handicapped *someone/person with a disability, the disability/disabilities* (not "disabled") *community, persons with disabilities* (not "the disabled"). Good example of correct usage: the 1990 Americans with Disabilities Act. Do not use "handicapped" as a noun or adjective referring to any of the forty-three million Americans with disabilities. The difference between a "disability" and a "handicap" is crucial: a disability is a condition; a handicap is an obstacle. Someone with multiple sclerosis has a disability; the two flights of stairs leading to a classroom present a handicap to that person. Use "handicap" to describe a situation or barrier imposed by society, the environment, or oneself. Use "disability" for a functional limitation that interferes with a person's ability to walk, hear, talk, learn, etc. Guidelines in writing and speaking about disabilities: (1) Do not mention a disability unless it directly bears on your material. (2) Speak of the person first, then the disability; emphasize abilities, not limitations. (3) An illness is a disease; a disability is a condition. Do not refer to cerebral palsy, epilepsy, arthritis, etc., as diseases; they are conditions. (4) Do not define a multifaceted human being in terms of a disability. Avoid: an arthritic, a diabetic, an epileptic, a hemiplegic, a hemophiliac, a paralytic, a paraplegic, a quadriplegic. Use instead: *someone with arthritis/diabetes*, etc. (5) Do not refer to people by their missing part or surgical procedure (amputee, laryngectomee, mastectomee, ostomate). (6) In connection with disabilities avoid or replace: abnormal; atypical; birth defect (*congenital disability, someone born with...*); burden/drain; defect/defective; deformed/deformity (*orthopedic/physical disability*); fit (*seizure*); gimp; hare lip (*cleft palate*); healthy (*nondisabled, able-bodied*); invalid; lame (*uses a cane/walker, nonambulatory, mobility-impaired*); learning disabled (*someone with/who has a learning disability*); maimed; normal (*nondisabled, able-bodied*); patient (use only for someone in a hospital or under a doctor's immediate care); physical handicap (*physical disability*); plight; poor; spastic/spaz (*someone who has cerebral palsy*); stricken with (*incurred*); stutterer (*person with speech impediment*); unfortunate; withered. (7) Avoid condescending euphemisms like "physically challenged" or "mentally different." (8) Avoid portraying those who succeed as especially courageous or superhuman; this raises false expectations that all people with disabilities should achieve at this level. Also avoid giving excessive and patronizing praise or attention to persons with disabilities. *See also* afflicted with; amputee; blind; cerebral palsied; crip/cripple; deaf/deaf and dumb; handicappism; idiot/ idiocy; insane/insanity; leper/leprosy; mongolism/mongoloid; paraplegic/quadriplegic; "people first" rule; retard/retarded; schizophrenic; suffers from (a condition); victim; wheelchair-bound.

handmaid/handmaiden *servant, personal attendant, attendant.*

handyman *odd/general jobber, repairer, fixer, fixer-upper, do-all, do-it-yourselfer, odd-job laborer, maintenance worker, carpenter, janitor, custodian, caretaker; handywoman and handyman* if used gender-fairly. People with a classics bent might like *homo habilis* (Latin for "handy human being") or *factotum*, Latin for "do everything" and meaning a person having many diverse activities or responsibilities.

hangman *executioner, public executioner, lyncher.*

harbor master *harbor chief/superintendent/officer/commander.*

hardhat *See* construction worker.

hard master *tyrant, iron hand/ruler, despot, martinet, disciplinarian, oppressor, stickler, dictator.*

harebrained *See* scatterbrained.

harem although the harem is negatively perceived in the West as a place of confinement for women, it is not always so negatively perceived by women in those cultures. Two caveats in using this term: do not use it without understanding its many culture-specific ramifications; do not refer to a man's several women friends as his "harem." This ethnocentric and incorrect use of "harem" is demeaning to women and fosters the inappropriate sense of men owning women. *See also* owner; purdah; sex object.

harlot/harlotry *prostitute/prostitution.* "Harlot" (from the Old French for "rogue") used to refer only to male vagabonds, rascals, vagrants, entertainers, etc. Later it was used for a person of either sex, and finally became restricted to women.

harpy/harridan (woman) avoid. *See also* shrew.

harvestman leave as is for the arachnid. Its common alternative is equally male: "daddy long legs." For the machine used for harvesting or the person doing the harvesting, use *harvester.*

hatcheck girl *hatchecker, hatcheck attendant/clerk, hat attendant/clerk, checkroom/coatroom attendant/clerk.*

hatcheryman *hatchery owner/worker.*

hatchet man *hatchet, hired hatchet/killer/attacker/assassin, killer, professional killer, murderer, slayer, executioner, mercenary, assassin, attacker, liquidator, terrorist, gangster, racketeer, mobster, hoodlum, cutthroat, thug; character assassin, scandalmonger; someone who gives you the axe or does a hatchet job on someone.*

hats off to based on the male custom of doffing one's hat to indicate respect or appreciation, this term is used today without sex bias—perhaps because hat-wearing is no long so closely associated with one sex.

hausfrau although this term means "housewife" for both the Germans and those English-speaking peoples who have borrowed it, its use is neutral-to-positive in Germany but largely pejorative in English-speaking countries. Use it only in Germany.

hautboy nonsexist; comes from the French "bois" for "wood."

hayseed this term tends to be used more of a man than of a woman, although it is in itself not gender-specific. Along with such words as "bumpkin," "clod/clodhopper," and "plow jockey," it is pejorative and anti-farmer, and should be avoided. More sex-neutral and less pejorative terms include: *country cousin, rustic, tiller of the soil, provincial.*

he (pseudogeneric) never use "he" when you mean "he and she," or when you are referring to someone who could be a man or a woman (for example, "the consumer/he"). Make your sentence plural, circumlocute, or use one of the suggestions given in the Writing Guidelines.

headman *head cager/worker; traditional chief; overseer, supervisor.*

headmaster/headmistress *private-school/school director/principal, principal, director, head administrator, head.* In some instances (e.g., an old-fashioned, conservative, or British boys'/girls' school) "headmaster" or "headmistress" might be correct.

head of family/head of household 28% of all households are headed by a woman. *See also* bring home the bacon; family man; headship; housewife; provider.

head of state female heads of state have included Golda Meir (Israel), Indira Gandhi (India), Margaret Thatcher (Great Britain), Gro Harlem Brundtland (Norway), Vigdis Finnbogandottir (Iceland), Violeta Chamorro (Nicaragua), Corazon Aquino (Philippines), Benazir Bhutto (Pakistan), Edith Cresson (France), and Mary Robinson (Ireland).

headship this word is used by fundamentalists in particular to denote the father's rightful and God-given status as undisputed head of the family. In the many woman-headed households today, headship properly belongs to women and in non-fundamentalist two-parent families, headship is either shared or is not an issue. The caveat is to avoid using the word lightly or without knowledge of its significance to your audience.

headsman *executioner, public executioner, beheader.*

headwaiter man or woman.

heart disease heart disease death rates are about 77% higher among men than among women; for both sexes, death rates are significantly higher among blacks than among whites, although the disparity has narrowed substantially in the past twenty years. A 1990 study reported that many men see a heart attack as a sign that they have worked hard and done a good job, and so although they are more prone to heart attacks than women, they recover more quickly. A woman (and society along with her) tends to see her heart attack as a failure; she has not "coped" with her situation.

heavyweight in the sense of an important or successful person, a heavyweight can be either sex. There is, however, a male cast to the word, because of wrestlers and because for so long all the important people were men. Use instead *VIP, big shot/wheel, bigwig, dignitary, personage, high-muck-a-muck.*

hector although based on the Trojan champion slain by Achilles, this term is used inclusively and probably not one person in a million thinks of Hector while saying it.

Heidelberg man *Homo erectus, early human.* The physical remains are referred to as the Heidelberg jaw or the Heidelberg fossil.

heiress *heir.*

heist man *armed robber, professional thief.*

helmsman *pilot, steerer, navigator.*

helpmate/helpmeet avoid these terms; they are most often used for women and they imply a certain existential inferiority. While still in the White House, Louisa Adams wrote, "Man's interpretation of the word 'helpmate' as used in the Bible means this: Women made to cook his dinner, wash his clothes, gratify his sensual appetites, and thank him and love him for permission to drudge through life at the mercy of his caprices. Is this the interpretation intended by the Creator, the father of all mercy?" Probably not. Modern scholars say the original Jewish term that has been translated as "helpmate" (someone "to assist Adam in life") was actually "suitable partner," someone to walk side by side with him. *See also* Adam's Rib; Eve.

he-man avoid, first, because there is no parallel for women and, second, because it perpetuates stereotypes and expectations of men that are often false and damaging. Use instead precise adjectives: *aggressive, hardy, rugged, husky, hearty, robust, powerful, muscular, domineering, capable, dynamic, energetic, physical,* etc.

henchman *sidekick, hireling, underling, flunky, lackey, thug, hood, tool, puppet, accomplice, stooge, hanger-on, ward heeler, minion, myrmidon; follower, supporter, subordinate, helper, aide, right-hand, cohort; groom, attendant, page.*

hen party *all-women party, women-only party.* The use of "hen party" follows the "insider/outsider" rule: women may call their gatherings hen parties; others may not so label them. "Hen" has been a slang word for a woman since 1626.

henpecked *bossed around, bullied, browbeaten, soul not one's own, passive, submissive, dominated, subjugated, under someone's thumb, led by the nose, at one's beck and call, ruled with an iron hand, in leading strings.* These terms can apply to men or women.

herculean despite its obviously male provenance, the use of "herculean" doesn't function as a biased word. If you want something less sex-specific use *heroic, extraordinary, great-hearted, valiant, stalwart, invincible, unswerving.*

herdsman *herder, sheepherder, shepherd, swineherd, swineherder, cattle herder, herd breeder, livestock manager/breeder/tender, rancher.*

hermaphrodite true hermaphroditism in human beings (someone with both male and female reproductive organs) is rare (some 400 cases have been documented). Use "hermaphrodite" only in its scientific sense.

hero/heroine use "hero" for both men and women even though it is the masculine form of the Greek word, while "heroine" is the feminine (although one of mythology's best-known couples was Hero and Leander, and Hero was *not* the manly half). In English, a heroine is defined as "a female hero"—that is, a subset of hero. Some sensitive writers and speakers feel there is a certain acceptability for a gender-fair use of "hero" and "heroine," but given the record of the serious devaluation and discounting of woman-associated words in our society, it seems best to support one neutral term. If "hero" feels too masculine try instead *protagonist, central/main character, champion, celebrity, notable, rara avis, star, superstar, model, paragon, good example, demigod, saint, benefactor, salt of the earth, one in ten thousand, one of the best, winner, leader, ideal, shining example, luminary, dignitary, personage, figure, public/popular figure, social lion, big name, big cheese, idol, matin e idol, principal, principal character/role, title/starring/lead role, feature attraction.*

herstory although this term is not recognized by any standard dictionaries, it appears in print and has validity as a naming of all that has been left out of "his story." (Note that the "his" in "history" is an English/American-language accident and has nothing to do with the male pronoun or with any male-based word.) *See also* history.

heterosexism attitudes, behaviors, and policies that assume everyone is heterosexual constitute heterosexism. Writing or speaking as though all homeowning couples involve a woman and a man, for example, is heterosexist.

heterosexual this is the acceptable term to describe a person of either sex with an opposite-sex sexual and emotional preference.

hetman (Cossack leader) leave as is (historical term).

he who hesitates is lost *they who hesitate are lost, once you hesitate you are lost.*

he who laughs last laughs best *they who laugh last laugh best, when you laugh last you laugh best.* A variant of this expression is "he who laughs, lasts," which was *Reader's Digest*'s forerunner to "Laughter, The Best Medicine," another good alternative.

he who lies down with dogs rises with fleas *they who lie down with dogs rise with fleas.*

he who lives by the sword dies by the sword *they who live by the sword die by the sword, if you live by the sword you will die by the sword.*

he who seeks finds *they who seek find, seek and you shall find.*

highboy nonsexist; comes from French "bois" for "wood."

high man on the totem pole *number one, second to none, front-runner, star, the favorite, person on top, high-ranking individual, someone with seniority, winner, top scorer, cream of the crop, influential person, big shot/boss/wheel/ cheese, hotshot, bigwig, someone at the top of the ladder/heap/tree.* This term is ethnocentric as well as sexist. *See also* lord it over someone.

high priestess *high priest.* But retain "high priestess" when discussing ancient or present-day goddess religions; it has significance and weight as a sex-specific term.

high-risk group *high-risk behavior.* It is not the group people belong to (needle-users, gay men, heterosexuals with multiple partners) that puts them at risk for AIDS, but rather their behavior: sharing needles, unprotected sex, etc.

highwayman *highway robber/bandit, robber, bandit, road agent, footpad, brigand, marauder, thug, outlaw, desperado, ruffian, rogue.*

highway patrolman *highway officer/patrol officer, motorcycle officer/police.*

hijack/hijacker the origin of these terms is unknown, although one story has it that they come from thieves ordering victims to raise their hands by saying, "High, Jack!" They are, however, used for both women and men and have no functional sexist connotations.

hillbilly this is used in a nonsexist manner today even though it was originally based on a man's name. However, its use is generally derogatory and should be avoided.

him never use "him" when you mean "her and him," or when "him" might refer to either a man or a woman (for example, "the taxpayer/ him"); replace with the plural, circumlocute, or *see* the Writing Guidelines for suggestions.

himself never use "himself" when you mean "herself and himself," or when it might refer to either a man or a woman (for example, "the priest/himself"); replace with the plural, circumlocute, or *see* the Writing Guidelines for suggestions.

hired man *farm hand/worker, hired/field hand, hand, helper.*

his never use "his" when you mean "hers and his," or when it might refer to either a man or a woman (for example, "the plumber/his"); replace with the plural, circumlocute, or *see* the Writing Guidelines for suggestions.

his bark is worse than his bite *her/their/its bark is worse than her/their/its bite, all clouds and no rain, all sound and no fury, empty threat, sham.*

his own man, be *stand on one's own two feet, someone who can't be bought, be inner-directed/self-governing/independent, be one's/your/her/his own person, be her own woman/his own man.*

his own worst enemy *one's/your/her/his own worst enemy.*

Hispanic rarely used by the community it purports to identify, this term is primarily a government invention and often renders invisible specific groups within it: people of Mexican origin make up 62% of the total "Hispanic" population; of Puerto Rican origin, 13%; of Central and South American origin, 12%; of Cuban origin, 5%. The remaining 8% are either from Spain or are people who have been in the United States for so long that they no longer claim a specific country of origin. Whenever possible, replace "Hispanic" with a specific designation. *See also* Chicana/Chicano; Latina/Latino.

history from the Greek "historia" meaning "inquiry/knowing/ learning," the word "history" itself is not male-based and has nothing to do with the masculine possessive pronoun "his." The writing of history has been extremely sexist, however, which is why women have coined the term "herstory" to "emphasize that women's lives, deeds, and participation in human affairs have been neglected or undervalued in standard histories" (Casey Miller and Kate Swift, *Words and Women*). Until recently, history was written by men about men.

"Where women do appear in traditional accounts of the past, they emerge as adjuncts of the masculine world being recorded, as supporting players, seen only in their male-related roles as wife, mother, daughter, or mistress. History thus related occurs around them rather than with them" (Carol Ruth Berkin, in *The Underside of American History*, ed. Thomas R. Frazier). Rosalind Miles (*The Women's History of the World*) says women have always been prominent but were never credited with the significance they deserved. It is commonly thought that there is little history by and about women because women did not write any or participate in any. Eleanor S. Riemer and John C. Fout (eds., *European Women: A Documentary History, 1789-1945*) describe the wealth of women's writings they found in "books, women's magazines, and periodicals written, edited, and sometim es typeset and printed by women, for women.... If historians until now have not used women's own sources to reconstruct women's past, it is only because they have not looked for them." Sara M. Evans (*Born for Liberty: A History of Women in America*) shows how women shaped vital political and social issues and did not always stay in the private sphere where they "belonged," but developed their own associations that fell neither in the private nor public spheres. *See also* herstory.

hit man *hired/professional/armed killer, hired gun/assassin, assassin, killer, murderer, sniper, slayer, gunslinger, gunsel, executioner, liquidator, mercenary, thug, gangster, sharpshooter, attacker, outlaw, terrorist, mobster, racketeer, hoodlum, trigger, croaker, enforcer.*

hobo woman or man. *See also* knight of the road; road sister.

Hobson's choice when you use expressions like this, be aware of how many are male-based. Balance them with female-based expressions, creative expressions of your own, or alternatives: *no choice, no choice at all, not a pin to choose between/from.* *See* Writing Guidelines for a discussion of sex-linked expressions.

hoistman *hoist operator.*

hoity-toity *highfalutin, pretentious, pompous.* "Hoity-toity" is invariably used of a woman.

hold the purse strings *hold all the cards, lay down the law, run the place/show, call the shots/plays, be in the saddle/driver's seat, have under control, wear the crown, be the boss.*

holdup man *armed robber, thief, purse-snatcher, mugger, roller.*

Holy Father (pope) in the past and at the present, this gender-specific term is correct.

holy roller *fundamentalist.*

Holy Spirit (Ghost)/he do not use masculine pronouns for the Holy Spirit, replacing them with descriptive adjectives, or, in prayer, with direct address ("you" and "your"). At other times, circumlocution will be necessary. The Hebrew "ruah" or "ruach," meaning "wind, breath, spirit," is grammatically feminine, and the Greek word for "spirit," "pneuma," is neuter, which is why some writers and speakers refer to the Holy Spirit as "she" or "it." However, the most theologically and linguistically correct approach is to avoid gender-specific pronouns.

homebody man or woman. *See also* family man; homemaker.

homeboy/homegirl all usages of these colloquial terms seem to be sex parallel.

home economics use this only for groups that so label their work. Despite a wide range of academic and professional pursuits, home economists are stuck with a gender stereotype: women in aprons. Preferred terms include *domestic science, human ecology.* "Human ecology" was the term used by ecologist Ellen Swallow, who pioneered the field, and "domestic science" indicates the field's professional, technical, and scientific aspects, which include health care and education, aging, nutrition, dietetics, AIDS, alcohol and drug abuse; food production, processing, supplies, and technology; design and textiles; family and social sciences, safety, housing; finance and planning, farm business development; consultation with government and industry.

homemaker this unisex term is positive in itself. Use it to describe men as well as women, but examine the context in which you use it for hidden biases and prejudices that may tend to belittle homemakers.

homeowner 21% of homeowners are women. "Homeowner" may become a classist term: fifteen years ago it took 23% of the median income of young families to buy a home; today it takes over 56%.

homeroom mother *homeroom parent/aide/helper.*

homeworker sociologists define a homeworker as a woman who does low-level office and factory work at home. Although industrial homework has been banned in the United States for the past forty-five years, homework exists in the form of middle-class white-collar workers in the U.S. and has mushroomed in Latin America and Asia, where women assemble component parts, sew clothing, and perform hundreds of other piecework operations. Many American women consider themselves entrepreneurs or "independent contractors" (which employers call them to avoid paying benefits and social security), but homeworkers generally work long hours for lower wages while still being primarily responsible for housework and childcare.

homicide this word comes from the Latin for "man," but it is defined and used today inclusively.

hominid anthropologists use this word inclusively, and it is functionally fairly nonsexist. It is a problem only when it is defined or used as referring to "man" instead of to "human being," which is the meaning of its Latin root. For example, one dictionary defines it as "any of a family (Hominidae) of bipedal primate mammals comprising recent man, his immediate ancestors, and related forms" (*Webster's Ninth New Collegiate Dictionary*). The unambiguous choice here would have been: "recent human beings, their immediate ancestors, and related forms."

homo- words beginning with "homo-" come from the Greek word meaning "same" or "equal" and are not sexist—for example, "homosexual" does not refer to a man but to someone whose sexual orientation is toward persons of the same sex.

homo (gay man) avoid.

Homo erectus this "homo" (*see* homo-) comes from the Latin for "human being." The confusion and ambiguity of the English "man" also tars the Latin "homo," and gives it a sexist look. However, the term is well established—and used inclusively—in anthropology. The main problem with it is that it is so often followed by references to "man" and "mankind" when the correct references should be "human being" and "humanity." When you see "Homo erectus," check the surrounding material for sexist language.

homophobia defined as an irrational fear of gay and lesbian acts, persons, and sentiments, today this term includes hatred, prejudice, and discrimination and covers a range of anti-gay behavior and attitudes. (The "homo-" here is not sexist; it refers to "same" as in "same-sex," not to "man.") Surveys indicate that almost all lesbians and gay men have suffered some form of verbal abuse, while 25% of all gay men and 10% of all lesbians have been physically assaulted because of their sexual orientation. According to researchers, gay men and lesbians are the target of more open and more intractable discrimination than that directed at any other minority group. Abuse ranges from verbal harassment to physical assaults and murder (in 1988 there were 7,248 incidents of harassment and assault, including 70 murders). Many so-called gay bashings go unreported because victims fear retaliation, publicly identifying themselves, or being blamed for provoking the assault. There is a particularly high social tolerance for abuse and discrimination, partly because, unlike other minority groups, lesbians and gay men are still victims of legalized bias; they are, for example, barred from the armed services and in many states their sexual activities are illegal. Although there has been a great increase in anti-gay bias since the beginning of the AIDS epidemic, it appears that AIDS has not created the new level of hostility, but rather has given bigots an excuse to act out their hatred. Research indicates that some men use hostility and violence against gay men to reassure themselves about their own sexuality. *See also* violence.

Homo sapiens this scientific name for the human species is based on the Latin word "homo" ("human being"). It is thus inclusive, although it is sometimes heard as adult-male man rather than human-being man, especially because its common definition ("mankind") underlines the males-only flavor. When using this term in nonscientific material, it is less ambiguous to use short, direct English words: *human beings, humans, humanity, humankind, people.* **See also** mankind.

homosexual this term refers to both women and men with same-sex emotional and sexual orientations and can be used when paired with "heterosexual" or "bisexual," but in other uses it is seen as clinical, sexually objectifying, and limiting. For the cultural terms by which people choose to identify themselves use *lesbian, gay man.* **See also** gay man; lesbian (noun/adj.).

honcho/head honcho big *shot/boss/wheel/cheese, leader, boss, hotshot, person in charge.* Although a honcho can be either sex (it comes from the Japanese meaning "group leader"), we have tended to reserve it for men, which is why you may want to use alternatives. The semi-facetious "honcha" is incorrect.

honey/hon these terms are often acceptable to people in intimate relation-ships who have implicitly or explicitly approved their use. Accord-ing to one study, "honey" was the overwhelming favorite term of endearment for both men and women. The second favorite, how-ever, was no endearment at all. People just called their significant others by their names. "Honey" and "hon" are always demeaning, incorrect, and unwelcome when used for strangers or slight acquain-tances. It is the person in the lower-power position in any relation-ship who gets called "hon," "honey," or "dear." The use of these terms by one person in an interaction implies that the other is inferior socially, intellectually, financially, or some other way. If the second person wouldn't dare call the first one "honey," it is a sure indication of an inequality in the relationship. (Imagine responding in kind to a boss, professor, or customer who has just called you "hon.") **See also** courts (judicial); dear/dearie.

honor this term has traditionally meant different things for men and women and often has done neither sex any good. Russell Baker (*About Men: Reflections on the Male Experience*) says, "Honorable is peculiarly a man's word, as are its antonyms: dishonorable, ignoble, base, vile, swinish, caddish. Such words are rarely applied to women. Even the phrase 'a woman's honor,' referring to the high-toned sexual morality once demanded of the American female, sounds like a man's invention for burdening women with heavier moral luggage than men chose to bear . . . . They lay that honor business on you when you're just a little boy, long before you guess what it's leading up to, long before you can possibly know that if you don't live by that little-boy code someday a general may slap your face and call you a coward or order a firing squard to dispose of you as a disgrace to your sex and hence a menace to your country. So the idea of honor becomes a vital part of a man's boyhood experience." *See also* virtue.

honorary fraternity *honorary society/honorary Greek society.*

hooker *prostitute.* "Hooker" originally referred to a prostitute from "the Hook" area of New York City. Later, during the Civil War, Union General "Fighting Joe" Hooker's troops fought to defend the nation's capital and also frequented prostitutes in such numbers that the women were referred to as one of Hooker's Divisions. The area where the men were bivouacked was called "the plague spot of Washington" and included 109 houses of prostitution ("hook shops") and 50 saloons.

Horatio Alger story based on the 120+ enormously successful boys' books written by the Unitarian cleric Horatio Alger, this phrase refers to the poor but honest newsboys and bootblacks who by hard work and virtuous living overcame obstacles and achieved success. Because of the term's male orientations, you may sometimes need an inclusive alternative: *rags-to-riches story, personal success story; rise up/get on in the world, make one's fortune, work/make one's way up.* This concept has contributed greatly to the myth that anyone can make it in the United States. *See also* classism.

horny despite its reference to the penis (horn), this term is used for both sexes.

horseman/horsewoman acceptable terms; they have not been used in sexist ways. If you want an alternative use *equestrian, horseback rider, horse rider/lover, rider, trainer, cavalier, jockey, horse breeder, hunter.*

horsemanship *riding/equestrian skills, equitation.*

hoseman *firefighter, hose carrier.*

hostess *host.* Also: *social director, tour guide, attendant, receptionist.* There are no talk show "hostesses." There are also, it appears, very few guestesses; according to researcher Mark Harmon, the guest list on "Meet the Press" since the start of the program in 1947 has been dominated by white men, although slight progress has been made in inviting members of minority groups. The percentage of women guests in any given decade held between 3% and 5%.

hotelier women now represent nearly 65% of the membership of the hospitality industry's largest professional organization, the Hotel Sales and Marketing Association International. They also make up 60% to 65% of the students enrolled in U.S. hotel and restaurant schools.

hotelman *hotel proprietor/owner/manager/worker, hotelier.*

Hottentot *Khoi-Khoin.* The correct term is always the one by which a people refer to themselves.

houri retain to refer to the women who feature in Muslim beliefs; do not use to refer to a voluptuous young woman.

houseboy/housegirl for "houseboy" use *servant*; for "housegirl" use *prostitute*. Note lack of parallel.

househusband this relatively new term may or may not find a place in the language. Househusbands are rarely the true equivalents of house-wives; although a few men care for children and are home full-time from choice, for most it is not a primary career. They are either forced into it (unemployment or ill health) or they are involved in salaried work done at home. And so far it appears more socially acceptable to be a "workwife" than a "househusband." This reflects what has also happened in the workplace; while women go into male-intensive occupations (and generally enjoy higher status for doing so), men are not going in great numbers into female-intensive occupations (and they report raised eyebrows when they do). How-ever, in a 1990 *Time* magazine poll of men and women ages eighteen to twenty-four, 48% of the young men expressed an interest in staying home with their children. The decision is not yet in on "househusband."

housekeeper not sexist per se, "housekeeper" is too often used as an all-purpose label for a woman. Professionals who manage others' homes call themselves *household technicians/workers/helpers, home managers*.

housemaid *servant, domestic worker, cleaner, house cleaner, household helper, housekeeper*.

housemaid's knee *inflammation of the kneecap*.

houseman *caretaker, janitor, house cleaner, odd jobber, fixer-upper*.

housemother *houseparent, counselor, monitor, cottage parent, chaperon, resident assistant*. There has never been a term "housefather."

housewife *homemaker, householder, homeowner, consumer, woman who works at home, woman, home/household manager, customer, shopper, parent*. Roseanne Barr refers to herself as a *domestic goddess*. "Housewife" marries a woman to her house, and should be avoided because it identifies someone by gender and marital status (both often irrele-vant in the context) and because of the practically endless possibili-ties for using it in sexist ways. *See also* househusband; housework; moonlighter; second shift, the; working mother; working wife; working woman.

housewifery *homemaking, housekeeping, home/household management*.

housework make no assumptions about the nature and ownership of housework. As the woman sings in the black musical "Don't Bother Me, I Can't Cope": "Show me that special gene that says I was born to make the beds." Housework is a relatively recent invention, arising from changes brought about by the industrial revolution. In 1737 in England, for example, more than 98% of married women worked outside the home. By 1911, more than 90% were employed solely as housewives. This pattern was repeated throughout the industrialized world. Today housework "chore wars" are one of the commonest features of marriage. Ellen Goodman writes, "He is doing more than his father and feeling underappreciated. She is doing more than her husband and feeling undervalued. There is a friction between women whose lives have changed faster than the men they share them with. There is a stalemate over the household." Statistics proliferate on who does what around the house but they all come down to the same thing: women still have the primary responsibility for maintaining the home and caring for the children. Debbie Taylor (in *New International*), says, "Men perceive that equating love and domestic work is a trap. They fear that to get involved with housework would send them hurtling into the bottomless pit of self-sacrifice that is women's current caring role." In *The Handbook of Nonsexist Writing*, Casey Miller and Kate Swift (with credit to Marjorie Vogel for the insight) point out that "many women do not use the term *work* to describe their housekeeping or homemaking activities. Nor, in general, do members of their families. A woman 'stays home' rather than 'works at home.' She 'fixes dinner' rather than 'works in the kitchen.' In contrast, activities men traditionally undertake around the house are usually dignified by the name *work*. A man 'works on the car' or 'does his own electrical work.' He may have a 'workshop' in the basement." *See also* housewife; man's work; moonlighter; second shift, the; working father; working mother; working wife; working woman.

hoyden (girl) avoid. This word once referred to members of both sexes. *See also* tomboy.

hubby you may refer to your own, but not anyone else's, husband this way. "Hubby" came from "husband" just as "hussy" came from "wife" ("huswif") but with far different connotations. *See also* husband (noun); husband and wife; wife/husband.

hula dancer woman or man.

human (noun) "human" refers to both sexes, although it's been a near thing for women at times. In 585 at the Council of Mâcon, forty-three Catholic bishops and twenty men representing bishops debated the topic "Are Women Human?" After much lengthy argument, the vote was 32 yes, 31 no. By one vote women were declared human. Native Americans and African Americans have not fared any better. The early settlers "considered the original inhabitants of the continent as somewhat lower than human beings, a species of animal" (Ann H. Beuf, in *Racism and Sexism* by Paula S. Rothenberg). To maintain the institution of slavery, blacks were described as subhuman heathens, and in 1857 the U.S. Supreme Court labeled them "beings of an inferior order." "Human," which comes from the Latin "humanus" for "ground," has been used as a noun since 1533 and is used and perceived today as an inclusive term, although some dictionaries include the incorrect "man/men" instead of "human being(s)" to define it.

humanity/humankind these terms come from the Latin "humanus" ("ground") meaning "human being" and are used and understood today as inclusive terms.

humor humor that demeans others often masks a great deal of hostility as well as a sense of inferiority. When others don't laugh at sexist, racist, or homophobic jokes/remarks, the jokester is quick to level the one accusation guaranteed to sting: "You don't have a sense of humor." It is particularly damaging to joke about violence to women, gay men and lesbians, or minorities. When good people, nonviolent and loving people, make jokes about violence, rape, sexual harassment, and putting people down, it provides a cultural tolerance for bias and gives tacit permission to the name-caller, the gay-basher, the abuser, the rapist, even the murderer, to think: "It isn't just me. All these people think it's not only all right, it's downright funny to hurt people."

hunk yes, this is sexist (there is no truly comparable term for a woman) and yes, it tends to make sex objects of men, but so far its use seems good-natured and complimentary. If you want an inclusive alternative try *dreamboat, centerfold, pinup, smoothie, greatest thing since* (fill in your own "sliced bread" equivalent).

huntress *hunter.*

huntsman *hunter, hunt manager.*

husband (noun) the "hus-band" was the Old English mate of the "hus-wif" ("hus" meaning "house") although the word "husband" fared a great deal better than either "housewife" or "wife" in terms of prestige and acceptability—possibly because "man" was used so often instead of "husband" (as in the outrageous "man and wife"). Today, just as many men are redefining the husband role in positive ways, there is a subtle discounting of "husband"; advertisers portray the husband in stereotypical ways and more and more jokes and one-liners are putting down husbands. Check the material around "husband" for bias. *See also* househusband; hubby; husband and wife; wife/husband.

husband (verb) *conserve, ration, measure, preserve, lay/put by, economize, store, reserve, accumulate, hoard, stockpile, stock, save, save for a rainy day, stow/squirrel/salt/sock/lay away.*

husband and wife vary this phrase half the time to "wife and husband." Male grammarians asserted centuries ago that the male was more important than the female, and should always be placed first in any sentence. We thus have husband and wife, Mr. and Mrs. (just try saying Mrs. and Mr.), boy and girl, king and queen, etc. English jurist Sir William Blackstone was a man of their kidney: "Husband and wife are one, and that one is the husband."

husbandlike/husbandly these vague words leave us little the wiser about the person so described; there are as many kinds of husbands as there are husbands. Choose instead specific adjectives: *solicitous, gentle, supportive, intimate, knowing, sensitive, protective*. These are not synonyms but rather what the culture often understands by "husbandlike/husbandly."

husbandman *farmer, agriculturist, agronomist, farm scientist, vintager, horticulturist, citriculturist, gardener, florist, cultivator, tiller of the soil, sower, reaper, grower, forester, breeder.* See also cattleman; herdsman; nurseryman.

husbandry *household thrift, thrift, thriftiness, good housekeeping, frugality, frugalness, careful management, conservation, economizing, conserving; agriculture, agronomy, agronomics, agribusiness, farming, farm management, cultivation, tillage, forestry.* Or, be specific: *arboriculture, floriculture, horticulture, landscape gardening, viniculture.*

hussy replace this word with adjectives that convey whatever meaning this has for you: *bold, brazen, seductive, shameless, immodest, immoral, indecent, bold-faced,* etc. Derived from "housewife," this word has taken the low road while its innocuous, affectionate mate, "hubby," has taken the high road. *See also* femme fatale; Jezebel/jezebel; loose woman.

hustler used of either sex, although a male hustler is a man successful with women or, in some instances, a prostitute, while a female hustler is always a prostitute. In the sense of a go-getter or a con artist, a hustler is either sex.

hymn a number of religious groups are giving their hymns an inclusive look. The United Methodist Church, second largest U.S. Protestant denomination, recently revised their hymnal to reflect respect for women, blacks, and people with disabilities (although they retained "he" for God), changing such phrases as "his power and his love" to "God's power and God's love"; "pleased as man with men to dwell" to "pleased with us in flesh to dwell"; "sons of men and angels say" to "earth and heaven in chorus say"; "Good Christian Men Rejoice" to "Good Christian Friends Rejoice"; "God of our Fathers" to "God of the Ages." Washing people "whiter than snow" was eliminated because of the negative inferences for blacks. Newly added were hymns from African American, Latina/Latino, Asian, and Native American traditions.

hyphenated names hyphenated surnames are not always ideal (computers often don't recognize hyphens and some names are too long for most forms) but they have provided a way for couples to mark their relationships and for children to carry their dual heritage. Even hyphenation doesn't assure gender fairness: the Nebraska Supreme Court ruled that the father's surname has to precede the mother's in hyphenated children's names. Hyphenation somewhat resembles the centuries-old custom in Spain, Portugal, and other Latin countries. Children are given two fully functional surnames, the mother's and the father's (husbands and wives do not have the same last name after marriage). However, the father's name is the first surname (in between the first name and the mother's name) and it is this name that carries greater social weight and is passed on to the next generation. *See also* matronym/matronymic; patronym/patronymic.

hysteria/hysterical based on the Greek for "womb" (hysteria was thought to be caused by disturbances in the womb), these terms are used almost entirely and often inappropriately of women. For the medical condition, use *histrionic personality disorder*. For the noun use *fear, frenzy, emotional excess, wildness, outburst, explosion, flare-up, seizure, eruption, delirium*. For the adjective use *angry, outraged, irate, incensed, enraged, furious, infuriated, livid, upset, agitated, fit to be tied, delirious, beside oneself, carried away, raving, raging, seething, distracted, frantic, frenetic, frenzied, wild, berserk, uncontrollable*.

i

I reckon there's as much human nature in some folks as there is in others, if not more.

Edward Noyes Westcott

I am not my brother's keeper use "my brother's keeper" when quoting or referring to the biblical story (when God asks Cain where his brother is after Cain has killed Abel, Cain answers, "I do not know. Am I my brother's keeper?"). If you want alternatives for the contemporary meaning use *don't look at me, it's none of my business, it's not my responsibility, I can't help what anyone else does, I'm not responsible for anyone but myself, I'm not her/his/my sister's/my brother's keeper.*

ice-cream man *ice-cream vendor.*

iceman *ice route driver, ice deliverer/carrier/seller.* Retain "iceman" in historical contexts. For slang meaning "killer" use *liquidator, hired gun, executioner, cutthroat, assassin, racketeer, butcher, mobster, thug, gangster, sharpshooter.*

idea man *idea machine, thinker, creative thinker, wizard, brain, brains, intellectual, genius, mental giant, think tank, sage, oracle, theorist, philosopher, savant, conceptualizer, visionary, daydreamer, expert, authority, ratiocinator, ideator.*

idiot/idiocy *someone with a mental impairment, a person who is mentally disabled; mental impairment/disability.* The term "idiot" is unscientific, highly demeaning, and always unacceptable. Also avoid abnormal, backward, feeble-minded, freak, imbecile, moron. *See also* handicapped; retard/retarded.

idiot savant *man/boy* or *woman/girl;* the French is grammatically masculine but has always been used for both sexes.

if you can't stand the heat, stay out of the kitchen despite the kitchen, this sentence is used for both men and women and carries no sexist sting.

I'll be/I'm a monkey's uncle this term could be reduced to "Well, I'll be!" although it doesn't need to be taken too seriously. Anyone who wants to be a monkey's uncle is probably not a threat to the language. (Correspondent par excellence Bob Considine wrote of female war correspondents: "In Korea, they landed with both feet, and if they aren't in war to stay, I'm a monkey's aunt.")

illegal alien *undocumented worker/resident.* ***See also*** alien.

illegitimate/illegitimate child *child of unmarried parents/unknown father.* No human being is "illegitimate." Except for narrow legal uses, avoid these terms. Examine the need to mention the circumstances of a person's birth; they are most often irrelevant. Of all children born each year, 22% are born to unmarried parents. Pejoratively labeling the children does nothing to help a situation with far-reaching social implications, and is sexist insofar as it is the mothers who, along with their children, are usually the targets of community disfavor. Being abandoned by the children's fathers further diminishes the status of both mother and children.

imam this Muslim cleric is always a man.

impotent use "impotent" only to describe a man unable to achieve erection; someone who is sterile or infertile may be potent, but unable to father children because of, for example, a low sperm count. Impotence in a man is not the same as "frigidity" in a woman. ***See also*** frigid; infertile; sterile.

impregnable *impenetrable, unassailable, invulnerable, safe, secure, invincible, indomitable, unyielding, irresistible, unconquerable, all-powerful.* "Impregnable" is surely innocent enough in spite of its sex-specific base. Alternatives are offered for times when its actual meaning might overcome its metaphorical use.

impregnate *fertilize, fecundate, generate, create; implant, infuse, imbue, infiltrate; permeate, saturate.* ***See also*** impregnable.

impresario woman or man; for terms that may not hit the ear with as masculine a sound as "impresario" try *promoter, producer, director, manager, talent coordinator, talent agent, booker, advance agent.*

inamorata *lover.* There is no male equivalent for "inamorata." ***See also*** boyfriend; girlfriend.

inclusive language inclusive language includes everyone. Nobody hears or reads it and thinks, "Where am *I* in all that?" Inclusive language may contain sex-specific words, but they will be used in ways that are unbiased, balanced, and gender-fair (as opposed to gender-free). Inclusive language is advocated by the prestigious Modern Language Association, has been used to revise government job titles, and is mandated in most publishing houses, government offices, businesses, and higher educational institutions.

Indiaman *India trader, East India trading ship, merchant ship, trader;* or retain as is in historical context.

Indian *Native American, American Indian.* Whenever possible use a specific tribe name (there are 443); "Native American" is approximately as specific as "European." It is redundant to use "Indian" after a tribe name (use, for example, "Lakota"). "Native American" is not universally accepted by American Indians because the federal government now includes Samoans and Hawaiians in that category. When using "Indian" to refer to the people of India, do not include peoples of the former British Empire (e.g., Burmese, Bangladeshis, Pakistanis, Sri Lankans) and do not use the incorrect, colonialist "East Indian."

Indian file *single file.*

Indian giver *sorry/repentant giver, back-pedaler, two-faced, take-backer, wishy-washy giver, someone who reneges/changes one's tune/backs down.*

infantryman *infantry soldier, footsoldier, member of the infantry, soldier, infantry; infantryman and infantrywoman if used together.*

infertile this term is used for both men and women, although most often it modifies "couple" ("an infertile couple"). "Infertile" refers to the lack of offspring in people who have been having unprotected intercourse for a certain length of time. "Sterile" usually indicates that a cause for the infertility has been found. Infertile people are not necessarily sterile. Sterile people are always infertile. Infertility is often treatable; sterility generally is not (unless, for example, a tubal ligation or vasectomy can be reversed). Do not confuse "sterile" with "impotent" or "frigid." *See also* barren; frigid; impotent; sterile.

ingenue this well-established and rather narrowly defined role in the theater has no real male counterpart; "ingenu" for a man is rarely heard. When using the term in its broader sense, substitute *novice, amateur, beginner, tyro, neophyte, newcomer, innocent, greenhorn, tenderfoot, initiate, fledgling, apprentice, trainee.*

inheritress/inheritrix *inheritor.*

inkman *inker.*

inner man *inner person/self/core, soul, heart, private self; appetite, stomach.*

innocent victim this phrase often implies that other victims are not so innocent. When an infant or blood-transfusion patient dying of AIDS is referred to as an innocent victim, other people with AIDS are seen as less "innocent." Delete the "innocent." *See also* afflicted with; victim.

innocent women and children *civilians, innocent civilians.* In accounts of bombings, terrorism, guerilla warfare, and other atrocities, one often finds references to "innocent women and children," the implication being that men somehow deserve what happens or that it is "natural" that they would be caught up in such death and destruction. Do not subscribe to this sexist view of the relative value of human life.

insane/insanity do not use "the insane" as a collective noun or "insane" as an adjective to describe a person with a mental disorder or an emotional disability. As per the "people first" rule, use, for example, *a person with anorexia, a person with obsessive-compulsive disorder.* Avoid nouns like paranoiac, schizophrenic, manic-depressive, anorexic, bulimic, etc., that label the whole person by the disorder or disability. Replace "insanity" with the medical diagnosis. Avoid unscientific and demeaning terms like crazy, maniac, mentally ill.

insane asylum *psychiatric hospital.*

"insider/outsider" rule certain terms used by people within a group are considered derogatory and unacceptable when used by people outside that group. For example, "crip" appears in *The Disability Rag*; this does not mean that the word is available to anyone who wants to use it. "Big Fag" is printed on a gay man's T-shirt. He may use that expression; a non-gay may not so label him. A group of women talk about "going out with the girls," but a co-worker should not refer to them as "girls." The rule that governs labels or descriptors says (1) people may call themselves whatever they like; (2) others should refer to them by terms chosen by the named parties. It is very possible that within a few years this "insider/outsider" rule will be superfluous; groups that suffer from discriminatory and bigoted labels are slowly reclaiming and rehabilitating many of the offensive terms. The hope is that eventually even very negative terms will have lost their power to wound.

inspectress *inspector.*

instructress *instructor.*

insurance man *insurance agent/sales agent/representative/rep.*

insurance rates the term is nonsexist, but according to some estimates, a lifetime of auto, health, disability, income, and whole life insurance and annuity coverage costs women an average of $20,176 more than men in higher premiums and lower paybacks. Although race and religion could also meet practical and statistical standards for insurance rate classifications, the marketplace would find using them highly offensive; basing rate classifications on sex is equally untenable. Currently efforts are underway to prohibit unfair sex classifications.

intercourse *See* sexual intercourse.

in the arms of Morpheus when you use expressions like this, be aware of how many are male-based. Balance them with female-based expressions, creative expressions of your own, or alternatives: *fast/sound asleep, sawing wood, dead to the world, out like a light, sacked out.* **See** Writing Guidelines for a discussion of sex-linked expressions.

Irishman *Irishwoman and Irishman, native of Ireland, inhabitant of Ireland.* Plurals: *the Irish, Irishfolk, natives of Ireland, inhabitants of Ireland, Irishmen and Irishwomen/Irishwomen and Irishman* (but not "Irishmen and women").

iron man *iron woman/iron man.* Originally referring to a baseball pitcher of superior endurance, this term has come to mean anyone of unusual physical staying power. Except for roundabout phrases (someone "with the strength of ten," "with stamina"), there are no good alternatives for this pithy term.

ironmaster *ironsmith, ironmonger, iron manufacturer/worker.*

irrational this term is too often used as a rebuttal of women's arguments or applied inaccurately to women as a catch-all condemnation; use carefully in reference to women. It is not used in the same way for men. *See also* emotional.

Isle of Man "Man" is thought to come from a Keltic word meaning "mountain"; it has nothing to do with human beings.

it is a wise father that knows his own child leave as is. The old truth to this sex-specific proverb is that a mother can know with 100% certitude that a child is the child of her body but a father has no such biological certainty.

it's a man's world this blatant generalization would be rejected by many men—the unemployed or homeless, victims of street violence, soldiers fighting in the front lines in wars of someone else's making, men who wonder why they die an average of eight years earlier than women, divorced fathers who see their children only rarely. The clich has some use, however, as a means of expressing relative well-being: in a 1989 *New York Times* poll 56% of the women and 49% of the men said American society hadn't changed enough to allow women to compete with men on an equal basis; in a 1990 *Time* magazine poll, 65% of men and 59% of women agreed it's still a man's world.

it's not over 'til the fat lady sings *it ain't over 'til it's over.* The sentence attributed to Yogi Berra is at least as succinct and colorful as the sexist, weightist, anonymous "The opera is never over until the fat lady sings."

Ivy Leaguer may be either sex.

j

The difference between the right word and the almost right
word is the difference between lightning and the lightning bug.

Mark Twain

jack/jack-/-jack although the word, prefix, and suffix "jack" came from
Jacob and often meant a man/boy, they have come to refer without
any particular gender overtones to certain tools (e.g., bootjack,
hydraulic jack, jack, jackhammer, jackknife, jackscrew, and tire jack),
plants and animals (jackdaw, jackfish, jackfruit, jack-in-the-pulpit,
jack mackerel, jack pine), nouns (jackboot, jackstay, jackstraw), and
verbs (jack up prices, jack game). All these can be used as they are.
See also ball the jack; before you can say Jack Robinson; crackerjack
(adj.); every man jack; flapjack; Jack Frost; jack-in-the-box; Jack Ketch;
jackleg; jackman; jack of all trades, master of none; jack-o-lantern;
jackpot; jack rabbit; jacks (child's game); jack-tar; lumberjack/
lumberman.

jackass this word, meaning male donkey, is defined as a foolish or stupid
person, but is reserved for men. It's doubtful that people shouting
"jackass!" really want alternatives, but more neutral-sounding terms
do exist: *donkey, yo-yo, fool, nincompoop, blockhead, nitwit, dumbbell.*

Jack Frost when using expressions like this, be aware of how many are
male-based. Balance them with female-based expressions, creative
expressions of your own, or alternatives: *the Frost Goblin, Jack and Jill
Frost, the Frost Fairy.* Also: *frost, winter. See* Writing Guidelines for a
discussion of sex-linked expressions.

jack-in-the-box the clown that pops up in the box is generally male, which
makes this term acceptable; the toy has no inclusive name.

Jack Ketch seventeenth-century Jack Ketch, who hung people for a living
but whose occupation was listed as "civil servant" for his protection,
lives on in this phrase that refers to someone whose job title hides
their true and sinister task—a phrase for which there is no good
gender-free equivalent.

jackleg *amateur, makeshift.*

jackman *printing-roller handler.*

jack of all trades, master of none this expression is nearly impossible to replace; it's familiar, pithy, and rhythmic. If its sex-specificity jars in your context, try *good at everything, expert at nothing; good at all trades, expert at none; generalist; all-around expert; many-talented; someone who knows a little bit about a lot of things and not much about any of them. See also* handyman.

jack-o-lantern *carved/Halloween/hollow pumpkin, pumpkin face.*

jackpot not functionally sexist although "jack" derives from a man's name. Alternatives include *pot, pool, kitty, stakes, bank.* For "hit the jackpot," use *break the bank, score a success, succeed, turn up trumps, strike it rich, hit the mark.*

jack rabbit leave as is to refer to several genuses of large hares. However, to mean a male rabbit, be sure it is male and that its sex is relevant to your material.

jacks (child's game) nonsexist; originally called jackstones, the "jack" is from a corruption of "chuck" meaning "pebble."

jack-tar *sailor.*

jailbait (underage female sexual partner) avoid. Using "jailbait" perpetuates the Eve-tempting-poor-Adam myth, implying a certain victimization and unwilling cooperation on the part of the man, and obscures the fact that the man is engaging in criminal activity (and laying the foundation for a statutory rape charge).

jailbird technically either sex, a jailbird is generally perceived as male, probably because men have always greatly outnumbered women in prison. *See also* juvenile delinquent; prisoner.

jake *restroom, toilet.*

jane *restroom, toilet. See also* drugs.

Jane Crow Pauli Murray said this term "refers to the entire range of assumptions, attitudes, stereotypes, customs, and arrangements which have robbed women of a positive self-concept and prevented them from participating fully in society as equals with men. Traditionally racism and sexism in the United States have shared some common origins, displayed similar manifestations, reinforced one another, and are so deeply intertwined in the country's institutions that the successful outcome of the struggle against racism will depend in large part upon the simultaneous elimination of all discrimination based upon sex. Black women, faced with these dual barriers, have often found that sex bias is more formidable than racial bias."

Jane Doe acceptable legal term; use with John Doe.

Jane Q. Citizen/Jane Q. Public acceptable terms; use with John Q. Citizen/John Q. Public. *See also* average man; common man; John Q. Citizen/John Q. Public, man in the street.

janitress/janitrix *janitor.*

JAP/Jewish American Princess these terms, which portray Jewish women as self-centered, materialistic, manipulative, and sometimes dishonest, appear in jokes and everyday conversation as well as in anti-Semitic graffiti. Many people use the terms without realizing their powerfully damaging effects; tolerance of them has been puzzlingly strong. Some claim it is no coincidence that the terms appeared at a time when Jewish women were beginning to establish a place for themselves in Judaism, serving as rabbis and cantors, as well as in the commercial world.

Java man *Homo erectus, early human, early human found in Java, ancestral hominid, archaic homo sapiens.* Remains are called *Java fossil, Java skull.*

jazzman *jazz musician/player, member of jazz band.*

Jekyll and Hyde when using expressions like this, be aware of how many are male-based. Balance them with female-based expressions, creative expressions of your own, or alternatives: *split personality, alter egos. See* Writing Guidelines for a discussion of sex-linked expressions.

jerk technically available for both sexes, "jerk" seems to favor men. In a Men's Rights, Inc. study of hundreds of advertisements in which both women and men appeared, every perceived jerk was a man. Since the advent of the women's movement, it has become less politically correct and much riskier to make women look feeble in advertisements, but since much of lowbrow humor depends on putting someone down, men have become the targets.

jerrican/jerry can "jerry" does not refer to a man's name but to the nickname for Germans, to reflect the can's German design. Even though it involves an ethnic reference, the term is not functionally ethnocentric.

jerry-built although its origins are unclear (either a builder named Jerry known for his poor work or the apparently flimsy walls of Jericho), this term is functionally nonsexist. If a more neutral-looking term is needed use *shoddy/flimsy/careless construction, cheaply/hastily/shoddily built.*

Jesus Christ when writing about Christ, the masculine pronouns are, of course, correct. However, you may want to avoid all unnecessary ones because "theological tradition has virtually always maintained that the maleness of Jesus is theologically, christologically, soteriologically, and sacramentally irrelevant" (Sandra M. Schneiders, *Women and the Word*). Given the era and culture in which he lived, it is not surprising that Jesus came as a male; the same message from a woman would not have been accepted. However, there have been few individuals in history as completely androgynous as Christ, and it does his message a disservice to overinsist on his maleness.

Jewess *Jew.*

Jezebel/jezebel avoid. The biblical story of Jezebel shows a murdering, controlling, rapacious person. She is primarily an amoral manipulator and only secondarily a woman. Instead of focusing on Jezebel's viciousness, the dictionary definition of a jezebel emphasizes her sexuality (a shameless or abandoned woman) when in fact Jezebel did not in any way trade on her sex to carry out her evil deeds. Use instead *evil influence, villain, murderer, bully, plotter, scourge of the human race, devil in human form/shape.*

jiggerman *potter.*

Jim Crow avoid. *See also* Jane Crow.

jim-dandy when using expressions like this, be aware of how many are male-based. Balance them with female-based expressions, creative expressions of your own, or alternatives: *terrific, super, wonderful, marvelous, fantastic, sensational, fabulous, stupendous, out of this world, far out, extraordinary. See* Writing Guidelines for a discussion of sex-linked expressions.

jimjams/jimmies/jimmy the origins of these terms are unclear, but because they look sex-linked alternatives may be preferred. For "jimjams," use *jitters.* For "jimmies" use *candy sprinkles.* For "jimmy" (noun/verb) use *crowbar/burglar's crowbar; pry/pry up.*

jobmaster *supervisor, watch manufacturing supervisor.*

job titles both statutory and administrative law now clearly prohibit the use of sex-, race-, and age-referents in employment practices.

jock (athlete) although both sexes are referred to as jocks today, the tendency is still to think first of a man when one hears the word. And for good reason. The old "jock/jockum" meant "penis." Its meaning is particularly clear in "jockstrap."

jockette some racing stewards have actually used this silly and demeaning term—a pitiful thing to have done to a decent word like "jockey" and to the talented women who have made it into the ranks of professional jockeys. ("Jockey" does not come from the same root as "jock"; it developed from a nickname for John.)

joe/Joe Blow/Joe Schmo "joe" and "Joe Blow" have long meant an average, typical, or ordinary man, while "schmo" comes from the Yiddish for "jerk." These are sexist insofar as there are no parallel terms for women. Less casual inclusive synonyms for both sexes are *Jane Doe/John Doe, Jane Q. Citizen/John Q. Citizen,* and *Jane Q. Public/John Q. Public.*

john (man) *prostitute's customer.* Our language is nowhere less descriptive of reality than when dealing with prostitution (*see* discussion in the Writing Guidelines). We have no word equal to "prostitute" in weight, significance, and high moral judgment that describes the prostitute's customer. Prostitutes carry the economic, psychological, physical, social, and linguistic burden for a system that could not exist without "customers." The continuation of prostitution depends absolutely on the continued participation of customers; language ought to reflect this responsibility. Instead there are scores and scores of pejorative terms for prostitutes, but only three relatively innocuous terms for prostitutes' customers: john, date, and trick. While some people see the association of "john" with a toilet sufficiently evocative of the john's seedy activities, the fact remains that John is a nice all-American name—a little too good for prostitution and certainly not parallel to the term "prostitute." Using "prostitute's customer" at least ties the person to the activity.

john (toilet) *bathroom, restroom, toilet, washroom, privy, water closet, lavatory, W.C., comfort station, outhouse.*

John Bull (England) some countries are personified by men (the United States' Uncle Sam), while others are personified by women (France's Marianne). You can balance the male John Bull image with a female one: Great Britain is personified by Britannia, a far more familiar and widely used national symbol who represents all of Great Britain, not just England.

John Doe acceptable legal term; the female form is Jane Doe. Do not use "John Doe" pseudogenerically to mean "average man." *See also* average man; common man; man in the street, John Q. Citizen/John Q. Public.

John Hancock *signature, name, moniker.*

johnny *hospital gown.*

johnnycake nonsexist; the term seems to have come either from an Indian word or from "journeycake." For more neutral-appearing words use *journeycake, cornbread, corncake.*

Johnny-come-lately when using expressions like this, be aware of how many are male-based. Balance them with female-based expressions, creative expressions of your own, or alternatives: *newcomer, new arrival/face, upstart, nouveau riche, arriviste, outsider, social climber, rookie, greenhorn.* See Writing Guidelines for a discussion of sex-linked expressions.

Johnny-jump-up (flower) leave as is.

Johnny-on-the-spot when using expressions like this, be aware of how many are male-based. Balance them with female-based expressions, creative expressions of your own, or alternatives: *friend in need, guardian angel, deus ex machina, right hand, at the ready, good Samaritan, benefactor, ministering angel, there when you need her/him.* See Writing Guidelines for a discussion of sex-linked expressions.

Johnny Reb *confederate soldier.* Or, leave as is.

John Q. Citizen/John Q. Public acceptable when used with Jane Q. Citizen/Jane Q. Public, these terms are sexist when used pseudogenerically to refer to the average citizen. Use instead *the average citizen/person.* *See also* average man; common man; man in the street.

jointress leave this very specific British legal term as is until it is changed or replaced.

journeyman in the general sense, this word can be replaced by *journey worker, journeyed/trained/trade/craft worker, trainee, beginner, assistant, helper, subordinate; average performer; skilled craftworker; journey level* (adj.). Or, use a specific title. However, in labor law or in the trades, "journeyman" has certain specific and so far irreplaceable meanings. It may be possible in some such cases to use *journeyman and journey-woman* or *journeyperson*. ("Journeyperson" is very much a choice of last resort, but it may have some limited usefulness while the term is in transition.)

judas when using an expression like "judas" or one of its derivatives, be aware of how many figures of speech are male-based. Balance them with female-based expressions, creative expressions of your own, or alternatives. For "judas" use *false friend, betrayer, deceiver, traitor*. For "judas goat" use *bait, lure, decoy, trap, baited hook*. For "judas hole/judas window" use *peephole*. For "judas kiss" use *kiss of betrayal*. *See* Writing Guidelines for a discussion of sex-linked expressions.

judeo-christian avoid using this term in an exclusive manner; in recent years "judeo-christian" and "christian" have come to be casually used as inappropriate synonyms for morality. Use instead *ethical, moral, decent, upstanding, righteous, upright, high-minded, honorable, principled, conscientious, moralistic, right, good*. *See also* christian.

judgette *judge*. "Judgette" was actually used to refer ("all in good fun") to Justice Sandra Day O'Connor.

jumping jack the child's toy remains a "jumping jack" when the figure is a man; if it is a clown, use *jumping clown*. For the conditioning exercise, use *side-straddle hop*.

jumpmaster *jump director*.

junior/Jr. only boys/men are juniors; neither girls/women with feminized versions of their father's names nor girls/women named for their mothers get legal tags indicating a name relationship. The old attitudes that go with "junior" children have been more closely associated with boys (laws of primogeniture, the handing on of father-son farms, firms, businesses, etc.) but have been slowly evolving to include girls. Much consciousness has been raised about the power and significance of naming; it remains to be seen what individuals will do with "juniors."

junior executive *executive trainee*. "Junior trainee" is ageist and demeaning.

junior miss *young woman, teenager, high school student, adolescent*. This term is ageist, sexist (no parallel term for boys), coy, old-fashioned, and conveys certain unrealistic cultural stereotypes.

junkman *junk dealer/collector, rag picker*.

jury foreman *See* foreman (jury).

juryman *juror*.

juvenile delinquent *juvenile offender*. Of 1989 juvenile arrests, 1,027,567 were boys/young men, 289,399 were girls/young women. In 1987, 6.9% of the 25,024 young people incarcerated in juvenile institutions were female.

k

Language . . . is one of the instruments of domination. It is carefully guarded by the superior people because it is one of the means through which they conserve their supremacy.

Sheila Rowbotham

kaffeeklatsch in Germany this expression is completely sex-neutral and refers to informal gatherings of both sexes to visit and drink coffee. In the United States, however, it is a belittling, patronizing term for gatherings of women. Use instead: *get together, tea, coffee, coffee break, gathering, social hour, visit, talk, open house, party.*

Kaffir *Xhosa*. The correct term is always the one by which a people refer to themselves.

kaiser roll *Vienna roll*. Also, *hard roll, hamburger roll*. There's nothing much wrong with using "kaiser roll" to describe this crusty bread with its poppy seeds and distinctive crown-like appearance, but alternatives are offered because it is, strictly speaking, a sexist term. Introduced at the 1873 World's Fair in Vienna and named after the kaiser, Emperor Franz Joseph, the rolls were brought to the United States by German and Jewish immigrants.

kapellmeister *choir/orchestra conductor/director/leader.*

keelboatman *keelboater, keeler, keel/barge worker.*

keelsman *See* keelboatman.

keelson probably of Scandinavian origin, this word has nothing to do with male offspring.

keep a stiff upper lip avoid. Although a woman may occasionally be given this sort of advice, it is something of a cultural imperative for men. It's never been clear why repressing feelings and putting a false face on things is desirable; it is far more likely to be unhealthy. *See also* act like a man/be a man/take it like a man.

kennelman *kennel owner/operator/attendant, dog breeder.*

kept woman this term is highly offensive because of (1) the woman's supposed passivity (she is "kept") and (2) the lack of a word to describe her partner. Although two people are involved, only one of them is labeled pejoratively—or even labeled at all. The assumption is that the man is behaving "normally" and thus is still just a man, while the woman's behavior (no different in important respects from his) is "deviant" enough to require a special term. *See also* gigolo.

key man *key person/individual/executive, linchpin, number one, numero uno, leading character, leader, chief, chief cook and bottle washer, pivotal person, cornerstone, focal point, axis, heart, prop, center, main ingredient, vital part.* Try using "key" alone as an adjective or noun: *she's absolutely key to the project, he's the key to this transaction.* Or, choose a punchy adjective: *crucial, critical, pivotal, essential, vital, indispensable.*

kilnman *rotary-kiln operator, kiln worker/supervisor, annealer.*

Kinder, Küche, Kirche the "children, kitchen, and church" slogan was used by the Nazis to reconfine women to their supposed biological roles. The phrase has since been used to describe women's "rightful place" in the scheme of things. Many woman do, in fact, find deep satisfaction in children, kitchen, and spirituality. The problem is applying this "ideal" to every woman, just because and only because she is a woman.

king use only when it is the correct formal title. Otherwise, use *monarch, ruler, sovereign, crowned head, majesty, regent, chief of state, leader, governor, chieftain, potentate, commander, protector; autocrat, tyrant, despot, dictator.* In religious writings, "Sovereign" is often used for God as King, while "ruler" is used for a human king. For its meaning as a superlative use *best, top, expert, superstar, boss, chief, leading light, dean, mogul, nabob, tycoon, high-muck-a-muck, big wheel, big cheese.*

kingcraft *statecraft, diplomacy, political savvy, leadership, politics, the art of governing, holding firmly to the reins of government, wielding the scepter.*

kingdom *realm, land, country, reign, rule, monarchy, domain, dominion, nation, state, world, sovereignty, principality, territory, protectorate, empire, commonwealth, republic, world.* "Reign," "realm," and "dominion" are particularly good for references to the kingdom of God. "Kindom" is sometimes used to express the meaning of "kingdom" without the triumphal and male overtones. "World" can serve in quasi-scientific uses, for example, the animal, mineral, and plant worlds (but retain the biology term "kingdom" in scientific writing). Note that during the reigns of even the most powerful and influential queens (e.g., Queen Elizabeth I), no one ever used the word "queendom."

kingdom come *the next world, paradise.* For the phrase "from here to kingdom come" use *from here to eternity.*

kingliness *nobility, royalty, authority, dignity, gallantry, charisma, greatness.*

kingly *regal, dignified, majestic, imperial, aristocratic, autocratic, courtly, gallant, charismatic, sovereign, royal, dynastic, royalist, monarchical, imperialistic.*

kingmaker *power behind the throne/scenes, power broker, wheeler-dealer, a mover and a shaker, strategist, executive maker, earthshaker, someone with political clout, string-puller, operator.* Plural: *the powers that be.*

king of the hill/king of the mountain Or, *queen of the hill/mountain.* Other possibilities: *big wheel, bigwig, magnate, someone on the top of the heap, monarch of all they survey.*

king of the jungle *monarch/ruler/majesty of the jungle.*

kingpin *linchpin.* See also key man.

king post specific architectural term with no substitute; leave as is.

king's blue *cobalt blue.*

King's Counsel when a queen is on the throne, it's *Queen's Counsel.*

king's English *perfect/standard/correct/pure English, standard usage, correct speech.* When a queen is on the British throne, one ought to hear "the Queen's English," and one does hear it in Great Britain. In the United States "King's English" is used, although it has not been correct since early 1952 when Elizabeth II acceded to the throne.

kingship *monarchy, majesty, royal position, royal office, dignity; statecraft, leadership, diplomacy.*

king-size *jumbo-size, jumbo, super-size, oversized, outsized, gigantic, enormous, huge, extra-large, of heroic proportions, larger than normal/life.* Terms like "king-size" give new meaning to the roles of kings and queens as "rulers." Retain "king-size" when referring to beds and bed linen as the standard use of "single," "double, "queen," and "king" is probably here to stay. But let the objection be stated: who says the king is always larger than the queen?

kinsman/kinswoman use as they are, or, for gender-free terms: *relative, blood relative, relation, cousin, kin, kinsfolk, kith and kin, connection.* Plurals: *kinfolk, relatives, kin.*

knave historically this was a man or boy in roughly the same pejorative sense that "boy" has been used in English for a man. For a tricky, deceitful person, use *mischief-maker, rascal, trickster, troublemaker, sneak; double-crosser, four-flusher, cheater; crook, villain, evildoer, traitor, betrayer.*

knavery *mischief, mischievousness, monkeyshines, shenanigans, hanky-panky, rascality; trickery, roguish trick; baseness, villainy, unscrupulousness, deviltry, wrongdoing.*

knight (noun) the knight of the Round Table was always a man, and there was no equivalent for a woman. Women members of British orders of knighthood are called ladies and addressed as dames (for example, Dame Agatha); only men are called knights and addressed as sirs. For inclusive modern-day alternatives to the metaphorical use of "knight," use *champion, hero.* Full membership in groups with "knight" in their title (for example, the Knights of Columbus) is generally reserved for men. The word "knight" is not always a clue to noble deeds and high-mindedness; the most visible (so to speak) of the infamous kind are the Knights of the Ku Klux Klan.

knight (verb) either a woman or a man may be knighted today, although this was not always the case. *See also* knight (noun).

knight errant *rescuer, champion, hero errant; dreamer, idealist, romantic; philanthropist, altruist, humanitarian.*

knight-errantry *gallantry, nobility, bravery, quixotism, generosity, altruism, philanthropy, kind-heartedness.*

knighthood in the past, reserved for men; today both women and men may be raised to knighthood. *See also* knight (noun); knight (verb).

knight in shining armor this is still used, although there is no good parallel for a woman; perhaps the closest is "woman of my dreams."

knight of the road *vagabond, hitchhiker, hobo. See also* road sister.

knockout avoid. This word, used colloquially to mean a wonderful thing or person, takes on new meaning today: an ad for a woman's shelter asks, "Does your husband think you're a knockout?" Numerous men have been killed or severely injured as a result of knockouts in the "sport" of boxing. *See also* violence.

knock someone up/knock up someone this crude slang expression for getting a woman pregnant is not often used by anyone with any sensibilities, but is included here to illustrate a fairly common street attitude toward women that is at the same time violent and passionless (unfeeling); women are little more than passive, throwaway objects to such a speaker.

The little rift between the sexes is astonishingly widened by simply teaching one set of catchwords to the girls and another to the boys.

Robert Louis Stevenson

lackey historically, lackeys were men. In today's sense of a servile follower, servant, gofer, or toady, a lackey can be either sex.

lad use with "lass." Or: *child, youth.*

ladder man *firefighter.* An old synonym was "shepherd" because of the staff-like rescue hooks carried up the ladders by these firefighters.

ladder man (gambling) *ladder supervisor, overhead spotter/checker, supervisor, spotter, checker, guard, casino employee.*

ladies and gentlemen when used to address an audience, this will probably not set most teeth on edge although it is old-fashioned and the correct pair for "gentlemen" is "gentlewomen," not "ladies." Use contemporary, inclusive terms: *friends, family and friends, colleagues, members of —, staff members,* etc. Or, omit what is often a meaningless phrase and begin directly, "Welcome." *See also* gentlewoman; lady (noun).

ladies' auxiliary the concept is very sexist, but as ladies' auxiliaries become less common, the need for the term will disappear. In the meantime, use it only for women who so name themselves.

ladies' man *popular/successful with the women/the men, heartbreaker, smooth operator, God's gift to men/women.* "Ladies' man" is sexist because there is no equivalent for women ("gentlemen's woman"?) and because of the use of "ladies'." *See also* lady (noun); playboy; womanize/womanizer.

ladies' room *women's room.* The parallel term is "men's room." Although the ratio of men's rooms to women's rooms in most public places is 1:1 there is often a higher combined total of urinals and toilets in men's rooms than toilets in women's rooms. This effectively discriminates against women who for biological reasons generally need more sanitary facilities. Men are more efficient, thanks to their particular physiology, while for women, more complicated clothing, pregnancy, menstruation, and caring for small children mean additional time. To achieve what has been termed potty parity, there is talk of more than doubling the number of toilets in women's rooms in convention halls and performing arts centers.

lady (adj.) *woman.* A sex-identifying adjective is often unnecessary; would you use the adjective "gentleman" for a man in a similar situation? *See also* lady (noun).

lady (noun) *woman.* Many good people have had trouble understanding the objections to "lady." "But isn't that a *nice* word?" they ask. "Lady" defines women as ornaments or decorations rather than real people, as arbiters of both manners and morals, as members of some leisured class, as needing protection from real life, as "too good" or "too special" to "dirty their hands." According to the unspoken operating instructions that come with a "lady," a "lady" doesn't go into combat, do construction work, organize a union, argue publicly with a co-worker, make more money than the men she knows (or even earn a salary at all), or pay for her own lunch. "To want 'equal pay for equal work' and at the same time to be treated 'like a lady' are inconsistent and incompatible objectives" (Laurel Richardson, in *Feminist Frontiers: Rethinking Sex, Gender and Society*). "Lady" is classist, condescending, trivializing, anachronistic, and oppressive. It has served to keep women on a tricky pedestal, in a neatly disguised servanthood—and out of the workplace. Fran Lebowitz says: "The word LADY: Most Often Used to Describe Someone You Wouldn't Want to Talk to for Even Five Minutes." *See also* chivalry.

lady beetle/ladybird/ladybug leave as they are.

ladyfinger leave as is.

ladyfish leave as is.

lady friend/lady love avoid; for alternatives *see* girlfriend. *See also* lady (adj.).

lady-in-waiting *servant, attendant, personal attendant/servant.* Use "lady-in-waiting" when it is an official title.

lady-killer this is sexist (because there is no equivalent for a woman and because of the use of "lady") and unacceptably violent; the term has moved from metaphor to ugly reality as a shocking number of men murder women (one said, "I just wanted her to like me"). One use of "lady killer" that is hard to quarrel with: the American Cancer Society has used it in anti-smoking ads as the cigarette industry targets women to boost sales in a shrinking market. For the usual meaning use instead *popular/successful with the women/the men.*

ladylike avoid. The word "lady" is generally unacceptable, and "ladylike" conveys different meanings according to people's perceptions of what a woman ought or ought not to do, say, think, wear, feel, look like. These subjective cultural judgments have nothing to do with sex and everything to do with gender (*see* the Writing Guidelines for a discussion of the difference between gender and sex). Choose instead precise adjectives: *courteous, well-mannered, civil, polite, tender, cooperative, neat, soft-spoken, gentle, aristocratic, cultured, elegant, proper, correct, gracious, considerate, refined, well-bred, kind, well-spoken.* All these adjectives may be used equally appropriately of a man; they are not synonyms for "ladylike" but rather what people most often mean when they use it. *See also* lady (noun).

lady luck *luck.*

lady of easy virtue/of pleasure/of the evening/of the night *prostitute.* These terms are sexist (there are no parallels for men), coy, and imprecise. Note the irony of the word "pleasure"; more often, the prostitute experiences degradation, pain, or unpleasantness.

lady of the house *head of the house, householder, homeowner, registered voter, taxpayer, citizen, consumer. See also* housewife.

ladyship used of a woman with the rank of lady; the equivalents for a man are "lord/lordship."

lady's maid *attendant, personal attendant/servant.*

lady's slipper/lady's smock/lady's thumb (plants) leave as they are.

laird *landed proprietor,* except where "laird" has specific use and meaning in Scotland.

landlady/landlord *proprietor, owner, land owner, property owner/manager, manager, lessor, manager, building/apartment manager, superintendent, householder, realtor.*

landsman *landlubber. See also* compatriot.

Lapps *Sami.* The correct term is always the one by which a people refer to themselves.

lass use with "lad." Or: *child, youth.*

Latina/Latino use these words correctly ("Latina," female, "Latino," male); they are the terms of choice (greatly preferred to "Hispanic" and "Spanish"). Avoid using "Latino" or "Latinos" as generics; use instead "Latinas and Latinos," for example. The adjective "Latino" is a problem—is "Latino art" the work of only men? In such cases circumlocate or reword to make clear the presence of both women and men.

laundress *launderer, laundry worker. See also* laundryman/laundrywoman.

laundryman/laundrywoman *launderer, washer, clothes washer, laundry attendant/worker/hand/collector/deliverer, dry cleaner.*

lawman *lawmaker, lawgiver, law officer/enforcer, law enforcement officer/agent, defender/upholder/arm/officer of the law.* Or, be specific: *sheriff, deputy, judge, attorney, officer, FBI agent, detective, marshal, police/patrol/peace/ traffic/highway officer, magistrate, justice, constable, warden, bailiff, guard.*

lawyer 20% of the nation's lawyers are women as are 40% of law students. According to a number of studies, women still face many obstacles in the legal profession: pay inequities (a 1990 Minnesota State Bar Association compensation survey showed women attorneys earning a little more than half what men attorneys earned—a "terrific discrepancy" with no acceptable explanation, according to bar officials); lack of litigation (most trial lawyers are men) and other high-visibility work assignments; inability to fulfill their client development obligations because of being excluded from the old-boy network, all-males clubs, sporting events, and after-hours socializing; greater difficulty finding mentors to guide their careers; difficulty in achieving partnerships—the most prestigious law firms will hire women in 22% to 35% of their apprenticeships, but the rate of female partners rarely exceeds 2% or 3%; sexual harassment (in one survey 60% of the women reported unwanted sexual attention); greater conflicts in juggling work and home life than their male colleagues. *See also* courts (judicial).

"lay"/"easy lay"/"good lay" (sex partner) no. Don't. Forget it. Referring to someone like this makes of them an object, an incidental scratch for the speaker's itch. *See also* score.

layman *layperson, laic, member/one of the laity, lay Christian, congregation member, parishioner; amateur, nonprofessional, nonspecialist, nonexpert, the uninitiated, outsider; civilian, secularist; average/ordinary person.* Plurals: *laypeople, the laity, layfolk, congregation members/membership, members of the congregation, the lay public.* Although "-person" words are generally not recommended, "layperson" has gained common acceptance and is one of the few "-person" words that does not seem to jar.

layman's terms *plain/nontechnical/ordinary/uncomplicated/ informal language, common/simple/nontechnical/easy-to-understand/layperson's/lay terms.*

layout man *layout artist/planner/worker, graphic artist, patternmaker, designer, typographer.*

lay-up man *lay-up worker, stocklayer.*

lazy Susan *revolving/relish tray.*

leading lady/leading man *lead, principal.* Note the nonparallel "lady/ man."

leading seaman "seaman" is still an official rank in the U.S. Navy—for both sexes.

leadman *group leader, supervisor; star. See also* foreman (jury).

lead-off man *lead-off batter.*

leadsman *sounder, depth sounder/reader.*

leaseman *lease buyer, leaseholder.*

leatherneck (Marine) woman or man.

lecher/lech by definition a man, "lecher" has no precise inclusive synonyms, but "lech" is used casually for women and there are several
sex-neutral related terms: *sex maniac/fiend, make-out artist, libertine,
debaucher, swinger, bedhopper, seducer.*

lefthanded *backhanded, offhanded, ambiguous, dubious, insincere, clumsy,
awkward.* Do not use "lefthanded" metaphorically; it perpetuates
subtle but age-old negative associations for those who are physically
left-handed. If it's true that we favor the half of our brain opposite
our hand preference, left-handed people may be the only truly "right-
minded" ones among us.

legionnaire invariably a man. In the American Legion, women are "full
members" in the auxiliary but are not called legionnaires.

Legion of Honor/Legion of Merit all orders are awarded to both women
and men.

legislator 1,256 state legislators (16%) are women as are 30 members of
the House of Congress.

legman *gofer, assistant, clerk, courier, runner, carrier, messenger, deliverer,
page; reporter, correspondent.*

leman *lover.* Oddly enough with its "-man," this is usually defined as a
"mistress" (sexual sense).

leper/leprosy *person with Hansen's disease; Hansen's disease.* We no longer
name the whole person by something that is only part of them, nor
do we say someone is "suffering from" or "a victim of" Hansen's
disease. A chronic, infectious germ-caused disease, Hansen's is still
one of the least contagious of all communicable diseases; only about
4.5% of the world's population is even susceptible to it. There are
approximately 11 million cases in the world (about 5,000 in the
United States).

lesbian (noun/adj.) this acceptable gender-specific word, the term preferred by most of the estimated six to thirteen million lesbians in the
United States, is derived from Lesbos, the Greek island that was
home to the poet Sappho and her students. Respect the distinction
between "gay" (men) and "lesbian" (women); with the concurrence
of the women's liberation movement and the gay rights movement,
lesbians have chosen to assert their independence from men of either
sexual preference. When "gay" appears alone, you may generally
assume it refers only to men. Occasionally "gay" is used as an
adjective to include both women and men, but most often "lesbian
and gay" is the inclusive adjectival form, for example, Lesbian and
Gay People in Medicine, the Institute for the Protection of Lesbian
and Gay Youth, the Lesbian/Gay Health Conference. Do not use
"lesbian" as an adjective unless it is truly necessary to your material;
mention of a person's sexual preference is often gratuitous. *See also*
gay (adj); Gay Rights Movement; heterosexism; homophobia; homosexual.

lesbie/lesbo/lezzie these terms fall under the "inside/outsider" rule, which means it's acceptable for lesbians to use the terms positively among themselves, but it is rarely acceptable for someone outside the group to use them.

let 'er rip *let it rip/go/roll/start! There's the signal! Time to start!* Maurice Sendak's contribution (*Where the Wild Things Are*): *let the wild rumpus start!*

let George do it *let somebody else do it, pass the buck.*

letterman *letterholder, letter winner, lettered athlete; letterwoman and letterman* if used fairly.

leverman *lever operator.*

lib/libber *liberationist, feminist, member of the women's liberation movement.* "Lib" and "libber" are derogatory and offensive, and they generally indicate hostility on the part of those who use them.

librarian about 15% of librarians are men as are less than 10% of elementary school librarians.

liegeman *servant, subject, fiefholder, vassal.* Historically a liegeman was always a man; his wife and children were assumed to be part of him, not separate "liegemen."

lifemanship *put-down artistry, superiority complex.* This is a difficult term to replace with one word; circumlocution, elaboration of the characteristic, or showing the person's orientation instead of just telling about it are possible solutions.

life of Riley although "leading/living the life of Riley" probably came from Pat Rooney's 1883 comic song, "Is That Mr. Reilly?" (which tells what a suddenly rich Mr. Reilly would do, such as sleeping in the president's chair and buying up hotels), it has long since been used of both sexes.

liftman (British) *lift operator.*

like a man replace this impossibly vague cultural stereotype with precise descriptions: *with a high/strong hand, with a head for mechanics, resolutely, courageously, competitively, self-confidently, in a straightforward manner,* etc.

like father, like son *the acorn doesn't fall far from the tree, a chip off/of the old block, spit and image, spitting image, birds of a feather, the very image of, for all the world like, as like as two peas, take after, follow in the parent's footsteps, take a leaf from the parent's book, like parent like child.*

limp-wristed this stereotypical adjective is inaccurate most of the time and objectionable all of the time.

line foreman *line supervisor.*

lineman (sports) *line player, offensive/defensive tackle/guard/center; line umpire.* As long as football players continue to be boys or men, "line man" is acceptable; because some sports have female umpires, it is better to use "line umpire."

lineman/linewoman (job title) *lineworker, line installer/repairer/fixer/main-tainer/erector/installer-repairer/supervisor, line-service attendant, rigger, electrician.*

linesman *line tender/judge/referee.*

linkboy/linkman *torch carrier, light attendant.* Or, retain in historical contexts as they were boys/men. For "linkman" as used chiefly in Great Britain, *see* anchorman (newscasting).

linksman *golfer, golf player.*

little boys'/little girls' room unless found in a preschool daycare center, these terms are too too cute. In elementary schools, for example, use *boys' room/girls' room.* In most other cases use *women's room/men's room.*

little Hitler avoid. This term is largely reserved for men but, more important, it trivializes World War II and desensitizes us to something that we need to continue to regard with horror.

little lady it is never correct to refer to an adult woman this way, and there is no acceptable substitute because the very notion is demeaning. It is also incorrect to refer to a child this way because (1) a child is not an adult and should be allowed to be a child while she is a child and (2) telling a child she is a little lady almost without exception is an attempt to perpetuate some cultural stereotype, e.g., sitting quietly and neatly in the background. There is nothing wrong per se with this behavior, but "little lady" tells the child this is the desired, best behavior for all occasions.

Little League open to both boys and girls, although of its 2.5 million members, only several thousand are girls so far.

little man unlike "little woman," which can also be used to refer to an adult woman, "little man" is reserved for boys. Avoid it because (1) a child is not an adult and should be allowed to be a child while he is a child and (2) telling a child he is a litle man almost without exception is an attempt to perpetuate some cultural stereotype, e.g., not showing emotions. There is nothing wrong with occasionally suppressing fear or refraining from crying, for example, but a boy should not be taught that this is the desired, best behavior in all circumstances.

little shaver *youngster, tyke, child.* Although the origins of this expression may not be as masculine as they sound ("shaver" deriving perhaps from the chip-off-the-old-block kind of shaving rather than from whisker shaving), it is defined either as a youngster or as a boy and it is perceived as masculine.

little woman, the *spouse, partner, wife.* Never use this, even (especially) as intended humor.

liveryman *livery worker, vehicle-rental service operator; liveried retainer.*

living doll unlike other uses of "doll," this one refers to both sexes. Although it seems that there ought to be a general rule not to refer to people as dolls (because of all the implications of making objects of them), this particular expression has always been fairly benign, and there seems to be no difference in tone, intent, or significance between references to men and women.

lobsterman *lobster catcher/fisher/farmer/grower/cultivator/dealer.*

Lolita *sexually precocious; underage and seductive.* There is no parallel for a boy. The Lolita stereotype of a child who wants and can sustain a sexual relationship has been immeasurably harmful. It's not only beauty that's in the eye of the beholder; some people see desire where there is none. Several groups argue for "sexual freedom" for children, maintaining that children actually want and need sexual experience with an adult. Kiddie sex is a flourishing business in various parts of the country, but it is not the runaway street children who want sex (although they do want the money, food, or drugs it brings them), but the unhealthy, twisted adults. *See also* pornography.

lone wolf woman or man.

longbowman *archer, longbow archer.* Or, retain in historical contexts.

longjohns *woolies, winter underwear, BVDs.*

longshoreman *longshore worker, stevedore, dockhand, dockworker, shorehand, shoreworker, wharfworker, wharfhand, ship loader.*

looksism "Most women are still judged primarily by their beauty or attractiveness, whereas men are judged primarily in terms of their achievements. We still live in a society where more money is spent on women's looks than on social service programs" (Nijole V. Benokraitis and Joe R. Feagin, *Modern Sexism*). Although Americans give lip service (and some actually believe) that health, happiness, intelligence, effort, talent, and achievements are more important for a woman than looks, over 80% of those having cosmetic surgery are women and the most popular operations are breast-related: in one recent year there were 95,000 breast augmentations, 16,200 breast lifts—and 4,500 hair transplants for men. However, plastic surgery for men is increasing rapidly, particularly in the area of pectoral implants. "It opens up a whole new field of changing the body to fit accepted norms," says Beverly Hills plastic surgeon and pectoral implanter Dr. Mel Bircoll. The *Wall Street Journal* reported in 1990 that the number of teenagers undergoing plastic surgery doubled in five years; plastic surgeons now do 25% of their business with people not old enough to vote. The media perpetuate looksism by including irrelevant information and descriptors of women's appearance when to do so for men would be considered ludicrous. *See also* body image.

loose woman if you mean prostitute, use *prostitute.* If you mean a woman of questionable morals (which is a questionable judgment) say exactly what you mean using inclusive words: *promiscuous, sexually active, indiscriminating,* etc. The language has no such expression as "loose man," yet a "loose woman" must, by definition, have a partner; avoid judging one sex by criteria not applied to the other.

Lord retain "Lord" when referring to the Lord Jesus Christ, as that is part of who he is (the masculine pronoun referring to Jesus is of course correct). However, "Lord," when referring to the Godhead (not the person of Christ) can be replaced with *Advocate, Almighty/the Almighty, Author, Being, Creator, Creator of all things, Defender, the Deity, Divine Light, the Eternal, Eternal One, Ever-present God, First Cause, Friend, God, Godhead, God my Rock, God my Rock and my Redeemer, God of Abraham and Sarah, God of Grace, God of Heaven, God of Hosts, God of Israel, God of our ancestors/forebears, God of the Nations, Good Parent, Guide, Heavenly Creator, Heavenly Parent, Holy One/the Holy One, Holy One of Israel, the Infinite, Just One, Liberator, Living God, Maker, Merciful God, Mighty One, Most High/the Most High, Most Loving God, Nurturer, O God my God, O Gracious God, Omnipotent One, our Refuge and our Strength, Powerful One, Preserver, Providence, Redeemer, Rock, Rock of Refuge, Ruler, Savior, Shepherd, Shepherd of Israel, Source/the Source, Source of Life, Sovereign, Spirit, Supreme Being, Sustainer, Wisdom.* Avoid masculine pronouns referring to God. *See* God/he; God/ himself; God/his. *See also* Father (God); Father, Son, and Holy Spirit/Ghost; God; Holy Spirit (Ghost)/he; Lord's Prayer, the; Son of Man (Christ).

lord and master (husband) avoid, even if you think it's cute or funny (attitudes that will date you).

lord it over someone *dominate, domineer, boss around, browbeat, bully, intimidate, tyrannize, overshadow, overpower, oppress, wear the crown, ride herd on, be hard upon, rule with a high hand, have the upper hand, deal hardly with, call the shots, run the show, keep a tight rein on, lay down the law, bend to one's will.*

lordliness *stateliness, dignity, majesty, elegance, splendor; high-handedness, arrogance, haughtiness, imperiousness, insolence, overconfidence, conceit, condescension, pomposity.*

lordly *stately, imperial, imposing, dignified, noble, majestic, august; haughty, arrogant, insolent, overbearing, imperious, condescending, high-handed, domineering, arbitrary, peremptory, dictatorial, tyrannical, presumptuous, overconfident, snobbish, commanding, pushy, bossy.*

lord mayor leave as is where used officially (as in Great Britain).

lord of the manor, play *swagger, give oneself airs, act big, ride a high horse, act the high-and-mighty, be insolent/haughty/overbearing/pretentious/self-important/pushy/snobbish/pompous/high-handed.* *See also* lord it over someone.

Lord's Day *Sunday.*

lordship used of a man with the rank of lord; the equivalent for a woman is "ladyship."

Lord's Prayer, the some people feel that the two sex-linked words in this prayer ("Father" and "kingdom") are not sexist, but are instead theologically and scripturally sound and necessary. Others disagree, and feel that the spirit of the prayer is in no way violated by replacing "Father" with "God," "Mother/Father," or another title, and "kingdom" with "dominion" or other synonym. That the word "Father" is even what was intended is doubtful. Neil Douglas-Klotz, who transliterates the "Our Father" from Syriac Aramaic, says that where we say "Father," the original was something like, "O Thou from whom comes the breath of life" or "O Thou, the Breath, the Light of All"; the words are neither male nor female. An inclusive Lord's Prayer might look like this: *Our God in heaven, holy be your name. Your dominion come, your will be done, on earth as it is in heaven. Give us this day our daily bread. Forgive us our trespasses, as we forgive those who trespass against us. Let us not be led into temptation, but deliver us from evil. For the dominion, the power, and the glory are yours, now and forever. Amen.*

Lothario if you need inclusive alternatives use *heartbreaker, seducer, deceiver, libertine, lover, great/dashing lover, make-out artist, smooth operator, swinger, flame, admirer, flirt.*

lounge lizard *social parasite.* This phrase is functionally sexist because it's used only of men.

love, honor, and obey (wedding ceremony) *love, honor, and cherish; love, respect, and cherish; develop mutual love and respect; love, honor, and reverence; love, encourage, and accept; love and honor; love and cherish.*

lover acceptable and useful sex-inclusive term describing individuals of any sexual orientation.

lowboy nonsexist; "boy" comes from the French for "wood," "bois."

lowerclassman *beginning student, first- or second-year student.* **See also** freshman.

low man on the totem pole *lowest ranking individual, new kid on the street, someone with no seniority/clout, the last one in, washout, loser, three-time loser, hard-luck case, defeatee, the low scorer, also-ran, plebian, neophyte, proletarian, rookie, beginner, tyro, gofer.* The phrase is ethnocentric as well as sexist.

lumberjack/lumberman *lumber worker/cutter, logger, tree cutter, woodcutter, log roller, timber worker, forester, sawyer, woodchopper.*

lust properly (or improperly) attributed to either sex.

m

The subtlest and most pervasive of influences are those which create and maintain the repertory of stereotypes. We are told about the world before we see it. We imagine most things before we experience them. And those preconceptions, unless education has made us acutely aware, govern deeply the whole process of perception.

Walter Lippmann

ma'am used in the same way "sir" is used for men, this contraction for "madam" is practical, appropriate, and in no way derogatory. *See also* madam.

macho by definition, only men can be macho; there is no parallel for women ("macha" is incorrect). Because "macho" is so often used derogatorily and stereotypically, it may be better to replace it: *overly aggressive, defensive, proud, overbearing, overconfident, show-off, arrogant,* etc. The word "machismo" has been used of both sexes: Betty Friedan (*The Second Stage*) says "female machismo . . . hides the same inadmissible self-hate, weakness, sense of powerlessness as machismo hides in men."

madam "madam" is a valuable term, used for a woman in the same way "sir" is used for a man. Use it to address women you don't know or know only very slightly. At one time it appeared to be losing its respectability because of its other meaning: female head of a house of prostitution. Like so many of the female words in male-female word pairs, it had been deeply discounted. (Notice how nice "sir" has always been.) For someone connected with prostitution, use *prostitute, owner/head of house of prostitution*. Use "madam" only for social address.

mad as a wet hen this is harmless enough, but if you need a sex-neutral expression try *mad as a hatter/hornet/as a bear with a sore head/as blazes*.

mademoiselle use only for a Frenchwoman who calls herself "mademoiselle." In France, "mademoiselle" is generally reserved for women in their teens or early to mid-twenties while "madame" is used for older women—in both cases irrespective of their marital status. This was once also the case with "Miss" and "Mrs." *See also* Miss/miss/missy; Mrs.; Ms.

madman/madwoman avoid. These terms are gender-fair but they are psychologically inaccurate and insubstantial. If a person's mental condition must be mentioned, use *a person with obsessive-compulsive disorder* or whatever the correct medical terminology is; avoid identifying the whole person with one aspect of their existence. *See also* insane/insanity; insane asylum.

maestro *conductor, orchestra leader; expert.*

Mafia *organized crime, the underworld.* "Mafia" is often carelessly and incorrectly used for any organized crime groups.

magdalen *reformed prostitute.*

magsman *safecracker.*

maharaja/maharani acceptable sex-specific words.

maid *household servant/worker/cleaner/helper, houseworker, servant, housekeeper, room attendant, attendant, cleaner, house cleaner/servant, custodian, janitor.* *See also* charwoman; handyman.

maid/matron of honor *attendant, best woman, attendant of honor, honor/wedding/bride's attendant.* Whichever term you choose, be sure that the groom's attendant is referred to with a parallel term, for example, *best woman and best man, bride's attendant and groom's attendant.* *See also* best man.

maiden (adj.) *first, inaugural, initial, premier, earliest, new, untried, untested, untapped, unused, fresh, intact, inexperienced; single, unmarried, unwed, unwedded, celibate.* Use terms like "single" and "unmarried," only if this information is necessary. *See also* maiden voyage.

maiden (noun) use only when quoting or in historical contexts.

maidenhead *hymen, virginity.* However, beware of some strange cultural attitudes about these terms. *See also* virgin/virginity.

maidenhood *youth, innocence, adolescence.* There is little reason to use the outdated and problematic "maidenhood"; avoid it. *See also* virgin/virginity.

maiden lady *See* spinster.

maidenly this is so vague that using it is not good communication; your audience will be no wiser. Decide what qualities you mean to convey and use them.

maiden name *birth/given/birth family/family/former/original name, family of origin name.* "Birth name" is the most commonly used term. A Rhode Island probate court judge surprised a woman who thought her birth name was hers by ruling that a wife could not use her birth name without her husband's permission; the American Civil Liberties Union challenged the ruling.

maiden voyage *first/premier voyage, first trip.*

maid of all work *general servant.* *See also* charwoman; cleaning girl/ cleaning lady/cleaning woman; handyman; maid.

mailboy *mail messenger.*

mailman *mailcarrier, letter carrier, mail handler/deliverer/clerk, postal worker/ clerk/officer.* Both the National Association of Letter Carriers and the National Postal Mail Handlers Union use inclusive terms. About 22% of mailcarriers are women.

mail order bride use as is in historical contexts; there has never been anything remotely parallel for men.

main man (slang) *best friend, mentor, hero, partner.* "Main man" has such a particular meaning that in most cases it is probably irreplaceable if you are writing or reporting street talk.

maintenance man *maintenance worker/engineer/mechanic/repairer/ specialist, maintainer, repairer, cleaner, office cleaner, custodian, janitor, porter, factotum, odd/general jobber, fixer, fixer-upper, troubleshooter.*

maître d'hôtel *dining room/restaurant host, host, head waiter, majordomo, hotel manager/steward/proprietor.*

majordomo man or woman; this term comes from the Latin for "elder of the house."

majorette *drum major, baton twirler, marching band leader, major.*

make a man of *be the making of, do a world of good, improve, mature, toughen up.*

makeup girl/makeup man *makeup artist.* Note the nonparallel "girl/ man."

malapropism from Mrs. Malaprop in Richard B. Sheridan's comedy *The Rivals* (1775), the word "malaprop" has passed into the language with no rival (although "spoonerism" is a near relative) and with no pithy substitute or alternative. Few people perceive the term as sex-linked. *See also* spoonerism.

male (adj.) use only when you would use "female" or when it is necessary for clarification; this adjective is often inserted gratuitously, for example, "male nurse," "male secretary," "male model," "male prostitute." Watch particularly for nonparallel usage, for example, "three male dancers and one woman dancer." *See also* male (noun).

male (noun) avoid the use of "male" as a noun except in technical writing, for example, medicine, statistics, police reports, sociology. It is most often reserved for biological or nonhuman references. When using "male" as a noun, beware of nonparallel constructions, for example, "three women and two males." *See also* male (adj.).

male bonding writing in *The New Republic*, Robert Wright says it's unclear "whether the intense bonds formed during war, and all the valor and sacrifice they inspire, result from 'male bonding' or simply 'person-under-fire bonding.'" The traditional meaning of male bonding is being replaced by a new and vigorous sense of what it means to men to be with other men as friends, brothers, and companions on the journey.

male chauvinist/male chauvinist pig *chauvinist, sex-chauvinist*. "Chauvinism" used to refer to the view that one's own country was vastly superior, right or wrong, to all other countries. Dictionaries now also define "chauvinism" as the view that one's own sex is vastly superior. Either a man or a woman can be a sex-chauvinist.

male-dominated society *dominator system, dominator model of society, hierarchy, hierarchical society*. The first two highly recommended alternatives are from Riane Eisler (*The Chalice and the Blade*). There is perhaps good reason to speak of a male-dominated society and especially a male-dominated language, although not in terms of the actions of individual men but rather in terms of an ethic that has supported the supremacy of all things male: "inasmuch as the masculine sex is the superior and more excellent"; "the male being, according to our ideas, the nobler sex"; "in all languages, the masculine gender is considered the most worthy" (quoted in Francine Wattman Frank and Paula A. Treichler, *Language, Gender, and Professional Writing*, p. 83). However, it is far more helpful today to think in terms of dominator versus partnership societies rather than in terms of male versus female systems. *See also* chivalry; matriarch/matriarchy; patriarch/patriarchy.

male ego *ego*.

male menopause *climacteric*. By definition menopause is the cessation of human egg production, and thus specific to women. However, there is a corresponding period in men called the climacteric. Although levels of testosterone do not usually decline significantly until around age seventy, some men in their fifties and sixties experience a gradual waning of the sex urge and occasional sleep problems, mood swings, depression, and anxiety—which could also be related to a mid-life crisis. *See also* mid-life crisis.

"male privilege" a few of the benefits men have traditionally enjoyed primarily because they are men generally include being paid more for comparable work, being able to ignore what women say and to interrupt them more frequently than women interrupt them, to be deferred to in group situations, to be called on more frequently in the classroom, within reason to go where they like without fearing assault, rape, or sexual harassment, to do a disproportionately smaller share of housework and childcare, and even, in many cases and over centuries, to define reality. Along with all this, however, has come the "privilege" today—simply because they are men—of registering for the draft, fighting in combat, dying earlier than women, and generally wearing the "provider" hat for wife, children, and extended family. Certain men may be privileged—as are certain women; it is incorrect, however, to refer stereotypically to "male privilege" as though it were a fact of life. Herb Goldberg (*The Hazards of Being Male*) reports that "every critical statistic in the area of [early death], death, suicide, crime, accidents, childhoood emotional disorders, alcoholism, and drug addition shows a disproportionately higher male rate."

males-only draft "no form of sex discrimination, against either gender, has been as devastating and deadly as the military draft" (Mel Feit, *University of Dayton Review*, Winter-Spring 1986-87). Feit speaks for many men when he says bitterly: "We live in a strange society in which conscripted men have been deprived of their freedom and comfort, stripped of their dignity and civil rights, forced to leave their family and friends, compelled to interrupt their careers, brutally trained to kill or be killed, murdered and maimed in warfare, and where the public perception is that the victims of sex discrimination have been women. Incredible." Whether it benefits us to discuss who has been the most discriminated against, there is no denying the horrific gender genocide in the males-only draft and males-only combat laws. Ellen Goodman said: "Are Americans ready to see women come home in body bags? I hope not. But . . . [w]hy are we ready to see men come home in body bags? . . . In the end, this must be said: Any war that isn't worth a woman's life isn't worth a man's life." Who is served by our cavalier attitude toward "disposable" men and the continuing acculturation of men as warmakers? The answer might include people with traditional values and mindsets, but it must also include those who profit from war, those who understand that as long as only men die in wars, wars will remain facile solutions to small and large problems. The charge that "men make wars" and that therefore it is only right that they (and not women) fight in the front lines of the wars does not hold water. For one thing, there are the men who make the wars and the men who actually go to war; of the 56,886 Americans killed in the Vietnam War, there were 0 lawmakers. For another thing, women, from Queen Elizabeth I to Maggie Thatcher, have sent men into wars. It is not particularly women who resist doing their part; in a *Glamour* magazine survey, 70% of women between eighteen and thirty-five believe that women should be drafted if men are, especially in the event of a crisis, and 60% don't think military women should be kept out of a combat. *See also* armed forces; combat; coward/cowardly/cowardice; draft dodger; serviceman (armed forces); sexism; warrior.

mama's boy *spoiled/immature/irresponsible person*. "Mama's boy" is an unfortunate cultural stereotype that keeps many parents from giving their sons the nurturing they need (and that they continue to seek, often in inappropriate ways, throughout life). Daughters, on the other hand, are encouraged (also with sometimes unfortunate results) to be clinging and dependent.

mammal Eugene R. August of the University of Dayton points out that "by categorizing animals according to the female's ability to suckle the young through her mammary glands, *mammal* clearly omits the male of the species."

"mammy" avoid. This term is sexist (there is no parallel term for a man), racist, and a stereotype that was probably always highly mythical.

man (adult male human being) this narrow definition is the only acceptable nonsexist usage for the noun. Dictionaries list two major definitions for "man": (1) adult male, (2) human being. However studies have shown that people "hear" only the first meaning of the word. *See* Writing Guidelines for a discussion of pseudogeneric man. *See also* bad guy; coward/cowardly/cowardice; gender roles; males-only draft; "male privilege"; Man/man (pseudogeneric); provider; sex differences.

man (chess, checkers, games) *piece.*

man- many words beginning with "man-" come from the Latin for "hand" and are not sexist: manacle, mandate, maneuver, manger, mangle, mangy, manicure, manifest/manifestation, maniple, manipulate, mansion, mantel, mantis, manual, manufacture, manumission, manure, manuscript. Other words that begin with "man-" have nonsexist roots: manciple (from Latin for "purchase"); mandrake (from a Greek term for the plant); manege (from Italian for "horse training"); manes (from Greek for "spirit"); mangrove (from Spanish for the tree); Manhattan (from Native American word for "island"); mania (from Greek for "spirit"); Manichaeism (from Mani, the Iranian founder); manifold (from Old English for "many"); manor/mansion (from Latin for "dwell"); mantle (from Latin for "cloak"). *See also* Isle of Man; mandarin.

Man/man (pseudogeneric) *person/s, people, human/s, human being/s, the human race/family, civilization, society, individual/s, one, creature/s, creation, all creation, mortal/s, body, somebody, someone, anyone, soul/s, living soul/s, all living souls, society, all of us, ourselves, everyone, humankind, humanity, human society/nature/species/creatures/populations, early peoples, we, us, mortality, flesh, all generations, folk/s, the public, the general public, the world, community, the larger community, nation, state, realm, commonweal, commonwealth, republic, body politic, population, resident/s, inhabitant/s, adult/s, citizen/s, taxpayer/s, worker/s, member/s, partipant/s, hand/s, party/parties, earthling/s, worldling/s, our ancestors, figure (snow figure, underworld figure), women and men.* Or, be specific: *Neolithic peoples, early settlers, fifteenth-century Europe, civilization as we know it,* etc. Although many people, including both women and men, insist that "man" is a generic term, that usage was declared obsolete in 1971 by both the National Council for Teachers of English and the *Oxford English Dictionary*, and a close reading of books published before the 1970s shows that "man" never was truly generic. Erich Fromm wrote that "man" needs food, shelter, and access to females. The "man/men" in our own constitution couldn't have been generic since it took two constitutional amendments to give the vote to those who were not white men. A well-educated young man of the 1990s explained that his western civilization textbook used the terms "man" and "mankind" because "women were dogs. They didn't contribute anything. You might as well say 'men and their dogs plowed the field.' That's why my book uses 'man' and 'mankind.'" *See also* man (adult male human being); manhood.

man/manned for the verb use *operate, staff, run, supply a crew/personnel for, supply with/furnish with personnel/crew, people, populate, work, serve at/ on, control, cover, occupy, equip, hire, employ, station, arm, brace, fortify, garrison, prepare, protect.* For the adjective use *staffed, crewed, peopled, populated, operated, serviced, stationed, worked, run, covered, handled.*

-man/-men not all words that end in "man/-men" are sex-linked. For example, "dolman" is from "dolama," a Turkish robe; "ottoman" from the French for "Turk"; a Roman or a German may be either female or male; "talisman" from Greek for "consecration"; "whatman" is named after James Whatman; "amen" comes from the Hebrew for "truly" or "certainly"; "catechumen" from the Greek for "someone being instructed"; "tegmen" from the Latin for "covering"; "gravamen" from the Latin for "burden." When in doubt, see a dictionary. *See also* dragoman; Pullman car/pullman porter.

man about town *worldly person, sophisticate, socially active person, swinger, mover, high-liver, high-flier.* Any of the foregoing can be used for either sex whereas there is no phrase for women parallel to "man about town." A woman who has "been around" is not being complimented—au contraire. *See also* ladies' man; playboy; rake; womanize/womanizer.

man after one's own heart, a *someone after one's own heart, someone for whom you have a soft spot, persona grata, favorite, general favorite, apple of one's eye.*

"man against man, man against himself, man against nature" *the individual against self, other, and nature; literary characters may experience conflict within themselves, with others, or with nature.*

manageress *manager.* Although "manager" is nonsexist (it comes from Latin, "hand"), many women say the word feels sexist to them because the "man" in the word is so reinforced by management practices, by the glass ceiling for women, and by the fact that management remains, in many areas, a male bastion. Although the number of women holding middle management jobs increased from

14% in 1965 to over 33% twenty years later, the percentage of women in senior management, as well as the number who are members of corporate boards, has barely changed in twenty-five years (Edith Gilson with Susan Kane, *Unnecessary Choices: The Hidden Life of the Executive Woman*). A 1990 *Fortune* magazine study found that in the highest echelons of corporate managers, fewer than one-half of 1% are women. Women themselves aren't optimistic about their opportunities: *The Harvard Business Review* polled managerial women in 1965 and again in 1985, and the number who felt that women had equal opportunities for advancement within their own companies dropped from 40% to 33%. *See also* directress; executive; glass ceiling; wage earner.

man alive! *good grief! gee! gee whiz! gosh! golly! wow!*

man among men *one in a million, salt of the earth, one of the best, oustanding human being, ace, hero, champion, paragon, shining example, trump, marvel, a real lifesaver, a one-off.*

man and wife never use this; it is a nonparallel construction. Use instead *man and woman/woman and man, wife and husband/husband and wife, spouses, mates, partners, married couple.*

man-at-arms *warrior, soldier, combatant.*

man bites dog story there is currently no good gender-free substitute for this colorful phrase; it conveys something very particular that would be lost in translation. That doesn't mean, of course, that someone won't eventually come up with an equally pithy and evocative—but inclusive—phrase.

man-child use with "woman-child," not "girl-child," as is generally done. If "girl-child" is used, then "boy-child" is the equivalent, not "man-child."

mandarin when this term refers to a public official in the Chinese Empire, it is always male (but not because of the "man," which is part of the Sanskrit word for "counselor"). Its other uses are nonsexist.

man-day *worker-day, workday, labor-day, average worker day.*

man does not live by bread alone *we/you/people do not live by bread alone, one does not live by bread alone, not by bread alone do we/does one live.* According to the New Revised Standard Version of the Bible, approved for use in the nation's major Protestant churches, this phrase is rendered, "One does not live by bread alone."

man-eater/man-eating *people-eater, human-eater, flesh-eater, carnivore, omnivore, cannibal; people-eating, human-eating, flesh-eating, carnivorous, omnivorous, cannibalistic, dangerous, deadly.*

man for all seasons *a person of many parts, woman for all seasons and man for all seasons, a Renaissance individual, all-around expert.*

man-for-man *player-for-player, one-on-one.*

man Friday *assistant, office/administrative/executive/program assistant, aide, clerk, right hand, secretary, gofer; man Friday and woman Friday if used* gender-fairly, although the convention generally remains limited to "woman Friday" and even then it seems difficult for people to use "woman Friday" instead of the familiar "girl Friday." Note the nonparallel "man/girl."

manful/manfully for these vague cultural stereotypes substitute precise words: *strong/strongly, resolute/resolutely, brave/bravely, courageous/ courageously, mighty/mightily, vigorous/vigorously, robust/robustly, sturdy/sturdily, powerful/powerfully, potent/potently, indomitable/indomitably, husky/huskily, energetic/energetically, bold/boldly, defiant/defiantly, unflinching/unflinchingly, inexorable/inexorably, dogged/doggedly,* etc. All these adjectives/adverbs can be used for both sexes; they are not synonyms for "manful/manfully," but they are what is most commonly meant by the terms.

manhandle *abuse, mistreat, maltreat, mishandle, damage, maul, batter, push/ kick/knock around, paw, maul, subdue, force, handle roughly, rough up, beat up, pummel, thrash, strike, injure.*

man-hater/woman-hater these sex-specific terms are acceptable if used in their narrowest sense and not as a stereotypical put-down. *See also* misanthrope/misogynist.

manhole *sewer hole, utility access hole.* Also, *utility/access hole, sewer access, streethole, vent hole, utility tunnel, exit port, sewer viewer, peephole, underground service access hole.*

manhole cover *sewer cover, street hole cover.* Also, *utility/utility-hole/access/ sewer-hole/access-hole/street/utility-access/sewer-access cover, sewer cover/ top.*

manhood "manhood" has four dictionary definitions. (1) Do not use it to mean "the condition of being human"; this is a pseudogeneric. A useful and popular alternative is *personhood.* (2) Do not use "manhood" to mean "human beings"; this is also a pseudogeneric. (3) When you are referring to manly qualities in a man, its use is correct although your sentence will almost always benefit from more specific words: *pride, self-confidence, vigor, strength, courage, maturity,* etc. (4) Use "manhood" anytime to mean the condition of being an adult male human being. ("Womanhood" is the parallel term.) *See also* man (adult male human being); Man/man (pseudogeneric); mankind.

man-hours *total hours, hours, worker/work/working/staff/labor/ operator/typist/ employee hours, hours of work, hours worked, work/staff time, labor, time, labor time.*

manhunt *dragnet, chase, fugitive/person hunt, search for a fugitive, search, hunt.* "Manhunt" is one of the more difficult sexist words in that there currently exists no equally brief and descriptive inclusive term. When possible avoid it by circumlocution.

manikin/mannikin *miniature person.* "Manikin" not only looks masculine, it means "little man." There is no parallel term for a woman. *See also* mannequin.

man-induced *artificially/humanly induced, human-caused, manufactured, of human genesis/origin(s).*

man in motion *player in motion.*

man in office *person in authority/office, official.*

man in the moon *face in the moon.*

man in the street *average person/citizen/human/human being/voter, common person/citizen/human/human being/voter, ordinary person/citizen/human/ human being/voter, citizen, voter, layperson, taxpayer, resident, homeowner, householder, landowner, passerby, nonspecialist, commoner, one of the people/masses, rank and file, average/typical worker; average woman and average man if used gender-fairly.*

man is known by the company he keeps, a *people/we/you are known by the company they/we/you keep, one is known by the company one keeps, birds of a feather flock together, we are judged by the company we keep, show me your company and I'll tell you who you are.*

man-killer *killer, murderer, slayer, assassin, cutthroat, sniper, silencer, dispatcher, liquidator, hired gun, bloodshedder.* **See also** gunman.

mankind *humanity, humankind, people, human beings, humans, human society/nature/species/creatures/populations, the human race/family, civilization, society, individuals, one, creatures, creation, all creation, mortals, body, somebody, someone, anyone, souls, living souls, all living souls, society, all of us, ourselves, everyone, early peoples, we, us, mortality, flesh, all generations, folks, persons, the public, the general public, the world, community, the larger community, nation, state, realm, commonweal, commonwealth, republic, body politic, population, residents, inhabitants, adults, citizens, taxpayers, workers, members, participants, hands, parties, earthlings, worldlings, our ancestors, women and men.* Or, be specific: *Neolithic peoples, early settlers, fifteenth-century Europe, civilization as we know it,* etc. *See also* Man/men (pseudogeneric).

manlike/manly avoid these vague cultural stereotypes. By definition, whatever a man does is manly or manlike because a man is doing it. Choose instead precise adjectives: *courageous, strong, brave, upright, honorable, mature, noble, resolute, straightforward, vigorous, adventurous, spirited, direct, competitive, physical, mechanical, logical, rude, active, self-confident,* etc. These words apply equally well to either sex.

manly art of self defense if you want a cliché, use *the noble art of self defense.* Both expressions came from eighteenth-century advertisements for boxing lessons taught in Great Britain by prizefighter Jack Broughton. Self-defense has also of necessity become a womanly art.

manmade *artificial, handmade, human-made, hand-built, synthetic, made, manufactured, fabricated, machine-made, homemade, produced, mass-produced, machine-produced, crafted, constructed, custom-made, simulated, machine-simulated, plastic, imitation, bogus, mock, spurious, counterfeit, fictitious, contrived, human-constructed, of human origin, result of human* *activity*. "Manmade" can often be left out entirely without affecting the meaning of the sentence. It is one of those words that we tend to believe is irreplaceable, yet much of our resistance to replacing it is habit; if you say "human-made" about fifty times it begins to sound quite "natural" and "right."

manmade fibers industry *synthetic fibers industry*.

manned space flight this phrase currently has no equally pithy and inclusive description of space flight crewed by both women and men. Circumlocution is one solution ("the Columbia space flight with six astronauts aboard"). In print, "crewed space flight" works well, but in broadcast journalism, "crude" will be heard. Other possibilities include: *piloted/staffed/live/ astronaut-controlled space flight*. And, finally, it is possible, reasonable, and comprehensible to speak simply of *space flight*. *See also* man/manned.

mannequin *model, dressmaker's/tailor's dummy, display figure, window display figure*. "Mannequin" and "manikin" come from the same Dutch word, which means "little man."

mannish replace this meaningless term with adjectives that convey your precise meaning: *brusque, blunt, abrupt, direct, square-jawed, aggressive*, etc.

man of action *human dynamo, ball of fire, take-charge person, active/energetic/ determined/ambitious/action-oriented person/individual, someone on their toes, woman of action and man of action*.

man of affairs avoid; the ersatz parallel for women doesn't sit well in polite society. Use instead *entrepreneur, mover, wheeler-dealer, someone with fingers in many pies/many irons in the fire*. *See also* businessman.

man of all work *caretaker, odd-jobber*. *See also* handyman; maintenance man.

man of business, one's *agent, factotum, caretaker, bailiff, factor, tax preparer, steward, clerk, attorney, broker, representative*.

man of distinction *important personage, person of distinction/note/mark/ consequence/importance, prominent/high-ranking individual, pooh-bah, nabob, man of distinction and woman of distinction*.

man of few words *strong, silent type; person of few words; close-mouthed individual*.

man of God *See* churchman; clergyman.

man of his word/man of honor *honorable person, trustworthy individual, someone as good as their word, someone on the up and up/as honest as the day is long/tried and true, truth-speaker, truth-dealer, truth-lover, square-shooter, straight-dealer; woman of her word and man of his word*.

man of letters *writer, author, scholar, literary giant, one of the literati, pundit; woman of letters and man of letters*.

man of means *wealthy/rich/powerful/moneyed individual/person, plutocrat, capitalist, moneybags, nabob, millionaire, billionaire; woman of means and man of means*.

man of my kidney, a *my kind/sort/type of person, a person after my own heart.*

man of straw *See* straw man.

man of the church/man of the cloth *See* churchman; clergyman.

man of the hour *honored guest, star of the show, center of attention; woman of the hour and man of the hour.*

man of the house *homeowner, head of the household.* "Man of the house" and "woman of the house" have been so abused that even if they are used gender-fairly they still have a subtle sting. *See also* family man; homebody.

man of the world *sophisticate, person with wide experience, practical/sophisticated/worldly/worldly wise/well-rounded/well-traveled/experienced person, someone who gets around/who knows the ropes.*

man of the year *newsmaker/citizen/member/entertainer/ humanitarian of the year; man of the year and woman of the year.*

man-of-war retain in historical context. Otherwise use *warship, battleship, ship of war/of the line, war vessel.* Or, be specific: *cruiser, destroyer, gunboat.*

man on the street *See* man in the street.

man overboard! *overboard!, person/someone overboard!*

manpack *backpack, one-person pack.*

manpower *workforce, personnel, human resources, staff, available workers, workers, employees, labor, people, labor supply/force, staffing, human/people power/energy, staff time, payroll; muscle power, human power/energy.* "Womanpower" is seen occasionally ("the new womanpower in Japanese politics") and is a good sex-specific term, but it is not parallel in meaning or scope to "manpower."

manpowered *muscle-/human-/people-powered.*

manpower planning *human resources planning.*

man proposes, but God disposes *creation proposes, but the Creator disposes, we/people/you/the world/the individual propose(s), but God disposes, the Missourians propose but the Kansans dispose.*

manrope *handrail.*

man's best friend there is no good substitute for this phrase because it is associated like none other with the dog, whereas we all know that a woman's best friend are diamonds, and the friend of the people could be anything from Smokey the Bear to General Electric to Karl Marx. Try instead: *the devoted dog, our canine friend, our faithful canine friends, a human's best friend.*

manservant *servant, attendant, assistant.*

-manship avoid words with this suffix. *See* airmanship; brinkmanship/ brinksmanship; chairmanship; craftsmanship; gamesmanship; grantsmanship; horsemanship; marksmanship; salesmanship; sportsmanship; statesmanship; workmanship; yachtsmanship.

man's home is his castle, a *my home is my castle, a person's home is a castle, a woman's home is her castle/a man's home is his castle, our home is our castle; home is where the heart is, there's no place like home.* Look for fresh ways to replace this phrase, for example, "Home is the place where, when you have to go there,/ They have to take you in" (Robert Frost). "My heart is turning home again,/ and there I long to be" (Henry Van Dyke).

man's inhumanity to man *inhumanity, the inhumanity of the human species turned upon itself, our inhumanity toward each other; a house divided against itself.* See also evil men do, the; only man is vile.

man-size(d) *large-size(d), oversized, enormous, hefty, husky, big, ample, large, comfortably large, sizeable, massive, weighty, impressive, considerable, capacious, towering, voracious, immense.*

man's job, a *an adult job, adult-sized job, a big job.*

manslaughter this term has a specific legal meaning—use it in that sense until a nonsexist legal term is developed; in its broader sense, use *murder, homicide, killing, butchery, wholesale killing/slaughter, assassination, bloodletting, slaughter, carnage, massacre, slaying.*

manslayer *slayer, murderer, assassin, killer, liquidator, dispatcher, bloodshedder, hired gun.* See also gunman.

man's man, a this term—usually defined as someone who doesn't threaten other men's egos and is accepted by them but who perhaps is not very comfortable in the presence of women—has no functional parallel for women but it doesn't seem biased against either sex.

man's work *work.* The only "work" biologically limited to men is the work they do in helping propagate the species and so far it is rarely referred to as work. All other "men's work" is based on cultural stereotypes. However, around the world and across centuries men's work has been valued more highly than women's. Margaret Mead pointed out that there have been villages in which men fish and women weave, and villages in which women fish and men weave, but in either type of village, the work done by men is valued more highly than the work done by women. This may be due to (1) the association of women with nature and men with culture; (2) women's reproductive activities keeping them closer to home where their activities are domestic and largely invisible while men's activities are public and highly visible and thus command more cultural respect; (3) boys/men defining themselves by distancing themselves from and disdaining women and women's work. If men's work has been more highly valued it has also traditionally been very toxic; the responsibilities of the provider role, the lack of family or leisure time, and rigid and narrow expectations of what is "masculine" have denied men their full human range of expression and may be responsible for the sex difference in death rates. Today many women are also taking on toxic work loads. In self-preservation, both women and men need to change the cultural norms for success and for what constitutes an appropriate work load and a balance between work, self, and family. *See also* Mother Nature; provider; woman's work.

man the barricades *mount/defend the barricades.*

man to man *one to one, heart to heart, person to person, one on one, face to face, straight from the shoulder, on the level, candidly, frankly, privately, confidentially.*

man-to-man combat *hand-to-hand/one-on-one/face-to-face combat.*

man-to-man defense *player-to-player/one-to-one/person-to-person/one-on-one/ person-on-person (POP) defense.*

mantrap *booby/death trap, snare, trap.*

mantrap (woman) avoid this tempter-Eve/helpless-Adam stereotype.

manward *peopleward, toward/in relation to people/human beings, with respect to humans.* Many words that end in "-ward" with the meaning of "toward" are awkward and should probably be replaced anyway.

man who is his own doctor/lawyer has a fool for a patient/client, a *those who are their own doctors/lawyers have fools for patients/clients, if you insist on being your own doctor/lawyer, you have a fool for a patient/client.*

manwise *humanwise, peoplewise* (if you must). Using the "-wise" suffix is Madison Avenue-ese (another example) that is better replaced or circumvented.

mare's nest *false alarm, hoax, delusion, great disappointment, worthless, much ado about nothing; chaos, mess.*

margrave/margravine; marchioness/marquise; marquess/marquis use these sex-specific titles when necessary.

marine 5% of the U.S. Marine Corps are women.

marketing man *marketer, marketing associate/rep/representative.*

market man *stock market expert.*

marksman *sharpshooter, crack/good/dead/expert shot, first-class shot/aim; markswoman and marksman. See also* gunman.

marksmanship *riflery skills, shooting ability/expertise/skill, sharpshooting.*

marry/marriage until recently it was not "correct" to say a woman married a man. He married her; she "was married" (Francine Wattman Frank and Paula A. Treichler, *Language, Gender, and Professional Writing*). When writing or speaking about marriage keep in mind: that she and he marry/get married/are married (there is no direct object); that by using "couples" or "relationships" you can include unmarried and same-sex couples as well as married ones; that the responsibility for the marriage is not the woman's alone (Gloria Steinem says, "I have yet to hear a man ask for advice on how to combine marriage and a career"); that marriage is not the end-all and be-all for everyone (cultural assumptions point to marriage-as-norm); that the average married man is not trapped, henpecked, or unhappy (in fact, married men report a significantly higher level of well-being than those who are not married, earn an average of 30.6% more than umarried men, and are half as likely to die during any ten-year period as unmarried men).

masculine avoid this vague stereotype that conveys different meanings to different people according to their perceptions of what a man ought or ought not to do, say, think, wear, feel, look like. These subjective cultural judgments have nothing to do with sex and everything to do with gender. Use instead precise adjectives: *strong, upright, charming, robust, hearty, direct, straightforward, deep-voiced, protective, nurturing, attentive,* etc. These are not synonyms for "masculine" but are rather what people usually mean by it.

masculine mystique where the feminine mystique referred to society's narrow definition of women as housewives whose primary competence lay in the domestic sphere, the masculine mystique refers to society's narrow definition of men as providers/protectors whose primary competence lies in the workplace. Lucile Duberman (*Gender and Sex in Society*) says men are pressured to be strivers—in their jobs, in physical exploits, and in areas of leadership. *See also* gender roles; provider.

masculinity what cultural (but not biological) truth is there in this old saying? "Women have their femininity as a birthright. Men have to prove their masculinity all their lives."

masculist one of several terms used with varying degrees of acceptance by members of the men's movement, this label should be used only for those who so identify themselves.

masher since a masher is a man who makes passes at women, there is no synonymous inclusive term. Today's masher is often found in sex harassment cases. For inclusive alternatives use *flirt, someone who comes on strong, sex harasser.*

Mason (member of fraternal organization) *See* Freemason.

massacre distinguish carefully between "massacre" and "battle" or "victory" to avoid ethnocentric or chauvinistic bias.

masseur/masseuse *massager, massage therapist.*

master (adj.) *expert, accomplished, proficient, skilled, excellent, competent, gifted, dextrous, adroit, deft, resourceful; controlling, main.*

Master (Christ) *Teacher.*

master (noun) *owner, manager, chief, head, leader, governor, superior, director, supervisor, employer, boss, commander, captain, controller; sovereign, ruler, monarch, autocrat, dictator, potentate; expert, authority, artist, adept, proficient, specialist, connnoisseur, professional, genius; mentor, teacher, trainer, instructor, educator, tutor; victor, conqueror, winner, champion; householder, proprietor, landholder.* "Master" has some inclusive meanings (owner, employer, teacher, scholar, artisan, victor, etc.) but because it is perceived as a masculine word and because other meanings of the word are incontrovertibly masculine (e.g, "male head of household"), it is ambiguous. And there is no parallel for a woman. (In the once-parallel word pair "master/mistress" the prolific male word has spawned entire pages of "master"-based words in the dictionaries while the female word has shrunk to describe only the sexual function of the woman.) Because "master" is used as noun, verb, and adjective as well as a compound in many other words, its overwhelmingly masculine and hierarchical flavor seasons a good bit of our language. "Master" should probably be avoided except for its applications in trades where it has specific meaning and no currently acceptable substitutes. For all other forms of the word there are many appropriate and easy-to-use alternatives.

master (verb) *excel in/at, grasp, learn, understand, comprehend, be successful at, be proficient in, acquire proficiency at, learn inside and out/backwards and forwards, get a good grasp of, be on top of; conquer, subdue, defeat, subject, vanquish, tame, subjugate, subordinate, suppress, get the upper hand, overcome, overpower, overwhelm, overthrow, surmount, humble, triumph over; rule, dominate, govern, control, command, dictate to, boss/order around.* For "master the fine art of" use *make a fine art of.*

master/master mariner (sailing vessel) retain in official use; some marine occupational titles using "master" are used by the U.S. Employment and Training Administration. Otherwise use *captain.*

master bedroom/suite almost without exception these are the currently used terms. You could, however, use *main bedroom/owner's/principal/largest bedroom/suite.* Or, refer to bedrooms by their location, as do some designers and architects: *the northeast/southwest bedroom.*

master builder *expert/award-winning/skilled/professional builder.* This may refer to either sex.

master class an advanced art, music, or dance seminar led by a recognized expert (of either sex), "master class" is difficult to replace with a term that is equally concise, descriptive, and meaningful in those fields. An alternative sometimes used is *artist class* (it is not limited to the visual arts).

masterful *expert, skilled, articulate, authoritative, competent; powerful, commanding, domineering, sweeping, imperative, imperious, arbitrary, overbearing, arrogant, haughty.*

master hand *expert, genius, major talent, professional, authority, adept, proficient, whiz, dab hand.*

master key *universal/all-purpose/main/controlling/skeleton key, passe partout.*

master list *overview, key, main/complete/primary/reference list.*

masterly *accomplished, skilled, knowledgeable, consummate, matchless, excellent, distinguished, experienced, crack, ingenious, able, felicitous, shrewd.*

mastermind (noun) *genius, brilliant thinker, intellectual/mental prodigy/giant, inventor, originator, creator, brains; plotter, organizer, creative organizer, instigator, planner, leader, director, head, someone who pulls the strings.*

mastermind (verb) *oversee, direct, head, guide, lead, coordinate, plan, contrive, engineer, launch; originate, invent, devise, have the bright idea.*

master of ceremonies/mistress of ceremonies *host, emcee, leader/coordinator of ceremonies, speaker, main/guest speaker, facilitator, moderator, introducer, announcer, marshal, parade marshal.* Although "emcee" comes from these sex-specific terms, it is used for both sexes and is perceived as neutral.

master of one's fate *captain of one's soul/fate.*

master of the situation *in charge, in control, on top of things, reins firmly in hand, finger on the pulse.*

masterpiece *great/greatest/best work, work of art/genius, stroke of genius, consummate art, chef d'oeuvre, magnum opus, cream of the crop, crème de la crème, piéce de rèsistance, flower of the flock, nonpareil, acme of perfection, perfection, brilliant achievement, ne plus ultra, tour de force, coup de maitre, model, monument, standard.*

master plan *overall/comprehensive plan, overview.*

master print *original film.*

"master race" use this term only in its historical context and put it in quotation marks to indicate its lack of validity.

master's degree *M.A., graduate/advanced degree, first advanced/first graduate degree.* The spelled-out "master's degree" is still used in many cases; there is no current substitute for it.

master sergeant this official armed forces term might refer to either sex.

masterstroke *trump card, clever idea, good move, bold/lucky stroke, checkmate, stroke of genius, coup, complete success, stunt, exploit, victory.*

master switch *control/lead/main switch, circuit breaker.*

master tape *pattern/final tape, template.*

master teacher leave as is where custom and usage require it. A substitute sometimes seen is *artist teacher* (not restricted to the visual arts). A master teacher can be either sex.

masterwork *See* masterpiece.

mastery *proficiency, understanding, knowledge, accomplishment, acquaintance with, competency, firm grasp, excellence, facility, advantage, adeptness, skill, dexterity, deftness, expertise; rule, sovereignty; victory, ascendency, supremacy, authority, subjugation, conquest, control, domination, dominance, upper hand, reins in one's hands, command, order, sway.*

matador *See* bullfighter.

mate used for both sexes in the sense of "partner," "spouse," or "lover" and also in navy and coast guard ranks. The popular Australian "mate" is used for both sexes.

mater/materfamilias acceptable sex-specific terms, although the Latin is more often replaced with "mother/matriarch." *See also* pater/paterfamilias.

materialman *material supplier, supplier.*

maternal unless you mean motherlike or mother-related ("maternal grandfather"), use *parental, ancestral; kindly, kindhearted, loving, devoted, indulgent, solicitous, concerned, fond, protective, sympathetic.*

maternal instinct *instinct.*

maternity leave *parental/family/childcare leave.* "As of mid-1989, U.S. parents remain in the unenviable position of living in one of the two countries in the industrialized world that do not have laws requiring job-protected leave for care of the newborn" (*The American Woman 1990-91: A Status Report*, ed. Sara E. Rix). According to a 1990 survey of 250 U.S. companies, 42% offer unpaid parental leave; 5% offer paid parental leave. Another study shows 37% of working women offered unpaid maternity leave while 18% of men are allowed unpaid paternity leave. Sweden provides parents 90% salary reimbursement for the first nine months after birth; President Bush vetoed a 1990 bill that would have provided three months of *unpaid* parental leave.

matman *wrestler.*

matriarch/matriarchy these correct sex-specific terms are sometimes used judgmentally. Because patriarchy is seen as the norm, a matriarchy tends to be viewed with suspicion, alarm, and disapproval; it doesn't seem "natural." In fact, the opposite of a patriarchy is not a matriarchy. Both matriarchies and patriarchies involve an imbalance of power between the sexes and are called dominator societies by Riane Eisler (*The Chalice and the Blade, The Partnership Way of Life*). The true opposite of a matriarchy or a patriarchy is a partnership society. Until we reach the point where neither sex needs to dominate the other, use "matriarchy/patriarchy" terms cautiously. The word "matricentric" puts the mother at the center of the family or system without the hierarchical overtones of "matriarchal." Sex-neutral alternatives for "matriarch" include *ancestor/family elder, head of the family, family head. See also* patriarch/patriarchy.

matrilineal use "matrilineal" when referring to descent through the mother's line.

matrimony *marriage, union, nuptials, wedlock.* "Matrimony"—from Latin "mater" for "mother"—is sex-specific and is also part of the oddly nonparallel word pair "matrimony/patrimony" (which may not be so odd given that historically money was handed down to the men in the family while the women were expected to marry it). "Marriage" is also sex-linked (from Latin for "a woman's dowry") but less directly and obviously than "matrimony."

matron *warden, attendant, police officer, deputy sheriff, bailiff, guard, prison/ jail/custodial guard, superintendent, supervisor, overseer; principal, chief, director, head, manager.* In its narrow legal sense, "matron" must be used until a nonsexist legal term is developed. In the sense of a middle-aged woman, replace "matron" with words that more precisely describe the person. Note the widely different status and meaning of the word pair "matron/patron."

matronly replace this vague word with precise, inclusive terms: *dignified, gracious, ponderous, heavy-set, established, grave, comfortable-looking, serene, slow-moving, well-dressed, mature, sedate,* etc. There is no such word as "patronly."

matron of honor *See* maid/matron of honor.

matronym/matronymic referring to a name derived from the mother or a maternal ancestor, these are correct sex-specific terms. They also have a little-recognized historical accuracy: the practice of passing the father's name on to the children hasn't always been in force nor is it universally practiced in the Western world. For example, Nelson is "Nell's son," Allison is "Alice's son," and Babson is "Barbara's son." Charles Panati (*Browser's Book of Beginnings*) says, "Seemingly, when surnames originated, few traces of male chauvinism historically were involved." *See also* hyphenated names; patronym/patronymic.

maverick although this term comes from a man's name—a nineteenth-century Texas rancher named Samuel Maverick with a certain reputation for straying from the herd (he refused to brand his cattle)—its origins have been largely forgotten and it is perceived as sex-neutral.

mayoress *mayor.*

may the best man win *may the best person win.*

meathead just as Archie Bunker tied women to "dingbat," so he tied "meathead" to men.

meatman *butcher, meat vendor.*

mediatress/mediatrix *mediator.*

medical research most medical research studies on heart disease, aspirin use, cholesterol, smoking, aging, alcoholism, sports medicine, AIDS, and other important health issues have been carried out on men (or on male laboratory rats) and produce no data on women. The results are thought to be "possibly applicable to women." "The safety and effectiveness of drugs and treatments prescribed for everyone—men and women of all ages and ethnic backgrounds—are typically based on clinical trials using only middle-aged, white men" (Sue Woodman and Dianne Lange, in *Mirabella*, September 1990). A 1990 congressional hearing concluded that men are overrepresented in tests of new drugs, devices, and procedures, and in late 1990 the NIH opened an office on women's health. Ethicist Arthur Caplan says, "For centuries, male scientists and physicians have seen men as representing and illustrating what is normal and healthy about human beings. Male physiology and behavior define normal human physiology and behavior. Women . . . are seen as 'deviations.' Since scientists want to conduct research with subjects who are as normal, as 'typical' as possible, bias against non-male traits leads to the exclusion of women as suitable subjects . . . . Discrimination against women in research will not end until doctors, scientists, and legislators agree that it is normal to be female."

medical treatment women's medical treatment has traditionally been different from men's, even when women have the same symptoms. As one doctor put it, if a fifty-year-old man complains of chest pain, his doctor will schedule a stress test for the next day. A fifty-year-old woman complaining of chest pain will mostly likely be told to go home and rest. Women who have bypass surgery for heart disease are much sicker than men who have the surgery, slightly older, and more likely to die as a result—largely because they have been referred for surgery later in the course of their illness. "Experts" explained the sex differences in bypass surgery by suggesting that "the women might have taken medications that concealed the symptoms until they were very ill, or they might not have described their symptoms as men do, using words that might alert the doctor." They did not explain how the women obtained medications powerful enough to mask symptoms of serious heart disease, nor how women, traditionally very verbal, failed to find the simple words to describe chest pain and shortness of breath. Other studies have also indicated doctors were less likely to heed women's complaints of chest pains than men's.

medicine man *shaman, healer, magician, faith healer; medicine woman and medicine man.*

meistersinger "mastersingers," members of German middle-class guilds, flourished during the fourteenth to sixteenth centuries and were all men.

memsahib always a woman; the man is a "sahib."

men (pseudogeneric) *See* man (adult male human being); Man/man (pseudogeneric); mankind.

men- most words that begin with "men-" are not sexist, for example, menace (from Latin, "threaten"); menagerie (from French, "household"); menarche (from Latin, "month"); mendacious/mendacity (from Latin, "lie"); mendicant (from Latin, "beg"); menhir (from Breton, "stone"); menial (from Latin, "dwelling"), menorah (from Hebrew, "candlestick"); mental (from Greek, "spirit"); mention (from Latin, "call to mind"); menu (from French, "small"). *See also* man-; -man/-men; mench/mensch/mensh; menopause/menopausal; menses/menstrual/menstruation; mentor.

mench/mensch/mensh this variously spelled word is neutral (in Yiddish, "human being," in German, "person") although it is often used in English only for men. Use it for women too to mean a purposeful, upright, honorable person who stands up for the rights of others as well as for her own.

men of goodwill *people/those of goodwill.*

menopause/menopausal nonsexist; the "men" comes from Latin for "month." "Menopause" is a neutral term describing a physical reality that is very different for different women although a 1990 study says it does not appear to cause stress or depression in most healthy women, and may even improve mental health for some. Avoid stereotyping menopause, and do not describe a woman as menopausal unless it is germane to the discussion and unless you are sure she is.

menses/menstrual/menstruation these terms have nothing to do with men ("menses" is Latin for "months"), but they are correctly sex-linked because they are associated biologically only with women. Throughout history menstruating women have not had good press: in the Bible they were thought to be unclean; later they were thought to be diseased, animal-like, possessing supernatural powers, and responsible for rusted-out metal tools and weapons. Still later they were thought to be subject to mood swings that affected their judgment and mental abilities.

men's liberation/movement the women's movement's essentially negative view of men as oppressors was not, naturally enough, received well by men—and most especially by those who found themselves oppressed by the males-only draft, the provider role, rigid societal definitions of masculinity, unfair divorce and custody laws, and other biases in the culture. Men today report they are tired of criticism, frustrated with their limited roles compared to the options they see available to women, and confused about what it means to be a man or a father or a husband. Landmarks in the men's movement include: 1970 formation of the Men's Center in Berkeley; subsequent creation of other men's centers around the country; founding of MEN International, Men's Rights Incorporated, and Free Men; publication of *The Hazards of Being Male: Surviving the Myth of Masculine Privilege* by Herb Goldberg; appearance of voices like those of poet Robert Bly, anthropologist Michael Meade, Warren Farrell (*Why Men Are the Way They Are*), and Jungian psychologist James Hillmann, and members of activist divorce reform and father's rights groups. More and more men are examining and challenging the traditional male sex role in the belief that "men, not women, must define what it means to be a man" (Tom Williamson, in *Men Freeing Men*, ed. Francis Baumli). Goals and attitudes vary widely among members of the men's movement; it is not a homogeneous group so be wary of generalizing about it. *See also* "male privilege"; males-only draft; provider.

men's studies the first men's studies courses began in the early 1970s, and currently there are some 400 courses being taught in various disciplines. For further information see *Men's Studies Review*, published by the Men's Studies Association, and *Men's Studies: A Selected and Annotated Interdisciplinary Bibliography* by Eugene R. August. *See also* women's studies.

mental health according to Patricia Perri Rieker, Harvard University Medical School sociologist, "People don't realize the extent to which an implicit sexism permeates notions of how normal men and women ought to behave." In one study forty-seven therapists watched a videotape of a patient (actually an actor) describing his symptoms of depression. When the therapists were told that the man was an engineer whose wife stayed home with their children, they attributed his problems to work pressures, family problems, or biological causes. But when the man said his wife was an engineer and he stayed home with the children, the therapists diagnosed him as having severe depression and related his problems to the role he played at home. In another study, men being treated at psychiatric emergency rooms for depression were more likely to be hospitalized than were women with equally severe depression, presumably because their symptoms seemed more unusual. Women diagnosed as alcoholic were more likely to be committed to the psychiatric hospital than were men with equivalent diagnoses. Women are twice as likely to be diagnosed as depressed, men five times as likely to be diagnosed as alcoholic. Many psychotherapists work from stereotypes about which disorders are more "appropriate" for women and men. Symptoms like sexual promiscuity and diagnoses of histrionic personality disorder (formerly called hysteria) are generally assigned to women. Men are more reluctant to seek therapy and drop out of it earlier because of a conventional view of masculinity that says disclosing problems is a sign of weakness; men feel they "shouldn't" need help, show vulnerability, or talk about their feelings.

mentor the original Mentor was a male friend of Odysseus charged with the education of Odysseus' son, but the term is used today for both sexes.

men working *work zone/crew, crew/people/workers working, crew at work, workers, working.*

mercenary this is still largely a male field, although you will occasionally find female mercenaries.

merchantman *merchant, commercial ship, merchant ship/marine.*

mermaid/merman folklore and fantastic tradition have given us these creatures, along with nonparallel designations ("maid/man"). When possible use instead *merwoman/merman, sea creature, sea nymph, Nereid, sea god/sea goddess.*

meter maid (parking) *meter reader/attendant/monitor/tender/officer, parking monitor/officer/enforcer, parking enforcement officer.*

meter man (water/gas/electricity meter) *meter reader.*

Mickey Finn when using expressions like this, be aware of how many are male-based. Some of the time use female-based expressions, creative expressions of your own, or alternatives: *knockout drops. See* Writing Guidelines for a discussion of sex-linked expressions.

Mickey Mouse (adj.) when using expressions like this, be aware of how many are male-based. Some of the time use female-based expressions, creative expressions of your own, or alternatives: *cheap, cheaply insincere, inferior, insignificant, worthless, petty, trivial, trifling, piddling, simple, easy, childish, flimsy, paltry, trite, nonsense, time-wasting, sentimental, corny. See* Writing Guidelines for a discussion of sex-linked expressions.

Midas touch when using expressions like this, be aware of how many are male-based. Some of the time use female-based expressions, creative expressions of your own, or alternatives: *magic/golden touch, everything she/he touches turns to gold. See* Writing Guidelines for a discussion of sex-linked expressions.

middleman *go-between, agent, contact, third party, liaison, negotiator, intermediary, broker, mediator, arbiter, arbitrator, representative, messenger, factor, intercessor, intervener, umpire, referee, peacemaker, facilitator, contact, advocate, middle party; jobber, wholesaler, distributor, dealer, contract dealer, trader, reseller.*

mid-life crisis it is a natural part of human growth and development for individuals of both sexes to reorient themselves somewhere between the ages of thirty-five and fifty.

midshipman retain where this term is used officially; it can refer to either sex. Otherwise use *cadet, naval officer in training.* At the U.S. Naval Academy women (who make up 10% of the enrollment) are called "female midshipmen."

midwife (noun) this term is inclusive; it is used for both women and men practitioners and the "wife" does not refer to the person assisting but to the person giving birth ("mid" means "with"). However, the "wife" plus the term's long association with women (of the more than 3,300 certified nurse-midwives in the United States, only 14 are men) give it a feminine cast and you may sometimes want alternatives: *birth attendant, accoucheur.* The United States, Canada, and South Africa are the only industrialized nations in which midwives are not recognized and supported by the law and the medical community. Interestingly enough, in the five European countries with the lowest infant mortality rates, midwives supervise more than 70% of all births.

midwife (verb) *give birth to/beget, assist, support, conceive of/beget (ideas), bring for*th.

milady/milord sex-parallel historical terms.

military draft *See* males-only draft.

military man *soldier, member of the armed forces/the military, military officer.* *See also* armed forces; serviceman (armed forces).

military wife *military/soldier's/service member's spouse.*

militiaman *militia member, member of the militia, soldier, citizen soldier, Revolutionary War soldier, militiawoman and militiaman.*

milkmaid *milker, dairy worker/employee/hand/worker,* except for fairy tales or in historical contexts. A milkman sells or delivers milk while a milkmaid milks cows. (Note nonparallel "maid/man"). *See also* dairymaid/dairyman; milkman.

milkman *milk route driver, milk/dairy deliverer, milk truck. See also* dairymaid/dairyman; milkmaid.

milliner those who design, make, trim, and sell women's hats can be either sex.

milquetoast/milksop (man) *timid soul, someone scared of their own shadow, someone with cold feet, timid/meek/poor-spirited/fearful/unassertive person.* ("The Timid Soul" was the name of H.T. Webster's newspaper cartoon featuring Casper Milquetoast.) *See also* coward/cowardly/cowardice.

minister depending on the denomination, this might be a woman or a man. If you are unsure how to address a female minister, ask her; this may vary from denomination to denomination and from person to person within a denomination. In denominations ordaining women to full ministry (preaching the word and administering the sacraments) women constitute approximately 9% of the clergy. Among 221 denominations surveyed by the National Council of Churches, eighty-four ordain women and eighty-two do not (six do not ordain clergy at all and forty-nine are uncertain what to do). *See also* clergyman; priest; rabbi.

minstrel although most minstrels have been men, women belonged to some medieval troupes, juggling or acting out small parts. Troubadours, which flourished during the two centuries preceding the rise of the minstrels, also numbered some women among them (Meg Bodin, *The Women Troubadours*). At the height of the popularity of nineteenth-century Negro minstrelsy, women were impersonated by men (for example, in the "wench performances"), so there appeared to be women on stage, but there rarely were.

minuteman retain for minutemen in the Revolutionary War or for minuteman rockets. Or, *soldier, citizen soldier, revolutionary soldier, Revolutionary War soldier.*

misandrist/misanthrope/misogynist "misandrist" ("man-hater") and "misogynist" ("woman-hater") are acceptable sex specific terms. "Misanthrope," which refers to a cynic who hates or distrusts everyone, is often misused because dictionaries ambiguously define it as "man-hater" or "hater of mankind" where "man" and "mankind" are pseudogenerics (the Greek "anthropos" means "human being"). Social values are reflected in the asymmetry of this word pair; "misogynist" is a common term while "misandrist" is unfamiliar and seldom used (it generally appears only in unabridged dictionaries).

Miss/miss/missy avoid calling a woman/young woman a "miss" or "missy." And use "Ms." except for people who indicate a preference for "Miss." Dale Spender (*Man Made Language*) says, "Contrary to the belief of many people, the current usage of *Miss* and *Mrs.* is relatively recent, for until the beginning of the nineteenth century the title *Miss* was usually reserved for young females while *Mrs.* designated mature women. Marital status played no role in the use of these terms." Calling women "Miss" or "Mrs." labels them in relation to men although men have never been labeled in relation to women. *See also* mademoiselle; Mrs.; Ms.; salutations.

Miss America since 1921 the Miss America Beauty Pageant in Atlantic City has contributed to a competitive and unrealistic idea of beauty for women. Although making it to the pageant is a dream-come-true for many young women as well as the result of years of hard work, the pageant itself has much to answer for in its objectification of women and its unrelenting emphasis on externals and physical perfection (which the tolerance of injected, taped, and altered body parts falsely supports).

missus/the missus avoid.

mistress *lover.* If you mean "mistress of the house," use *householder, homemaker, head of the household. See also* girlfriend; kept woman; schoolmarm/schoolmaster/schoolmistress.

mistress of ceremonies *See* master of ceremonies/mistress of ceremonies.

mitochondrial mother *See* Eve.

mixerman *mixer tender.*

modern man *modern people/peoples/civilization/world, today's people, modern civilization, the modern age.* Use the term only for the Minnesota man who legally changed his name to Modern Man. *See also* Man/man (pseudogeneric); mankind.

modiste *clothier, clothing retailer, hatmaker, fashion/high-fashion/garment designer.*

moldman *machine molder, mold mover/maker/worker, fiberglass laminator.*

mollycoddle (noun/verb) because of "molly" (from the woman's name) but even more because the noun is defined as "a pampered, spoiled, effeminate boy or man," this word is thoroughly sexist. For the noun

use *spoiled/immature/irresponsible person, timid/gentle/sensitive perso*n.
For the verb, use *indulge, spoil, pamper, dote on, overprotect.* **See also**
mama's boy; sissy.

mommy track writing in the *Harvard Business Review* (January/February
1989), Felice N. Schwartz said that "the cost of employing women in
business is greater than the cost of employing men" (citing more
career interruptions, plateauing, and turnovers for women) and
suggested employers distinguish between "career-primary" and
"career-and-family" women managers and to devise policies so that
the latter could "trade some career growth and compensation for
freedom from the constant pressures to work long hours." Although
Schwartz did add that "The costs of employing women pale beside
the payoffs," her approach was quickly labeled the "mommy track"
(Schwartz herself never used the term) and criticized on a number of
grounds: except for two unpublished studies by anonymous corporations, Schwartz offered no data to support her claim about the costs
of employing women; she divided women into two groups while the
diversity of men was ignored; the paper reinforced the assumptions
that you can have either a family or a career but not both if you're a
woman and that it is always the woman's responsibility to care for
children; it tried to fit women into the existing culture instead of
questioning the values of the culture; her theory would perpetuate
the current situation in which women at upper levels of management
mostly do not have children while their male colleagues do. Management consultant Audrey Freedman points out that in the aggregate,
men cost corporations more than women; it is more often men who
are involved in drug abuse, lawlessness, corporate takeover battles,
incidents like the Valdez spill, and alcoholism, with its attendant loss
of performance and productivity (43% of men are classified as
moderate to heavy drinkers compared to 18% of women), but "the
male-dominated corporate hierarchy most often chooses to ignore
these 'good old boy' habits." It might be more profitable to abandon
female-male cost comparisons (since both sexes are obviously
needed) and concentrate on making the workplace less toxic and
more user-friendly for both women and men. **See also** executive;
glass ceiling; wage earner; working father; working man; working
mother; working woman.

monastery most monasteries house or housed monks, but some abbeys
and convents are also considered monasteries so not all those who
live in monasteries are male.

mongolism/mongoloid *Down syndrome; someone with Down syndrome.*

monk correct sex-specific term; the approximate equivalent for women is
nun. If you want a generic use *religious, recluse, ascetic, hermit,
solitary.* **See also** nun/nunnery.

monogamy either a woman or a man can enjoy monogamy. *See also* polyandry/polygyny; polygamy.

monsignor always a man; it means "my lord" or "my sir."

Montezuma's revenge when using expressions like this, be aware of how many are male-based. Some of the time use female-based expressions, creative expressions of your own, or alternatives: *dysentery, intestinal flu, travelers' tummy/scourge. See* Writing Guidelines for a discussion of sex-linked expressions.

Moonie *member of the Unification Church.*

moonlighter more than 40% of people who work two or more jobs are women. According to government studies, a woman who moonlights typically has to work more than a moonlighting man to earn the same pay. Most moonlighting men are married while most moonlighting women are divorced, separated, widowed, or never married.

Moslem *Muslim.* Followers of Islam call themselves Muslims; "Moslem" is an unacceptable westernized version of Muslim (which is both adjective and noun).

mother (noun) good sex-specific word. Two cautions: don't use "mother" when you really mean "parent" or "mother and father"; a woman expecting a child is a pregnant woman, not a mother (unless she has other children).

mother (pseudogeneric verb) *parent, nurture, support, protect, take care of, look after, care for, be responsible for, rear children, caregive, supervise.*

mother and father use "mother and father" carefully; many children live with only one parent, with a parent and stepparent, with a guardian, in a foster home, or with two parents of the same sex. According to the Census Bureau there are more than two million gay mothers and fathers. Most of their children are from earlier, heterosexual relationships, but some 5,000-10,000 lesbians are estimated to have borne children after coming out, and hundreds of gay and lesbian couples have adopted children. Except when speaking of a specific mother and father, use *parent(s), parent or guardian, family,* or, in casual material, *parental units.* Use "father and mother" half the time.

motherboard retain this very specific and currently irreplaceable computer term. *See also* daughterboard.

mother cell this biology term has a longstanding and specific meaning; leave as is. When mother cells split, they form daughter cells.

mother country *See* motherland.

mother deprivation this is acceptable when paired with "father deprivation." It has all too frequently been paired with the much less judgmental "father absence." If you use "father absence," use also "mother absence."

Mother Earth *Earth.* For the rationale on not feminizing nature, *see* Mother Nature.

mother hen *overprotective/indulgent/hovering person/parent.*

motherhouse correct sex-specific term for religious order headquarters, although there is no parallel "fatherhouse."

mother-in-law there are no father-in-law jokes and virtually no father-in-law put-downs.

motherland *homeland, native land/country/soil, home, home/birth country, land of one's ancestors, natal place, the old country.*

mother lode *main/principal lode.*

motherly replace this vague adjective with precise ones: *warm, nurturing, loving, kind, kindly, protective, supportive, caring, solicitous, considerate, interested, benevolent, good-natured, fond, affectionate, devoted, tender, gentle, demonstrative, sympathetic, understanding, indulgent, obliging, forbearing, tolerant, well-meaning, sheltering, generous.* These words also apply to men; they are not synonyms for "motherly" but rather what people seem to mean by it.

mother-naked *stark naked, naked, starkers, naked as a jaybird, without a stitch on, in the altogether/raw/buff, in one's birthday suit, au naturel, unclad.*

Mother Nature *Nature.* The earth is made easy to rape, exploit, and subjugate by being considered female; "in our culture, words matter: The masculine dominates the feminine. To consider the Earth in terms wholly female implies that it is to be acted upon at our will. Plowing fields, cutting timber, mining ore, burning rain forests, and dumping our garbage into landfills and oceans are actions that characterize this view of the Earth as an entity we dominate" (Mary Morse, *Utne Reader*, May/June 1990). Elizabeth Dodson Gray (*Creation*, May/June 1989) says giving nature a traditional feminine image is reassuring to us for "surely a mother will always be loving toward us, continue to feed us, clothe us, and carry away our wastes, and never kill us no matter how much toxic waste we put into the soil or CFC's into the ozone." In the same way Nature has been hurt by the association with the feminine, women have been discounted because of their association with Nature. Sherry B. Ortner ("Is Female to Male as Nature Is to Culture?" *Woman, Culture, and Society*, eds. M.Z. Rosaldo and L. Lamphere) attributes the secondary status of woman in society ("one of the true universals, a pan-cultural fact") to the way every culture distinguishes between "nature" and "culture" and then associates women with nature and men with culture. Woman is perceived as being closer to nature because of (1) her body and its functions—which place her in (2) social roles that are considered to be at a lower order of the cultural process than man's and which lead to a (3) psychic structure which is seen as being closer to nature; "proportionately more of a woman's body space, for a greater percentage of her lifetime, and at some—sometimes great—cost to her personal health, strength, and general stability, is taken up with

the natural processes surrounding the reproduction of the species."
In contrast, man, lacking natural creative functions, asserts his
creativity externally, "artificially," through technology and symbols.
"In so doing, he creates relatively lasting, eternal, transcendent
objects, while the woman creates only perishables—human beings."
The association of woman with second-class nature is reinforced by
her association with incontinent, unsocialized children (who are,
being "uncivilized," closer to nature) and by her traditional confinement to the domestic (originally because of bearing and nursing
children); the domestic sphere is always considered less than the
public sphere since society is logically at a higher level than the
domestic units of which it is composed. "Since it is always culture's
project to subsume and transcend nature, if women were considered
part of nature, then culture would find it 'natural' to subordinate, not
to say oppress, them."

mother of pearl (British) rhyming slang for "girl" although it usually
means wives or women friends; leave as is.

mother of pearl (mollusks) leave as is.

mother of vinegar leave as is.

Mother's Day proposed by Anna Jarvis, Mother's Day was first observed
on May 10, 1908, in Philadelphia. No florists, greeting card companies, or candy makers were involved at the time.

mother's helper *babysitter, childcare worker, family/parents' helper, live-in
babysitter, child minder/monitor/attendant, housekeeper.*

mother superior retain when it is someone's title.

mother tongue *native language/tongue, birth/first/original language.*

mother wit *native wit, natural wit/intelligence.*

motorman *driver, streetcar/railway/subway driver, dinkey/streetcar/motor
operator, motor-power connector, engineer, railway/railroad conductor,
motoreer* (a clever older word that was put together from motor +
engineer).

moundsman *pitcher.*

mountain man/mountain woman acceptable if "mountain man" is not
used as a pseudogeneric. Plural: *mountain people/folk.*

Mountie both men and women belong to the Royal Canadian Mounted
Police Force.

movie man *projectionist, exhibitor.*

Mrs. some women prefer this title; respect their wishes. When their
wishes or marital status are unknown, use "Ms." Dale Spender (*Man
Made Language*) says, "Contrary to the belief of many people, the
current usage of *Miss* and *Mrs.* is relatively recent, for until the
beginning of the nineteenth century the title *Miss* was usually reserved for young females while *Mrs.* designated mature women.
Marital status played no role in the use of these terms." "Mrs." and
"Miss" reflect a tradition of labeling women in relation to men

although the converse has never been true. While many married women are moving away from the custom of calling themselves by their husbands' names ("Mrs. Greaves Oakley"), this practice isn't necessarily preferred by African American women, "whose history denied them the legal right to that designation. What signifies bondage to one woman may mark freedom to another" (Francine Wattman Frank and Paula A. Treichler, *Language, Gender, and Professional Writing*). *See also* mademoiselle; Miss; Ms.

Ms. pronounced "miz" and originating in secretarial manuals of the 1940s, this social title is used for women where "Mr." is used for men. If you use "Mr. Seifert," use "Ms. Ayallah"; if you call Seifert by his last name, do the same for Ayallah. "Ms." is generally acceptable when you don't know what social title (Ms., Mrs., Dr., Miss) the person uses; you may also omit the social title for both sexes ("Dear David Koskenmaki"; "Dear Irene Nash"). The greatest objection to "Ms." has been that you can't tell if she's married or not. The only sensible reply is that we have managed for centuries without knowing whether a "Mr." is married or not. *See also* mademoiselle; Miss; Mrs.; salutations.

muezzin always a man.

multiculturalism the recognition in our writing and speaking that we come from, share the planet with, and are shaped by many cultures and individuals is called multiculturalism. Other ways of saying nearly the same thing include: *cultural diversity, diversity, pluralism, cross-culturalism, ethnic inclusiveness.* In its broad sense, multiculturalism means including everyone. To see if your materials ignore or offend certain groups, read it as though you were the other sex, another race, twenty years older or younger, gay if you are straight, straight if you are gay, disabled if you are not, able-bodied if you are disabled.

mum's the word this has nothing to do with "mum" ("mother") but with an old command to be quiet.

murderess *murderer*. About 5% of inmates in prison for murder are women. In 1989, 12,434 men and 1,676 women were arrested for murder in the United States.

muscleman *hired muscle, muscler, goon, thug, bully, menace, bruiser, ugly/ rough customer, enforcer, big tuna, hard case; powerhouse, weightlifter. See also* bad guy.

my proud beauty/me proud beauty use only in melodramas where the villain has a particularly long and twirly mustache.

n

In reality, all communication that debilitates females also
debilitates males, for if any system diminishes a part of the
species, it diminishes all of it.

Bobbye D. Sorrels

nabob historically the governor or deputy of a Mongol or Indian district
or town was always a man, and there was no parallel term for a
woman; in the broad sense of a wealthy, high-ranking, or prominent
person, it can be used of both sexes.

nag (noun) *grouch, grump, grumbler, fussbudget, crosspatch, faultfinder,
complainer, nitpicker, sorehead, crank, griper.* Avoid "nag"; it is used
only for women (with no parallel word for men).

nag (verb) *complain, gripe, criticize, scold, kvetch, badger, pick on, find fault,
pester, harass, grumble, grouse, irritate, harp at/on, bicker, drive up the
wall, fuss, raise a fuss, have a bone to pick with.* Do not use "bitch,"
"henpeck," or "whine." Although "nag" is not sexist per se, it has
been used only for women, while in the same situation men are said
to bully, chew out, complain, or just plain talk. *See also* bitch (verb);
henpecked; whine.

namby-pamby (noun/adj.) *softie, pushover, weakling, doormat, lightweight,
featherweight; insipid, inane, shallow, flimsy, weak, indecisive, anemic,
wishy-washy, colorless, milk and water, simpering.* Reserved almost
exclusively for men, "namby-pamby" comes from a nickname given
to the poet Ambrose (thus the rhyme with "Amby") Philips (1674-
1749) whose poems were much parodied. *See also* coward/cow-
ardly/cowardice; mama's boy; sissy; weak sister.

name *See* hyphenated names; matronym/matronymic; patronym/
patronymic.

nanny this sexist term (because there are no biological, only cultural,
reasons for its being limited to women) historically described a
woman servant who had charge of young children. In Great Britain
today it refers to a woman who has two or more years of formal
training, has passed a national examination, and sometimes has
served an internship. There are no certification boards or examina-

tions for nannies in the United States, but a few programs offer nanny training. A U.S. nanny is usually someone who cares for children full-time in the home. Otherwise use inclusive terms: *babysitter, live-in babysitter, family/parents' helper, childcare worker, child minder/monitor/attendant, nursery worker, tutor.*

nation/she *nation/it.*

natural/nature avoid applying these terms to sex roles, age, race, sexual orientation, disabilities, etc. It is difficult to know (scientifically, psychologically, philosophically) whether something is indeed "natural" and, secondarily, whether being natural is a good in and of itself. These terms are often a substitute for uninformed thought. Instead of "natural," use *automatic, instinctive, essential, idiosyncratic, usual, often-seen, common, habitual, accustomed, customary, established, time-honored, regulation, traditional, general, prevailing, frequent, popular, predictable, expected.* Instead of "nature," use *character, personality, individuality, essence, identity, quality, kind, type.*

"natural" father/"natural" mother *biological mother/father, birth father/mother.*

nature/she *nature/it.* For the rationale on not feminizing nature, *see* Mother Nature.

Neanderthal man *archaic human, Neanderthal, the Neanderthal, Neanderthals, early human.* The colloquial insult "Neanderthal" is sexist because it is reserved for men and ethnocentric because it unfairly represents early peoples.

necessity is the mother of invention *necessity gives rise to/fosters/breeds/spawns/provokes/generates invention.* Or, instead of quoting Richard Franck, William Wycherly, or the anonymous Roman, use "Necessity does the work of courage" (George Eliot); "Sheer necessity—the proper parent of an art so nearly allied to invention" (Richard B. Sheridan); "The stomach is the teacher of the arts and the dispenser of invention" (Persius).

née this French construction, indicating the name a woman was born with and weighted with sexist implications, has outlived its usefulness in most cases. Instead give both names: Joanna Morganthau Celletti or Joanna Morganthau-Celletti.

needlewoman *needleworker, tailor, mender, alterer, stitcher, alterations expert, custom tailor, garment worker/designer.*

Negress/Negro *African American, Afro-American, black.* If gender is necessary: *African American/Afro-American/black woman/man, man/woman of color.* Except in established titles (e.g., United Negro College Fund), the terms "Negro/Negress" are considered offensive, slavery-based, and contemptuous. *See also* African American/Afro-American; black-and-white (adj.); black/Black (noun); black/black-.

nerd because this tends to be used mostly for men/boys, you may want more inclusive alternatives: *square, wimp, twinkie.*

nervous Nellie *fussbudget, worrywart, handwringer, terminal worrier.*

newsboy *newspaper carrier/vendor. See also* paperboy.

newsman/newspaperman *reporter, newspaper reporter, journalist, news representative/writer, correspondent, representative/member of the press/ media/Fourth Estate, newscaster, newsmonger.* Or, be specific: *war/ special/foreign correspondent, columnist, commentator, wire/roving/ investigative reporter, feature writer, sportswriter, stringer, editor, publisher, radio correspondent, television commentator, anchor, news anchor/ director, announcer, reviewer, gossip columnist, photojournalist.* Women now account for nearly two-thirds of U.S. journalism degrees, almost half of new hires, and over half of all editors and reporters. However, newsroom staffs are still 93% white and 65% male, and of newspaper executives only 15% are women and 4% are from minority groups. Women make up approximately 8% of U.S. newspaper publishers; out of 132 publishers of newspapers with circulations over 100,000, only 4 are women. *See also* anchorman (newscasting).

New World replace this highly Eurocentric term with specific geographic areas, for example, *the North American continent. See also* "discovery" of America.

niggardly although by definition and derivation "niggardly" and "nigger" are completely unrelated, "niggardly" is too close for comfort to a word with profoundly negative associations. Use instead one of the many available alternatives: *stingy, miserly, parsimonious, skinflinty, cheeseparing, reluctant, ungenerous, grudging, begrudging, cheap, money-grubbing, grasping; scanty, skimpy, piddling, measly, puny.*

nigger deeply offensive, although you may hear it used positively among African Americans. For the completely unacceptable phrase "nigger in the woodpile" substitute *fly in the ointment, catch, hitch, snag, drawback.*

nightmare the original Night Mare was a beautiful creature who flew in dreams, bringing inspiration to the poet's bed. According to writer and Keltic mythologist Maureen Williams, the Night Mare became a horror when the patriarchy took over, reversing the polarity of everything good, lucky, and female. Since "nightmare" does not appear to function as a woman-biased term in everyday usage, it is probably not critical that we have no good alternative.

night watchman *night guard/watch, guard, watch, guardian, security guard/ officer, caretaker, gatekeeper, custodian, sentinel, sentry, lookout, patrol, patroller.*

no better than she should be this phrase reeks of judgment, sexism (there is no parallel for a man), and a conception of virtue based solely on sexuality.

nobleman *noble, member of the nobility, aristocrat, peer; noblewoman and nobleman.* Or, be specific: *countess, duke, princess, earl, marquis, baroness.*

no man is an island unless quoting Donne, use *no one is an island.*

no man is a prophet in his own country *no one is a prophet in their own country* (*see* singular "they"); *we are slow to see the prophet in our midst; prophets are not without honor, save in their own country and among their own kin and in their own house; prophets are seldom recognized in their own land; prophets go unhonored in their own country; people rarely recognize the prophet in their midst.* (The original phrase reflects earlier biblical translations; many current translations no longer use that version.)

no-man's-land *limbo, wasteland, Death Valley, nowhere land, uninhabitable/ unclaimed/lawless/noncombatant/unclaimed land/zone, demilitarized/buffer/ dead zone, hostile country, nowheresville, vacuum, dead space, in the crossfire, arid zone, the desert.* This is a difficult phrase to replace at times, not so much because there are no alternatives, but because we are seduced by its familiarity and by the ease with which it springs to mind.

noncustodial parent sometimes language automatically assigns this role to the father; don't assume anything. In the case of the noncustodial mother, beware of judgments. Our ideas of mothering and fathering are so narrow that we cannot conceive of a mother who would give up custody of her children or of a father who is devastated when he fails to get custody of his. The force of these sexist attitudes is enough to pressure some women into taking custody of children who might be better off with their fathers. Then, too, it is not always a straightforward matter of do-I-want-the-kids-or-not. In *How Could You? Mothers Without Custody of Their Children*, Harriet Edwards reports that three-quarters of her survey respondents of noncustodial mothers left because of bad marriages (75% had been physically or emotionally abused) but economics prevented them from taking their children (only five of the 100 women earned over $10,000, only seventeen had savings accounts—and fourteen of those amounted to less than $400, and only ten owned cars). They chose to avoid custody battles because they wanted to spare their children the conflict or because they were terrified of physical violence or of threats and harassment. One-quarter of them left because they didn't like mothering. Be especially careful of judging this last group; there is nothing in the genes that says all women have a bent for nurturing.

nonsexist language language that carries no cultural bias toward one sex or the other is nonsexist. It may or may not contain sex-specific words. "Irishwomen and Irishmen" is sex-specific but nonsexist.

nontraditional career/employment *female-intensive occupation/career, male-intensive occupation/career*. Using "nontraditional" implies work is unacceptable or abnormal for one sex. Statistics indicate that women's increasing interest in male-intensive occupations has not been matched by a comparable increase in men's interest in female-intensive occupations. And, despite two decades of social change, surveys show women in male-intensive fields still describe an inhospitable climate in which men ignore, discount, or sexually harass them—and advance more quickly to the more satisfying, higher-paid jobs. *See also* pink-collar job/worker.

nonwhite this term assumes white is the standard and lumps everyone else together without any individual identity. Replace the term with specifics.

noodle man *noodle-catalyst maker*.

normal man *normal individual/person*. The catch-all convention "normal man" is used, particularly in some medical and scientific writings, to designate a generic person; it is not a generic.

Norseman *ancient/early Scandinavian, Scandinavian, peoples of old Scandinavia, Viking, Norseman/Norsewoman, Northwoman/Northman, Norsefolk*. Inhabitants of Scandinavia since the tenth century are properly called Scandinavians. Before that they are Northmen and Northwomen. Scandinavian sea-warriors who plundered the coasts of Europe from the eighth to the tenth centuries are Vikings.

nosey parker this term is used for both women and men, and it is not based on anyone's given name. From the word "parker" (park keeper), a "nosey parker" was someone who hung about London's Hyde Park around the turn of the century for the vicarious thrill of spying on lovemaking couples.

nosy *curious, overcurious, supercurious, interested, interfering, intrusive, officious, snoopy, prying, spying, eavesdropping, tending/minding other people's business*. "Nosy" is used to describe women when men in the same situation are simply said to be curious.

not a fit night for man or beast *not a fit night to be out in/for two-legged creatures nor four-legged ones either/for humans or beasties, not a night to leave your fire by*.

not by bread alone does man live *not by bread alone do we/do you/does one live*.

now is the time for all good men to come to the aid of their party *now is the time for all good people to come to the aid of their country; the quick red fox jumps over the lazy brown dog*. The first alternative to the traditional (but sexist) typing drill is less partisan and the second is more effective (it contains all the letters of the alphabet).

nubile avoid; there is no parallel for a man. The biggest problem with this word is that it defines a woman primarily in terms of her readiness for a relationship with a man.

number-one man/number-two man *number one, boss, chief, head; number two, second in command, key/chief aide.* **See also** high man on the totem pole; right-hand man.

nun/nunnery acceptable sex-specific terms. The "sexist" religious orders system (i.e., restricted to one sex for other than biological reasons) has in fact been a positive one for women because (1) women themselves often chose to live this way; (2) inasmuch as the hierarchical church allowed any group autonomy, these women governed themselves; (3) religious orders offered women the first alternative to "belonging" to earthly father or husband; (4) nuns were some of the first women to work professionally outside the home (as teachers and nurses). Many nuns today consider themselves feminists and were among pioneers in the women's movement. The word "nunnery" is outdated; today nuns live in convents (or sometimes at the motherhouse), although increasing numbers live in apartments, shared houses, and other non-convent homes. In writing and speaking about nuns avoid stereotypes and acknowledge their contemporary work and status.

nuncio so far, always a man.

nurse 6% of nurses are men; they earn 10% more on average than women nurses.

nursemaid/nurserymaid *childcare worker, child minder/monitor/attendant, family/parents' helper, live-in babysitter, babysitter, nursery worker.*

nursery governess *teacher, private/in-home teacher, child minder/monitor.*

nurseryman *nursery owner/manager/operator/worker, tree farmer/grower, landscaper, gardener, horticulturist, florist, forester.*

nurture (verb) both men and woman can nurture.

nymph *nature god, sprite.*

nymphomaniac defined as a woman with excessive sexual desire, "nymphomaniac" is, in theory, paired with "satyr," a man with abnormal or excessive sexual craving. In practice, we hear "nymphomaniac"— or "nympho"—much more often (and used much less precisely) than "satyr." Unless you use both terms gender-fairly choose inclusive terms: *indiscriminate lover, oversexed/promiscuous/sexually active/ insatiable/senuous/sensual person, sex maniac/fiend, someone who sleeps around, bedhopper.*

O

A very great part of the mischiefs that vex this world arises from words.

Edmund Burke

oarsman *rower, boater, paddler, canoer, canoeist, oar puller.*

oblate woman or man.

odd-job(s)-man *odd-jobber, do-all, factotum, fixer, fixer-upper, repairer, do-it-yourselfer, general jobber, odd-job laborer, maintenance worker, carpenter, janitor, custodian, caretaker.*

odd man out *odd one out, loner, left out, third wheel, extra.*

Oedipus complex acceptable sex-specific term; the parallel is "Electra complex."

office boy/office girl *office worker/assistant/helper/staff member, staffer, assistant, right hand, aide, bureau assistant, co-worker, gofer.* Or, be specific: *secretary, clerk, bookkeeper, typist, receptionist, switchboard operator, messenger, courier, runner, deliverer, page. See also* girl Friday.

ogress *ogre.*

oh, boy! *wow! what a mess! whew! whoops!* "Oh, boy!" is not a dangerously sexist phrase; alternatives are included for those who want them.

oilman *oil company executive/sales representative, oil field worker, petroleum engineer, driller, wildcatter, wholesaler, retailer, refinery operator.*

old examine any use of "old" in describing people: how relevant and necessary is it to your material? Avoid these ageist, sexist terms: old bag, old bat, old biddy, old buzzard, old codger, old coot, old duffer, old fogey, old fuddy-duddy, old geezer, old witch.

old as Methuselah when using expressions like this, be aware of how many are male-based. Balance them with female-based expressions, creative expressions of your own, or alternatives: *old as the hills/as history/as time, an old chestnut. See* Writing Guidelines for a discussion of sex-linked expressions.

old boy/old girl these terms appear ageist and sexist, but they may be affectionate and complimentary in certain contexts. When there is any doubt about how they may be perceived, avoid them.

old-boys' network there may be times when this phrase is the one you want. However, it is becoming rare that a network is composed without exception of one sex, so it is often more correct to use *network, professional/career network, connections, business connections, contacts. See also* old-girls' network.

old-girls' network this tongue-in-cheek takeoff on the powerful and long-established old-boys' networks still often describes a reality for women who use one. The trend is to free the idea from sex roles so you may want alternatives sometimes: *network, professional/career network, connections, business connections, contacts.*

old lady/old man these terms have been used for generations (usually with "my") to refer disrespectfully to one's spouse, live-in partner, or parent. "Old man" has also been used to refer quasi-admiringly to one's boss or to a high-ranking male officer; "old lady" never was used this way. Note the nonparallel "lady/man." *See also* old woman.

old maid the correct alternative is *woman*. Unless a person's marital status is relevant, avoid even such apparently benign expressions as "unmarried woman" and "single woman"; they perpetuate the marriage-as-norm stereotype. Why have unmarried women gone from bachelor girl to spinster to old maid while men of all ages have simply been bachelors? *See also* bachelor; spinster.

old maid (card game) because commercial decks of cards for this child's game clearly mark the key card (which shows an old woman) as the "Old Maid," it is difficult to be anything but ageist and sexist when using a dedicated deck. The dreaded leftover card has not always been female; at times the game has been called Le Vieux Garçon (French for "the old boy") or Black Peter. Since the only known nonsexist name for the game is ageist (Old Miser), those who are passing it on to the next generation are encouraged to re-name the game. Remove three aces (leaving the ace of hearts) and call the game simply Ace. Or add a joker to the deck and call the game Joker, Wild Card, or The Cheese Stands Alone.

old-maidish replace this vague term with a more precise adjective: *particular, fussy, finicky, fastidious, pernickety, set in one's ways, solitary, precise, old-fashioned, repressed, nervous, fearful.* These adjectives can be used for both men and women and are associated with unmarried older women only insofar as they convey the inaccurate but stereotypical meaning of "old-maidish."

old maids (popcorn) *unpopped corn/kernels, no-pops.*

Old Man River/Ol' Man River leave as is.

Old Man Winter there is a long tradition of making a man of winter: "Barren winter, with his wrathful nipping cold" (Shakespeare); "Lastly came Winter . . . [c]hattering his teeth" (Edmund Spenser);

"winter [hath] his delights" (Thomas Campion); "Winter . . . [w]ears on his smiling face" (Coleridge); "O Winter, king of intimate delights" (William Cowper); "Winter . . . with all his rising train" (James Thomson). Why have winter, time, and death all been personified as men?

old masters since the old masters were all men, and they were masters in the Western European system of master-apprentice relationships, this term is historically correct. When not referring to painters and works specifically known as the old masters, use *distinguished/great painters/ paintings, the classics, thirteenth/fourteenth/fifteenth/sixteenth/seventeenth-century artists/works*. "Master" and "mistress" illustrate what commonly happens to male-female word pairs: the male word takes on new and broader meanings while the female word shrinks to refer only to a woman's sexual function. Lord Beaverbrook appreciated the absurdity of this word pair: "Buy Old Masters. They fetch a much better price than old mistresses."

oldster as a companion for "youngster," this term is not particularly demeaning. However, not everyone will like being so labeled; use it sensitively or reserve it for self-definition.

old-timer OK; this is more of an affectionate term of respect than a negative reflection on age.

old wives' tale *superstitious folklore/belief, superstition, myth, silly myth, misconception, tale*.

old woman this put-down does triple duty: it insults the man being so described, makes an epithet of "woman," and is also ageist. Use instead for both sexes *fussbudget, fuddy-duddy, weakling, worrywart, handwringer, worrier*. *See also* old lady/old man.

ombudsman *ombuds, ombud, ombudscommittee, watchdog, investigator, referee, representative, surveillant, intermediary, go-between, censor, monitor, guardian of the public good, regulatory agent, troubleshooter*. The Swedish word itself is inclusive—the "man" means "one"—but its English use is not. The *Oxford English Dictionary* defines "ombudswoman" as "a female ombudsman," thus indicating that "ombudsman" is sex-specific. University campuses now have Student Ombuds Services and at least one large metropolitan area has an ombudscop program under which police officers respond to neighborhood concerns.

one man, one vote *one person/citizen/member/legislator/voter, one vote, one vote per voter/person/citizen/member/legislator*.

One man's meat is another man's poison *one's meat is another's poison, one person's meat is another person's/another's poison*.

one-man/two-man/three-man, etc. (adj.) *one-person*, or substitutes such as *two-seater boat, two-way mayoral race, three-person tent, three-way contest, four-passenger plane*. Or use a noun: *two-seater, tent for two*. For "one-man" try: *individual, lone, solo, singlehanded, solitary*. Alternatives for "one-man show" include *one-person/solo/individual/single-artist show/ exhibition/exhibit/performance*. As there is no parallel nonsexist phrase for "one-man band" use *one-woman band or one-man band*.

one of the boys *one of the gang, a regular person.*

one small step for man, one giant leap for mankind unless quoting Neil Armstrong, use *one small step for a human being, one giant leap for the world/human race.*

oneupmanship *one-upping, the art of one-upping, going one better, keeping a jump ahead, getting the jump on, trying to get the best of, competitiveness, competition, competitive skill, rivalry, outdoing someone, quest for superiority, keeping up with the Joneses, vying for top honors.* With use, the shorter and punchier "one-upping" quickly begins to sound "right." It is not a new construction; Malcolm Forbes said, "Keeping score of old scores and scars, getting even and one-upping, always makes you less than you are."

only man is vile unless quoting Reginald Heber, use *only we/we mortals/ humans are vile, only humankind is vile.* See Writing Guidelines for suggestions on how to handle sexist quotations.

open 'er up! *open it up!*

opposite sex this phrase is sometimes used coyly in sexist contexts and also perpetuates an adversarial attitude toward female-male relationships. Give it a second look. Dorothy L. Sayers wonders why it has to be the "opposite" sex; why not the "neighboring" sex? *See also* "battle of the sexes."

orchardman *orchardist, tree grower/farmer, nursery owner/manager/operator/ worker, citriculturist, arborist, arboriculturist.*

orderly *nursing/nurse assistant, N.A.* Traditionally aides and orderlies did the same work, but all aides were women and all orderlies were men. Most hospitals and nursing homes now use the inclusive terms.

organization man "One of the interesting changes that has taken place in today's business climate is that many organization 'men' are now women" (Don Ethan Miller, *The Book of Jargon*). Until a more compact, inclusive term appears, use *organization woman/women and organization man/men.* *See also* company man.

Oriental *Asian American, Asian.* Or, be specific: *Japanese, Vietnamese*, etc. "Oriental" is particularly unacceptable as a noun, but even the adjective and the term "Orient" are considered imprecise and stereotypical and in disfavor with most Asian Americans.

Our Father (prayer) *See* Lord's Prayer, the.

outcall service *prostitution business.*

outdoorsman *hunter, nature-lover, outdoors enthusiast/person, fresh-air lover/ type, fan of the great outdoors; outdoorswoman and outdoorsman.* Or, be specific: *camper, fisher, hiker, birdwatcher, canoer, mountain climber.*

out-Herod Herod when using expressions like this, be aware of how many are male-based. Balance them with female-based expressions, creative expressions of your own, or alternatives: *outdo, outweigh, surpass, excel, exceed, transcend, outrank, get ahead of, be superior to, outstrip, beat one's own record, put into the shade, have the upper hand, go to any length. See* Writing Guidelines for a discussion of sex-linked expressions.

outing publicly disclosing the homosexuality of prominent people thought to be heterosexual is advocated by some gay activists who want to out those gay men and lesbians who are believed to have harmed—or at least refused to help—their own community (for example, a gay lawmaker who votes against AIDS funding or a gay record producer who handles a notorious gay-bashing comedian). The thinking is that when admired neighbors and public figures are seen to be lesbian or gay, the public will come to accept homosexuality; these outed people can then also serve as role models for younger people. Those who favor outing also feel that the death toll taken by insufficiently funded AIDS research and the rising rate of violence against lesbians and gay men justify a new militancy. They say that gay men and lesbians who frequent public places where gays gather have outed themselves and should not rely on some assumption of a "privacy zone" to protect their closet status. However, most mainstream gay political groups oppose outing and support the right to privacy. Sexual orientation is nobody else's business, they say, and individuals have the right to come out (if they do) in their own idiosyncratic time, place, and manner. Outing, on the other hand, is an aggressive act, forced upon people against their will "for their own good"—a controlling, violent, and dominating act. Dragging unwilling victims to the sacrificial table went out of style a long time ago.

ovenman *oven tender/operator, malt roaster.*

overlord *supervisor, overseer, boss. See also* master (noun).

overman (noun) *leader, arbitrator, referee. See also* forelady/foreman/forewoman.

overman (verb) *overstaff, oversupply. See also* man/manned.

overmaster *overpower, overcome, overset, outwit, outflank, out-maneuver, defeat, conquer, vanquish, discomfit, confound.*

overmastering *overpowering, overwhelming, all-powerful, irresistible, invincible, unconquerable, indomitable, unquenchable, incontestable.*

oversensitive *sensitive, considerate, thoughtful; thin-skinned, touchy, easily hurt.* "Oversensitive" is usually reserved for women; use the alternatives for both sexes.

owner an issue that once divided this country and left scars that still haven't healed (one human being owning another) was considered good fun by *Esquire* magazine when it offered its readers a tear-out section entitled, "Your Wife: An Owner's Manual" (June 1990). A number of works have documented women's treatment as property, along with the consequences, which range from petty humiliation to murder. One study of women's deaths at the hands of lovers and husbands showed that the critical moment often occured when the woman tried to leave. Chuck Niessen-Derry, who works with batterers through an intervention project, says the man who is so obsessed by a woman that he would sooner kill her than have her go off and live a life of her own is neither mentally ill nor out of control. "When a man kills his wife, he's on the same continuum as the rest of us, only on the far edge. It's like the ultimate expression of sexism, of ownership: 'If I can't have you, nobody can.'" There is only one person entitled to an owner's manual on a woman (an example of the proper use of this concept is The Diagram Group's publication, *Woman's Body: An Owner's Manual*).

oysterman *oyster farmer/grower/cultivator.*

p

Opinions founded on prejudice are always sustained with the greatest violence.

Francis Jeffrey

packman *peddler.*

page boy *page.*

pageboy (hairstyle) *bob, page-style hairdo, roll-under hairstyle.*

pal from the Romani for "brother" or "friend," "pal" is more often used of boys/men, but is also correctly used of girls/women.

paladin historically a man; for an outstanding champion of a cause, a paladin could be either sex.

palimony this court-ordered allowance may be made to either member of a former relationship.

pallbearer woman or man.

Pandora's box the majority of our sex-linked metaphors, expressions, and figures are male-based; female-based ones, like this one, are very often negative. "Pandora's box" has immediate and graphic associations for us, and it is often the best choice. If you want sex-neutral alternatives use *opening a can of worms, the curiosity that killed the cat, unforeseen consequences, the unknown, mischief, the ills that flesh is heir to, machinations of the devil, all hell breaking loose.*

panjandrum man or woman.

pantryman *pantry worker/clerk.*

paperboy *newspaper/paper carrier/deliverer, news carrier, newspaper vendor; paperboy and papergirl* (if sex-specificity is necessary and if the carriers are under the age of thirteen or fourteen).

paramour from the French, "par amour" ("by way of love") "paramour" is used of either sex.

paraplegic/quadriplegic *someone with/who has paraplegia/quadriplegia.* Question the need to mention a disability. When it is highly relevant to your material, information can be conveyed neutrally without labeling the whole person by something that is only part of their life.

parent too often the inclusive "parent" is used when the surrounding text makes it clear that only the mother is being addressed. Material on infant care is addressed "Dear Mother" and an ad for a new adhesive tape makes "diapering so easy, even Dad can do it." Beware of sex bias toward parents; while the reality may be that more women are active parents than men, it is also reality that many more men than before are becoming involved and should be given the name as well as the game. A step in the right direction: the new Target Greatland stores have diaper-changing counters in both the men's and the women's restrooms. In the plural do not assume that both parents live with the child, are related to the child, or are the same sex. *See also* babysitter; mother and father.

parlormaid servant. *See also* cleaning girl/cleaning lady/cleaning woman; maid.

parson depending on the denomination, this may be either sex.

parts man *stock clerk, parts clerk/worker.*

pasha retain as a male term in the context of Turkish or North African political life. However, there is no contraindication to the colorful and metaphorical use of "pasha" to describe a powerful or high-ranking official of either sex.

paste-up man *paste-up editor/copy editor, camera operator.*

past master *acknowledged expert, expert, adept, champion, genius; ex-champion; experienced/accomplished artist/writer/bricklayer,* etc. This may also refer to the holder of a Freemason office or to a specific title in a guild or society, in which case it should be used as it is.

pastor depending on the particular denomination, a pastor may be either sex.

pater/paterfamilias acceptable sex-specific terms, although the Latin is more often replaced with "father/patriarch." The original paterfamilias, head of the clan, tribe, or family, had unlimited power over his wives, concubines, children, slaves, servants, animals, and property. In the classical era, his power extended even to deciding who would live and who would die (girl children, for example, or disobedient wives or slaves). Be sensitive to the history and legacy of this concept when using these terms.

paternal unless you mean fatherlike or father-related ("paternal grandmother"), use *parental, ancestral; kindly, kindhearted, loving, devoted, indulgent, solicitous, concerned, fond, protective, sympathetic.* "Paternal" has been overused, and has unpleasant associations with such words (and the attitudes behind them) as "paternalism" and "patronizing."

paternalism (pseudogeneric) *parentalism, authoritarian parentalism, authoritarianism, political intrusion.* "Paternalism" is entrenched in certain academic, philosophic, and political circles, and is thus difficult (but not impossible) to replace with a commonly recognized one-word term. The concept of paternalism is offensive to many women and minorities; paternalistic societies, laws, churches, and husbands have

been a fact of life throughout history. Former U.S. Supreme Court
Justice William Brennan wrote that "Our nation has had a long and
unfortunate history of sex discrimination . . . rationalized by an
attitude of 'romantic paternalism' which, in practical effect, put
women not on a pedestal, but in a cage." Retain the term when
speaking or writing about the historical fact of male hierarchical
domination; avoid it when the sex of the dominators is not germane.
See also chivalry; male-dominated society.

patient as Job when using expressions like this, be aware of how many
are male-based. Some of the time use female-based expressions,
creative expressions of your own, or alternatives: *long-suffering,
stoical, forbearing, uncomplaining, longanimous, abiding, patient, extraordinarily patient, patient as the grave, through fire and water, keeping the
faith.* (Incidentally, the Book of Job does not contain the word
"patient.") *See* Writing Guidelines for a discussion of sex-linked
expressions. *See also* patient Griselda.

patient Griselda *someone who is long-suffering/submissive/ humble/patient/
extraordinarily patient/patient as the grave/passive/abiding/stoical/forbear-
ing, someone who endures through thick and thin/through fire and water.*
Griselda is probably Job's opposite number, but she does not, to put
it mildly, provide a particularly acceptable or admirable model for
today's woman, and it is better to avoid her. *See also* patient as Job.

patriarch/patriarchy originally seen as divinely authorized, the social
systems traditionally referred to as patriarchal form "the basic
principle of all major relationship systems in the western world"
(Sandra M. Schneiders, *Women and the Word*). Schneiders, theologian
Rosemary Ruether, former president of the World Council of
Churches Visser't Hooft, and others say that this principle supports
racism, colonialism, ageism, classism, and clericalism as well as
sexism. Today replace "patriarchy" with *dominator system/society,
dominator model of society, hierarchy, hierarchical/authoritarian society*
(the first two terms from Riane Eisler, *The Chalice and the Blade, The
Partnership Way of Life*). While it is true that dominator models of
society have been established and maintained almost entirely by men,
it was not their maleness that was destructive and oppressive as
much as their hierarchicalness and their abuse of power. In addition,
not all men were involved in the dominator system; many of them,
especially those who did not conform, suffered under it. It is entirely
possible to be a father (patriarch) without being oppressive; continuing to use terms like "patriarch" and "patriarchy" as synonyms for
"oppressor" and "oppressor system" is not recommended. Note
incidentally that the opposite of a patriarchy is not a matriarchy.
Both matriarchies and patriarchies involve an imbalance of power
between the sexes and are thus dominator societies; the true opposite

of a matriarchy or a patriarchy is a partnership society (Riane Eisler). Until we reach the point where neither sex needs to dominate the other, use "matriarchy/patriarchy" terms cautiously. Sex-neutral alternatives for "patriarch" include *ancestor/family elder, head of the family, family head*. The word "patricentric" puts the father at the center of the family or system without the hierarchical overtones of "patriarchal." *See also* chivalry; male-dominated society; matriarch/ matriarchy; paternalism (pseudogeneric).

patrician this word shares the same Latin root ("pater") as other "father" words and there is no parallel "matrician." It is not overtly sexist, but you may sometimes want alternatives: *blue-blooded, noble, elegant, well-bred, formal, stately, graceful, courtly, debonair, delicate, decorous, majestic, exquisite, polite, seemly, refined, genteel, cultivated, urbane, sophisticated, worldly, stylish, cosmopolitan, classy*. The best alternative for the noun is *aristocrat*, although we tend not to use "patrician" in that sense, perhaps because of our democratic underpinnings.

patrilineal use "patrilineal" when referring to descent through the father's line.

patrimony *inheritance, heritage, legacy, inherited property, estate, family estate, portion, share, lot*. Note the amazingly nonparallel "patrimony/ matrimony." *See also* matrimony.

patriot/patriotic/patriotism from Latin for "land of my father," these terms function today as inclusive words. If you need alternatives without sex-linked roots try *nationalist, lover of one's country, chauvinist, flag-waver, jingo, jingoist, loyalist, hundred-percenter; nationalistic, loyal, allegiant, jingoistic, chauvinistic, flag-waving, public spirited, civic-minded; national loyalty, good citizenship, nationalism, allegiance, jingoism, chauvinism, love of country*.

patrolman *patrol/highway/law enforcement/peace/police/traffic officer, patroller, state trooper, trooper, officer, police*.

patron both women and men are patrons today, and the word functions fairly inclusively, but it comes from the Latin for "father"; it has been used more of men than of women; it is part of the exceedingly imbalanced word pair "matron/patron"; and it has some fairly sexist relatives ("patronage," "patronize," "patronymic"). For those reasons you may want alternatives: *benefactor, sponsor, backer, donor, supporter, promoter, philanthropist, booster, champion, partisan, angel, guardian angel, bankroll, advocate, mentor, helper, protector; library user, customer, shopper, buyer, purchaser, subscriber, client*. *See also* matron.

patronage *sponsorship, support, auspices, advocacy, defense, championship, assistance, encouragement, promotion, protection, influence; business, trade, custom, customers, clientele, commerce, shopping, trading*. "Patronage" comes from the Latin for "father," has no word pair "matronage," is closely related to "patronize," and reflects centuries of "father"-

inspired domination. These associations suggest it is better to replace the word. *See also* patron.

patroness *patron.* "Patron" may not always be the word of choice but it is far better than "patroness." *See also* patron.

patronize *support, favor, uphold, promote, defend, sponsor, show favor to, defer to, tolerate; condescend to, treat condescendingly, underestimate, disparage, discount, look down on, talk down to, deign, stoop, be overbearing/arrogant; trade with, buy/purchase from, do business with, give business to, shop at, frequent.* "Patronize" has highly sexist roots and associations and should be avoided. *See also* patron.

patronizing *condescending, scornful, supercilious, overbearing, snobbish, superior-acting, offensive, humiliating, haughty, presumptuous, insulting, insolent.*

patron saint *namesake/guardian saint, special saint* (e.g., "Saint Appollonia, special saint of dentists").

patronym/patronymic referring to a name derived from the father or a paternal ancestor, these are correct sex-specific terms. If you mean the term in the generic sense use *surname, last name, birth name.* Author Une Stannard believes that giving children their fathers' surnames sprang from ignorance about the facts of life. Before the female ovum was discovered in 1827, people assumed that men contributed the seed of life while women's wombs simply provided the soil in which it grew. "Since the female role in generation was thought to be negligible, it seemed only logical that children would receive their names from their fathers, seen as their sole progenitors." There is currently no law that requires a child's birth certificate to bear the father's last name. In most states, you can name a child whatever you want as long as you have no dishonest intentions. In 1988 in Nebraska, however, a couple were prevented, by state bureaucrats and judges, from giving their daughter a last name different from either the father's or the mother's. According to the ruling, parents have no fundamental right to choose their children's names. A dissenting judge wrote, however, that "a person's name is, in a sense, her identity, her personality, her being. There is something sacred about a name. It is our own business, not the government's." Sharon Lebell (*Naming Ourselves, Naming Our Children: Resolving the Last Name Dilemma*) proposes the "bilineal solution" whereby boys are named after their fathers, girls after their mothers, or vice versa, thus ensuring that both names get passed on. *See also* hyphenated names; matronym/matronymic; surname.

patsy the origins of this word do not appear sex-linked and it is not perceived as particularly gender-specific. For a more neutral-appearing term use *scapegoat, goat, loser, born loser, sucker, dupe, nebbish, victim, mark, target, laughingstock, sad sack, doormat, sap, hard-*

luck story, pigeon, pushover, fool. **See also** fall guy/fall man; whipping boy.

Paul Pry when using expressions like this, be aware of how many are male-based. Some of the time use female-based expressions, creative expressions of your own, or alternatives: *snoop, busybody, stickybeak, eavesdropper, nosey parker*. For a discussion of sex-linked expressions, *see* Writing Guidelines. **See also** nosey parker.

pay equity *See* equal pay/equal pay for equal work.

paymaster *pay/payroll agent, payroll supervisor, purser, treasurer, bursar, receiver, steward, accountant, cashier, teller*.

peace on earth, good will to men *peace on earth, good will to all*.

peacock/peafowl/peahen use the generic "peafowl" instead of the male "peacock" when referring to both males and females.

Peck's bad boy *enfant terrible, in the avant garde, innovative/unorthodox/ unconventional/nonconforming director/artist/musician*, etc., *heretic* (in nonreligious sense), *questioner; embarrassment; mischievous child*. **See also** enfant terrible.

Pecksniffian when using expressions like this, be aware of how many are male-based (Pecksniff was a male character in Dickens). Some of the time use female-based expressions, creative expressions of your own, or alternatives: *pharisaical, hypocritical, insincere, crocodilian, mealy-mouthed, double-dealing, two-faced, smooth-tongued, sanctimonious, self-righteous, unctuous, canting, pietistical*. **See** Writing Guidelines for a discussion of sex-linked expressions.

pederast *child molester/abuser, habitual child molester*. The Greek root word means either "child" or "boy," but "pederast" is defined today as a man who uses boys as sex objects, and thus is correctly sex-linked; there is no parallel for women/girls. The suggested alternatives for "pederast" are inclusive but, more important, they also make clear exactly what a pederast does. **See also** pedophile.

pedophile *child molester/abuser, habitual child molester*. "Pedophile" is not sexist per se, but it is often associated with men since they are the principal abusers. Use alternatives because they appear more inclusive but, more important, they do not dress up an ugly practice with a fancy name that is indecipherable to many people. **See also** pederast.

peeping Tom *peeper, peeker, window peeper, voyeur, ogler, eavesdropper, breather, fetishist, pervert*. Although "peeping Thomasina" is seen occasionally, it is unnecessarily coy and not a good parallel for "peeping Tom." The male peeper is not the harmless voyeur he has been thought to be. Statistics indicate that such individuals are usually involved or will be involved in more harmful deviant behavior including rape and other sex crimes. Avoid treating this offender lightly or humorously.

peeress *peer*.

Peking man *early human, Peking fossil, Homo erectus*.

penman *writer, author, scribe, calligrapher*.

penmanship *handwriting, writing, longhand, hand, script, calligraphy, manuscription*.

penwoman *writer, author, scribe, calligrapher*, except for members of the National League of American Penwomen, an organzation of professional women writers and editors.

"people first" rule Haim Ginott taught us that labels are disabling; intuitively most of us recognize this and resist having labels put on us. The disability movement originated the "people first" rule, which says we don't call someone a "diabetic" but rather "a person with diabetes." Saying someone is "an AIDS victim" reduces the person to a disease, a label, a statistic; use instead "a person with/who has/living with AIDS." The 1990 Americans with Disabilities Act is a good example of correct wording. Name the person as a person first, and let qualifiers (age, sex, disability, race) follow, but (and this is crucial) only if they are relevant. For years women and minorities have been asking writers and speakers to delete unnecessary sex-specific and race-specific identifiers. Readers of a magazine aimed at an older audience were asked what they wanted to be called (elderly? senior citizens? seniors? golden agers?). They rejected all the labels; one said, "How about 'people'?" When high school students said they didn't like to be called kids, teens, teenagers, youth, adolescents, or juveniles, and were asked just what they *would* like to be called, they said, "Could we just be people?" *See also* handicappism; victim.

people of color use this term (or variants of it) when groups or individuals use it for themselves; it is often a term of pride. When used by the dominant culture to label others from without, it is problematic, masking people's individuality and diverse origins.

perky copyeditor Nancy Greiner says, "No more stories describing women athletes or other women as 'perky,' please. It is demeaning." A similar caution might be applied to "pert."

person not sexist; the Latin "persona" means "human being." Although using "-person" as a suffix has been helpful in making the transition to inclusive language, it should be avoided whenever possible; it is awkward, contrived, and unnecessary. *See* Writing Guidelines for a discussion of -man, -person, and -woman. Women-Are-Persons-Too Department: in 1988 a federal judge ruled against the U.S. Department of Agriculture, which claimed that a farm couple was only one person. Although a father and his son or a brother and a sister farming in partnership were regarded as two people, a husband and wife were counted as only one person for USDA purposes. U.S. District Court Judge Joyce Hens Green officially rejected "the archaic notion that husbands and wives are one 'person.'" African Americans have had great difficulty with personhood; for years they were designated "nonpersons" in order to maintain the institution of slavery. *See also* human.

pervert technically inclusive (referring to a person given to some form of sexual perversion) "pervert" tends to most often call to mind a man. The other problem with it is defining "sexual perversion"; it has often been used to mean prostitution or same-sex sexual activity. Use the term cautiously and infrequently.

peter/peter out (verb) *give/run out, become exhausted, trail/drain off, dry/use up, dissipate.*

Peter Pan collar this term is so immediately evocative of a certain collar that it is difficult to replace. Sometimes you can use *round collar.*

Peter Pan syndrome described by Dr. Dan Kiley in a book of the same name and subtitled *Men Who Have Never Grown Up*, this syndrome includes such traits in adult males as narcissism, impulsivity, poor adjustment to reality, dependence on other people's approval, "self-assertion" by means of temper tantrums, and taking love for granted while never learning to give it.

Peter's pence *church tax, donation, alms, honorarium, gratuity, offering.* Use "Peter's pence" when it refers specifically to the (in most dioceses) annual papal collection in the Roman Catholic Church.

petite avoid; it is used only of women, and its masculine companion, "petit," has a rather important and meaningful life in the legal world—an example of yet another female/male word pair that bit the dust. If size is relevant use inclusive terms: *small, tiny, miniature, pint-sized, teeny, short, trim, slight, slender, thin, lean.*

pharaoh the word "pharaoh" means "king"; women married to a pharaoh or who served as regents were called queens. However, at least one woman reigned with the full powers of a pharaoh and was even portrayed with the stylized pharaonic beard. Hatshepsut, who reigned from 1503 to 1482 B.C., devoted herself to commerce, peace, and the construction or completion of monuments and temples. After her death, her nephew, Thutmose III, defaced her cartouche, left unfinished her tomb, smashed statues of her, and otherwise rendered her and the fruits of her reign as invisible as possible. Christiane Desroches Noblecourt (*La femme au temps des pharaons*) notes that Egyptian women of the pharaonic periods contributed to society in politics, religion, and daily life. They had as many rights as men, being able to rule, teach, and make their own decisions.

philanthropic/philanthropist/philanthropy *See* anthropology.

pickup (woman) never use this; it not only says that the woman is passive (she is "picked up") but it also implies (by giving her, but not her partner, a special derogatory label) that she is the guilty party. We pay lip service to the two-to-tango notion, but our language says that a man's actions are literally unremarkable while the woman's actions deserve a judgment. Removing words like "pickup" from the language will not also do away with the double standard, but it is a necessary part of the process.

pied piper in the well-known fairy tale, the pied piper was a man, but the term itself is gender-free.

pikeman *pike bearer/wielder, soldier; tollbooth operator; miner.* Or, leave as is in historical contexts.

Pilgrim Fathers *Pilgrims.*

pimp by definition a man.

pink from babyhood onward, this color has traditionally been associated with girls/women. Unlike blue, which can be worn by female infants, girls, and women with impunity, pink has remained largely associated with the feminine; men generally wear it only in small discreet doses. According to European legend, girl babies were found inside pink roses (the same legend situated newborn boys in blue cabbages), thus giving rise to the pink-for-girls "rule" and reinforcing the blue-for-boys. *See also* blue; sexism.

pink-collar job/worker "pink-collar" refers to that small number of jobs (30 out of 500) into which 80% of all salaried women fit (and that proportion has changed very little over the past twenty-five years): secretaries, household workers, nurses, waiters, librarians, health technicians, elementary school teachers, bank tellers, etc. Most women remain segregated in relatively low-paying, low-status, female-intensive occupations. "Pink-collar" is currently a valid sex-specific sociological term; the hope is that a changing reality will eventually render it obsolete. The clustering of women in certain jobs negatively affects earnings: a 1% increase in the proportion of female college graduates in an occupation reduces earnings by .42%; among women without college degrees clustering accounts for 30% of the wage difference between the sexes. The few men in such pink-collar jobs as nursing, childcare, secretarial work, or teaching say "their hardest job is combatting the poor image that society gives them for taking these jobs" (Mike Kelly, "Men Who Wear 'Pink Collars'," *Men Freeing Men*, ed. Francis Baumli). The men are perceived as unaggressive, unmasculine, and not career-oriented, they feel they have to perform better on the job than women, and they are constantly chided for doing "women's work." *See also* nontraditional career/employment.

pin money an outdated term for an outdated concept whereby husbands gave their wives spending money (literally to buy pins).

pinup girl *model, photographic/calendar model.*

pioneer we too often incorrectly assume that all pioneers were not only male, but white.

pirate noted pirates (or buccaneers or freebooters) included Anne Bonney, Mary Read, and Grania O'Malley.

pitchman *sidewalk vendor/seller, barker; hawker, promoter, high-pressure seller, celebrity endorser.*

pitman (automobile) *connecting rod.* The "man" in "pitman" refers to the adult male, so the word's origins are sexist.

pitman (industry) *pit/underground miner, miner.*

pivotman (basketball) *post/pivot player, pivot, center.*

placeman *bureaucrat, government official, functionary.*

plainclothesman *plainclothes/undercover officer/detective, detective, investigator, police officer.*

plainsman *plains dweller/inhabitant; plainswoman and plainsman.*

platform man platform attendant/loader.

playboy *swinger, bedhopper, philanderer, mover, hustler, free spirit, flirt, libertine, seducer, high-roller, high-liver, high-flier, hedonist, fun-seeker, pleasure-lover, good-timer, sport, gadabout, party animal, dissolute/promiscuous/sexually active person, someone who sleeps around, make-out artist, lover. See also* ladies' man; man about town; rake; womanize/womanizer.

playfellow *playmate, friend.*

playgirl/playmate *centerfold, model, nude model.* If you mean "playgirl" in the same way "playboy" is used, *see* playboy for alternatives.

playmate (woman) avoid; highly demeaning and objectifying.

plowboy/plowman *plow driver/operator, farm worker, farmer, cultivator, sower.*

plumber fewer than 1% of U.S. plumbers are women.

poetess *poet.*

poilu this World War I French soldier was always a man, with at least one known exception: Marie Marvingt, the Frenchwoman known as the Fiancée of Danger, disguised herself as a poilu and fought in the front lines for three weeks until she was discovered.

point man *high-scoring player/ballplayer, high-scorer, scorer.*

policeman *officer, police, police/peace/law/highway/patrol/law enforcement/beat/traffic officer, officer/agent/arm of the law; policewoman and policeman.* Or, be specific: *sergeant, detective, sheriff, chief, deputy, lieutenant,* etc. Some 13% of U.S. police officers are women. There have been policewomen since 1910 when former social worker Alice Stebbins Wells was appointed to the Los Angeles Police Department. Invariably accused of using her husband's badge for the then-free streetcar rides offered all police officers, she was finally issued "Policewoman's Badge No. 1." *See also* patrolman; stick man (police).

policeman of the world *watchdog/police officer of the world, world's cop.* "Policeman of the world" has a specific and instantly recognizable sense in some disciplines. However, with a little effort one could get used to an alternative or construct a new one. Headline writers like "world's cop" for its brevity.

politics makes strange bedfellows unless quoting Charles Dudley Warner, use *politics makes strange bedmates.*

Pollyanna if you need a sex-neutral term use *irrepressible/eternal/persistent/ unflagging/perennial/cockeyed/foolish/incurable optimist, daydreamer, romantic, visionary, castlebuilder, utopian, idealist, victim of terminal cheerfulness, one who lives in a fool's paradise, wearer of rose-colored glasses.*

polyandry/polygyny correct sex-specific terms. *See also* polygamy.

polygamy this term means a marriage in which either spouse may have more than one mate at the same time. We tend to use it as though it means "several wives" instead of "several mates"; the correct term for "several wives" is "polygyny."

pom-pom girl *pom-pom twirler/artist, cheerleader.*

pontiff so far, always a man.

pontificate *orate, declaim, hold forth, harangue, expound, wax pompous, declaim; preach, lecture, sermonize, dogmatize.* "Pontificate" comes from the Latin, sex-neutral "bridge-building," but has been so associated with the male papacy that alternatives are offered.

pooh-bah although the original character from *The Mikado* (1885) was a man, this term can be used to describe a self-important person of either sex who occupies a high position, holds several positions at once, or wields great influence.

poor as Job/poor as Job's turkey when using expressions like this, be aware of how many are male-based. Some of the time use female-based expressions, creative expressions of your own, or alternatives: *poor as a church mouse, destitute, penniless, indigent, poverty-stricken, on one's uppers, down and out, out at the elbows, down at the heels. See* Writing Guidelines for a discussion of sex-linked expressions.

population control *reproductive responsibility/freedom/rights/information, birth control, contraception, family planning, fertility control.* The term "population control" reveals a paternalistic, patronizing attitude (masculine terms are intended) toward people in general, toward peoples in nonaligned countries, and most particularly toward women. The alternatives shift the emphasis to the control people have over their own choices. *See also* birth control.

pornography in *The Pornographer,* John McGahern says, "It [pornography] is heartless and it is mindless and it is a lie." For Susan Brownmiller (*Against Our Will*), "Pornography is the undiluted essence of anti-female propaganda." Susan Sontag (in *Perspectives on Pornography,* ed. Douglas A. Hughes) says it drives "a wedge between one's existence as a full human being and one's existence as a sexual being—while in ordinary life one hopes to prevent such a wedge from being driven." Pornography is often associated with the rising tide of sexual crime against both children and adults, the desensitization of individuals toward the horror of violence and rape, and the inability of many men to relate to women with any mutuality or respect because of their pornography-inspired (but unrealistic) expectations of women as physically perfect, willing servants to any sexual fantasy. Susan Griffin (*Pornography and Silence*) says pornography teaches men that sex has nothing to do with emotions. Child porn flourishes, and is even defended by a few well-organized political pressure groups (e.g., the North American Man-Boy Love Association and the Rene Guyon Society, whose motto is "Sex by Age 8 or It's Too Late"). As many as one million children have been used to create the child porn in some 275 monthly magazines (Carol Gorman, *Pornography*). Addiction is also a factor. (Harriet Beecher Stowe said it best many years ago: "Whipping and abuse are like laudanum; you have to double the dose as the sensibilities decline.") Men may buy pornography but women pay for it—in terms of exploitation, rape, violence, and a society that sees them as disposable sexual objects. Pornography associates women with pain, inferiority, and humiliation; the assumption for the user is that this is real and normal. Good sex is also a victim; a graduate of The School of Pornography is a sex-illiterate. (D. H. Lawrence says, "Pornography is the attempt to insult sex, to do dirt on it.") Erotica differs from pornography in that it celebrates rather than degrades human sexuality. It preserves the mutuality of sexual activity, is not exploitative, controlling, objectifying, addictive, a "using" activity, or effected for prurient interests. It also does not embarrass you if you are found reading it by a friend you admire. *See also* rape; sex object; violence.

portress *porter.*

poseur this grammatically masculine French term is used (in French and English) for either sex. If it seems too masculine, try *pretentious person, mannerist, lump of affectation, charlatan, quack, humbug, pedant, pedagogue, pseudo-intellectual.*

postboy *postilion.*

postman *See* mailman.

postmaster/postmistress retain for titles in current use; otherwise use *postal chief/manager, post office supervisor/manager.* When the official title for men in the same position is "postmaster," use that for women (it is less sexist than "postmistress") but you might want to add "[sic]" after it.

postmaster general retain for current titles; otherwise use *federal postal chief/supervisor.*

potboy retain in historical contexts. Otherwise use *barroom attendant, tavern helper, bar assistant.*

potentate   in certain contexts today, this could be either sex; historically it was always a man.

poultryman   *poultry farmer/breeder, chicken farmer.*

poundmaster   retain for official titles or add "[sic]" after it; otherwise use *poundkeeper, pound officer/chief/supervisor.*

poverty   the term is inclusive; the issue is both sexist and racist. A white male head of household has a one-in-nine chance of living in poverty; a black female head of household has a one-in-two chance; nearly one-third of urban-dwelling Native Americans and nearly one-half of those in rural areas live below the poverty line. *See also* classism.

powder room   *restroom, washroom, lavatory, bathroom, lounge.* This word is paradoxically sexist: the "powder" in the phrase comes from the powder men used on their wigs in colonial times, yet today the powder room is reserved for women. Avoid the term; it is coy and exclusive. *See also* john (toilet).

prattle   "prattle" and most alternatives ("chatter," "babble," "jabber," etc.) are used of women and children, and rarely of men. Examine your material to see if by choosing "prattle" you are making a subtle statement about women. For more inclusive-sounding alternatives use *rattle, rattle away, ramble, blabber, blather, spout, spout off, run off at the mouth, talk nonsense, talk through one's hat, talk idly, shoot the breeze, make chin music, bend someone's ear.*

preacher   depending on the denomination, may be a woman or a man.

pregnant   nonsexist word, but beware the surrounding context and attitudes. Is pregnancy treated as an illness, disability, misfortune, or inferior state of being? Is the pregnant woman assumed to be more moody and less capable than other people? Are expectant mothers penalized in the workplace? For sex-neutral terms for "pregnant" meaning fullness or suspense use *meaningful, profound, momentous, ominous, expectant, suspenseful, waiting, teeming.*

prehistoric man   *early peoples/humans, fossil humans.* "Prehistoric" itself is a problematic, unscientific, ethnocentric term, used to indicate the period before written history, although anthropologists do not observe any such artificial break in the timeline. "Prehistory" has been used, for example, by colonialists and explorers in reference to indigenous groups.

prehominid   *See* hominid.

prelate   so far, always a man.

premenstrual syndrome/PMS   acceptable sex-specific term that describes a recognized medical condition. Never ascribe a woman's behavior to PMS; the woman herself is the only one able to say what is PMS and what is not.

premier danseur   a "premier danseur" is the principal male dancer in a company; his opposite number is the "prima ballerina." Retain "premier danseur" for its narrow meaning within ballet companies, but describe a man who dances ballet nonprofessionally as *lead dancer, principal dancer, first dancer, ballet dancer. See also* ballerina; danseur/danseuse; prima ballerina.

pressman *press operator/tender/feeder/worker, presser, compositor, typesetter, typographer.*

prick (man) avoid. The-Title-Says-It-All-Department: "'Pricks' and 'Chicks': A Plea for 'Persons,'" by Robert Baker (in *Philosophy and Sex*, eds. Robert Baker and Frederick Elliston).

priest in some churches (Episcopal, The Reorganized Church of Jesus Christ of Latter Day Saints, for example) a priest may be a man or a woman. Priests in other churches (Anglican, Roman Catholic, for example) are men. Although one properly hesitates to call female priests by the traditional "Father," one isn't too sure what to replace it with. The most common practice seems to be the use of first names for both female and male clergy. Some women clergy are comfortable being called "Mother," while others say they are not disturbed when they are called "Father"; they accept it pro tem in the spirit in which it is meant. It is never in poor taste to ask a priest what she or he likes to be called. This is a time of transition and few people, including the clergy themselves, have hard and fast guidelines as yet. (Neither male nor female priests are properly addressed orally as "Reverend," however.) There does not appear to be a biblical or first-generation Christianity basis for the ban on women priests; the four biblical passages often quoted to defend the ban (1 Cor. 11, Eph. 5:22, I Tim. 2, and I Cor. 14) do not address the issue directly and cannot be defended by an indirect approach. The requirement that priests resemble Christ has been taken to mean only his maleness; it is not equally required that they be short, bearded Jews. Food for thought: "If you ain't gonna ordain 'em, don't baptize 'em" (Anonymous). *See also* clergyman; minister; rabbi.

priestess retain "priestess" in historical or present-day contexts where the term reflects a reality that is very positive for women, for example, in the goddess religions. In many instances the term is not second-best but one that offers a model of power and inspiration for women; when "priestess" is just a subset of "priest" use *priest.*

prima ballerina gender-specific terms are still used in professional ballet companies to distinguish between the female first dancer ("prima ballerina") and the male first dancer ("premier danseur"). Retain the narrow usage when referring to members of professional ballet companies, but use inclusive language for others: *ballet dancer, first dancer, star dancer, principal dancer. See also* ballerina; danseur/danseuse; premier danseur.

prima donna *lead, lead opera singer, opera star, leading role, opera/lead/principal singer.* There is no parallel for men. When describing an overly self-absorbed and temperamental person, it is used (in spite of its plainly feminine cast) for both sexes, and it's a toss-up as to who is put down more thoroughly, men or women.

primitive do not refer to early peoples, indigenous peoples, or those from other cultures as "primitive"; anthropologists renounce the term as unhelpful and "loaded."

primitive man *early people/peoples/human being, Cro-Magnon, Neanderthal, Stone Age people.* Avoid the ethnocentric "primitive."

primogenitor *ancestor, forebear.* Because the "genitor" comes from the word for begetting, "primogenitor" refers to male ancestors.

primogeniture in its narrowest sense (the inheritance rights of the first-born son), "primogeniture" is the correct term to use, although the concept is very sexist. In the larger sense of being the firstborn of all the children of the same parents, use *firstborn, firstborn child, eldership, seniority, the rights of the firstborn.*

prince correct sex-specific term for royalty; avoid in its generic sense. Its supposed feminine parallel ("princess") has quite different connotations and there are no female equivalents for such expressions as "he's a prince," "a real prince," "a prince of a fellow," "a prince among men." For inclusive alternatives use *a real paragon, an ace, the acme of perfection, a trump, a marvel, a real lifesaver, a one-off, one in a million, salt of the earth, one of the best, outstanding human being, hero, champion, shining example.*

princely replace with precise, inclusive adjectives: *generous, liberal, bounteous, magnanimous, lavish, profuse, sumptuous, rich, abundant; luxurious, glorious, brilliant; noble, stately, grand, august, awesome, majestic, dignified.*

princess use only for royalty. *See also* prince.

prioress generally retain; "prioress" denotes a woman with power and stature usually equal to that of a prior's. For the generic sense of "prioress" or "prior," you might use *religious, ascetic, superior, administrator, director.*

prisoner men outnumber women more than 17 to 1 in prison, more than 9 to 1 in jail. The percentage of women prisoners increased from 4.2% in 1981 to 5.6% in 1989—primarily because of drugs; 60% of all women in federal prisons are there on drug convictions, but other crimes—prostitution, theft, armed robbery—are drug-related. There is a disproportionate number of minority prisoners; several states are questioning whether statutes, rules, or practices in the court systems cause unfairness. Other groups are looking at social causes.

prizeman *prizewinner, prizeholder.*

prizemaster *prize officer.* Retain in historical contexts.

problem expressions like "the Indian problem" and "the black problem" have incorrectly associated victims with the results of their abuse. There was no "black problem" until four million people were brought to this country as slaves (and without racism and discrimination there would be no "black problem" today); there was no "Indian problem" until virtually an entire people was killed, dispossessed, impoverished, or isolated. Identify instead the real problem: *oppression, discrimination, racism, poverty, race relations, restitution for stolen lands, violence,* etc.

pro-choice this is the term preferred by those who believe that women (not government, not doctors, not clergy) should make the choice about abortion; the term "pro-abortion" is highly offensive to this group, which includes both men and women. Some of the bitterness of the abortion debate has focused on the terms "pro-life" and "pro-choice." Alternatives have been suggested (usually by each group for the other) and vigorously rejected. The ambiguity of two opposing groups being "pro-" (shouldn't one be "anti-"?) seems difficult for people to accept. But the rule here is to call people by the terms they use for themselves. *See also* pro-life.

proconsul Roman proconsuls were all men, as are almost all modern administrators of colonies, dependencies, and occupied areas.

procreate procreation is shared equally by men and woman. When speaking of it, sometimes use "beget" and sometimes use "give birth to."

procuress *procurer.*

prodigal son *returned prodigal, the prodigal one, the prodigal, one who returns to the fold; profligate, wastrel, squanderer, scattergood, waster, spendthrift, high liver.*

professional man *professional.* According to the U.S. Labor Department, the nation's 13.8 million professional jobs are held almost equally by women (6,938,000) and men (6,909,000). Although women in general slightly outnumber men, there are more male professionals at the tops of their professions. "Professional" (and "pro") used to be very complimentary when used of men, but were often synonymous with "prostitute" when used of women. This usage is no longer so prevalent, but avoid using the terms when they might be ambiguous. *See also* businessman; executive; glass ceiling.

professor emeritus "emeritus" is the male form; women are called "professor emerita."

pro-life this is the term preferred by those who oppose abortion; pro-life stances range from opposing abortion for any reason whatsoever (and also opposing birth control) to favoring birth control and accepting abortion as a possibility in a few narrowly delimited instances. Some pro-lifers are one-issue people (abortion only) while others define "pro-life" by a wide spectrum of issues (death penalty, poverty and justice, global peace, etc.). Both men and women are involved in the pro-life movement. Some of the bitterness of the abortion debate has focused on the terms "pro-life" and "pro-choice." Alternatives have been suggested (usually by each group for the other) and vigorously rejected. The ambiguity of two opposing groups being "pro-" (shouldn't one be "anti-"?) seems difficult for people to accept. But the rule here is to call people by the terms they use for themselves. *See also* pro-choice.

prolocutrix *prolocutor.*

promiscuous avoid; this term is reserved almost entirely for women.

propertyman/prop man *property attendant/handler/coordinator/ supervisor.*

prophetess *prophet.*

proprietress *proprietor.*

prostitute/prostitution a prostitute may be either sex. Use the clear, simple word "prostitute" ("sex worker" also clearly describes what is involved) instead of the hundreds of demeaning or euphemistic street terms like: baggage; bawd; call girl; chippie/chippy; doxy; drab; fallen woman; fancy girl/woman; floozy; pavement princess; pross/prossie/prostie/prosty; round heels; sidewalk hostess; streetwalker; strumpet; trollop; trull; woman of easy virtue/ill fame/ill repute. There are, of course, male prostitutes, but the (male-dominated) language has been slow to name them, which is why all the foregoing words apply only to women. Some 600,000 prostitutes see approximately 2,000,000 men per week; prostitution is a "business" with annual grosses of over $1 billion. *See* Writing Guidelines for a discussion of our language on prostitution. *See also* camp follower; demimondaine; grisette; harlot/harlotry; hooker; houseboy/ housegirl; kept woman; lady of easy virtue/of pleasure/of the evening/of the night; loose woman; madam; sex industry; slattern/ slut; tart; tramp (woman); wench; whore.

protectress *protector.*

protegé/protegée protegé for both sexes. "Protegée" is defined in most dictionaries as "a female protege," thus removing women one step from the real thing. Usage today tends away from feminine endings (poetess, directress, etc.). *See also* divorcé/divorcée.

provider just as the caregiver role—as the primary option—has limited, dehumanized, and oppressed some women, the provider role—as the primary option—has limited, dehumanized, and oppressed some men. Men do bring home more bacon than women, but many of them consider the economic benefits associated with their gender to be a mixed blessing. The notion that "it's a man's world" has obscured the fact that along with benefits have come severe lifestyle restrictions, stress, economic pressures and responsibilities, unrealistic social expectations, and being judged by criteria not applied to women. As more and more women providers join men in taking on toxic work loads, personal and societal goals may need to be reevaluated to help fashion a more lifegiving balance between work life and non-work life. The following words are theoretically inclusive, but we use them largely to penalize men for not being providers or "good enough" providers: also-ran, born loser, deadbeat, derelict, do-nothing, down-and-outer, dud, failure, freeloader, goldbricker, good-for-nothing, hard-luck case, idler, layabout, lazybones, light-weight, loafer, mooch, ne'er-do-well, nonstarter, parasite, piker, prodigal, schlemiel, schmo, shirker, skinflint, slacker, sponge, wash-out, wastrel. Traditionally a male "loser" is a financial failure—someone who can't "provide"; a woman who is a "loser" fails to be sexually attractive. *See also* breadwinner; bring home the bacon; bum; gender roles; "male privilege"; success object (man).

provocative when describing ideas or intellectual properties, "provoca-tive" is nonsexist. In a social or sexual situation, however, the word's connotations make it difficult to use fairly and factually. Too often it is women who are "provocative"—eternal Eves luring endless numbers of passive Adams. *See also* provoke.

provoke this word crops up frequently as a "reason" for beating, raping, and even killing women. A man in a domestic violence program explains, "I know I shouldn't hit her, but I can't seem to stop. The bitch really asks for it, you know. She really provokes me." When Carol S. Irons, the first female judge in Kent County, Michigan, was shot to death in her chambers by her estranged husband, the jury convicted him of a lesser crime (voluntary manslaughter instead of the first-degree murder charge) because, as one juror put it, "Every-body felt he was provoked by his wife to do this." A judge ruled that a five-year-old girl was a "temptress" in "provoking" a sexual encounter with a twenty-year-old man (Nijole V. Benokraitis and Joe R. Feagin, *Modern Sexism*). After Linda Simmons's husband, a hospital pathologist, killed her as she was walking out the door with their two young children, he told police, "She just wouldn't quit bugging me"—presumably about his severe and longstanding alcoholism. Nineteen-year-old John Paul Mack invited a customer into the storeroom to pick out some new blinds, then blocked the door and told her to lie down. When she refused (thus provoking him), he repeatedly smashed her skull with a hammer, stabbed her five times, slashed her throat many times, put her body in a car, drove around, then parked and went to a movie. Mack later de-scribed this as "just blew my cool for a second." Mack believed that he had "reacted in a way in which any man would perhaps react under similar circumstances" (he was working long days and his marriage was in trouble). After serving less than twenty-seven months in a county jail, he went on to become "arguably the most powerful staff member on Capitol Hill" (*Washington Post*) as House Speaker Jim Wright's aide. *See also* "she asked for it."

prudent man (legal) *prudent person/individual.* *See also* reasonable and
   prudent man (law).

pseudogeneric words that purport to include everyone, but that in fact do
   not are pseudogenerics. Erich Fromm wrote that "man" needs food,
   shelter, and access to females. Although he is assumed to be speaking of human beings, the reference to "access to females" shows that
   "man" doesn't really include both sexes. *See* Writing Guidelines for
   more information about pseudogenerics. *See also* he (pseudogeneric); Man/man (pseudogeneric); mankind.

public relations man *publicist, public relations/P.R. agent/practitioner/*
   director/executive/representative/specialist, promoter, publicity/press agent,
   booster, advance agent, propagandist, public information manager/officer,
   publicity writer. *See also* adman; spokesman.

puerile the Latin "puer" refers to either a boy or a child. If you want
   alternatives use *juvenile, childish.*

Pullman car/pullman porter named after George Pullman. You can avoid
   the masculine look of "pullman porter" with *porter, train attendant, red*
   cap.

pumpman *pumper.*

purdah purdah (literally, "curtain") is the pattern of veiled and secluded
   domesticity that characterizes the lives of certain Muslim, South
   Asian, and Hindu women. When using the term, be sensitive to
   cultural differences. Emily C. Smith, member of Muslim Women of
   Minnesota, says, "Muslim women do not aspire to feminism on the
   Western model. Instead, they pursue the rights guaranteed to them
   in their own religious law, which 1,400 years ago granted them
   independent legal status and rights of voting, inheritance, and
   divorce. The adoption of Islamic dress is often a political statement
   by which the wearer rejects the sexual exploitation of women while
   reaffirming that she does not need to mimic customs and manners
   foreign to her own culture. To assume that the Muslim woman is
   universally oppressed is an insult which disregards the achievements
   of millions of our Muslim sisters worldwide." The Action Committee
   of Women Living Under Muslim Laws tries to raise consciousness
   among Muslim women about the difference between what is really
   Islamic and what is being passed off as Islamic by religious and
   political vested interests to reinforce male political and social domination over women. *See also* harem.

putty man *puttier.*

pygmy there are no peoples who call themselves "pygmies"; replace this
   ethnocentric, Eurocentric term with specific, authentic peoples'
   names (Mbuti, Twa, etc.).

q

And now we come to the magic of words. A word, also, just like an idea, a thought, has the effect of reality upon undifferentiated minds.

Emma Jung

quail (girl/woman) this perpetuates the notion of girls/women as prey and as sex objects. Similar labels include the fowly related "bird" and "chick" and words like "score" and concepts like "notches on the bedpost." In all of them, the female is the "natural" heterosexist prey of the male hunter. In *The Chalice and the Blade*, Riane Eisler unseats the myth that these images are legacies of our ancestors; in fact, many early societies were based on female-male partnerships in which neither sex dominated (or hunted) the other. *See also* score; sex object.

Quakeress *Quaker*.

quality-control man *quality-control engineer/evaluator/ inspector/supervisor*.

quarryman *quarrier, quarry worker*.

quartermaster in the Army this term refers to a field of specialization, not to an individual; members of this branch include supply sergeants, supply officers, and supply NCOs. In the Navy and Coast Guard, "quartermaster" is a job title or rank used for both women and men involved in navigation. Civilian equivalents might include: *navigator, small craft/large ship operator*. The Air Force and the Marine Corps do not use the term "quartermaster"; they call their supply branches Individual Equipment (Air Force) or Supply (Marines).

queen (gay man) this homophobic term is unacceptable and derogatory when used by those who are not gay. Gay men might use it among themselves. *See* "insider/outsider" rule.

queen (royalty) acceptable sex-specific word. If you need a gender-free term try *ruler, monarch, sovereign, crowned head, leader*. Edward Gibbon points out the subtle irony for many queens throughout history: "a woman is often acknowledged the absolute sovereign of a great kingdom, in which she would be deemed incapable of exercising the smallest employment, civil or military."

queen (verb) women apparently "queen it over" their friends while men "lord it over" theirs. Inclusive alternatives: *have the upper hand, hold something over someone's head, wear the crown, hold court, have/get it all one's own way, have the game in one's own hand/corner.*

queen bee correct when referring to the inhabitant of a hive. Its metaphorical usage is not particularly negative, but if you need to convey this idea in a gender-neutral way, try *big wheel.*

queen consort in referring to the wife of a reigning king, it is acceptable to drop the word "consort" except in some narrow circumstances (legal or historical references and official titles).

queenlike/queenly there is nothing very biased about these sex-specific words, but they are, like most stereotypes, vague and uninformative. You may want to replace them with more precise adjectives: *regal, imperial, noble, dignified, imposing, impressive, stately, majestic, commanding, haughty.*

queen-size terms like this give new meaning to the roles of kings and queens as "rulers." For a gender-free way of describing size use *small, medium, large, extra large*—unless referring to beds and bed linen, in which case the standard use of "single," "double," "queen," and "king" is probably here to stay. But let the objection be stated: who says the king is always larger than the queen?

queer/queer as a three-dollar bill/queer beer although these terms have some everyday uses (meaning strange, phony, or odd), they are homophobic, hostile, and derogatory when used to refer to a gay man or, occasionally, a lesbian. However, "queer" is being reclaimed and rehabilitated by some lesbians and gay men, especially in the formation of Queer Nation; watch for changes in the usage of this word.

quizmaster *quiz show host.*

r

If thought corrupts language, language can also corrupt thought.

George Orwell

rabbi women are rabbis in the Conservative, Reform, and Reconstructionist branches of Judaism, and they are addressed like men rabbis: "rabbi." There are no women rabbis in the Orthodox branch.

racism any attitude, action, social policy, or institutional structure that discriminates against a person or a group because of their color constitutes racism. Racism is specifically the subordination of people of color by white people because racism requires not only prejudice but power. "The history of the world provides us with a long record of white people holding power and using it to maintain that power and privilege over people of color, not the reverse" (Paula S. Rothenberg, *Racism and Sexism*). Michael Harrington (*The Other America*) says, "The American economy, the American society, the American unconscious are all racist." Johnetta B. Cole (*McCall's*, October 1990) says poverty alone will not explain why more college-age African American men are in prison, jail, or on parole than in college, that poverty and sexism alone will not explain why a black woman has only one chance in 21,000 of receiving a doctorate in mathematics, engineering, or the physical sciences. Only racism can explain why a young African American woman has one chance in five of dropping out of high school, and three chances in five of becoming pregnant before age twenty, why a black baby has nearly one in two chances of being born poor, and why a black infant is twice as likely as a white baby to die before its first birthday.

racketeer functionally sexist term; although women may be involved in racketeering, there are not so many of them and they are rarely called racketeers. *See also* bad guy.

raconteur this French word is grammatically masculine (the "raconteuse" stayed in France) but is used in English for both sexes. More inclusive-sounding alternatives are *storyteller, anecdotist, teller of tales, taleteller, talespinner, spinner of yarns, romancer, narrator*.

radarman *radar operator.*

radioman *radio operator/repairer.*

raftsman *rafter.*

ragman *ragpicker, rag collector, junk dealer/collector.*

raise Cain when using expressions like this, be aware of how many are male-based. Balance them with female-based expressions, creative expressions of your own, or alternatives: *make mischief/a fuss, carry on, lose one's temper, fly off the handle, flare up, run amok, raise a rumpus/a storm/a hue and cry/the devil/hell, castigate, lecture, rail, fulminate, find fault; be boisterous/loud/rowdy/disorderly, disturb the peace.* For a discussion of sex-linked expressions, *see* Writing Guidelines.

rajah always a man; his wife is a "rani."

rake this term is reserved for men, and there is no parallel for women. Use instead: *libertine, swinger, bedhopper, free spirit, high-roller, dissolute person. See also* ladies' man; man about town; womanize/womanizer.

rallymaster *rally director/organizer.*

rambo based on the film character Rambo, this term is used for someone of great physical strength and powers for destruction. While its popularity and implications for society might pose serious questions, the term itself is descriptive and useful, sex-specificity and all.

ranchman *rancher. See also* cattleman; cowboy.

randy usage reserves this adjective for boys/men, although it has no connection with a male name (it comes from "to rant"). Inclusive alternatives: *horny, turned on, hot and bothered, aroused, sexually excited. See also* horny.

rape women constitute over 99% of all rape victims. Current data indicate that a woman is raped every six minutes in the United States, that one of three women is raped during her lifetime, that 25% of college women have been victims of rape or attempted rape, and that the rape rate is increasing four times as fast as the overall crime rate. One study found 44% of the respondents had been victims of rape or attempted rape, but only 10% had ever reported the incidents to police. Perhaps as many as half of all sex crimes go unreported. Insights into the alarming increase in rape: one of eight Hollywood films has rape scenes; men who watched R-rated films were less likely to think a woman was being brutalized during a re-enactment of a rape than those who hadn't seen the movies; people have become desensitized to the horror of rape (discussing a TV rape episode, actor Michael Paré said, "It's not going to be a violent rape, where the guy rapes her and kills her. It's going to be a friendly rape"); one of twelve men surveyed in one study admitted to acts that met the legal definition of rape; in another study a majority of children surveyed thought rape was acceptable; New York City rape arrests of thirteen-year-old boys increased 200% over two years; less than 3% of charged rapists go to prison; a man who admitted raping a woman was given no prison time (despite guidelines and a plea agreement for at least four years in prison) because a Florida judge knew the woman from a divorce case he handled several years earlier and thought she was "pitiful" (the judge advised the man to be more careful in choosing women); police departments are either ill-equipped or ill-motivated to pursue rapists—in 1990 the Oakland, California, Police Department had to reopen 203 rape cases that had been dropped without even minimal investigation; in Boston rapes went uninvestigated because the police department had been out of rape testing kits for several months; less than half the states have laws allowing charges of spousal rape. Obstacles to dealing effectively with rape include the myths surrounding it. One says that nobody can be sexually assaulted against their will; in fact, 87% of all adult rape victims are faced with weapons, death threats, or threats of bodily harm, and nearly one-fifth of all rapes involve two or more assailants. In almost 90% of the cases, victims attempt such self-protective measures as physical force, threats, or calling for help. Rape victims range from infants to people over eighty; about one-fifth of all rape victims are aged twelve to fifteen. It is highly possible to be raped against one's will. Although another myth says women "ask for it" by dressing or behaving seductively or by being in the wrong place at the wrong time, studies indicate that 60% to 70% of rapes are planned in advance; the woman's actions have little effect on the outcome. Since rape does not involve sexual desire, but rather violence and power, "seductiveness" is not a factor. We tend to react differently to property crimes than to crimes against persons. A prosperous-looking man who is robbed is rarely accused of "asking for it" by the way he was dressed (rape victims' attire and manner are often a big issue in court); when a man gives frequently to charity, we still call it a crime if someone robs him on the theory that he doesn't appear to mind "giving it away" (women's sex lives are often cited against them in rape cases on the theory that this wasn't anything they hadn't done before); if a man gives money to members of his family, it is still wrong for his wife and children to steal from him (women who report date rape or husband rape are told that since they have previously been willing to have sex, they have no recourse when sex is forced on them). The racist twist to rape is not the one of myth: "the rape of black women by white males has been far more commonplace than the white fantasy about black men raping white women suggests" and it is "still a serious problem for black women in some parts of the United States" (Nijole V. Benokraitis and Joe R. Feagin, *Modern Sexism*). *See also* date rape; provoke; rape victim; sexual harassment; "she asked for it"; victim; violence.

rape victim woman/girl or man/boy. Although the percent of male rape victims is too small to be statistically significant (.2/1000), the fact remains that men are raped, particularly in prisons where rape is a common way of maintaining an inmate power structure; do not exclude men from the term "rape victim" and do not assume that victim and violator are of different sexes. *See also* date rape; rape victim; sexual harassment; "she asked for it"; victim; violence.

"real" father/"real" mother *biological mother/father, birth father/mother.*

reasonable and prudent man (law) *reasonable and prudent person/individual; reasonable, prudent person; the ordinary, reasonable, prudent person (ORP person); the average person; objective standard of reasonableness.*

rector depending on the denomination, this may be either a woman or a man.

red hot mama avoid. It makes a sex object of a woman and there is no parallel for a man.

red light district *prostitution district.* One hundred years ago some brothels burned red lights in their windows.

red man *Native American, American Indian, first American. See also* Indian.

redneck *bigot.* "Redneck" is classist, judgmental, inflammatory, and used mostly of men.

reformed alcoholic *recovering alcoholic.*

regal/regalia/regent these words are based on the Latin "rex" for king, but they no longer have any strong male associations, except perhaps for those who know Latin. Either a woman or a man may be regal or a regent.

reinsman *driver, coach/sulky driver, horse racer.*

remainderman *remainderer, remainder agent, reversioner.* "Remainderperson" is seen on rare occasions, but is not recommended.

remember, man, that thou art dust and unto dust thou shalt return *remember that thou art dust, and unto dust thou shalt return.*

Renaissance man *a multi-talented/well-rounded, self-actualizing individual, a person of many parts; Renaissance woman and Renaissance man.*

repairman *repairer, service rep, servicer, adjuster, technician, mechanic, fixer, troubleshooter, custodian.* Or, be specific: *plumber, electrician, carpenter, roofer,* etc. In England a "repairman" is a "fitter," a neat, useful -er word.

repo man *repossessor, the repo.*

restaurateur woman or man.

retard/retarded *person with mental disability/impairment, someone with developmental delays; mentally disabled, developmentally delayed. See also* handicapped; idiot/idiocy.

retreat master *retreat director.*

reverend (adj.) depending on the denomination, this title may be used for a woman or a man. Use "The Reverend Dinah Morris" when writing, but in general do not use "reverend" as a noun, as in "How are you today, Reverend?" Use instead the person's first name or the title the person prefers. Clergy today welcome a question like "What shall I call you?" *See also* clergyman; minister; priest.

rewrite man *rewriter. See also* newsman/newspaperman.

Rhodesian man *the Rhodesian, early human, Homo erectus.*

rich as Croesus when using expressions like this, be aware of how many are male-based. Balance them with female-based expressions, creative expressions of your own, or alternatives: *well-to-do, made of money, worth a bundle/a pretty penny, rolling in money, on Easy Street, has a gold mine, has money to burn, flush, someone whose ship has come in.* For a discussion of sex-linked expressions, *see* Writing Guidelines.

rich man's sport *rich person's sport, a sport for the rich, a sport for rich blood.*

rifleman *sharpshooter, carabineer, crack shot, sniper, sharpshooter, shooter, gunner, soldier. See also* gunman.

right-hand man *right hand, deputy, lieutenant, assistant, right-hand/chief/ invaluable assistant, aide, key aide, helper, attendant, co-worker, sidekick, subordinate.*

ringman *bettor, gambler, gamester.*

ringmaster *ringleader, ring supervisor, circus announcer/leader/producer, announcer, host, leader. See also* master of ceremonies/mistress of ceremonies.

Rise of Man, the *the Rise of Civilization/Humanity/Culture.*

riverman *river logger/jobber.*

road sister *hobo.* When girls/women first became hoboes in the 1930s, they were called road sisters, a colorful historic term that may sometimes be preferred to the nonsexist term. *See also* knight of the road.

rob Peter to pay Paul *See* borrow from Peter to pay Paul.

rob the cradle in the case of a partner below the age of consent, there are legal terms with associated criminal penalties that are more accurate. In the case of adult couples with an age difference, both women and men marry and date younger people so the phrase isn't sexist, but it is ageist, judgmental, and unwelcome. *See also* toyboy.

rodman *See* gunman.

roger *OK, that's right; over and out.* Although based on a man's name (from the old communications code for the letter "r"), this well-established term is not functionally sexist.

Romeo when you need an inclusive term use *lover, great/doomed lover.*

roommate inclusive term describing someone you share quarters with; so far it is not generally used as a euphemism for lover.

roscoe *handgun, revolver.* Although based on a man's name, "roscoe" is a fairly harmless sex-linked term. What is not harmless is the roscoe itself; 1988 statistics show 7 handgun deaths in Great Britain; 8 in

Canada; 13 in Australia; 19 in Sweden; 25 in Israel; 53 in Switzerland; and 8,915 in the United States. Every day in the United States a child or teenager is accidentally shot.

roughhouse/roughneck although culturally reserved for men, particularly because one meaning of "roughhouse" is "an oilfield worker" (a traditionally all-male field), this term may also be used for women.

roundsman *relief cook.*

roustabout a roustabout is invariably a man, and there is currently no similar word or occupation for women.

routeman *route worker/supervisor, driver, newspaper carriers' supervisor, delivery person, deliverer.*

rowdy can be said of women/girls or boys/men, although the default is male; girls are often reproached for being rowdy, while in boys it is considered "natural."

royal/royalty although these terms are based on "roy" ("king"), they no longer have perceived male associations.

rube based on a man's name and used more of a man than of a woman, this term is also a pejorative, anti-rural stereotype and should be avoided. More sex-neutral and less pejorative terms include *country cousin, rustic, tiller of the soil, provincial.*

rule of thumb there are several explanations of the origin of this "rule": in a letter to *Ms.* (July 1986), Claire Bride Cozzi wrote that its derivation was painfully sexist: English common law allowed a man to chastise his wife with a switch "no thicker than his thumb." Other explanations are more accepted and acceptable: since the last joint of the thumb is about an inch it was commonly used as a measure; artists used a thumb to gauge perspective; the thumb was used to test the degree of fermentation of malt in making beer in nineteenth-century England; the thumb was used as a tiny writing pad to calculate the exchange of Spanish dollars for French francs by French contractors in the early 1800s in southern France.

rule the roost this phrase is sexist because the roost is invariably "manned" by a rooster, but paradoxically the expression refers to a woman who dominates her family. The original expression is not sexist; it comes from the British variant "rule the roast" where "roast" refers either to a governing body or to the roasted beef served for Sunday dinner (and it is moot who ruled it: the woman who roasted it or the man who carved it). Use instead *call the shots/the tune/the plays, wear the crown, sit on the throne, wield the scepter, have it all one's way, lay down the law, be in the driver's seat, hold all the cards, be in the saddle.*

S

Prejudices, it is well known, are most difficult to eradicate from the heart whose soil has never been loosened or fertilized by education; they grow there, firm as weeds among stones.

Charlotte Brontë

Sabines an ancient people of the Appenines, the Sabines are sometimes mistakenly thought to be women only—probably because of the infamous abduction and rape of the Sabine women.

saboteur this grammatically masculine French word is used for both sexes in French and in English.

sacristan depending on the denomination, a sacristan may be either sex.

safety man *safety inspector/engineer.*

sahib always a man; the woman is a "memsahib."

salad girl/salad man *salad maker.* Note the nonparallel "girl/man."

salesgirl/saleslady/salesman/saleswoman *salesclerk, clerk, sales associate/ rep/agent/representative/broker/manager, agent, seller, door-to-door seller, canvasser, commercial traveler, vendor, seller, dealer, marketer, merchant, retailer, wholesaler, trader, estimator, driver, soliciter, shop assistant, peddler.* These terms are not interchangeable: "salesclerk" is appropriate for a retail store employee, while "sales representative" describes someone employed by a large manufacturing company who is a combination business manager, product specialist, and sales trainer. For "salesmen" use plurals of the alternatives given as well as *sales force/staff/personnel, salespeople.*

salesmanship *sales ability/expertise/technique/skill, high sales potential; vendorship, sales record; hucksterism.*

salutations when you know the person's name but not their sex or social title (Ms., Dr., Prof., etc.), write Dear C. Busby; when you don't have a name, either address yourself to the company (Dear Gates-Porter) or to a job title (Dear Credit Manager) or to a role (Dear Neighbor). The trend is toward replacing the salutation with a subject line (Re: enclosed contract). *See* Writing Guidelines for more information on salutations.

salvage man *salvage worker/inspector/repairer, salvager, parts salvager.*

sampleman *sampler, sample collector/worker/reworker, raw sampler.*

samurai always a man.

sandboy *sand/beach flea.* Or, leave as is.

Sandman, the *the sleep/sand fairy, sleep, sand sprinkler, the sleep genie, the Sander, Sandy Eyes.* Derived from an old European tale, the Sandman is harmless enough in himself; the problem is that so many of his ilk are male (Santa Claus, Jack Frost) and small children are especially susceptible to the subliminal messages about maleness and femaleness in a world overrun with "he"s.

sandwich girl/sandwich man *sandwich maker.* Note the nonparallel "girl/man."

sandwich man *sandwich board advertiser.*

sanitation man *sanitation worker/engineer.*

San Quentin quail (underage female sexual partner) avoid. Labeling the girl/young woman this way (while failing to label the man) incorrectly places the onus for the relationship on her, perpetuates the Eve-as-tempter/helpless-Adam stereotype, and implies a certain victimization of the man, obscuring the fact that he is engaging in criminal activity (and laying the foundation for a statutory rape charge).

Santa Claus Father Christmas, Père Noel, Saint Nicholas, Kris Kringle, and Santa Claus are better left as they are, even with the acknowledgment that these male figures reinforce the cultural male-as-norm system. Mrs. Claus goes largely unrecognized; she doesn't even have a first name. There is nothing inherently wrong with a male Santa Claus; the problem is that nearly every cultural rite of this magnitude is male-dominated. The solution is to promote female heroes along with rituals that feature women. Consider introducing Befana, or La Befana, the Italian version of Santa Claus, who carries a cane and a bell and traditionally drops down the chimney on the twelfth night of Christmas.

Satan/he *Satan/it.*

satyr *libertine, bedhopper, swinger, lover, seducer. See also* nymphomaniac.

savage avoid this racist, ethnocentric, sexist term. By labeling Native Americans "savages," the colonists justified invading, dispossessing, and subjugating entire populations. They called the Indian manner of defending themselves "savage" and referred to Indian victories as "massacres" (their own unprovoked attacks and indiscriminate killing were simply "battles" or "victories"); "any attempt to evaluate war as 'civilized' or 'savage' usually depends on which side one is on" (*The Underside of American History*, ed. Thomas R. Frazier). Slavery was also made possibly by labeling kidnapped Africans "savages." Today men are sometimes called savages where women are not. Altogether a very unpleasant word. Avoid also heathens, pagans, primitives. *See also* "discovery" of America.

savant the French word is grammatically masculine but is used in French and English for both sexes.

say uncle *surrender, give up, throw in the towel/sponge, knuckle under, raise the white flag, draw in one's horns, cry quits/barley, strike sail, throw oneself on the mercy of, pack it in, throw up one's hands, capitulate, eat one's words.*

scarlet woman avoid. There is no parallel term—nor any expressed condemnation—for the men who are the "partners in crime" of scarlet women.

scatterbrained *out to lunch, space ranger, flake, out of it, on another planet, with one's head in the clouds, not all there, missing some marbles, with a mind like a sieve, impractical, irresponsible, slaphappy, woolgathering, dreamy, mindless, brainless wonder, dense, muddleheaded, shallow, inane, foolish.* Along with airhead, birdbrained, emptyheaded, feather-brained, and harebrained, this word is used invariably of girls/women and not boys/men.

schizophrenic *person who has/with schizophrenia.* Replace the colloquial use of "schizophrenic" with *divided, torn in two, of two minds,* etc. **See also** handicapped; insane/insanity.

schoolboy/schoolfellow/schoolgirl *schoolchild, schoolmate, classmate, peer, youngster, elementary school child, child.*

schoolman/Schoolman *scholastic, teacher, school administrator, pedagogue, academician, academist, professor, scholar, savant.* "Schoolman" is historically correct for a Scholastic.

schoolmarm/schoolmaster/schoolmistress *schoolteacher, teacher, educator, instructor, tutor, trainer, principal.*

scientist 28% of employed scientists are women.

scold (woman) according to Abby Adams's *An Uncommon Scold* (quotations by women), a common scold was legally defined as a troublesome, angry woman who broke the public peace (and the law) with her brawling and wrangling and was punished by public ducking. A U.S. woman was booked (but not convicted) on a common scold charge as recently as 1971.

score the concept of scoring (a man "getting" or "having" a woman sexually) underlies much that is skewed with female-male relations. "Man is the hunter; woman is his game," wrote Alfred, Lord Tennyson (*The Princess*)—and many men agree with him. Thinking of a woman as prey makes her an object, a game, a notch on the bedpost—she is not a partner in any meaningful sense. The characteristic that betrays an imbalanced relationship or a "score" is the lack of mutuality; beware the sentence where "man" is the subject and "woman" is the object. "Score" is also an inclusive term for the client of either sex of a male or female prostitute. *See also* "lay"/"easy lay"/"good lay" (sex partner); sex object; sexual conquest.

Scotchman *See* Scotsman, which is preferred.

Scotsman *Scot, Scotlander, inhabitant of Scotland.* Plural: *Scots, the Scottish, Scotlanders, inhabitants of Scotland.*

scoutmaster *scoutleader.*

scowman *scow hand/worker.*

scrapman *scrap worker/separator/collector.*

script girl/script man *script reader.* Note the nonparallel "girl/man."

Scrooge when using expressions like this, be aware of how many are male-based. Balance them with female-based expressions, creative expressions of your own, or alternatives: *tightwad, money-grubber, penny pincher, pinchpenny, miser, skinflint, cheapskate, piker, cheeseparer.* *See* Writing Guidelines for a discussion of sex-linked expressions.

scrubwoman *janitor, cleaner, office cleaner, household helper, custodian, domestic worker, char, charworker, maintenance worker.*

scullery maid retain in historical context. Or, *scullery worker.*

sculptress *sculptor.*

seafaring man *seafarer.*

seamaid *See* mermaid/merman.

seaman *seafarer, sailor, enlisted sailor, naval recruit, mariner, marine, navigator, pilot, argonaut, tar, salt, gob, captain, skipper, mate, first mate, crew member, deck hand, boater, yachter.* "Seaman" and "seaman recruit" are official U.S. Navy terms, but refer to either sex; 9.1% of the Navy are women.

seaman apprentice *apprentice sailor/crew member, marine apprentice.* "Seaman apprentice" is an official Navy term used for both sexes.

seamanlike/seamanly *shipshape, sailor-like.* Or, be specific: *tidy, orderly, skilled,* etc.

seamanship *navigation/ship-handling skills, marine strategy, sailing techniques, navigational expertise.*

seamstress *sewer, tailor, mender, alterer, stitcher, alterations expert, custom tailor, clothier, dressmaker, fashion sewer, garment worker/maker/designer, needleworker.*

second baseman *See* baseman (baseball).

second shift, the from *The Second Shift* by Arlie Hochschild, this term refers to the unpaid job a woman comes home to after finishing eight hours of paid work each day. Hochschild says that because husbands generally do little more housework or child care than their fathers did, even though wives now work outside the home, wives spend fifteen fewer hours at leisure each week than their husbands and, over the course of a year, work the equivalent of an extra month of twenty-four-hour days. Most men in two-career marriages—even those who believe in equality—do not really do enough child rearing, cooking, cleaning, food shopping, or other chores to count. They still "help out" with the housework—an expression that explains whose job it really is. One of the couples in Hochschild's book devised an

equal "division of labor": he took care of the dog and the garage; she
took care of the child and the house. Couples who did share housework equally were found to be the happiest, although it's unknown
whether they were already happier and thus shared more, or
whether the sharing made them happier. However, men who "win"
the argument about housework, whose wives work that extra month,
lose a good deal to exhaustion and resentment; the second most
common reason women cited for wanting to divorce (after "mental
cruelty") was their husbands' "neglect of home or children." This
was mentioned more often than financial problems, physical abuse,
drinking, or infidelity. The idea that women work two—or three—
shifts is not new. In 1918, Alexandra Kollontai wrote, "The wife, the
mother, who is a worker, sweats blood to fill three tasks at the same
time: to give the necessary working hours as her husband does, in
some industry or commercial establishment, then to devote herself as
well as she can to her household and then also to take care of her
children. Capitalism has placed on the shoulders of the woman a
burden which crushes her: It has made her a wage earner without
having lessened her cares as a housekeeper and mother" (quoted in
European Women, eds. Eleanor S. Riemer and John C. Fout). The
second shift is not limited to women, but they work it in far greater
numbers than men, and both men and women are acculturated to
women working it. *See also* housewife; housework; moonlighter;
working father; working mother; working wife; working woman.

second-story man *cat burglar, burglar, housebreaker, professional thief.*

secretary although the number of men in this pink-collar occupation has
doubled over the past five years, 99% of all secretaries are still
women—which is a switch; until the 1870s, when the typewriter was
introduced, the secretarial profession was considered strictly men's
work. From the time of the Middle Ages a "secretarius" (from the
Latin for "secret") was a confidential male officer who could be
trusted with state secrets. When the YWCA hired eight women to be
"typewriters" in 1873, physicians were brought in to certify that the
women's physical and mental abilities could withstand the pressure;
many people predicted the women's minds would snap. In 1880, the
all-male First Congress of Shorthand Writers issued a statement
saying, "Some day women will be smart enough to write shorthand."
Lt. Uhura of the "Star Trek" series spent a lot of time placing Captain
Kirk's calls and was called the "communications officer"—apparently
future-speak for secretary. According to an article in *New Woman*,
"Many secretaries feel the title [secretary] is so pejorative and deficient in conveying their responsibilities (which have shifted from
clerical positions toward those of middle management) that it should
be amended or replaced." Preferred titles include *executive secretary,*

executive assistant, administrative assistant, administrative coordinator, office administrator. The largest professional association for secretaries, Professional Secretaries International, is thinking of changing the title "secretary" as well as its own name and predicts that "secretary" will probably be replaced by "office administrator." *See also* girl Friday; pink-collar job/worker.

Secret Service man *Secret Service agent, member of the Secret Service, bodyguard, intelligence agent/officer, plainclothes officer, undercover/secret agent, spy.*

seductive both men and women can be seductive; don't limit the word to women.

seductress *seducer.*

see a man about a dog/horse *see somebody about a dog/horse.* Or, replace the phrase with whatever you really mean. This Victorian circumlocution was designed to avoid mentioning anything inconvenient or embarrassing: visiting the restroom, going to a bar or tavern for a drink, seeing a prostitute.

seedsman *sower, seed dealer, seed store owner, seed company representative.*

seeress *seer.*

seigneur/seigneury retain in historical context. Alternatives: *member of the landed gentry, feudal property owner, elder, local authority; landed estate, manor house.*

selectman *representative, city representative, commissioner, council member, member of the council, councilor, municipal/board officer, board member, chancellor, ward manager; selectwoman and selectman.*

self-made man *self-made individual/person, entrepreneur, go-getter, hardworker, rags to riches story; self-made woman and self-made man.*

self-mastery *self-control, self-discipline.*

seminal *germinal, germinative, creative, original, inventive, innovative, primary, primal, primordial, prototypal, prototypical, exemplary, fresh, novel, unprecedented, precedent-setting, first of its kind, initial, earliest, unorthodox, nonconforming, unconventional, rudimentary, inceptive, fundamental, source, productive, catalytic, far-reaching, potential, possible, probable, likely, unrealized.* Alternatives are given because "seminal" is the adjectival form of "semen," and nothing could be more male. Using the word underscores the notion that only men have important, "seminal" ideas.

seminary both sexes have attended seminaries in the past, but their experiences have not been parallel. Seminaries for women enrolled high school-aged girls while seminaries for men trained clergy. The former is now a rarity, while the latter includes women, depending on the denomination. At least one-third of the student population at the leading interdenominational divinity schools are women; at Yale and Harvard, it's more than half.

semination *sowing, planting, cultivating, cultivation.* **See also** seminal.

sempstress *See* seamstress.

senator ninety-eight of the one hundred U.S. senators are men; ninety-eight are white.

senior airman this official U.S. Air Force term is used for both sexes.

senior citizens/seniors although not universally liked, these terms are probably here to stay ("seniors" may be a little more popular). A possible alternative: *older adults.* Avoid referring to age unless it is necessary to your material. Phrases such as "elderly woman dies" or "car stolen from elderly man" appear routinely in newspapers. If it seems ridiculous to say "middle-aged woman dies" or "car stolen from middle-aged man," don't use the reference to "elderly." Labels to avoid: the elderly (offensive), Golden Agers (suffers from cuteness), retirees (they often are not truly retirees and the implication is that they are idle). If you need to refer to age, use a specific age ("a 78-year-old man") or age group ("those between 65 and 74") instead of imprecise terms like "the aged."

separate the men from the boys *separate the sheep from the goats/wheat from the chaff/professionals from the amateurs/strong from the weak/good from the bad/able from the incompetent/mature from the immature.*

serf man or woman.

serve two masters *serve God and mammon, have divided loyalties, be torn in two.*

serviceman (armed forces) *service member, member of the service/armed forces, enlistee, recruit, officer, sailor, soldier, Marine, flyer; servicewoman and serviceman.* Or, use specific service titles—all of which may now refer to either a woman or a man. Some of the following sample titles still appear "masculine" as we are unaccustomed to women in these ranks—and woman may not to date have filled all of them—but they may potentially be held by either sex: *adjutant, admiral, brigadier general, captain, colonel, commandant, commander, command sergeant major, commodore, corporal, ensign, field marshall, first lieutenant/sergeant, fleet admiral, general, gunnery sergeant, lance corporal, lieutenant/ lieutenant colonel/lieutenant commander/lieutenant general/lieutenant junior grade, major, major general, military police, NCO (noncommissioned officer), paratrooper, petty officer, private/private first class, rear admiral, second lieutenant, senior naval officer, sergeant/sergeant at arms/sergeant first class/sergeant major, squadron commander/squadron leader, staff officer/staff sergeant/staff sergeant major, subaltern, technical/top sergeant, vice admiral, warrant officer, wing commander.* **See also** specific titles such as airman; aviation survivalman; corpsman; wingman. **See also** armed forces; combat; males-only draft; warrior.

serviceman (repair) *servicer, service contractor, repairer, technician, maintenance/repair worker, troubleshooter, fixer, mender, adjuster; gas station/ service station attendant, mechanic.*

service wives *military/soldiers'/service members' spouses.* Today a number of service spouses are men.

session man (music recording session) *session player/musician, free-lance musician; session man and session woman.*

set-up man *set-up mechanic/operator, setter, preparer, press/kick press/machine setter, setter mechanic/worker; denture mounter.*

sewer-bottom man *trench trimmer.*

sewing woman *sewer, tailor, mender, alterer, alterations expert, stitcher, garment worker/maker/designer, fashion sewer, custom tailor, clothier, dressmaker, needleworker.*

sex an understanding of the difference between sex and gender is crucial to the correct use of language. Sex is biological: people with male genitals are male, and people with female genitals are female. Gender is cultural: our notions of "masculine" tell us how we expect men to behave and our notions of "feminine" tell us how we expect women to behave—but these may have nothing to do with biology. When deciding whether a word is restricted to one sex or the other, the only acceptable limitation is genetic sex. A woman cannot be a sperm donor because it's biologically impossible. It may be culturally unusual for a man to be a secretary, but it is not biologically impossible. To assume all secretaries are women is sexist because the issue is gender, not sex. Gender signifies an individual's personal, legal, and social status without reference to genetic sex; gender is a subjective cultural attitude while sex is an objective biological fact.

sex change operations of the 7,000–12,000 operations since 1979, one-half have been male-to-female and one-half female-to-male.

sex differences in 1947, Dorothy Sayers wrote, "The first thing that strikes the careless observer is that women are unlike men . . . . But the fundamental thing is that women are more like men than anything else in the world." In 1955 Ivy Compton-Burnett observed, "There is more difference within the sexes than between them." Forty-five years later a *Newsweek* article concurs: "Social scientists agree that the sexes are much more alike than they are different, and that variations within each sex are far greater than variations between the sexes." According to *The Opposite Sex* (ed. Dr. Anne Campbell), "As soon as we finish with sexual anatomy and move on to questions about behavior, abilities and social roles, 'obvious' differences [between the sexes] turn out to be not nearly as obvious as we may have thought at first." In *The Third Sex* Patricia McBroom writes, "Few sex differences survive the test of crosscultural analysis. Martin and Voorhies examined aggression, intelligence, dependency, ambitiousness, and nurturance, finding all these traits to be culturally variable. Anthropologists do, however, recognize that endemic warfare is a virtually exclusive male activity. Crosscultural patterns in gender personality do exist, but they are neither innate nor universal." The differences between the sexes can be examined along three axes: (1) anatomy, or how we are physically different from each other; (2) biology, or how we behave innately differently from each other because we are male or because we are female; (3) culture, or how we live out certain social roles as women/girls and men/boys. A sperm donor is always a man, not because of the culture, but because of anatomy and biology. A CEO today is far more likely to be a man than a woman, not because of anatomy or biology, but because of culture. It is easy to see when anatomy determines behavior (only women give birth, only men can impregnate women). It is not quite so easy to see when culture determines behavior and when biology determines it. Are girls innately better at verbal tasks and boys innately better at spacial tasks? Or is it the culture that determines the small statistical test-score variations between the sexes? (Sex differences in abilities are only averages, which means that men/boys can do as well on verbal abilities as the best women/girls, and girls/women can do as well as the best boys/men on spatial abilities.) Is it biology or culture that determines who is "the weaker sex"? Research shows that when adults are told a baby is a girl, they view the child as delicate, fragile, or small in size. But when told the *same* child is a boy, they think of him as strong, alert, and large. Increasingly, social scientists emphasize that society as much as nature turns girls into women and boys into men. Writing in the *Newsweek* "My Turn" column, James M. Dubik explains how he came to see, via his two daughters and his experiences teaching male and female cadets at West Point, that "Many of the characteristics I thought were 'male' are, in fact, 'human.'" Infant psychiatrist Dr. Taghi Modarressi says, "When we talk about inborn, intrinsic maleness and femaleness, we really don't know what we're talking about." Our western, hierarchical thinking says that if two things are different, one must necessarily be better or worse, higher or lower, than the other. Applied to the differences between the sexes, this attitude has been particularly malignant. (Which is "better," an apple or an orange, a lake or a river, geology or astronomy, the way women think or the way men think?) Deborah Rhode (*Theoretical Perspectives on Sexual Differences*) says we can deny sex differences, we can celebrate them, or we can "dislodge difference as the exclusive focus of gender-related questions." Anatomically, there are great differences between the sexes; biologically, there are some interesting differences (among the possibilities are that men generally appear to have greater muscle mass, cardiovascular capacity, more lefthandedness, and a higher concentration of red blood cells while women generally have more good cholesterol, handle stress better, sing and smell better, and live longer—in addition, neurobiologists report structural differences in at least two regions of the human brain); culturally, there remain great differences in attitudes, behaviors, opportunities, and expected roles for women and men. Anatomy and biology may be immutable; culture is not. *See also* gender roles.

sex discrimination *See* sexism.

sex industry the multi-billion-dollar sex industry is blatantly sexist. Those who profit from it financially are almost all male and the majority of victims are female, although boys/young men are also victims. One of the most vicious and appalling aspects of this "industry" is the large number of children involved. According to one insider, "The word on the street [in New York] is johns prefer chickens—kids." There are upwards of 25,000 street kids in New York alone each year. The most common scenario involves a middle-class surburban male who pays for sex with underagers. Abuse, degradation, drugs, disease, poverty, and death are facts of life for the young victims of this man's idea of "consensual sex."

sexism both boys/men and girls/women are objects of discrimination based on their sex; "sexism" is an inclusive term when viewed primarily as discrimination. However, sexism is often defined specifically as the subordination of women by men. "While some women may dislike men intensely and treat them unfairly and while some women may be equally guilty of prejudice toward other women, the balance of power throughout most, if not all, of recorded history has allowed men to subordinate women in order to maintain their own privilege" (Paula S. Rothenberg, *Racism and Sexism*). Unequal, discriminatory treatment of the sexes touches almost every aspect of society, from such life-and-death issues as the males-only draft and males-only combat positions, to survival issues like the feminization of poverty, the disparity in income between women and men, and the glass ceiling for many working women, to everyday issues like lifestyle ("workwives" are a lot more socially acceptable and admired than "househusbands"), clothing (women can wear just about anything men wear, including for a while, boxer shorts, while men aren't culturally approved for skirts, dresses, or most women's wear), and activity (girls can be "tomboys" but boys better not be "sissies"). Nijole V. Benokraitis and Joe R. Feagin (*Modern Sexism*) say, "Although both men and women can be targets and victims of sex discrimination, a vast literature indicates that being a woman is frequently a better predictor of inequality than such variables as age, race, religion, intelligence, achievements, or socioeconomic status." In all but two respects that is true: today people with same-sex orientations are likely to be more discriminated against than any other group; the males-only draft and combat laws provide a stunning inequality for men. *See also* blue; combat; emotional; glass ceiling; males-only draft; pink; wage earner.

sexist (adj.) use this to describe attitudes, practices, behavior, language, codes, laws, cultures, etc., but avoid using it of people. Instead of "Dale is so sexist," say, "she uses sexist language" or "he encourages sexist practices in the office" or "your attitude seems very sexist to me."

sexist language sexist language promotes and maintains attitudes that stereotype people according to gender; it favors one sex and excludes the other. Writing for members of the Foreign Service Institute, Mortimer D. Goldstein sums up the status of sexist language in his chapter title, "Sexist Language Is Yesterday's Style: Besides, It's Against the Policy" (*Disciplined Writing and Career Development*).

sex object for centuries women have been treated as sex objects ("piece of ass"), things ("skirt," "doll"), possessions ("my woman"), and commodities ("birds," "chicks"). Heavily reinforced by advertising, which uses women's sexuality to sell everything from razor blades to cars, this concept has had invidious results: prostitution, rape, laws and societies that "protect" women and relegate them to the status of children, words and attitudes that label women solely by their sexuality, even murder when the mythic cultural promise that women exist for the sexual pleasure of men goes unfulfilled. An article on male friendship before marriage (*Esquire*, June 1990) says, "You compete for women"—as if women were passive things for the having. *See also* gender roles; owner; score; success object (man).

sexpot avoid; used only for women, "sexpot" supports the stereotype of woman as tempter and narrows her entire personhood to her sexuality.

sex roles *See* gender roles.

sexton woman or man.

sexual assault *See* rape.

sexual conquest whether by one sex or the other, is "conquest" an appropriate term for a relationship that should ideally be more partnership than domination? *See also* "battle of the sexes"; score; sex object.

sexual harassment sexual harassment consists of unwelcome, unsolicited, nonreciprocal sexual advances, requests for sexual favors, sexually motivated physical contact, or communication of a sexual nature, usually by someone who has power over another; it includes comments, jokes, looks, innuendos, and physical contact, and asserts a person's sex role over their function as a worker. Between 70% and 90% of working women have experienced sexual harassment in the workplace as have 20% to 30% of women students in educational settings. A Pentagon study reported that one-third of U.S. military women surveyed experienced some form of direct harassment (rape, pressure for sexual favors, touching) and 64% said they had been sexually harassed either directly or indirectly. A federal government report puts the annual cost of sexual harassment among federal workers at $95 million—not including legal fees or settlements. However, most sexual harassment is unreported and less than 5% of victims seek institutional remedies. Men also experience sexual harassment although to a much lesser degree; in the Pentagon survey, 17% of the men said they had been sexually harassed by male or female colleagues (the study did not break down the sex of the harassers). Almost worse than the harassment are responses to it: the person "asked for it"; they should have been flattered; it wasn't such a big deal anyway; victims are oversensitive—it was all in fun; "can't you take a little joke/a little teasing?"; the person is "imagining" it or "too uptight"; in the case of sexual harassment by fraternities and male sports teams, "boys will be boys" and "it's just youthful highjinks." In a stunning flight of fancy, Phyllis Schlafly says "For the virtuous woman, sexual harassment is not a problem, except in the rarest of cases." She also says, "If it is perfectly clear that the answer is 'no,' the man doesn't ask. A man doesn't need to be told more than once." In case he does, however, there is now a remedy: sexual harassment is against the law. *See also* battered wife/woman; date rape; provoke; rape; rape victim; "she asked for it"; victim; violence.

sexual intercourse when discussing sexual activity in general, replace this heterosexist term with *sex, sexual activity*.

shaman woman or man.

shamus although this could refer to either sex, it tends to be heard as masculine, and so do its equally "neutral" alternatives: *cop, copper, flatfoot, gumshoe, private eye, shadow, sleuth, tail*. With the advent of good fictional female gumshoes (*see* gumshoe), these words are beginning to seem more inclusive.

shantyman *shanty dweller*.

"she asked for it" this corrupt and specious "explanation" has been used to excuse everything from unwanted sexual attentions to rape. No woman ever asks to be harassed, abused, or violated. *See also* battered wife/woman; date rape; provoke; rape; rape victim; victim; violence.

sheikh/sheik always a man. If you want an inclusive alternative use *heartthrob, someone who is easy on the eyes*.

shepherdess *shepherd*.

shiftless avoid; this highly objectionable word has been curiously reserved for blacks/African Americans.

ship/she *ship/it*. In the early days of sailing, a new ship was customarily dedicated to a goddess, under whose protection it sailed. Referring to ships and boats as "she" today is outdated, unnecessary, and unacceptable because of the association of the feminine with men's possessions. Everything that dominator societies have traditionally run or overpowered has been imaged as female: church, nations, nature, ships, cars, etc.

shipman *sailor. See also* seaman; shipmaster.

shipmaster *ship captain/commander/officer, sea captain, merchant marine officer/captain.*

shoeshine boy *shoeshiner.*

shogun always a man; no parallel for women.

shoot the bull this phrase doesn't refer to the male animal, but probably comes from "boule" meaning "fraud/deceit." To avoid its masculine bias (it is almost always used of men rather than women) use *shoot the breeze. See also* gossip.

shop girl *shop clerk/assistant/employee/manager/owner, salesclerk, clerk.*

shoreman *shorehand, dockworker, dockhand, stevedore, shoreworker, longshore worker, wharfworker, wharfhand.*

shovelbill/shovelman *shoveler, shovel hand.*

showgirl *dancer, performer, performing artist. See also* showman.

showman *performer, entertainer, limelighter, razzle-dazzle/stage artist, theatrical person, exhibitionist, someone with a flair for the dramatic, ham, show-off, actor, theatrician, show manager/producer/stager, impresario.* Note the nonparallel "man/girl" and the differences in prestige and type of work between a showgirl and a showman. *See also* showgirl.

showmanship *showcraft, razzle-dazzle, performing/staging skills, production genius, virtuosity, dramatics, theatercraft, theatrics, showiness, flair for the dramatic.* None of these terms may feel as satisfactory as "showmanship." Try showing what you mean (by examples, description) rather than just telling.

shrew *grouch, grumbler, crosspatch, faultfinder, fire-eater, complainer, pain in the neck, nitpicker, troublemaker, bad-tempered/peevish/cranky/petulant person.* Nonsexist per se, "shrew" is in practice reserved for women; avoid it.

shylock *loan shark, usurer, extortionist, shyster, moneylender, parasite.* "Shylock" is both sexist and anti-Semitic; avoid it.

sibyl retain in historical contexts and in those present-day contexts where the term finds validation among women. If you need an inclusive alternative use *prophet, fortuneteller.*

sideman *musician, member of the band/orchestra, band/orchestra player/ member.* Or, be specific: *bassist, drummer, clarinetist, violinist,* etc.

sight-effects man *sight-effects specialist/technician.*

signalman *signaler, signal operator.*

silk stocking district *posh neighborhood, wealthy/aristocratic area, deluxe section/fashionable part of town, the Gold Coast.*

silly more women than men are described as "silly." Doris Day notes that "If a man does something silly, people say, 'Isn't he silly?' If a woman does something silly, people say, 'Aren't women silly?'"

Simon Legree "Simon Legree" and its common synonym "slave driver" have extremely negative associations with slavery, but are not easily replaced with terms as familiar and evocative. Reword or use an alternative: *ogre, stickler, drill sergeant, tough/strict boss, martinet, severe disciplinarian, oppressor.*

simon-pure when using expressions like this, be aware of how many are male-based. Some of the time use female-based expressions, creative expressions of your own, or alternatives: *pure, genuine, untainted, sterling, honest, truthful, pure-hearted, flawless, upright, highminded, reliable, real, veritable, authentic, exact, precise, credible, worthy, clean as a whistle. See* Writing Guidelines for a discussion of sex-linked expressions.

Sioux *Dakota/Lakota people.* Terms like "Sioux" and "Sioux nation," which come from the Ojibway via French and mean "deadly/poisonous snake," are considered derogatory, belligerent, and ignorant when used by the dominant society.

single mother/single father *single parent, parent.* There are times when it is necessary to specify "single"; most of the time it is not. There are also times when it is better to use "single father" or "single mother." "Single parent" is too often thought to refer to a woman. The inclusive term may also obscure the gender breakdown: 13,700,000 children under eighteen live with a single mother; 1,793,000 children under eighteen live with a single father.

single-sex colleges there are ninety-five women's colleges (down from 224 in 1969) and some half-dozen males-only private liberal arts, military, or seminary colleges. Any group that excludes any other group—for whatever reason—is viewed as discriminatory today. Private institutions justify single-sex status by their specific alternative missions, lack of federal support, and, in the case of women's colleges, an affirmative action rationale. There is much to be learned from studies showing that single-sex colleges are highly advantageous for women—and questions to be raised about practices in coeducational institutions. Compared to students enrolled in the latter, women in single-sex colleges participate more fully in and out of class, develop measurably higher levels of self-esteem, score higher on standardized achievement tests, choose more male-intensive majors, and are more are likely to graduate. Women graduates of single-sex colleges are more successful in their careers (e.g., hold higher positions, are happier, earn more money), are twice as likely to receive a doctoral degree, six times more likely to be on the boards of Fortune 500 companies, and even appear to have lower divorce rates. While graduates of women's colleges constitute only 5% of all college-educated women, they make up 44% of female members of Congress. *See also* education.

singular "they" since medieval times "they," "their," and "them" have been used as singular pronouns (for example, Jill Ruckelshaus's "No one should have to dance backward all their lives"). The National Council of Teachers of English has said, "In all but strictly formal usage, plural pronouns have become acceptable substitutes for the masculine singular." Others go further: *Random House Dictionary II* forthrightly endorses the use of "their" with a singular antecedent like "everyone." "However negatively one may react to this recourse, it is of long-established use" (Robert N. Mory, Assistant Research Editor, *Middle English Dictionary*). Singular "they" was proscribed in 1746 on the theory that the masculine gender was "more comprehensive" (whatever that means) than the feminine. But it wasn't until the nineteenth century that prescriptive grammarians tried to enforce it; many writers continued to use singular "they." Casey Miller and Kate Swift (*The Handbook of Nonsexist Writing*) say that "the continued and increased use of singular *they* in writing as well as speech—and the restitution of the status it enjoyed before grammarians arbitrarily proscribed it—now seems inevitable."

sins of the fathers are visited on the children, the *the sins of the parents are visited on the children* (if you can stand to use this expression in the first place).

sir "sir" and "dame" are parallel sex-specific titles for those raised to knighthood. "Sir" and "madam" are parallel and useful sex-specific terms for everyday social exchanges.

siren *tempter.* Once again Woman lures Man to destruction—a stereotype that belittles both. "Tempter" at least allows that the temptee might resist the temptation—something not possible with a siren.

sissy *timid, gentle, sensitive; weakling, pushover, wimp, doormat, easy mark, weak stick.* "Sissy," which comes from "sister," is a negative term denoting excessive timidity. "Buddy," which comes from "brother," is a positive term describing a good friend. "Tomboy" is often paired with "sissy," but since it has the masculine connotation, society is much more tolerant of so-called tomboy behavior than it is of so-called sissy behavior. Dr. Eugene R. August points out that our language lacks "a favorable or even neutral term to describe the boy who is quiet, gentle, and emotional." *See also* coward/cowardly/cowardice; mama's boy.

sister (adj.) the use of "sister" in such constructions as "sister cities" and "sister plants" does not carry any negative bias, nor does the fact that "brother" doesn't operate similarly. If you need alternatives try *twin, co-, companion, affiliated, partner, allied, associate.*

sister (noun) do not use "Sister" to address a woman unless it is a title of respect for a religious.

sisterhood unlike "brotherhood," which has been badly overused as a pseudogeneric, "sisterhood" has high meaning for women as a description of a sex-specific and unique bond and should be retained in most instances. When you want an inclusive alternative use *unity, unity among humans, humanity, compassion, peace, companionship, goodwill, amity, friendship, comradeship, camaraderie, conviviality; family, the human family, kinship, shared/human kinship; community, society, association, organization, social organization, common-interest group, club, corporation, federation, union, group, partnership, society; sisterhood and brotherhood.* *See also* brotherhood (pseudogeneric).

sisterly this is a useful and accurate sex-specific word in most cases. Sometimes, however, it is used stereotypically when other words would be more descriptive: *affectionate, loving, caring, kindly, supportive, sympathetic, protective, indulgent, friendly, humane.*

skirt/a bit of skirt (woman) avoid; this makes of a woman an object, by inference a sex object, and there is no parallel for men.

skygirl *flight attendant.* The inappropriate "skygirl" was resurrected and bruited about for a while in 1989 following a column by retired *USA Today* founder Al Neuharth who wanted to "bring back the skygirls" to replace flight attendants who were no longer young, single, and nubile, but "aging women" or "flighty young men." *See also* steward/stewardess.

slagman *slag worker.*

slattern/slut for prostitute, use *prostitute.* Otherwise use *sloven, slob, unkempt person.*

slave girl never use. In addition to its unpleasant associations with slavery, this sexist, racist term perpetuates the false notion that most women secretly enjoy being enslaved. Susan Brownmiller says, "the glorification of forced sex under slavery, institutional rape, has been a part of our cultural heritage, feeding the egos of men while subverting the egos of women—and doing irreparable damage to healthy sexuality in the process."

slaveholders/slaveowners historically these were both men and women.

slumlord *slum boss, slumholder, slum owner/manager, absentee slum owner, absentee fat cat slum owner.*

smart aleck although this expression comes from the man's name Alexander and seems to be used more often of men than women, it is acceptable for both sexes. For alternatives with no masculine associations use *know-it-all, blowhard, egomaniac, braggart, big/swelled head, arrogant/conceited/mouthy person/individual.*

sneaky Pete when using expressions like this, be aware of how many are male-based. Some of the time use female-based expressions, creative

expressions of your own, or an alternative: *cheap wine*. *See* Writing
Guidelines for a discussion of sex-linked expressions.

snow man (job title) *defroster*.

snowman *snow figure/sculpture/creature/statue, snowwoman or snowman*.

sob sister *sob story writer/journalist, yellow journalist, advice columnist,*
bleeding heart; pushover.

social titles use the titles people use for themselves (if she calls herself
Mrs., use that; if it's Ms., use that). When you don't know, omit the
title (Dear Selina Vickers). In work situations, "Ms." is generally
acceptable. *See also* salutations.

social worker 66% of U.S. social workers are women.

socman *See* sokeman.

socmanry *socage*.

soda jerk may refer to either sex.

sokeman *tenant, landholder*. Use "sokeman" in historical contexts to refer
to an individual male landholder by socage.

soldier *See* armed forces; combat; draft dodger; males-only draft; serviceman (armed forces); sexism; warrior.

soldier of fortune generally a man.

soldier-statesman *soldier-politician/-diplomat/-lawmaker*.

solon from Solon, the Athenian lawgiver (sixth century B.C.), this term is
perceived as masculine more because of the preponderance of male
lawgivers than because of its origins; use it for both sexes.

sommelier traditionally sommeliers have been men, but today a handful
of the world's top sommeliers (known as "master sommeliers") are
women. For both women and men you can also use *wine steward/*
waiter.

sonarman *sonar technician*.

songbird *singer*.

songster/songstress *singer, vocalist, balladeer*. *See also* bluesman; chorus
boy/chorus girl; crooner; prima donna; torch singer.

sonny avoid this patronizing and sexist (there is no parallel expression for
girls/women) term.

son of a bitch avoid. This insult, aimed at a man, ricochets off a
woman—his mother. When you need an interjection or exclamation,
use *son of a gun! doggone! doggone it! rats! shoot! damn! good grief!*
There is generally no dearth of good swear words; replacing this
expression is a matter of choice. When you want to refer to a person
this way, use *ignoramous, saphead, stinker, ratfink, snake in the grass,*
creep, heel, jerk, bum, lowlife. When using the term to describe a
difficult job or situation, use instead *a tough one, uphill job*.

son of a gun most often a meaningless interjection or a cheery backslapping greeting between two men (preceded by "you old"), this relative
of "son of a bitch" is genial and unobjectionable most of the time.

Finding an alternative that women could use is difficult, mainly because women have their own ways of greeting each other in similar circumstances, few of which remotely resemble the male scenario. Vive la différence. For the rather meaningless interjection, you could use *good grief! doggone! See also* son of a bitch.

Son of God (Christ) *Beloved of God, Only Begotten, God's Own, Eternally Begotten, Chosen One.*

Son of Man (Christ) the original phrase, which translates simply as "member of the human race," emphasized the humanity as well as the divinity of Jesus Christ. Christ describes himself often with this phrase, underscoring its profound significance. Those rendering "Son of Man" inclusive will want to express "member of the human race" in a way that is theologically correct, scripturally sound, and acceptable to both congregations and hierarchies. This is a difficult phrase to retranslate, but there are several possibilities: *the Incarnate One, the One who became human/flesh, the One made human/flesh, Son/ Child of Humanity/Humankind/the People, one like you, one of you.* You can also reword, for example: *Christ, who was flesh and blood even as you and I are flesh and blood.*

sons (pseudogeneric) *children, heirs, offspring, progeny, daughters and sons/ sons and daughters.*

sonship *parent-child relationship.* There is no inclusive alternative for "sonship" that captures the fullness (or would-be fullness if it were inclusive) of this word. Until some creative mind comes up with a pithy inclusive word, circumlocute. (There is no "daughtership.")

sons of God *daughters and sons/sons and daughters of God, children of God, believers, the faithful.* "Children of God," although more attractive because of its brevity, is not always the best choice because of the difference between "children" and "adult children."

sons of man *children/daughters and sons of humanity/humankind, daughters and sons/children of the earth, our children/sons and daughters.*

sorceress *sorcerer.*

sororal from the Latin for "sister," this is the little-known and all-but-invisible companion to "fraternal." It is useful in describing all-women groups, activities, and friendships. Like other female-male word pairs, "sororal" and "fraternal" have developed along very different lines, with "fraternal" taking on many meanings, associations, and uses—some of them pseudogeneric. *See also* fraternal; fraternal order of; fraternal organization; fraternal twins; fraternization/fraternize.

sorority unlike "fraternity," which in the case of the Greek society is sometimes coed or which as a pseudogeneric refers to groups including both women and men, "sorority" refers strictly to women. If you want an inclusive alternative for the Greek society use *Greek society/*

system, *Greek-letter organization, Greek-letter society/group*. Otherwise use *organization, society, association, union, secret society, club, federation, fraternity and sorority, common-interest group*. **See also** fraternity; fraternity/frat (Greek).

soubrette retain for the well-defined stage and opera role; there is no precise synonym and no parallel for a man.

soul brother/soul sister acceptable, parallel sex-specific terms.

sound-effects man *sound-effects specialist/technician*.

sound man *sound controller/technician/specialist*.

sow wild oats both young men and young women do this while their parents pray for crop failure.

spaceman *astronaut, cosmonaut, astronavigator, celestial navigator, member of the space program/space exploration team, space explorer/traveler/aviator/ pilot/ranger/walker, rocketeer, spacewoman and spaceman; extra-terrestrial, person from outer space*.

spearman *spear thrower/carrier*.

special-effects man *special-effects technician*.

spend money like a drunken sailor *spend money like water, throw money around, squander one's money, spend foolishly/ extravagantly/outrageously/ lavishly/imprudently/immoderately*. This phrase perpetuates an out-dated stereotype.

sperm donor legitimate sex-specific term.

spin-cast-pipe man *centrifugal spinner*.

spinning jenny *spinning machine*.

spinster *woman*. Something that is only one part of a person's life (being single) becomes the whole of the person when "spinster" is used; references to marital status are also usually unnecessary. When they are necessary, use an adjective instead of a noun: *single, unmarried, unwed, celibate*. Even such terms as "unmarried" and "unwed," however, perpetuate the marriage-as-norm stereotype. Sometimes we act as though marriage and parenthood grant validity to a person when in fact married and unmarried often have more in common than not. Historically single women enjoyed more civil powers than married women who were dependent upon and secondary to their husbands. Note the nonparallel connotations of the two supposedly parallel terms, "spinster" and "bachelor." Women go from bachelor girl to spinster to old maid but men are bachelors forever.

spinsterhood *singleness*.

spoilsman *spoils advocate, supporter of the spoils system*.

spokesman *speaker, representative, source, publicist, company/union/White House official, prolocutor, company/White House/union representative, advocate, proponent, voice, agent, press/publicity agent, proxy, stand-in, intermediary, mediator, medium, go-between, negotiator, arbitrator, speechmaker, keynoter, promoter, aide, deputy, diplomat, mouthpiece,* *spokester, public information manager/officer, public relations director, news bureau manager.* "Spokesman" (first used in 1540) and "spokeswoman" (first used in 1654) are rarely used gender-fairly, and "spokesperson" (1972) is not only awkward and contrived, but is generally reserved for women. There are some excellent (and more descriptive) terms in the list of alternatives; "prolocutor," for example, is an exact synonym meaning "speaker for." You can also use *speaking for the group/on behalf of, representing.*

spoonerism switching the initial sounds of two or more words ("it is kisstomary to cuss the bride," "one swell foop," or "the queer old dean," in a reference to Queen Victoria) results in a spoonerism, named after Oxford educator William A. Spooner. Retain the term, even though it is is sex-linked; there is no substitute. Some sexual linguistic balance is provided by Mrs. Malaprop and the term that describes her own brand of confusion. *See also* malapropism.

sportfisherman *sportfishing boat.*

sporting gentleman *gambler.*

sport of kings *royal/noble sport.*

sportsman *sports lover, sport, sportster, sports/outdoor enthusiast, athlete, gamester, hobbyist, competitor; gambler; honorable competitor, good sport, honest/fair player; sportswoman and sportsman.* Or, be specific: *angler, hunter, fisher, tennis player, canoer, ballplayer, golfer.*

sportsmanlike/sportsmanly *sporting, fair, fair-minded.*

sportsmanship *sporting behavior, fair play, fairness, fair-mindedness, playing fair, sense of fair play, being a good sport/good loser, honor, honorable competition, competing honorably.*

sportsman's license *sporting/sports license.*

spot man *spotter.*

spouse "spouse" has had a straightforward, nonpejorative history; it has always referred to the marriage partner of either sex. Use it instead of "husband" or "wife" when the sex of the person is irrelevant to your material. When referring to the other person in a same-sex or nonmarried relationship use *partner, domestic partner, companion, housemate.* The rather officious "spousal equivalent" has been seen in some contexts.

spry avoid; reserved for older people to indicate that they are livelier than you would expect at their age.

squire (noun) always a man; there is no parallel for a woman.

squire (verb) *accompany, escort* (used of either sex).

stableboy/stableman *stable hand/worker/attendant.*

stage man *stagehand, stage manager.*

stag line a group of dateless, danceless men at a dance, the stag line is rarely seen today. It was, however, a terrifically sexist concept, burdening young men/men with the social duty of requesting dances of young women/women and restricting women to a passive object status. Compare "wallflower," applied to groups of dateless, danceless young women/women, to "stag line." *See also* wallflower.

stag movie *pornographic movie.*

stag party for men only, a stag party can mean simply a gathering of men unaccompanied by women (perhaps a parallel for "hen party") or it can mean a raunchy party where prostitutes perform, pornographic movies are shown, or other socially undesirable behavior occurs. "Going stag" (that is, attending a party or event without a partner) used to be applied only to men; women also use it now.

stand pat nonsexist; the "pat" is not a person.

starlet *aspiring/promising young actor, neophyte/novice/beginning/young/rookie actor, rookie/young performer, tyro screen star, newcomer to the stage/ screen, young/future star.* Or, use whatever term you would use for a male actor at the same level of professional experience.

statesman *political/world/government leader, diplomat, legislator, lawmaker, politician, public figure, political/government strategist, public servant/ official; stateswoman and statesman.* Do not use "statesperson"—so far it's been used only for women.

statesmanlike/statesmanly *diplomatic, politically savvy.*

statesmanship *statecraft, diplomacy, government/world leadership, leadership, political savvy.*

stationmaster *station manager.*

status of women according to *The American Woman 1990-91: A Status Report* (ed. Sara E. Rix), the status of women is far from equal that of men by all significant criteria. The independent Population Crisis Committee ranked about 100 countries according to the status of women and how their treatment compared with that of men and found that nowhere in the world do women enjoy equal status with men in the areas of health, marriage and children, education, employment, and social equality. And, "in the least developed countries of Africa, the Middle East, Asia, and Latin America, crushing poverty overlaid with longstanding patterns of discrimination create living conditions for women almost too harsh to imagine."

steeplejack *steeple builder/painter/repairer.*

steersman *pilot, navigator, steersmate.*

stenographer 99% are women. *See also* secretary.

stepmother, wicked leave this phrase for the old fairy tales and do not write any new ones using it. It is sexist because there is no highly developed wicked stepfather persona and its mythic influence has unnecessarily complicated many blended family situations.

stereotype "stereotype" comes from the printing process of duplicating printing plates made from set type. Stereotypes are a shorthand method of labeling and cataloging people—they are quick and convenient because they require no thought. For the same reason, they are often inaccurate—and racist, sexist, homophobic, ageist, handicappist, or ethnocentric.

sterile this term is used for both women and men. "Infertile" refers to the lack of offspring in people who have been having unprotected intercourse for a certain length of time. "Sterile" usually indicates that a cause for the infertility has been found. Infertile people are not necessarily sterile. Sterile people are always infertile. Infertility is often treatable; sterility generally is not (unless, for example, a tubal ligation or vasectomy can be reversed). Do not confuse "sterile" with "impotent" or "frigid." *See also* barren; frigid; impotent; infertile.

sternson nonsexist; from a Scandinavian word that has nothing to do with a male offspring.

stevedore nonsexist; from the Spanish for "to pack."

steward/stewardess *flight/cabin attendant, attendant, crew member.* Plural: *flight crew.* In spite of the attempt to equalize the job label, sexist, ageist terms for flight attendants still pop up in the popular culture: skygirl, dinosaur, senior mama, gold winger. *See also* skygirl.

stickman (gambling) *casino employee, stick/craps boss.*

stick man (police) *stick officer, police patrol officer, beat officer/patrol.*

stickman (sports) *stick player.* There is no substitute for this term in some games.

stickup man *armed robber, thief, mugger, purse-snatcher, roller.*

stillman (liquor) *distiller.*

stillman (oil) *refinery operator.*

stock boy/stock girl/stock man *stockkeeper, stock/stockroom clerk/assistant, stock gatherer.*

stockholder approximately 50% of stockholders are women.

stockman *rancher, cattle owner/raiser/breeder, sheep farmer/owner/raiser/ breeder.*

storageman *storage agent.*

storeman *storekeeper.*

straight (adj.) "straight" and "gay" are often used as an adjective pair to refer to people who have respectively other-sex and same-sex attractional orientations. Although "straight" appears generally acceptable to gay and non-gay populations, it is not particularly recommended as it appears to be based on the dictionary definition of "straight" as "exhibiting no deviation from what is established or accepted as usual, normal, or proper" (*Webster's Ninth New Collegiate Dictionary*). The informal "het" is sometimes used instead of "straight."

straight man *comedian, stooge, entertainer, the straight, comic's partner, feeder of straight lines.*

straw man *diversionary tactic, hoax, nonexistent problem, imaginary/weak opposition, carefully set up just to be knocked down, front, cover; red herring; nonentity, hot air, ineffectual person, weakling; sitting duck.*

strident *harsh, jarring, raucous, dissonant, discordant, unharmonious, clashing, sharp.* "Strident" is heard much more frequently today, primarily to describe women (and especially feminists). Because it has been used indiscriminantly and discriminatingly, it has become devalued and stereotypical, and should be avoided.

strongarm man *strongarm guard, the muscle, muscler, bodyguard; enforcer, goon, ugly/rough customer, bully, big tuna, hard case.*

strongman *dictator, tyrant, military dictator; weightlifter, powerhouse.*

stuffed shirt this term is appropriate for both sexes, but you may prefer more neutral-sounding alternatives: *big head, someone who is pleased with oneself, prig, person who is stuck-up/conceited/smug/self-important/ parochial/ provincial/supercilious/snobbish/puffed-up/complacent/self- satisfied.*

stunt woman/stunt man *stunt performer/driver/actor, professional acrobat, daredevil, breakneck, acrobat, aerialist, contortionist, gymnast; stunt woman and stunt man.*

subassemblyman *subassembler.*

subkingdom retain this biology term as it is.

submissive use cautiously with reference to women. Promoting submis- siveness as a "natural" attitude for women has often been based on the biblical injunction for wives to be submissive to their husbands. However, this use of "submissive" appears to have been a mistrans- lation; the original writings enjoin both husband and wife to respect and defer to each other.

success object (man) if women have traditionally been viewed as sex objects, men have traditionally been viewed as success objects; both roles are artificial, highly limiting, and destructive. For men, eco- nomic success is still the crucial criterion of self-worth—witness the bumper sticker "He who dies with the most toys wins." Avoid writing and speaking of men solely in terms of their achievements, finances, possessions, and social rank. This is not to belittle achieve- ment, hard work, or success, but it is to say that men are a lot more than machines that endlessly crank out "product" for the boss, the family, the neighborhood, and the IRS. *See also* provider.

suffers from (a condition) *someone who has (a condition), someone with (a condition).* In referring to people with disabilities avoid all forms of the afflicted with/suffers from/victim of construction. *See also* handicapped.

suffragette *suffragist.* Although women in Great Britain chose to call themselves "suffragettes," American women did not want the demeaning "-ette" ending ("majorette," "usherette," "farmerette," etc.) and were called "suffragettes" only by those periodicals and speakers hostile to the women's goals. The difference between "suffragist" and "suffragette" can be seen in the dictionary definitions; a "suffragist" is "one who advocates extension of suffrage esp. to women" and a "suffragette" is "a woman who advocates suffrage for her sex" (*Webster's Ninth New Collegiate Dictionary*). *See also* suffragist.

suffragist although it most often refers to a woman, this inclusive term describes anyone of either sex who works for the voting rights of others, especially those of women. In 1912 Mark Twain wrote of suffragists: "For forty years they have swept an imposingly large number of unfair laws from the statute books of America. In this brief time these serfs have set themselves free—essentially. Men could not have done as much for themselves in that time without bloodshed, at least they never have, and that is an argument that they didn't know how." *See also* suffragette.

sugar daddy avoid. There is no parallel word to describe a woman who supports a younger man, but a possible inclusive alternative might be *meal ticket*.

suicide more than three out of every four suicides are men.

suitor in affairs of the heart, this term has traditionally been reserved for men. Today, it is not so much the case that women may also be suitors as that the term is no longer necessary because forming a relationship tends to be a mutual activity. No longer is one person the supplicant, the pursuer, while the other is the "sued."

sultan/sultana acceptable sex-specific terms.

superhero/superheroine these denizens of popular comic book/strip genres might seem to be equals, but as long as "heroine" is defined as "a female hero," she is a sub-set and thus the lesser of the two. Call all such characters *superheroes*. *See also* hero.

superman/superwoman these are fairly equivalent gender-specific terms and they can be used as they are. The inclusive alternative is *superhero*.

surrogate mother a legitimate sex-specific word, although other terms are being advocated: *biological mother, gestational mother, egg donor*.

swagman *vagrant*.

swain *admirer*. "Swain" comes from "swein" meaning "boy" or "servant." *See also* boyfriend; suitor.

swami this word comes from the Hindi for "owner, lord," and is perceived as male. Unless you are using it in its narrowest sense, substitute *teacher, religious teacher, ascetic, pundit, seer, mentor, leader, guide, spiritual guide, guru*.

swashbuckler this term seems ineradicably associated with men, although there have been women who have behaved like swashbucklers, among them pirates Anne Bonney, Mary Read, and Grania O'Malley and the French daredevil Marie Marvingt. More neutral-appearing words include *daredevil, adventurer, sensation-seeker, thrill-seeker, show-off, exhibitionist, fire-eater*.

swear like a trooper troopers and soldiers include both sexes now, but if you want something that sounds less masculine try *turn the air blue, cuss a blue streak, curse up hill and down dale/up one side and down the other, badmouth.*

sweater girl if it is truly necessary to describe a woman in terms of her voluptuousness, use adjectives instead of a noun so that a piece of clothing (emphasizing one part of the woman) does not become the whole woman. "Sweater girl" implies a great deal more than what the woman looks like: it also hints at her lifestyle and her intelligence, all on the basis of how she looks in a sweater. Avoid making an issue of women's physical appearance when this is so rarely done for men. *See also* body image.

sweet sixteen (and never been kissed) as this always refers to a young woman, it is sexist. Avoid it. No sixteen-year-old wants to hear it anyway.

sweet william leave as is.

switchman *switcher, switch/switchyard operator, technical equipment operator/ technician, switching equipment technician/operator.*

swordsman *sword fighter, fencer, dueler, duelist, swashbuckler; swordswoman and swordsman.*

swordsmanship *fencing/sword fighting skills/expertise.*

t

Words, like eyeglasses, blur everything that they do not make clearer.

Joseph Joubert

tail (woman) avoid. The slang use of "tail" ("Get off my tail") is nonsexist.

tailor woman or man.

take it like a man *See* act like a man/be a man/take it like a man.

take off one's hat to this formerly male custom has all but disappeared; the term is used today inclusively.

talesman *substitute juror.*

talk to like a Dutch uncle *talk to bluntly, rebuke, upbraid, admonish, chide, reprove, reprimand, reproach, scold, chew out, lecture, lay down the law, remonstrate, call on the carpet.*

tallboy nonsexist; "boy" is from the French for "wood," "bois."

tallyman *tallykeeper.*

tapman *taproom attendant.*

tart *prostitute.* Originally "tart" was used as an endearment, much as "honey" or "sugar" is used.

taskmaster/taskmistress *supervisor, boss, job boss, task sergeant, disciplinarian, inspector, instructor, overseer, monitor, martinet, surveyor, superintendent, director, manager, employer.*

taximan *taxi driver.*

teacher there is an interesting breakdown by gender and race in the teaching profession: 98% of all preschool and kindergarten teachers and 85% of elementary school teachers are women, while 96% of public school superintendents are men (97% are also white) as are 76% of public school principals (90% are also white) and 62% of college and university teachers. Tenure for the latter is also sex based: as of 1988, 69% of male and 46% of female faculty members were tenured. The percentage for women was the same as in 1975 while the percentage for men had increased 5%. Representation by race is also highly imbalanced (for example, only 2% of full-time medical-school faculty positions are held by African Americans).

teach one's grandmother to suck eggs *teach a bird to fly/fish to swim, reinvent the wheel, take coals to Newcastle.*

tease (woman) avoid. The dangerous myth that women are "teasing" when they say no to a man's advances has been responsible for much grief, criminal behavior, and even murder. The notion of woman-as-tease is often in the eye (and other body parts) of the beholder.

teen/teenager acceptable age-specific terms, but avoid using them in generalizations. Young people (the term they prefer) reject a one-size-fits-all label. They particularly dislike being called kids, girls and boys/boys and girls, youths, adolescents, juveniles, or teenyboppers (which is also sexist, as it's reserved for girls). Older teens can be called *young adults*, and secondary students can be called *high schoolers*. One career teacher addresses his high school students as *scholars*.

teleman *communications officer; petty officer in charge of communications or petty officer, communications; sparks.*

telephone man *telephone installer/repairer/worker.* Some 12% are women.

telephone operator 10% are men.

television sexist, racist, homophobic, ageist, handicappist, and violent, television is not an equal opportunity medium—not perhaps surprising considering that over three-quarters of television writers are white men. Men are featured much more often, in more lead roles, and for a wider range of roles. While men are shown more often at work, women are usually presented in family roles and given explicit marital status (most female characters are married, about to be married, or in a serious relationship with a man, while most male characters are single). Men are more likely to dominate women than vice versa, and even when they have equal status, men are more likely to assume control, both physically and emotionally. Men are the movers and shakers who earn the money; women are responsible for the well-being and cleanliness of the family. A year-long study released in 1990 said that, despite exceptions, women are often shown as half-clad and half-witted, needing to be rescued by quick-thinking, fully clothed men. On the other side of the camera, women make up 25% of writers, 15% of producers, and 9% of directors. *See also* advertising.

tell it to the marines nonsexist since marines are now both women and men. Or use: *pull the other one.*

temptress *tempter.*

termagant *faultfinder, grouch, grumbler, crosspatch, fire-eater, loud/overbearing person.* "Termagant" is reserved for women and there is no parallel for men. *See also* shrew.

testatrix *testator.* "Testatrix" is still used for certain legal matters.

testicular fortitude *intestinal fortitude See also* balls.

testimony sometimes thought to be sexist because of its relation to "testes" ("ovarimony" is then suggested as a female partner), in fact terms like "testimony," "protest," "New Testament," and "testicals" all come from the Latin "testari" meaning to testify or to witness ("testes" developed as a supposed "witness" to virility). The connection between testes and testimony was reinforced by the old Roman custom whereby men swore oaths by laying a hand on their genitals while women swore by their breast. Freud was puzzled as to how women, not fearing castration, developed a conscience.

testosterone testosterone circulates in both sexes but is much more abundant in males; post-pubertal men have testosterone levels about ten times higher than in women. Avoid referring to testosterone as the male hormone and estrogen as the female hormone; in fact, it is the metabolic conversion of testicular testosterone to estrogen that actually masculinizes male brains. Some studies have indicated that testosterone is a likely source of aggression and that men who dominate in social situations have higher testosterone levels than their peers. While the presence of high levels of testosterone may have some behavioral consequences, scientists warn against generalizations and are sceptical that testosterone is a strong, direct cause of specific human activity when so many other social factors determine if and how testosterone translates into such behavior as aggression, dominance, or competitiveness. It appears, for example, that women can be as competitive as men, even with much lower testosterone levels. To imply that the violence men commit is inherent and unavoidable is not only unscientific but dangerous insofar as it gives a kind of permission to male acting out. With so little factual evidence, it is indefensible to accuse men ("jokingly" or not) of "testosterone poisoning." Just as menstrual cycles and menopause have been blamed for unrelated behavior in women, men are beginning to hear more unscientific remarks about their testosterone levels. Bite your tongue.

testy this comes from Latin for "head" and has nothing to do with testicles.

thinking man *thinker, thinking/reflective/intelligent/learned person, thinking/ intelligent being, intellectual, philosopher, sage, scholar, brain, highbrow.*

third baseman *See* baseman.

Third World *nonaligned/unaligned/developing/overexploited/ economically exploited countries/nations.* "The Third World is gone. . . . the countries once assigned to the Third World are still there, but the concept of the Third World is no longer connected to any reality" (Robert J. Samuelson, *Newsweek*, July 23, 1990). Introduced in 1952 by French demographer Alfred Sauvy, the term originally alluded to the tiers état (third state) of French society before the revolution of 1789, and described all those countries, differing greatly among themselves, that are marginalized in the current international system. Today the term "Third World" is increasingly criticized as simplistic, demeaning, and imprecise. Any country that doesn't belong to the bloc of industrial capitalist countries headed by the United States (the First World) or to the socialist bloc headed by the Soviet Union (the Second World) falls automatically into the catch-all "Third World" category. (Note the arrogance of the appropriated "First World" label.) The term "Third World" is much like "nonwhite": everyone who is not "us" must be a homogeneous "them." "Developing" may be a euphemism for some of these countries, but better alternatives will no doubt surface as people increasingly seek to replace the outdated "Third World."

three-man (adj.) *See* one-man/two-man/three-man, etc. (adj.).

thresherman *thresher.*

ticket girl *ticket taker, pricing clerk.*

tillerman *tiller, tiller operator.*

timberman *timber cutter/worker, logger, tree cutter, woodcutter, log roller.*

time-study man *time-study engineer.*

time waits for no man *time waits for no one.*

timothy grass leave as is.

tin lizzie *Model T.* The innocent-sounding "tin lizzie" has an unsavory history. Elizabeth (also Liza or Lizzie) was such a common first name for black women that, according to Stuart Berg Flexner (*I Hear America Talking*), it was used from the 1880s until the late 1920s as a generic name for any black woman, but especially a servant, maid, or cook. The name was given the car because it, like the maid, "worked hard all week and prettied up on Sundays."

tinman *tinsmith, tin manufacturer.*

tirewoman *personal attendant.*

T-man *Treasury agent.*

to a man *without exception, unanimously, of one mind/accord, with one voice, at one with each other, willingly, agreed on all hands, in every mouth, carried by acclamation/unanimously, to a one; like-minded; every last one of them, everyone.*

toastmaster/toastmistress these terms are difficult to replace as they have specific meanings and are deeply entrenched in the language, particuarly because of the many toastmasters clubs around the country. When possible replace with *emcee, host, speaker, announcer, introducer, lecturer, talker, guest lecturer, orator, declaimer, speechmaker, rhetorician, elocutionist, preacher, interlocuter.*

to each his own *to each their own* (*see* singular "they"), *there's no accounting for tastes, it takes all kinds, chacun à son goût, to each her own/his own.*

toff refers to men only; there is no parallel for women.

tollman *toll collector, toll booth operator.*

tomato *See* food names for people.

tomboy *active/agile/athletic/boisterous/adventurous/physically courageous/ competitive child, live wire, one of the gang, strong/vigorous/direct/spirited/ self-confident child, rude/blunt/messy/rough/tough child, logical/mechanically minded child,* etc. "Tomboy" once referred only to boys, then to both girls and boys, and now only to girls. In *Women of the World*, Julia Edwards says of foreign correspondent Dickey Chapelle: "Although she called herself a tomboy, she was better described as a tomgirl, for she didn't want to be a boy. She just wanted to do the things boys get to do." Sociologists and behavior experts suggest that the concept of tomboy is obsolescent; behavior that another generation found tomboyish is considered normal today. Sociologist Barrie Thorne spent eleven months observing boys and girls on a playground; only twice did she hear them use the word "tomboy," although adults did so fairly commonly. Many children were clearly unfamiliar with the term and several said they'd never heard of it. She predicts the word will disappear within the next decade. *See also* sissy.

Tom, Dick, and Harry, every *See* every Tom, Dick, and Harry.

tomfool (adj./noun) *foolish, imprudent, irresponsible, unwise, hasty, shortsighted, foolhardy, reckless, pointless, nonsensical, ridiculous, silly, crazy, daft, simpleminded, stupid, mindless, thick-witted; fool.*

tomfoolery/tommyrot *foolishness, nonsense, rubbish, shenanigans, monkeyshines, monkey business, mischief, hanky-panky, trick, buffoonery, silliness, malarkey, baloney, poppycock, balderdash, moonshine, gobbledygook, garbage, stuff and nonsense, hogwash, bunkum, craziness, goofiness.*

Tommy *British soldier.* Or, retain in historical contexts.

tommy gun nonsexist; named after John T. Thompson.

Tom Thumb when using expressions like this, be aware of how many are male-based. Balance them with female-based expressions, creative expressions of your own, or an alternative: *hop-o'-my-thumb.* For a discussion of sex-linked expressions, *see* Writing Guidelines.

tom-tom nonsexist; from the Hindi word "tamtam."

too big for one's britches said of both sexes.

tootsie (woman) avoid.

top banana/top brass/top dog use for both sexes.

torch singer this has always been a female singer with a husky, passionate voice who has generally lost her man. The term may include in the future male singers in gay bars. An inclusive alternative (although it is not an exact synonym) is *blues singer. See also* bluesman; crooner; songster/songstress.

tough cookie/tough guy *toughy/toughie, tough, bully, someone who is hard as nails, hard-nosed, callous, unsympathetic, hard-boiled, unfeeling.* Although of typically nonparallel construction ("cookie/guy"), these terms for, respectively, a woman and a man mean roughly the same thing.

tough titty *tough luck, tough, too bad, that's the breaks.* Its origins are unclear, but the slang for a woman's breast makes this a term to avoid.

towerman *tower tender/operator/erector/attendant.*

townsman *town-dweller, local, native, resident, citizen, townie, city slicker, urbane person.*

toyboy defined as a young, handsome man who dates older female celebrities, this term is ageist, highly judgmental, and as sexist as "kept woman." Our national obsession with other people's lives and our willingness to judge those we don't even know encourages the popularity of quick-fix stereotypes fashioned to sound-bite dimensions.

trackman *track layer/inspector, trackwalker; track athlete, runner, sprinter, relay/distance runner, track event entrant, member of the track team, athlete who competes in track events; discus thrower, high-jumper, hurdler, long-jumper, shot-putter.*

tradesman *shopkeeper, storekeeper, small business owner, merchant, retailer, dealer, store owner/manager/worker/employee, tradesperson, tradeswoman and tradesman; trades worker, skilled/construction worker, electrician, mason, machinist,* etc. Plural: *tradespeople, people in the trades.* Most of the trades have a participation rate by women of around 2% to 3%.

tradevman *training devices personnel.*

tragedienne *tragedian.*

trainman *train worker/operator/crew member, railroad employee, rail worker; train buff.*

traitress *traitor.*

tramp (hobo) woman or man. *See also* bum; hobo; road sister.

tramp (woman) for prostitute, use *prostitute.* For someone with questionable morals (a questionable judgment) or someone who is ill-kempt, use inclusive terms: *promiscuous/sexually active/indiscriminating person/individual; sloven, slob, unkempt person/individual.* "Tramp" is never used in these particular ways for men; avoid judging one sex by criteria not applied to the other.

transsexual woman or man.

transvestite although most dictionaries will say this is "especially a male," the term can be used of both sexes.

trashman *trash collector.*

traveling salesman *traveling sales agent/rep, commercial traveler. See also* salesgirl/saleslady/salesman/saleswoman.

trawlerman *trawler, trawler owner/operator.*

trencherman *hearty/heavy/serious eater; sponger, hanger-on.*

tribal warfare "Conflicts among diverse peoples within African nations are often referred to as 'tribal warfare,' while conflicts among the diverse peoples within European countries are never described in such terms. If the rivalries between the Ibo and the Hausa and Yoruba in Nigeria are described as 'tribal,' why not the rivalries between Serbs and Slavs in Yugoslavia, or Scots and English in Great Britain, Protestants and Catholics in Ireland, or the Basques and the Southern Spaniards in Spain?" (Robert B. Moore, in *Racism and Sexism* by Paula S. Rothenberg).

tribesman *tribe/tribal member, member of a tribe.* However, the use of "tribe" is generally considered ethnocentric or racist; it is particularly inaccurate and inadmissible with respect to African ethnology; use instead *people.* For Native Americans, use *nation, people*, or a specific group name. *See also* savage; tribal warfare.

trick *prostitute's customer. See* Writing Guidelines for a discussion of our language on prostitution. *See also* john (man).

trickmaster *trickster, magician, conjurer, illusionist, sleight-of-hand artist; hoodwinker, faker, cheat, imposter, swindler, fraud, bunko artist, charlatan, quack, sharpie.*

triggerman *professional/armed killer, killer, gangster, gun, hired gun, gunner, gunfighter, gunslinger, assassin, slayer, gun-wielder/-toter, sharpshooter, sniper, attacker, outlaw, bank robber, bandit, terrorist, racketeer, mobster, hoodlum, liquidator.*

Trinity, the *See* Father, Son, and Holy Spirit/Ghost.

trooper/trouper all meanings of these words are inclusive.

troop sergeant an outdated term, but if used today it could refer to either sex; in historical contexts, it was undoubtedly a man.

trophy wife introduced in *Fortune* magazine's 1989 article, "The CEO'S Second Wife," this term describes an (apparently) growing trend among chief executives to discard longtime spouses for women typically younger, "sometimes several inches taller, beautiful and very often accomplished." The article, written by a woman, appeared to support the idea that a wife was an accoutrement, and that first wives lost out because they "didn't keep up." Some observers feel that such an article could be written gender-free in a few years when top women executives begin to replace husbands who "don't keep up." One wonders if equality on this particular issue is a very interesting goal.

troubadour woman or man. For information on the little-known women troubadours, see Meg Bogin, *The Women Troubadours* (New York: Norton, 1976).

truck driver statistics vary, but it appears that from 2% to 10% are women.

truckman *trucker, truck driver; ladder truck firefighter.*

truckmaster historically always a man.

turfman *racetrack regular, horseracing/track fan, devotee of horseracing*.

tutoress *tutor*.

twinkie *space ranger, flake, brainless wonder*. Although "twinkie" could refer to both sexes, it's generally reserved for teenage girls/young women. *See also* airhead; scatterbrained.

twit man/boy or woman/girl.

two-man (adj.) *See* one-man/two-man/three-man, etc. (adj).

two-person single career introduced by Hanna Papanek in 1972, this term describes women's vicarious achievement through their husbands' jobs. Formal and informal institutional demands made of both members of a married couple (of whom only the man is employed by the institution) were prevalent for many years in middle-class occupations in the United States, and still exist today. Channeling the occupational aspirations of educated women into the noncompetitive "two-person single career" without openly injuring the concept of equality of educational opportunities, this phenomenon contributes to the stereotype of the wife as supporter, comforter, backstage manager, home maintainer, and main rearer of children. These wives' contributions to their husbands' work include status maintenance, intellectual contributions, and public performance. Their rewards consist of raises in salary and perquisites granted to the husband; open acknowledgment of collaboration is infrequent.

tycoon woman or man.

typist man or woman.

u

A trite word is an overused word which has lost its identity like an old coat in a second-hand shop. The familiar grows dull and we no longer see, hear, or taste it.

Anaïs Nin

ugly customer this "customer" is generally assumed to be male. Use the phrase, but let it inspire questions about what we are doing as a society that produces so many dangerous boys/men. *See also* bad guy; violence.

umpire/ump for some time Pam Postema has been the only woman umpire in professional baseball, but there are umpires of both sexes at other levels of baseball and in other sports.

unbrotherly replace this vague term with more precise words: *unkind, cold, uncaring, unfriendly, unfeeling, uncharitable, mean-spirited, hostile, distant*.

Uncle Sam while some countries are personified by men, others are personified by women (for example, France's Marianne and Great Britain's Britannia). If you need to replace "Uncle Sam," use: *the United States, the United States of America, the U.S., the U.S.A., the U.S. government; the armed forces, the military*.

Uncle Tom it is better to forego this term entirely; you may know exactly what you mean by it but your audience may not. As well as being sexist (there is no equivalent for a woman), it can be highly racist in many contexts. Gender-free substitutes include: *collaborator, traitor to one's race, toady, sycophant, stooge, backscratcher, bootlicker, puppet, rubber stamp, dupe, doormat, flunky, subservient/obsequious person*. Today we would speak of *someone who has been co-opted*.

underclassman *undergraduate*. Or, be specific: *first-year student, second-year student; class of 1994*. *See also* freshman.

undercover man *private eye, eye, plainclothes detective, sleuthhound*. *See also* G-man; gumshoe; plainclothesman.

undergraduette this word, common around 1930, is no longer used, but is included as an example of (1) how terminally cute the language can get and (2) how unacceptable terms tend to disappear over time.

Other "-ette" words (for example, "usherette") may still be found in dictionaries but are rarely used.

underlord *second in command, subordinate, subaltern, underling*.

undomestic nonsexist in itself, "undomestic" is sometimes used to reflect unfavorably upon those who don't fit the stereotype of what a woman "ought" to be. Give this word a second look.

unfeminine avoid this vague, self-contradictory cultural stereotype. A woman's clothes, behavior, words, feelings, and thoughts are, by definition, "feminine" because a woman is wearing them, saying them, feeling them, etc. Words like "womanly/unwomanly," "manly/unmanly," "feminine/unfeminine," "masculine/ unmasculine," "ladylike/unladylike," and "gentlemanly/ ungentlemanly" are based on cultural, not biological, expectations. Language should not underwrite this sort of illogic. The only truly unfeminine things are those things biologically reserved to men. Replace the unhelpful and inexact word "unfeminine" with descriptive adjectives: *cold, hard, selfish, abrupt, analytical, direct, competent, logical*. These adjectives can apply equally well to a man. They are not synonyms for "unfeminine" but rather reflect the cultural spin on this word.

ungentlemanly *See* "unmasculine" for an explanation of the subjective cultural meanings attached to this word. Try to define what you mean by "ungentlemanly" and choose a precise adjective: *impolite, crude, rude, insensitive, thoughtless, discourteous, poorly behaved, ill-mannered, uncivil, disagreeable, inconsiderate*. These adjectives (which can apply equally well to women) are not true synonyms for "ungentlemanly" but rather reflect the way this word is most often used.

Union Jack (British flag) leave as is. James I of England, who signed his name with the French "Jacques," was the first common ruler of Scotland and England; the flag may have been named after him and the historic union of England and Scotland. But the term may also come from "jack," a small flag hoisted on a jack-staff and used by naval vessels for signaling.

union man *union member, labor/trade unionist, unionist, union backer, member of a union*. Minnesota AFL-CIO President Dan Gustafson says that "women are becoming an increasingly larger and more important percentage of the permanent workforce and of union membership."

Unknown Soldier, the this World War I soldier is a man.

unladylike *See* "unfeminine" for an explanation of the subjective cultural meanings attached to this word. For the vague and often inappropriate "unladylike," substitute *insensitive, indelicate, awkward, uncharming, unkind, rude, undignified, ill-mannered, ungracious, impolite, abrupt*. These adjectives apply equally well to a man. They are not synonyms for "unladylike" but rather reflections of what society tends to understand by the word.

unman *unnerve, disarm, weaken, devitalize, incapacitate, disable, unhinge, undermine, frighten, paralyze, petrify, terrorize, appall, horrify, deprive of courage/strength/vigor/power, draw the teeth of, render hors de combat, attenuate, shatter, exhaust, disqualify, invalidate, muzzle, enervate, tie the hands of, spike the guns of, take the wind out of one's sails, clip the wings of, put a spoke in one's wheel, undo.* In the narrower sense of emasculate or castrate, use "unman" sparingly as it implies, unflatteringly, that the man is a passive victim. There are no terms referring to women parallel to "unman," "emasculate," and "castrate." *See also* castrate/castrating; emasculate.

unmanliness/unmanly *See* "unmasculine" for an explanation of the subjective cultural meanings involved here. Replace these limp terms with descriptive adjectives: *dishonesty/dishonest, cowardice/cowardly, deviousness/crooked, weakness/weak, fearfulness/fearful, timidity/timid.* These words can be applied equally well to a woman. They are not synonyms for "unmanliness/unmanly" but simply the stereotypical and unreflected notions of a sexist society on what it means to be a man.

unmanned *unstaffed, having no staff aboard, unpeopled, unpopulated, uninhabited, lacking crew, crewless, remote control, on automatic pilot; frightened, undone. See also* unman.

unmasculine avoid this vague, self-contradictory cultural stereotype. A man's clothes, behavior, words, feelings, and thoughts are, by definition, masculine because a man is wearing them, saying them, feeling them, etc. Words like "womanly/unwomanly," "manly/unmanly," "feminine/unfeminine," "masculine/unmasculine," "ladylike/unladylike," and "gentlemanly/ungentlemanly" are based on cultural, not biological, expectations. Language should not underwrite this sort of illogic. The only truly unmasculine things are those things biologically reserved to women. Replace the unhelpful and inexact word "unmasculine" with descriptive adjectives: *timid, craven, weak, indirect, fearful, soft, faint-hearted, gentle, overemotional, comfort-loving.* All these adjectives can apply equally well to a woman. They are not synonyms for "unmasculine," but stereotypical cultural notions of what it is to be a man.

unsportsmanlike *unsporting, unfair, unfair play/playing, unsporting behavior, dishonorable, underhanded, unprincipled, behavior of a poor loser.*

unstatesmanlike *undiplomatic, impolitic, imprudent, lacking stature/grace and diplomacy, showing poor political strategy/ineffective government leadership.*

unwed mother *single parent, mother, woman, head of household.* Or use whenever possible: *unwed parents.* The term "unwed mother" completely disregards the also unwed (at least to this woman) father. Statistically in this country, it's the woman who gets (1) the child, (2) the poverty, and (3) society's disapproval. According to a radio news item, "More women than ever before are living with men without being married to them. And more unmarried women than ever before are having babies." An inclusive and more accurate report would have said: "More men and women than ever before are living together without being married. And more unmarried couples than ever before are having babies." Annually, 24% of all infants are born to unmarried couples. This represents a large number of fathers and mothers; do not ignore half of them. If it's not possible to include a reference to the father (perhaps because he is no longer in the picture), at least do not linguistically accuse, try, and find guilty the woman who makes herself vulnerable to stigmatization by accepting the consequences of her actions. An "unwed father" shows no external signs of his fatherhood—and thus does not make a good target for society's strictures and moralizations. "Unwed mothers" and their children, on the other hand, are all too visible.

unwomanly *See* "unfeminine" for an explanation of the subjective cultural meanings attached to this word. Use instead *cold, hostile, sharp, unloving, ungentle, uncharming, ungiving, unsupportive, ill-mannered, unmannerly, ungracious, undignified, indecorous, unattractive, unappealing.* These adjectives apply equally well to a man. They are not synonyms for "unwomanly," but rather reflections of what society tends to understand by the word.

unworkmanlike *unprofessional, unskillful, slipshod, unskilled, inexpert, inexperienced, untrained, inefficient, unsystematic, unbusinesslike, incompetent, sloppy, careless, unsuitable, irresponsible, unhandy, imprecise, unproficient.*

up and Adam *up and at 'em.* "Adam" was a mistake.

upperclassman *upperclass student.* Or, be precise: *third-year student, fourth-year student; junior, senior; class of 1994.*

usherette *usher.*

utility girl/utility man *utility worker/hand/cleaner, typewriter repairer.* Note the nonparallel "girl/man."

V

The limits of my language stand for the limits of my world.
Ludwig Wittgenstein

Valentino for inclusive alternatives use *heartthrob, great/dashing lover, paramour.*

valet/valet de chambre *personal/room attendant.*

valley girl the valley girl seems to be history now, and as such the term is correct; there never was a "valley boy."

vamp (woman) *seducer.* Short for "vampire," this word posits hypnotic power for women and helplessness for men, which disserves both. "Vamp" was popularized by Theda ("Kiss me, my fool") Bara in the 1914 *A Fool There Was.* She and Pola Negri played many other vamps, strongly identifying the role with women.

varlet historically varlets were always young men. Alternatives include: *attendant, menial, page.*

vassal although taken to mean a man, this word is defined as "a servant, slave, dependent, or subordinate," and historically it included all members of the household of the feudal tenant, male and female.

vegetable man *vegetable peddler/vendor.*

venireman *venire/potential juror.*

verger man or woman.

verseman *versifier, poet, maker of verses.*

vestryman *vestry member, member of the vestry.*

veteran 1.3 million of the 27 million war veterans in the United States are women.

vicar depending on the denomination, a vicar may be either sex.

vice-chairman *vice-chair, second in command, deputy, deputy director, vice-president.*

viceroy traditionally a males-only rank; the "roy" comes from the French "roi," "king." For unofficial uses substitute *deputy, ruler, sovereign, governor.*

victim girl/woman or boy/man. The use of "victim" is problematic in three instances. (1) Do not describe people with disabilities as victims ("polio victim," "victim of multiple sclerosis"). Say instead *someone who has polio, someone with multiple sclerosis.* (2) Avoid blaming crime or rape victims. "We all want injustice to be the victim's fault" (Hortense Calisher). This twisted psychology is seen in reflections like "what was she doing at a bar at one o'clock in the morning?" or "why did he leave his car unlocked anyway?" Blaming the victim is particularly common in cases of rape. The myth is that most sexual assaults are provoked by the victim, when in fact 60% to 70% of all rapes are planned in advance; nothing the victim does or doesn't do can avert it. When Phyllis Schlafly makes the blatantly false assertion that "For the virtuous woman, sexual harassment is not a problem, except in the rarest of cases," she blames the victim's "nonvirtuousness" for the problem. (3) Be aware of the sex bias to crime. Men constitute about 80% of homicide victims, nearly 70% of robbery victims, and about 70% of the victims of aggravated assault. Black men are particularly vulnerable; in his lifetime an African American man has a 1 in 21 chance of being murdered by an unlicensed gun, compared to a 1 in 131 chance for a white man. *See also* date rape; handicapped; provoke; rape; "she asked for it"; violence.

victory for mankind *victory for the world, victory for humankind/all peoples/ everyone, our common victory. See also* one small step for man, one giant leap for mankind.

victress *victor.*

vigilante woman or man.

villainess *villain.*

violence this term has sexist implications. Violence is on the increase (latest figures show a 10% rise in violent crime in 1990 over 1989, including a 20% increase in murders), and men are more likely than women to be perpetrators of a wide range of violent activities; of all those arrested for violence in any year the great majority (for the United States the figure is around 90%) are men. They are also more liable than women to be victims of violence. Although most violence is not sex-biased in that the sex of the offender or victim is not a contributing factor in the violence, there is an exception. Women suffer disproportionately from violence by men, primarily because they are women. According to the Justice Department, three out of four women can expect to be victims of at least one violent attack in their lifetime. There is a high societal tolerance for abusing women; a nationwide Louis Harris Poll found that 25% of the men in the sample approved of a husband slapping his spouse. "Men are raised with a sense of entitlement, privilege and expectation that women can and should do what we want them to do," says Edward Gondolf, a researcher on male violence. "And if they don't we resolve the problem with aggression and force." The violence continuum includes sexist language, anti-woman jokes, abusive rap lyrics, film and TV violence against women, sexual harassment, pornography, wife beating, rape, and murder. Chuck Niessen-Derry of BrotherPeace says men need to "start making the connection between the rape joke on Tuesday and the rape on Thursday." Tolerance for the "milder" forms of violence permits the more serious forms. And the future doesn't look much better. More preteens surveyed could identify Jason and Freddy (of *Friday the 13th* and *Nightmare on Elm Street*) than George Washington, Abraham Lincoln, or Martin Luther King, Jr., and children eighteen and younger now are responsible for 70% of the hate crime committed in the United States. Experts agree that juvenile violence has become more vicious and more random and that the assailants are less remorseful afterward. Some think the increase in the murder, rape, and battering of women is a backlash by men as women gain more equality in society. Men are also abused by their wives and murdered by them, although in much smaller numbers. Many of the more serious assaults by wives have been reported as self-defense in response to abuse. This is not to discount the reality of abused men, but to give it perspective. When was the last time a man feared for his physical safety when he passed a group of women on the street? (Note that gay men as well as women may experience fear when approaching a group of men standing on a corner.) Our language reflects our institutionalized violence; it also helps perpetuate it. Consider avoiding violent expressions and metaphors, for example: knockout; kill two birds with one stone; crack the whip; kick something/an idea around; knock heads together; how does that strike/hit you; he's trying to hit on her; knock someone dead/for a loop; take a beating; sock it to 'em; I'd like to punch someone out/knock someone's block off/beat someone's brains out/beat the living daylights/the tar/the stuffing out of someone; give a black eye to; give someone a tongue lashing; haul someone over the coals; hit someone up for something; a slap on the wrist; hit below the belt; pin someone's ears back; skin someone alive; hit someone up the side of the head; I'd like to slap her/belt him; bite/snap/take someone's head off; big shot/gun; this'll knock 'em flat; smash hit; blast them out of the water; shoot down an idea; one thing triggers another. *See also* battered wife/woman; date rape; knockout; lady-killer; provoke; rape; sexual harassment; "she asked for it"; victim.

virago the first dictionary definition of "virago" is "a loud, overbearing woman: termagant." The second is "a woman of great stature, strength, and courage" (*Webster's Ninth New Collegiate Dictionary*) and as such is being reclaimed by some members of the women's movement.

virgin/virginity if you must use these terms for some logical reason, do so for both sexes with equal weight and meaning. The double standard still expects virginity or at least some measure of virginal behavior from women while rewarding men in subtle and unsubtle ways for being experienced. The concept of virginity is also heterosexist, euphemistic, and impractical: is the presence of a hymen the sine qua non of virginity in women? how is virginity defined in men without physical evidence? is the young nonsexual athlete with the torn hymen no longer a virgin? is the inexperienced woman no longer entitled to her virginity after rape? how virginal is a practicing lesbian with an intact hymen? Use these words with extreme caution.

virgin forest/virgin soil, etc. use only when necessary because of so-far unique meanings. Otherwise substitute *unspoiled, untouched, pristine.* "Virgin paper" is *nonrecycled paper.* The word "virgin" alludes to nature being unused by man (sex-specific word intended). *See also* Mother Nature.

virile this is a properly sex-specific word when it refers to a man's ability to function sexually. In its broader sense, use inclusive alternatives: *energetic, vigorous, forceful, strong, powerful, dynamic, spirited, daring, fearless, venturesome, courageous, intrepid, tough, audacious, dashing, potent, hardy, hearty, rugged, bold.*

virtue virtue for women has most often been defined by chastity, while for men it has always been far more free-ranging and has included such "manly" attributes as valor, courage, and a sense of morality. Assign "virtue" in its broadest sense to both sexes.

visiting fireman *visiting firefighter/colleague.*

visual-effects man *visual-effects specialist/technician.*

vizier has always been a man.

volunteer a volunteer can be either a woman or a man, but volunteer work has traditionally been apportioned along sexist lines: "For men it usually means serving in prestigious policymaking or advisory capacities, with the encouragement of the employer to take time off from work to serve as the company's 'goodwill ambassador' to the community. For women, volunteerism means providing direct services at their own expense (transportation, lunch). Second, because women volunteers work almost exclusively at the lowest levels of the volunteer hierarchy, they obtain little valuable work experience or training. Popular mythologies to the contrary, displaced homemakers have been continuously frustrated to find that their resumes, which have meticulously translated fifteen to twenty-five years of volunteer activities into marketable skills, elicit . . . negative responses from prospective employers . . . ." In general, "women volunteers are highly underutilized and underrated in terms of their intelligence, abilities, and credentials. It is not at all unusual, for example, for a female Ph.D. to be asked to spend fifteen hours a week laminating alphabet cards while the local hardware salesman is appointed to the Board of Education" (Nijole V. Benokraitis and Joe R. Feagin, *Modern Sexism*).

votaress *votary*.

voyageur history records only male voyageurs.

voyeur *See* peeping Tom.

W

The liberation of language is rooted in the liberation of ourselves.

Mary Daly

wage earner although the term is inclusive, what it means in dollars and cents is sex-biased: women working full-time have average annual earnings about 68% of those of men; based on median income, the figure is around 66%, virtually what it was in 1955; female college graduates make less than male high school graduates; minority women fare even less well—the average black female college graduate in a full-time position earns the same as the average white male high school dropout; corporate women at the vice presidential level or higher are paid 42% less than men with comparable titles; more than two-thirds of all minimum-wage workers are women; female-headed families (52% of all poor families) have average annual incomes of $14,620 compared with $24,800 for men; women who live alone have average annual incomes of $10,580 compared with $16,700 for men; wages become depressed when large numbers of women enter a previously male-intensive field.

waiter 83% of waiters are women.

waitress *waiter, server, attendant, table/restaurant server.* Also used in some areas: *wait, waitron, waitperson.* The plural *waitstaff* is being seen more and more.

Walkman unless referring to Sony's trademarked "Walkman," use *headset/ headphone radio/tape player, stereo/radio headset/headphones.*

wallflower avoid; although it could theoretically refer to either sex, it's reserved for women/girls and it reflects outdated customs and attitudes.

Walter Mitty when using expressions like this, be aware of how many are male-based. Some of the time use female-based expressions, creative expressions of your own, or alternatives: *daydreamer, escapist, secret adventurer. See* Writing Guidelines for a discussion of sex-linked expressions.

wanton this tends to be reserved for women, holding them to a higher arbitrary moral standard than men. If you must use it, do so gender-fairly to describe behavior but not people ("they behaved wantonly," but not "they were wanton").

war bride were there ever any war grooms? Retain in historical contexts.

wardress *warden.*

wardrobe mistress *wardrobe supervisor/manager/clerk/ handler/department/ coordinator.*

war hawk/warmaker/warmonger although studies show that the tendency toward warfare is characteristic of men across many cultures (the only nonbiological characteristic that can be attributed consistently to one sex), beware of generalizations; many men have devoted their lives to peace issues and some women are hawks. *See also* combat; males-only draft.

warlock *witch; conjurer, sorcerer, magician.* "Witch" and "warlock" are strong, evenly balanced, and not particularly sex-biased words.

warlord *supreme military leader, military leader/commander, militarist, warmonger, jingoist.*

warpaint (woman's makeup) avoid.

warrior both women and men have been and are warriors—whether this means fighting in battles or living out the warrior archetype. In *The Warrior Queens*, Antonia Fraser describes female warrior-rulers who have often been the focus for what a country afterwards perceives to have been its golden age, for example, Queen Elizabeth I of England, twelfth-century Queen Tamara of Georgia, or fifteenth-century Queen Isabella of Spain. In more recent times, women have taken part in every American military crisis since the Revolutionary War. Harriet Tubman planned and led a military campaign for the Union Army in South Carolina in 1863. At least some men—the traditional warriors—are becoming "new warriors" today. Exploring what it means to be fully a man and acknowledging the power within themselves, these men have no need to dominate others. They use their considerable energies in constructive, nonthreatening ways while renewing their connections with self, others, and the world. *See also* Amazon/amazon; combat.

washerman/washerwoman/washwoman *launderer, laundry worker, cleaner, drycleaner.*

WASP avoid; this acronym for White Anglo-Saxon Protestant has become a simplistic synonym for oppression, discrimination, and spurious superiority. It blames an entire group for something only some of them (as well as some from outside that group) may have been responsible for.

watchman *watch, night guard/watch, guard, security guard/officer/consultant, gatekeeper, guardian, sentry, sentinel, lookout, caretaker, custodian, patrol, patroller; crossing tender/guard.*

watchman's rattle *sentry's/lookout's rattle, alarm, warning, distress/danger signal.*

waterboatman (bug) leave as is.

water boy *water carrier.*

waterman *boater, ferry/watercraft operator.*

watermanship *swimming/boating/rowing/sailing/water sports skills, canoeing expertise.* Or, reword to describe the person with these skills: *competent swimmer, professional boater, skilled canoeist, veteran rower, proficient/expert/talented/ knowledgeable/skillful swimmer/boater.*

water witch *water dowser.*

way to a man's heart is through his stomach, the *the way to a person's heart is through their stomach* (*see* singular "they"); *the quickest way to the heart is through the stomach, the way to the heart is through the stomach.*

weaker sex, the avoid.

weak sister *weakling, weak link in the chain, weak reed to lean on, weak spot, one who blows hot and cold, unreliable/untrustworthy/half-hearted/wishy-washy/fickle person, someone who is weak as a child/weak as water.* Although this term is used to refer unflatteringly to both men and women (leaning more toward putting down men), the underlying assumption is extremely prejudicial to women.

wear the pants (woman assuming "masculine" role) avoid; outdated both in form and content.

weathergirl/weatherman *weathercaster, meteorologist, weather reporter/forecaster/prophet, forecaster, climatologist.* Note the nonparallel "girl/man."

wedlock far from the imagined imprisonment of facile wit, the "lock" in this word is from the Anglo-Saxon for "gift." "Wed" means "promise." Marriage, or wedlock, is thus the promised gift of happiness.

weighmaster *public weigher, licensed public weigher.* Sometimes the official job title "weighmaster" must be used.

weight man *thrower, throw, weight thrower.* Or, be specific: *shot-putter, discus/hammer/javelin thrower.* Both women and men are throwers.

welder approximately 5% are women.

welfare mother *welfare client/recipient.* Discuss welfare clients respectfully and carefully; myths, stereotypes, and unwarranted hostility abound. For example, although the prevailing public notion is that welfare families are larger than most, a 1989 study showed that women on welfare have fewer children than other women (45.8 per 1000 welfare recipients give birth each year compared to 71.1 for women in general). Other myths (welfare cheating, laziness, "immorality") are equally indefensible.

welsh/welsher *cheat, bilk, rip off, renege, default, skip town, back out, refuse to pay up; cheat, cheater, swindler, con artist, bilker, delinquent, defaulter.* The slur on the people of Wales makes these terms undesirable.

Welshman *inhabitant of Wales; Welshman and Welshwoman.* Plural: *the Welsh, people of Wales, Welshfolk, Welshwomen and Welshmen* (but never "Welshwomen and men").

wench retain in the earlier, historical sense ("young woman" or "female servant"). For prostitute, use *prostitute*.

wet nurse legitimate gender-specific word.

whaleman/whalerman *whaler.*

wharfman *wharfworker, wharfhand, dockhand, dockworker, stevedore, shoreworker, shorehand, longshore worker.*

wharfmaster *wharfinger, harbor manager.* The nonsexist "wharfinger" is actually the older term (1552); "wharfmaster" came into the language in 1618.

what evil lurks in the hearts of men? *what evil lurks in our/people's/human hearts? what evil lurks in the hearts of humans?*

what in (the) Sam Hill! *what in the heck/hell/world!*

whatsoever a man sows, that shall he also reap *whatsoever you sow, that too shall you reap; whatever we sow we will also reap.*

wheelchair-bound *wheelchair user, someone who uses a wheelchair.* Never use: wheelchair-bound, confined/bound/restricted to a wheelchair. A wheelchair is a tool, not a prison. *See also* crip/cripple; handicapped.

wheelman *cyclist; getaway driver.*

wheelsman *pilot, steerer, navigator.*

whine this word is functionally sexist since it is used primarily of women and children, while in similar circumstances men are said to complain, criticize, or just plain talk. Use instead *complain, grumble, grouse, gripe, criticize, harp on, fume, find fault, be dissatisfied, pester, harass, fuss, raise a fuss. See also* bitch (verb); nag (verb).

whipping boy *whipping post, scapegoat, goat, victim, target, dupe, tool.* In the historical sense, it was always a boy.

white when possible avoid the metaphorical use of this word to stand for purity, goodness, rightness (the opposite of all this being black). Never use "that's white of you"; replace terms like "white lie" (social lie); and circumvent others like "white knight," "white hope," and "white list." *See also* black/black-.

white man's burden one of the most outrageous expressions in the language (from Rudyard Kipling's 1899 poem of the same name), this refers to the alleged duty of white peoples to manage the affairs of "less developed" nonwhite peoples and has served to justify immeasurable horror and injustice. Lingering colonial/domineering/protectionistic/patriarchal attitudes stemming from this phrase still color much Western thought. Watch for subtle echoes, and delete them ruthlessly.

whore *prostitute.* "Whore" used to be a nonjudgmental term describing a lover of either sex.

widow/widower *surviving spouse.* It may be necessary sometimes to specify "widow" or "widower" for clarity. The ideal would be to have one word instead of two to describe a surviving spouse—"widow" preferably since it is the shorter, base word. "Widower" is one of the only male words that is the marked term—that is, the female "widow" is the unmarked or "default" word and the male word is based on it. Notice how often a woman is referred to in print as someone's widow—and how very seldom a man is referred to as someone's widower.

widow burning legally banned in 1829, widow burning or sati/suttee (literally, "good woman") was the custom of a Hindu widow who willingly or unwillingly was cremated on her husband's funeral pyre. *See also* bride burning.

widow lady *surviving spouse, widow. See also* lady (noun); widow/widower.

widow's mite *one's last cent/dime, giving of one's all, giving out of one's need, giving till it hurts.* Retain the term sometimes to balance the many male expressions in the language.

widow's peak this appears irreplaceable by an equally concise and descriptive term.

widow's walk leave as is. Or, *railed observatory platform.*

wife an acceptable word in itself (it comes from a general Germanic term meaning "female human being"), "wife" is sometimes used gratuitously or in very sexist ways. An effective test is to see if you would use "husband" in a similar situation. When *Esquire* offered its readers a special tear-out section entitled "Your Wife: An Owner's Manual," editor-in-chief Lee Eisenberg introduced it: "We are gathered together in the sight of our readers to come to grips with the subject of a man's wife, his partner, the little woman, the missus. . . ." The issue included a list of "synonyms" for "wife," some of which were positive or neutral and some, acknowledged as offensive, that illustrated what some men and some husbands think of wives: bitch, hussy, old lady, the gadget, Darth Vader, the hag, the nag, the rag, the bag, the spandex monster, my little piranha fish, the war department, twitface, the mouse queen, Evita, the terminator, the queen, the princess, Her Majesty, the boss, the worse half, exec-u-wife, the fishwife, the shrew, the mouth, the ballbuster, the creature, squaw, the powers that be, the ball and chain. *See also* farm wife/farmer's wife; husband and wife; owner; wife/husband; working wife.

wife/husband *spouse, mate, partner,* unless gender-specific terms are necessary. In Old English, the "hus-wif" and the "hus-band" ("hus" means "house") were exactly parallel terms, titles of respect and honor in the community, descriptors of the couple's partership as householders. The connotation for both terms was that of a "substantial person." Since that time, the words have taken different roads and were gradually replaced by one of the most glaringly unbalanced gender pairs in the language: "man and wife." Use instead *man and woman/woman and man, wife and husband/husband and wife.* **See also** couple; housewife; hubby; husband (noun); husband and wife; wife.

wifehood/wifelike/wifeliness/wifely our ideas of "wifelike," "wifely," "wifeliness," and "wifehood" depend entirely on subjective cultural stereotypes. Replace these terms with words that are gender-nonspecific, precise, and descriptive. For example, for "wifely" try terms like *companionable, helpful, supportive, sympathetic, sensitive, affectionate, intimate, loving, approving, admonishing.* These words would do equally well for "husbandly." **See also** wife; woman (noun); womanlike/womanliness/womanly.

wife-swapping *spouse-swapping.*

willy-nilly this term is male-based, but not because of a man's name; the original expression was "will he or nill he." Even so, it would be a rare individual who saw it as a sexist term.

wimmin/wimyn/womon/womyn some women favor alternative spellings for "woman" or "women" that leave out "man/men." These terms should be used for groups and individuals that so name themselves.

winchman *wincher.*

wingman *flyer.* "Wingman" is used in the Air Force for either a woman or a man. **See also** airman.

wingmanship *flying skills/expertise.* **See also** airmanship.

win one's spurs the strong masculine overtones probably come from knights being given golden spurs for their exploits. Use instead *earn one's wings, come of age, triumph, succeed, arrive, make a hit, pull it off, carry the day, come off with flying colors, have it all one's own way, have the world at one's feet, turn up trumps, have one's star in the ascendant.*

wireman *wirer.*

wise as Balaam's ass/Solomon when using expressions like this, be aware of how many are male-based. Some of the time use female-based expressions, creative expressions of your own, or alternatives: *wise as an owl/a serpent/a judge.* For a discussion of sex-linked expressions, *see* Writing Guidelines.

wise man/wise woman *wise person/one, elder, leader, sage, philosopher, oracle, mentor, luminary, learned person, pundit, scholar, savant, authority, expert, guru, thinker.* "Wise man" or "wise woman," which are currently used gender-fairly, will sometimes be the terms of choice.

wish is father to the thought, the *the wish gives birth to/begets/engenders/ brings forth/precedes/produces the thought.*

witch woman or man. Although the word "witch" has undeservedly negative connotations for many people, it is being reclaimed with pride by the estimated 150,000 witches in the United States who celebrate life in harmony with the Earth and are committed to doing good. Genuine benevolent witchcraft does not in any way include, let alone worship, Satan. Witches tend to be gentle people who believe in responsibility toward self, others, and the world.

wizard acceptable sex-specific term. Inclusive terms with related meanings are *sorcerer, magician, conjurer, witch.*

wolf (man) *flirt, seducer, predator, someone who comes on strong.* The distinctive "wolf whistle" is by definition sounded by a man, but women have not been shy about using it to tease male friends. *See also* lone wolf; womanize/womanizer.

woman (noun) the Old English word from which "woman" is taken ("wif-man") came from "wif" ("female") plus "man" ("human being"). Women continued to be "female human beings," which is fairly decent, but the word for "male human beings" ("wer-man") was gradually lost (it survives only in "werewolf") and men got to be human beings, period, full stop, no qualifications for sex. Although suggestions are made from time to time to replace the word "woman," it appears to be well entrenched in the language. What is more crucial today than where the word came from is how it is perceived. And functionally "woman" is a respected, acceptable term as long as the context in which it appears is not sexist. Women haven't always been regarded as individuals (*see* farm wife/farmer's wife) or even as human beings (*see* human), and in such roles as lovers, wives, sex partners, and wage earners (*see* girlfriend; prostitute/prostitution; wage earner; wife) the average woman has not been equal in status to the average man. A neat if perhaps facile summary of female-male history might be Theodor Reik's statement that "In our civilization, men are afraid that they will not be men enough and women are afraid that they might be considered only women."

woman/women (adj.) avoid using "woman" when you would not use "man" in a parallel situation. Phrases like "woman driver" and "woman scientist" are no-no's. If it is necessary to specify sex, use "woman" or "women" instead of "female"—for example, "women radical artists."

woman-hater *See* man-hater/woman-hater.

womanhood both definitions of this word are acceptable—"the state of being a woman" and "women or womenkind." "Manhood" has four definitions, two of which are falsely generic, the other two of which correspond to the two definitions for "womanhood." If you want a broader, sex-neutral term use *personhood, selfhood, adulthood, majority, maturity.* *See also* manhood.

womanish replace this vague and pejorative stereotype with descriptive words: *fussy, particular, overparticular, choosy, fastidious, anxious,* *overanxious, worried, nervous, timid, weak, indecisive, unathletic, vapid*. "Womanish" uses "like a woman" as an insult to put down men, thus disparaging both sexes with a single word.

womanist used by some black feminists, this term has been particularly associated with Alice Walker who says, "Womanist is to feminist as purple is to lavender" (*In Search of Our Mothers' Gardens: Womanist Prose*). African American women writers have been prolific; the Schomburg Library of nineteenth-century black women writers has assembled a thirty-volume collection of reprints of fiction, poetry, essays, and biographies by and about black women writers of the 1800s, with ten more volumes in the works.

womanize/womanizer *philander, bedhop, sleep around, seduce, be promiscuous/sexually active/sexually aggressive/indiscriminate, have many love affairs; swinger, philanderer, seducer, bedhopper, sensualist, free-lover, flirt, freethinker, free spirit, voluptuary, sybarite, hedonist, lover, big-time operator*. It's difficult to find and use good inclusive substitutes for "womanize" and "womanizer" because we so rarely need that exact word for anything except a man who pursues or courts women habitually or illicitly. Women who philander are either "man crazy" or "promiscuous." Gay men who have many affairs are also "promiscuous" or they have "one-night stands." Ellen Goodman says "manize" hasn't made it into the language because women have always associated sex with danger (rape, pregnancy, the double standard), because getting men on their backs isn't a power trip for most women, and because so far the power of older, successful women does not seem to act as an aphrodisiac on younger, good-looking men. There have been too few highly public and powerful women to know if "manizing" is something women would do (with reference to Golda Meir, Indira Gandhi, and Margaret Thatcher, it is difficult to imagine). *See also* ladies' man; man about town; playboy; rake.

womankind there may often be a legitimate use for "womankind" where "mankind" is problematic since it has been misused for so long as a pseudogeneric.

womanlike/womanliness/womanly these vague and subjective cultural stereotypes convey different meanings to different people according to their perceptions of what a woman ought or ought not to do, say, think, feel, and look like. They have nothing to do with sex and everything to do with gender. (*See* Writing Guidelines for a discussion of the difference between gender and sex.) Choose words instead that express precise characteristics: *gracious/graciousness, warm/warmth, gentle/gentleness, receptive/receptivity, supportive/supportiveness, tender/tenderness, charming/charm, sympathetic/sympathy, nurturing/nurturance, well-mannered/good breeding, considerate/consider-*

ation, kind/kindness, intuitive/intuition, strong/gentle strength. All these words may be used equally appropriately of a man. They are not synonymous with the sexist terms, but are rather what people generally seem to mean by them.

woman's place is in the home, a when a man's "place" is also in the home and when the woman truly wants to be there, this is a powerful sentiment. It also rings true if we substitute "heart" for "place" and apply it to both sexes. Unfortunately, this dictum has been used with all the finesse of a sledgehammer and promulgated as a "natural" law as well as a test of patriotism, "femininity," conjugal love, and right-thinking. Being physically at home is an excellent choice for many women and one that society ought to value and support with positive attitudes and practical assistance. The problem is that this expression has become a mandate for all women, and it ignores a man's involvement with the home. Avoid it.

woman suffrage movement this legitimate sex-specific term is the one used most often by historians.

woman's work avoid except when referring to what goes on during childbirth; there is no other work biologically specific only to women. "[I]t is a retrogressive idea to call any particular sphere of work 'Women's'. We do not know what women's work will be, we only know what it has been" (Caroline Boord, *The Freewoman*, 1911). *See also* man's work.

woman's work is never done, a in the case of a woman with a paid job and a family, this is particularly true, and usually more true than of a man with a paid job and a family. *See also* housework; second shift, the.

women women make up one-half of the world's adult population and one-third of the paid labor force. They perform two-thirds of the world's work, but earn only one-tenth of the world's income and own only 1% of the world's property. Sexist language both reflects and shapes statistics like these.

women and children pairing women with children is illogical, belittling to women, and a paternalistic attempt to perpetuate the subordination and powerlessness of women. The Napoleonic Code (1804) did much to legitimize the second-class status of European women. Among other things, the code grouped women and children with "persons of unsound mind," judging them all equally incapable of entering into contracts. This legacy is still seen today: the treatises on women in most law libraries are located between those on children and those on the insane. *See also* innocent women and children.

women and children first *those who need extra assistance first.* This expression probably arose not so much from some medieval idea of chivalry as from a more ancient fact of life: an early society's main chance for survival rested on its being able to reproduce itself. Men can father children every day but women need nine months to produce a child and a child represents a considerable investment in the future. Thus in times of crisis women and children were protected so as to ensure the future of the society. Today the future of our society depends on both sexes. *See also* innocent victim; women and children.

women's intuition *intuition.*

women's issues by using this vague label, politicians and others are able to discount and stereotype issues such as abortion rights, ageism, childcare, comparable worth, divorce, domestic violence, the Equal Rights Amendment, flextime, parental leave, poverty, rape, and sexual harassment, when they are in fact family, political, social, ethical, and human issues.

women's lib/women's libber *women's liberation movement, women's movement, feminism, feminist movement; feminist, supporter/member of the women's movement.* "Women's lib" and "women's libber" are not inherently pejorative terms; women use them among themselves positively. However, the terms are sometimes used in offensive, derogatory, patronizing, trivializing, and condescending ways by people who are hostile to women and their goals.

women's liberation movement the women's liberation movement, which grew out of leftist politics in the 1960s, was never one organized group, but its proponents generally espoused more radical issues than those of the women's movement or of feminism; they were the first to promote consciousness raising.

women's movement this term is not synonymous with "feminism," "women's rights movement," or "women's liberation movement," although all four have much in common. The women's movement, begun in the nineteenth century and all but forgotten for decades, is now a broad, generic, unstructured grouping of women concerned about issues that particularly affect women. In a 1989 survey 67% of the polled women agreed the United States continues to need a strong women's movement to push for changes that benefit women; 27% disagreed.

women's pages, the (newspaper) there is no rationale for a section aimed at one sex, and most daily newspapers have eliminated it. Even though many more men than women traditionally read the sports pages, they never were "the men's pages." What are now sometimes still called "the women's pages" might be designated instead *lifestyle, living section, features, family life, health and fitness, modern living, community news, consumer information,* or something generic like Variety, Express, Today, Viewpoint, etc.

women's rights movement this movement commonly dates from 1848 when women met in Seneca Falls, New York, to draw up the first public protest in the United States against the political, social, and economic repression of women. *See also* women's movement.

women's studies over two-thirds of all universities, nearly half of all four-year colleges, and about one-fourth of two-year institutions now offer women's studies courses. There are also over fifty centers or institutes for research on women, numerous professional journals, and over one hundred feminist bookstores across the country. *See also* men's studies.

woodsman *woodlander, forest dweller, backsettler; woodworker, carver, carpenter; forester, logger, woodchopper, woodcutter, woods worker; woodswoman and woodsman*. "Woodswomen" is becoming a strong, independent term, thanks to Woodswomen, an organization for outdoorswomen who like outdoor sports and adventure travel (trekking to Nepal, llama packing in the West, biking in Brittany and Cozumel, climbing in Alaska and Ecuador, rafting in the Northwest and Costa Rica). Rebecca A. Hinton writes in *Women's Outdoor Journal*, "Women have been enjoying the outdoors since the beginning of time, but if we'd all been wearing camouflage we couldn't be more invisible."

working father according to the Bureau of National Affairs, fathers still define themselves primarily as providers and continue to face traditional pressure to be good workers, but they are increasingly torn between work and family, wanting to connect with their children in stronger ways than their own fathers did. In one study 36% of fathers and 37% of mothers reported "a lot of stress" in balancing work and family. Men often keep quiet about their family interests because of workplace attitudes, but fear of reproducing their fathers' absence and detachment sets up conflicts for them as they move through their careers; 58% of the male workforce are men with children under eighteen. Companies are beginning to recognize this need and to consider benefits (time off, childcare facilities, flexible benefit programs, etc.) for both fathers and mothers. *See also* childcare; parent; provider.

working girl *worker, employee, jobholder, wage earner, laborer, day laborer, average/typical worker, blue-collar/industrial worker, professional*. Or, be specific: *programmer, mechanic, librarian, pipefitter, teacher, physician, electrician*, etc. "Working girl" is sexist (we have no "working boys"), inaccurate (if she's old enough to work, she's not a girl), and has unpleasant overtones; in the late 1940s it was synonymous with prostitute. *See also* businessman; career girl/career woman; working mother; working wife; working woman.

working man *worker, employee, jobholder, wage earner, laborer, day laborer, average/typical worker, blue-collar/industrial worker, professional*. Or, be specific: *programmer, mechanic, librarian, pipefitter, teacher, physician, electrician*, etc. Some 77% of all men age 16 or older are in the

workforce (the figure is 57% for women). *See also* moonlighter;
working father; workman.

working mother avoid this term to describe women who work outside
the home; it implies that women who work inside the home do not
really work. For mothers who work outside the home use *wage-
earning/jobholding/salaried woman/mother, woman/mother employed
outside the home/in the paid workforce, working-for-pay mother*, or her
specific job title. For women who work inside the home use
*nonsalaried woman/mother, woman/mother working/employed inside the
home/at home, at-home parent, home-working mother, home-employed
mother, woman who works as a homemaker, woman who is her own childcare giver* (the last two are used by the U.S. Department of Labor).
Question the need to specify gender and the existence of offspring;
most of the time your meaning will be served by a neutral term like
"jobholder." (At work, too often men with children are men, and
women with children are mothers.) If both partners work, use
inclusive terms like *working parents, a two-income/two-paycheck family,
two-earner/dual-career/dual-income couple*. Mothers who work inside
the home and those who work outside it both have their hands full;
William Safire points out that "motherhood begins with *labor*, and the
work does not end when the little job product is brought home."
Although working mothers have been criticized for destroying the
traditional family, they have, on the contrary, kept millions of children from sinking below the poverty line; two-thirds of the women in
the workforce today are either the sole support of their children or
have husbands who earn less than $15,000 a year. A survey called
"Don't Blame the Baby" (Wick and Co.) found that the majority of
women leave jobs to go to better jobs; only 7% leave to work at home.
See also housewife; housework; maternity leave; moonlighter; second
shift, the; woman's work; working wife; working woman.

working wife avoid this term to describe women who work outside the
home; it implies that women who work inside the home do not really
work. To describe the former use *wage-earning/job-holding/salaried
woman, woman employed outside the home/in the paid workforce*, or her
specific job title. To describe the latter use *nonsalaried woman, woman
working/employed inside the home/at home*. If both partners work, avoid
gender-specific distinctions and describe the couple as *working
parents, a two-income/two-paycheck family, two-earner/dual-career/dual-
income couple/household*. Lady L. McLaren pointed out in 1908, "The
great majority of wives are devoting their time to unpaid work, and
when the importance of the work is considered, it appears extraordinary that the services of wives have no money value placed on them.
. . . A wife who works diligently and devotedly to the family service
should be entitled to such wages of a servant or housekeeper as are

usual in that station of life in which she lives and this in addition to her board." According to a Canadian government advisory group study, the stress of combining unpaid work (in the home) and paid work (in the workplace) may be the number-one health hazard for women (as much as 80% of all illness can be linked to stress). *See also* housewife; housework; moonlighter; second shift, the; woman's work; working mother; working woman.

working woman *worker, employee, jobholder, wage earner, laborer, day laborer, average/typical worker, blue-collar/industrial worker, professional.* Or, be specific: *programmer, mechanic, librarian, pipefitter, teacher, physician, electrician,* etc. Some 57% of all women age 16 or older are in the workforce (the figure is 77% for men). From a 1919 *Smith College Weekly:* "We cannot believe that it is fixed in the nature of things that a woman must choose between a home and her work, when a man may have both." *See also* career girl/career woman; housewife; housework; moonlighter; second shift, the; working mother; working wife; workman.

workman *worker, artisan, crafter, employee, laborer, operator, hand, staff.* Or, be specific: *repairer, landscaper, etc. See also* handyman; odd-job(s)-man; repairman; working man.

workmanlike/workmanly *skillful, skilled, expert, professional, businesslike, competent, efficient, careful, precise, proficient, first-rate, top-flight.*

workmanship *artisanship, work, construction, handiwork, handicraft, artisanry, skilled-craft work, skill, technique, style, expertness, competence, proficiency, finish, quality, polish, execution, technique, performance.* "Workmanship" may need to be retained in the legal sense as case law often uses it.

workmen's compensation *workers' compensation.*

worth a king's ransom *priceless, beyond price, worth its weight in gold, above rubies, invaluable, matchless, peerless, inestimable, costly, of great price, precious, worth a pretty penny/a fortune.*

writing guidelines for help with bias-free language, *see* Writing Guidelines, beginning on page 3.

y

No dictionary of a living tongue ever can be perfect, since while it is hastening to publication, some words are budding and some falling away.

Samuel Johnson

yachtsman *yacht owner/captain, yachter; yacht club member; yachtswoman and yachtsman.* **See also** *seaman.*

yachtsmanship *yachting skills/techniques, yacht sailing techniques.*

Yahweh (YHWH) because this personal name for God is not gender-specific, it is popular with groups seeking inclusive terms for God. However, practicing Jews neither use nor speak this sacred word, and out of respect for this belief system, it is recommended that others forego its use also. Jews use instead "Ha-Shem" ("The Name"). Variant forms of address that Jews use for God include "Adonai," "Lord," and "Eloheinu"—but never "Jehovah," which was a hybrid name introduced by European Christian scholars centuries ago. *See also* Father (God); God; Lord.

yammer nobody yammers very much, but apparently men absolutely never do. For alternatives to this functionally sexist word, *see* gossip.

yardman *yard worker/laborer/supervisor, caretaker, odd-job laborer; gardener, landscaper; stockyard handler/laborer; railroad worker.*

yardmaster *yard manager/supervisor, railroad yard operations supervisor.*

yellow/yellow-bellied/yellow-bellied coward/yellow belly/yellow streak down one's back wholly reserved for boys/men, these insults indirectly discount girls/women (who have not been expected—or indeed often allowed—to accept challenges that call for courage, bravery, or risk-taking) and hold men/boys to impossibly high, dubious, and constantly shifting standards of courage. Boys/men are acculturated to be sensitive to taunts of "coward." Most people would not use these terms; they are included here to show the cultural bias that expects too much of men and too little of women. *See also* coward/cowardly/cowardice.

Yellow Peril avoid this particularly degrading ethnic slur. In historical contexts, set it in quotation marks to show its dubious validity or indicate in some way that it was not objective, but subjective, reality for those who coined and used it.

yenta this Yiddish word for a constantly talking, gossiping, meddling, or scolding woman is not used as negatively as it might appear. The Yiddish culture looks upon the yenta with a fond exasperation—after all, who else always knows what's going on? For inclusive alternatives *see* gossip.

yeoman/yeomanly/yeomanry/yeoman of the guard/yeoman's service some of these terms have historical or official meanings that defy substitution, but others can be variously replaced: *retainer, attendant; military corps personnel attached to the British royal household; smallholding farmer, freeholder; petty officer, clerical officer; clerk, paralegal, typist, copyist, transcriber.*

yeoman's job *impressive/remarkable/extraordinary/ outstanding/valiant/heroic/ superexcellent/first-class/bang-up/A-number-one job, massive/enormous effort.*

yes man *yea-sayer, toady, rubber stamp, sycophant, flunky, puppet, stooge, dupe, brown-noser, apple polisher, bootlicker, backscratcher, flatterer, hanger-on, follower, doormat, tool, minion, myrmidon.* According to Stuart Berg Flexner (*Listening to America*), the term came from a 1913 T.A. "Tad" Dorgan cartoon in which the "yes men" were assistant newspaper editors praising the word of the editor.

yessiree, Bob! *Yes indeed! Yessiree!* But feel free to use this harmless expression. To paraphrase Abbott and Costello, if Bob don't mind, why should we?

yogi woman or man. Indians call the woman a "yogini."

yokefellow *yokemate, partner, sidekick, helpmate, right hand, comrade, co-partner, co-worker, companion, opposite number.*

yokel although supposedly inclusive, this derogatory term is more likely to be used of a man. Most people avoid it anyway because of its inaccurate and demeaning stereotype of inhabitants of small towns and rural areas.

young lady *young woman.* For explanation *see* lady (noun).

youth girl or boy.

"You've come a long way, baby!" although this phrase looks gender-free it has been so profoundly associated with a cigarette advertisement aimed at helping women catch up to men's lung cancer and cardiac death rates that "baby" is assumed to be female. In addition, it is generally women who have been called by "endearments" that make of them babies, babes, girls, and other young, helpless dependents. If you want to defeminize it, men's groups have been known to use: "You've come a long way, Bubba!"